THE HERONS OF EUROPE

THE HERONS OF EUROPE

by

Claire Voisin

Illustrated by

G. Brusewitz, P.L. Suiro and F. Desbordes

T & A D POYSER

London

Contents

List of figures

List of tables

x *List of tables*

Acknowledgements

Three artists, to whom I am most grateful, have contributed their talents to enhance the interest and value of this book. The well known artist G. Brusewitz has painted the jacket and colour plates and drawn the chapter headings. P. Suiro has prepared all the maps and graphics, as well as the behavioural drawings of herons in the text. Finally, F. Desbordes drew the topographic drawings of a Grey Heron.

I am greatly endebted to Mrs Hélène Watson, to Dr A. Richford and to my husband Dr J. F. Voisin for their reading and constructive criticism of the manuscript.

My thanks go also to the following persons for their kind contribution to the chapter on protection: A. J. Binsbergen, comte C. Cornet, S. Eldoy, Dr Emonds, M. Ferenc, S. Dudley, Dr A. Grüll, O. Nord-Varhaug, P. Portelli, O. Preuss, J. Riofrio Aizpurua, H. Schmid, Dr A. Siefke, M. Spagnesi, R. Staav, E. P. Tsachalidis and M. Wieloch.

CHAPTER 1

Introduction

Herons are successful birds which have colonized all the world's continents with the exception of Antarctica. They are birds of beauty as well. The presence of even a single heron always enhances a landscape such as a river bank, a pool or a shallow lake. Even barren fields in autumn take on a hopeful aspect when Grey Herons rest upon them.

The heron family comprises about 60 different species, most of them inhabiting equatorial, tropical and subtropical regions. Only a small number of species are adapted to temperate climates and very few are able to live there all the year round. The most conspicuous heron species breed in colonies, or heronries, sometimes near human habitation, if they are not disturbed, but more often in remote or inaccessible wetlands. Large heronries are one of nature's most extraordinary sights — many hundreds, and sometimes many thousands, of birds nesting together. In warm countries, herons often breed in association with other birds such as storks, ibises, spoonbills, cormorants and anhingas. The birds usually nest in trees or bushes, in flooded freshwater areas. Aquatic vegetation thrives in such shallow, still waters and insects, particularly mosquitoes, are numerous during the birds' breeding season, which is usually at the end of the main rainy season. An extraordinary mixture of life and death haunts the colony. Many young die before fledging

1

and predators are numerous — in the main, aquatic snakes, but also crocodiles in Africa and Asia and caymans in the Americas.

In the morning and afternoon, the noise and movement in the colony is intense. A characteristic smell of bird faeces and decaying vegetation fills the air, often mixed with that of fish rotting in damp places or drying in the sun. Now and then, the visitor must also suffer the smell of a putrefied carcass. Even a very flat-bottomed boat is difficult to punt through the dense aquatic vegetation and between the bare muddy patches of ground which may appear on the way to the heronry. When the boat has become entirely stuck, the visitor has but one solution – to jump out and to push it by hand through the most difficult passages, often wading waist deep in the muddy water. However, many large heronries are impossible to visit since the risk of tropical diseases (such as bilharzia) may be too great, crocodiles or caymans too numerous or the ground a bottomless silt. In such cases, the birds can only be cencussed from a low-flying airplane.

The large flooded heronries are a strange world where the beauty of the birds flying to and from their nests, the noise of thousands of begging young and the penetrating smell amaze the visitor who nevertheless should not forget the dangers presented by the silty ground, the floating vegetation and the sticky branches which wait in ambush. The contrast between these large, glamorous birds, flying, displaying or quietly incubating, and the vision of more or less decomposed animals floating on the water or hanging in the branches, constantly amazes and appals the visitor. Here the struggle for life goes on with a tremendous intensity and ferocity. The most fascinating is the intense feeling of being in a very ancient world where man has no place. These heronries probably look much the same today as they did when neither man nor even the apes existed. These large colonies are really "the lost world" which still survives, but for how long?

The survival of most heron species and the continued existence of large heronries depends on the protection of wetlands. In Europe, only small patches of such areas remain, and they decrease each year as the struggle to defend them against reclamation for short-term benefit continues. Since people with cars and boats can now move so easily over great distances, colonially breeding herons are very exposed to human predation and can only survive if strongly protected. Protection is only recent in Europe, and for species like the Grey Heron, it is uncertain if it will be maintained. In continental Europe, fishermen and fish breeders have caused the disappearance of the Grey Heron in many areas as recently as the 1960s. At that time, Grey Herons succeeded in breeding successfully on only a few private estates. A better knowledge of the European herons, totally unknown to most people, seems necessary to build up strong public opinion to save them from extinction by persecution and reclamation of the last remaining wetlands.

This book sets out to summarize the available knowledge of the nine species of heron which breed in Europe. Should the reader wish to refer to the original literature, he or she will find references in the bibliography that will allow more thorough study of a particular point. Much still remains unknown and this is emphasized to ease and direct further research.

The book begins with seven short general chapters. The third, on the origin of the herons, follows P. Brodkorb's theories which I find the most convincing for the time being. In the chapter on breeding behaviour and biology, as in the chapter on feeding behaviour, I have tried to compare the nine species of European heron in order to highlight features common to all, and thus focus on characteristics of each genus or species, both in their biology and behaviour. An attempt to unify the vocabulary dealing with behaviour has been made in order to ease comparisons. Fortunately, A. J. Meyerriecks, in his book *Comparative Breeding Behaviour of Four Species of North American Herons* (1960a), took up this task in the 1960s and many observers have since used his vocabulary. This is particularly important since no progress can be made in comparative ethology if observers working on different species use different names for the same behaviour. However, the difficulty in this kind of standardized nomenclature is to understand to which behaviour the observed one is homologous. The observer must understand the purpose of a behaviour, particularly if interactions between individuals are involved, in order to describe it coherently and later to be able to determine to what other behaviours, seen elsewhere, the observed one is homologous. As this requires human interpretation, the intuition of the scientist plays an important part in the final success of the study. Incorrect interpretations may hinder the research for a while, but a new generation of scientists will sooner or later correct them and progress is made. A case in point is the aggressive displays of herons which were first taken for components of the nuptial displays.

Following these general chapters, I have devoted a chapter to each of the nine species which nowadays breed in Europe. The format of each chapter is the same, but their length varies greatly, according to the amount of information available for each. The recent range extension of Cattle Egrets is a particularly interesting event for which so much valuable data exists that I have chosen to present it in a separate chapter apart from the general one on Cattle Egrets. The book ends with a chapter on conservation giving the regulations currently prevailing in Europe, with the exception of countries in eastern Europe from which little information is available.

CHAPTER 2

The classification of herons

The scientific names of animals and plants are not established definitively, once and for all. Taxonomists must constantly adapt the naming and listing of species to reflect the progress made in comparative anatomy, physiology and behaviour. Changes may affect families and even orders, but such changes are not common in ornithology since birds belong to a group well known since the last century. However, changes are frequent at the lower taxonomic levels such as subfamilies, genera and species.

The family Ardeidae is one of the six families included in the order Ciconiiformes: the large wading birds. The other families are the Ciconiidae (storks), the Threskiornithidae (ibises and spoonbills), the Phoenicopteridae (flamingos), the Balaenicipitidae and the Scopidae. The two latter comprise only one monospecific genus each and were created respectively for *Balaeniceps rex* (the Shoebill Stork) and *Scopus umbretta* (the Hammerkop). The Ciconiiformes are medium- to large-sized birds. All have long necks, bills and legs, broad rounded wings and short tail feathers. Their lower tibias are bare. They are adapted to forage in marshes or other shallow water areas, though a few species have become accustomed to forage on dry land. The resemblance of their external features goes with important similarities of their internal ones. In particular, all Ciconiiformes have a similar

4

disposition of the cranial and palatine bones, good classification characters since they evolve very slowly.

The family Ardeidae differs from the other families of Ciconiiformes in several anatomical features, described more fully in Chapter 4. The particular articulation of several of the neck vertebrae, the movement of the eyes during the Bittern Stance, the insertion of all four toes at the same level on the tarsus and last, but not least, the possession of pectinated claws and well-delimited powder down patches are characteristic. Most Ardeidae have beautiful ornamental plumes during the breeding season, as do a few species of Threskiornithidae. Ardeidae and Threskiornithidae also share the same number of primaries, which is one less than the Ciconiidae and Phoenicopteridae.

In the family Ardeidae, the classification at subfamily level has not yet been definitively settled. Four distinctive groups of herons are recognized by all taxonomists: the bitterns, the tiger herons, the night herons and the day herons. J. Bock (1956) separated these four groups into two subfamilies, the Botaurinae comprising the bitterns, and the Ardeinae which includes the three other groups. Bock worked with anatomical characters, mainly plumage, but also considered behavioural features and thought the bitterns to be the oldest and most primitive group. He consequently placed them first in his classification, followed by the tiger herons. More recently, R.B. Payne and C.J. Risley (1976), working on osteological characters, found that the Botaurinae diverge more than the other subfamilies from the basic osteological features of the Ciconiiformes. They recognized the four groups mentioned above as subfamilies – the Ardeidinae, the Nycticoracinae, the Tigrisomatinae and the Botaurinae – and put the bitterns, which they found to be the most specialized, last in the classification, preceded by the tiger herons.

Later J. Hancock and J. Kushlan (1984) proposed that the Botaurinae had split from the others earliest, since the larger bitterns have a relict distribution throughout the world. In my view, this opinion seems justified and the traditional classification, with the Botaurinae first followed by the other subfamilies, has been followed in this book.

Among the European herons (Table 1), two species, the Great White Egret and the Cattle Egret, still have an uncertain taxonomic status, as has the Purple Heron, although to a much lesser extent.

The Great Egret, which is in many ways intermediate between the two genera *Ardea* and *Egretta*, has been put into a genus of its own (*Casmerodius*) by J.L. Peters (1931). Bock (1956) classified it with the egrets as *Egretta alba* on account of its external features and behaviour. Payne and Risley (1976) classified it with the large day herons as *Ardea alba* on osteological evidence alone, since the other "distinguishing" characters, i.e. scutallated tarsi and head-tilting, are common to both the genera *Egretta* and *Ardea*. Taking into account the possession during breeding of long scapular plumes characteristic of *Egretta*, as well as their pairing behaviour, which is quite like that of the Little Egret, the Great Egret will be termed *Egretta alba* in this book.

The Cattle Egret was put into a monospecific genus *Bubulcus* by Peters (1931). Bock (1956) placed it in the genus *Ardeola* since, with its short legs, relatively short and broad bill and rufous plumage during breeding, it looks rather like an *Ardeola*. On osteological evidence, Payne and Risley (1976) placed it in the genus *Egretta* and called it *Egretta ibis*. Recent observations of the breeding behaviour of the Squacco Heron *Ardeola ralloides* (Voisin 1980) clearly show that the behaviour of Cattle Egrets during pair formation is much more like that of the *Egretta* species than of *Ardeola*. In addition, the young of *Ardeola ralloides* seem to hatch synchronously, which is not the case for the Cattle Egret where the young hatch one after the other as is usual among herons. Thus Bock (1956) was probably wrong in putting the Cattle Egret into the genus *Ardeola*. However, as Cattle Egrets do definitely not look like the slender egrets the best course, for the time being, seems to leave them in the monospecific genus *Bubulcus*.

The Purple Heron, which was also placed in a monospecific genus (*Pyrrherodia*) by Peters (1931), was considered an *Ardea* by Bock (1956). Its status has been discussed regularly ever since. Payne and Risley (1976) considered it to belong clearly in the genus *Ardea*.

On anatomical grounds, Payne and Risley (1976) also proposed to suppress the genus *Butorides* and to include all the green herons (*Butorides* sp.) in the genus *Ardeola*, with the pond herons. The Green Heron, *Butorides striatus*, studied by Meyerriecks (1960) performs a typical Stretch Display during a pair formation. The Squacco Heron, *Ardeola ralloides*, uses the Foot-lifting Display during courtship (Voisin 1980), which is very different from the Stretch Display. Observations of the courtship displays of the Squacco Heron are up to now so few, that it is impossible to be sure that the species never uses the Stretch Display. However, as long as the Squacco Heron has not been observed using this display, the only known pairing displays of the Green Heron (Stretch Display) and of the Squacco Heron (Foot-lifting display) are so different from each other that these two species should be kept in different genera and the genus *Butorides* should be maintained on behavioural grounds.

Table 1. *The common names of European herons in seven European languages*

	Botaurus stellaris	*Ixobrychus minutus*	*Bubulcus ibis*	*Egretta garzetta*	*Egretta alba*
United Kingdom	Bittern	Little Bittern	Cattle Egret	Little Egret	Great White Egret
France	Butor étoilé	Blongios nain	Héron garde-boeufs	Aigrette garzette	Grande Aigrette
Germany	Rohrdommel	Zwergdommel	Kuhreiher	Seidenreiher	Silberreiher
Italy	Tarabuso	Tarabusino	Airone guarda-buoi	Garzetta	Airone bianco maggiore
Netherlands	Roerdomp	Woudaapje	Koereiger	Kleine Zilverreiger	Grote Zilverreiger
Spain	Avetoro común	Avetorillo común	Garcilla bueyera	Garceta común	Garceta grande
Sweden	Rördrom	Dvärgrördrom	Kohäger	Silkeshäger	Aigretthäger

	Ardea cinerea	*Ardea purpurea*	*Nycticorax nycticorax*	*Ardeola ralloides*
United Kingdom	Grey Heron	Purple Heron	Night Heron	Squacco Heron
France	Héron cendré	Héron pourpré	Héron bihoreau	Héron crabier
Germany	Graureiher	Purpurreiher	Nachtreiher	Rallenreiher
Italy	Airone cenerino	Airone rosso	Nitticora	Sgarza ciuffetto
Netherlands	Blauwe Reiger	Purperreiger	Kwak	Ralreiger
Spain	Garza real	Garza imperial	Martinete	Garcilla cangrejera
Sweden	Häger	Purpurhäger	Natthäger	Rallhäger

CHAPTER 3

The origin of herons

The living birds form a well-known group in comparison with invertebrates and even with the other vertebrate groups. No new genera have been discovered for a long time and new species are seldom described. On the other hand, the evolution of birds is not well documented, since fossils are scarce. The pneumatized bones of birds are very thin and thus very fragile, and do not fossilize easily. In addition, birds lack teeth, the most common fossil remains of other vertebrate groups.

The ancestor of birds is believed to be a small bipedal dinosaur that lived during the Trias, about 250 million years ago. In early Jurassic times, some 40 million years before the appearance of birds, the Pterosaurs were able to fly. They existed until the end of the Secondary Era, and were contemporary with birds for much of their history.

The oldest fossil bird ever found is the well-known *Archaeopteryx* from the upper Jurassic. Several complete skeletons with feather prints were found in the lithographic limestone of Solenhofen in Bavaria. The next oldest known fossil bird after *Archaeopteryx* is in fact a Ciconiiforme, which lived 3–25 million years later, during the lower Cretaceous, about 130 million years ago. The proximal part of a femur, the only fossilized remains of the bird, was found in a deposit of Neocomian age near Auxerre, France. According to

Brodkorb (1963), this fossil, named *Gallornis straeleni*, belongs to the now extinct family Torotigidae, in the suborder Phoenicopteri, order Ciconiiformes. This bird, living during the Secondary Era was thus a primitive flamingo and a wading bird. Since only a part of the femur is known, reconstruction of the bird is impossible.

A gap of about 50 million years exists between *Gallornis straeleni* and the next Ciconiiformes discovered at the end of the Cretaceous. During that period, a tiny ibis, *Plegadornis antecessor*, smaller than any living member of this suborder, was found in Alabama and two other fossil birds, again belonging to the suborder Phoenicopteri, were found; one, *Parascaniornis stensiöi*, in Sweden and the other, *Torotix clemensi*, in Wyoming. The bird fauna at the end of the Cretaceous has a modern appearance, the archaic bird genera such as *Hesperornis* and *Ichthyornis* having become extinct, and the new fauna includes the ancestors of divers, grebes, cormorants, flamingos, ibises, rails, sandpipers and a pelican-like bird, *Laornis*.

The first true flamingos, ibises, storks and herons arose during the Eocene (Tertiary Era). These birds, living 60–38 million years ago, were probably not very different from those living today.

These fossils are principally a Phoenicopterid (*Elornis anglicus*), a Threskiornithid (*Ibidopsis hordwelliensis*), five Ardeids (*Proherodius oweni, Eoceornis ardetta, Botauroides parvus, Proardea amissa, Goliathia andrewsi*) and three Ciconids (*Pelargopappus stehlini, Pelargopappus trouessarti* and *Propelargus cayluxensis*). They show the worldwide distribution of the order Ciconiiformes. However, during the Tertiary Era, Europe seems to have had a particularly rich fauna of water birds as many of the fossils found came from Europe, and especially from England and France.

○ *Elornis anglicus*: Eocene (Hordwell beds). England: Hampshire: Hordwell;
○ *Ibidopsis horwelliensis*: Eocene (Hordwell beds). England: Hampshire: Hordwell;
○ *Proherodius oweni*: Eocene (London clay). England: Middlesex: Primrose Hill and St-James' Park;
○ *Eoceornis ardetta*: Eocene (Bridger formation). Wyoming: Uinta County: Henrys Fork;
○ *Botaurides parvus*: Eocene (Bridger formation). Wyoming: Sweetwater County: Spanish John's Meadow;
○ *Proardea amissa*: Eocene or Lower Oligocene (Phosphorites du Quercy). France: Dept. Tarn et Garonne: Chaux;
○ *Goliathia andrewsi*: Eocene or Lower Oligocene (Fayum series). Egypt: Fayum;
○ *Pelargopappus stehlini*: Eocene or Lower Oligocene (Phosphorites du Quercy). France: Plateau of Quercy;
○ *Pelargopappus trouessarti*: Eocene or Lower Oligocene (Phosphorites du Quercy). France: Plateau of Quercy;
○ *Propelargus cayluxensis*: Eocene or Lower Oligocene (Phosphorites de Bach). France: Dept. Lot: Bach.

Two extant genera had already appeared during the late Miocene, more than 7 million years ago. Three species belonging to the genus *Ardea* have been found from the upper Miocene (*Ardea aurelianensis, Ardea perplexa* and *Ardea brunhuberi*) and one species belonging to the genus *Ibis* (= *Mycteria*): *Ibis milne-erwardsi*. The other extant genera seem to have appeared during the Quaternary Era, some of them such as *Nycticorax* (*Nycticorax fidens*) and *Ciconia* (*Ciconia gaudryi*) in the early Quaternary.

Unfortunately, usually only one bone of these fossil birds has been found and the determination has been done only from that bone. Thus the systematic position of these fossils is often debated. New authors change the systematic position of the fossil, thinking it belongs to another genera or family and sometimes even to another order (Olson 1985). However, many water birds, and among them the Ciconiiformes, seem to have evolved only slowly since the end of the Eocene. To emphasize the length of the period from the Eocene to the present, one must remember that the first ape appeared only during the Oligocene, about 35 million years ago, and thus the whole evolution of primates and man has taken place since that time. The Ciconiiformes, adapted to extensive shallow water areas, probably first appeared and evolved at a time when the large Mezozoic seas and lagoons still existed. The more xeric conditions which prevailed during the Tertiary, when most of the land was sharply separated from the sea, probably slowed down their evolution, favouring instead the true sea birds and land birds.

CHAPTER 4

The general appearance and special features of herons

Herons vary greatly in size, ranging from the small Zigzag Heron *Zebrilus undulatus* (30 cm long) and the Green Heron *Butorides striatus* (40 cm long), to the very large species such as the Imperial Heron *Ardea imperialis* (127 cm long) and the Goliath Heron *Ardea goliath* (140 cm long), the largest of all the herons.

Herons, particularly the day herons, have slim bodies and long necks and legs. Night herons are a little stouter with relatively shorter necks and legs. They fly with retracted necks and slow, but strong, regular wing-beats. The bills of herons are, except for a few species, long, straight and sharply pointed, but the precise structure is strongly related to the feeding ecology of each individual species. The edges of the mandibles are usually slightly serrated, which is typical of carnivorous birds hunting a great variety of prey. The larger the bill, the larger the prey taken. Thus a relatively small heron such as the Night Heron which has a proportionally large bill, takes large prey for its size. Short-billed herons, such as the Cattle Egrets, have more terrestrial habits than the long-billed ones, and herons with long and slender bills, such as the Little Egret, are adapted to catch small, swift prey.

The skeleton of the neck is adapted to allow both a folded position in a sharp S curve at rest and in flight, and a rapid forward lunge, typical of herons when

11

capturing prey. The characteristic kink of the neck is caused by a modification of the articulations of the fifth, sixth and seventh vertebrae. The muscular insertions on the vertebrae of both the long and short muscles are very numerous. The elongated and thin muscles of the neck, added to the very long, strong tendons, permit the extraordinarily rapid unfolding of the neck, the whole mechanism having evolved to produce the rapid forward lunge necessary for successful hunting. To maintain the strength of the very long neck, lateral movements are very reduced; the vertebrae being strongly connected to each other by large, short muscles (Boas 1929, Pls 2, 11, 15 and 20).

Herons are anisodactyl, that is to say they have four toes, three directed forwards and one (the first) backwards (a configuration already established by Archaeopteryx). In all herons, the middle forward toe is the longest. In the subfamily Botaurinae, the outer toe is shorter than the inner one, whereas in the subfamily Ardeinae, the outer toe is the longer one. A very characteristic feature is the existence of a pectinated claw. The claw of the middle toe of all herons is provided with a serrated, comb-like edge on its inner side, an anatomical peculiarity related to the strong development of powder down, which is also very characteristic of the group. Two reduced webs occupy the base of the three forward-pointing toes. The tree-nesting species have relatively shorter toes and more strongly curved claws compared to the marsh-nesting ones, which have very long toes and only slightly curved claws. Lord Percy (1951) described how marsh-nesting species walk through the marsh, above water level, by grabbing the reeds between their long toes at each step.

The musculature of the eyes of the bitterns and tiger herons has evolved to permit binocular vision over a large area in front of the bird during the Bittern Stance (see the chapter on the Bittern). The eyes of the bird in the Bittern Stance are directed forwards and downwards as much as possible, and really bulge out on each side of the base of the vertical bill when the bird looks forward, facing danger. This movement of the eyes in their sockets, which is quite exceptional among birds, is an adaptation that makes binocular vision, and hence the ability to judge distance, possible. The bird, while staying stiffly upright, bill pointing vertically towards the sky, is able to appreciate the distance between it and a predator in front. Hunted birds usually flee at the last moment, but a few individuals, particularly among Little Bitterns, are so frozen in their position that they get caught despite the good view that they have of the predator.

The wing has ten well-developed primaries (only nine in the Boat-billed Heron) and an eleventh, minute one. Primaries 7, 8, 9 and 10 are the longest. The number of secondaries varies from 15 to 20. The wing is diatataxic, that is, every pair of major coverts except the fifth embraces a remex. The tail is usually slightly rounded but a few species have a square tail. The undertail-coverts are nearly as long as the tail feathers. The aftershafts are well developed and the plumage is loose. The feather tracts are narrow and the down is confined to the apteria, areas of skin without contour feathers. Herons attain adult plumage in their second, third or fourth calendar year.

In herons, plumes are found in both sexes during the breeding season. Herons have two kinds of specialized plumes: lanceolated ones and aigrettes.

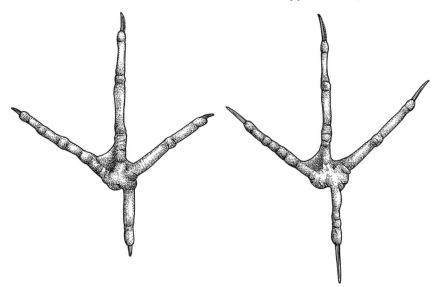

The sole of the left foot of a Grey Heron (left) compared to the one of a Great Bittern (right). The Bittern and the Grey Heron though of different body sizes have approximately the same size of feet but the claws of the Bittern are much longer. The large feet and long claws of the Bittern are adapted to move in reed beds. The bird grasps as many stems as possible in each foot to sustain itself when walking through the reeds.

An important difference between the two species is the comparative lengths of the inner and outer toes. The outer toe of the Grey Heron is longer than the inner one, on the contrary the outer toe of the Bittern is shorter than the inner one. The two subfamilies of Ardeidae, the Botaurinae and the Ardeinae (Bock 1956) can be distinguished on this character, the Botaurinae having the outer toe shorter than the inner, the contrary being true for the Ardeinae.

Lanceolated plumes are found on the crown and at the base of the foreneck of most species and, in a few (*Butorides virescens, Egretta ardesiaca*), even the scapular feathers are lanceolated. Lanceolated feathers have a long rachis and very short barbs firmly held together by barbules. Aigrettes, which are typical of the genus *Egretta*, but are also found in the genus *Ardeola*, are long and airy plumes and are very beautiful. Their rachis and barbs are both long. The distinctive look of these feathers is due to the barbules having degenerated, leaving the barbs free.

The genus *Ardea* does not have true aigrettes, but somewhat less elaborate plumes. The scapulars are not particularly elongated. The proximal part of the feather has an ordinary feather structure but, along the sides of its distal part and at its end, several rows of barbules have degenerated so that just a few barbs lock together. The distal part of the feather looks like several lanceolated feathers, which is not in fact the case. The proximal part is not visible, but is hidden by other contour feathers. In many other genera, such as

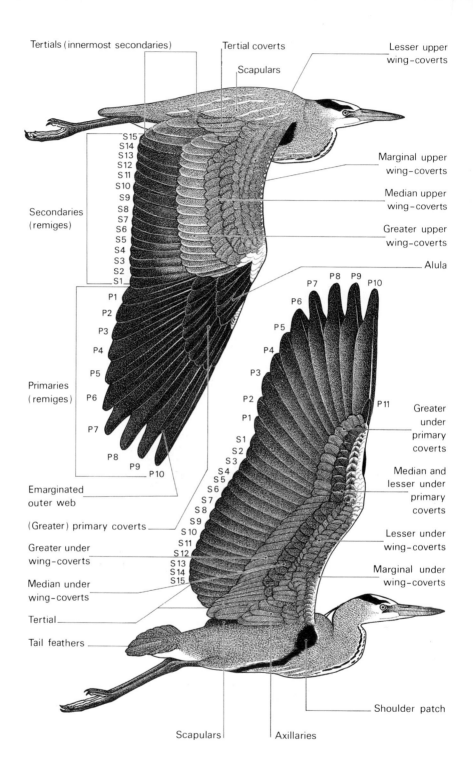

Tertials (innermost secondaries)

Tertial coverts

Scapulars

Lesser upper wing-coverts

Marginal upper wing-coverts

Median upper wing-coverts

Greater upper wing-coverts

Alula

S15
S14
S13
S12
S11
S10
S9
S8
S7
S6
S5
S4
S3
S2
S1

Secondaries (remiges)

P1
P2
P3
P4
P5
P6
P7
P8
P9
P10

Primaries (remiges)

Emarginated outer web

(Greater) primary coverts

Greater under wing-coverts

Median under wing-coverts

Tertial

Tail feathers

P7 P8 P9 P10
P6
P5
P4
P3
P2
P1
S1
S2
S3
S4
S5
S6
S7
S8
S9
S10
S11
S12
S13
S14
S15

P11

Greater under primary coverts

Median and lesser under primary coverts

Lesser under wing-coverts

Marginal under wing-coverts

Shoulder patch

Scapulars

Axillaries

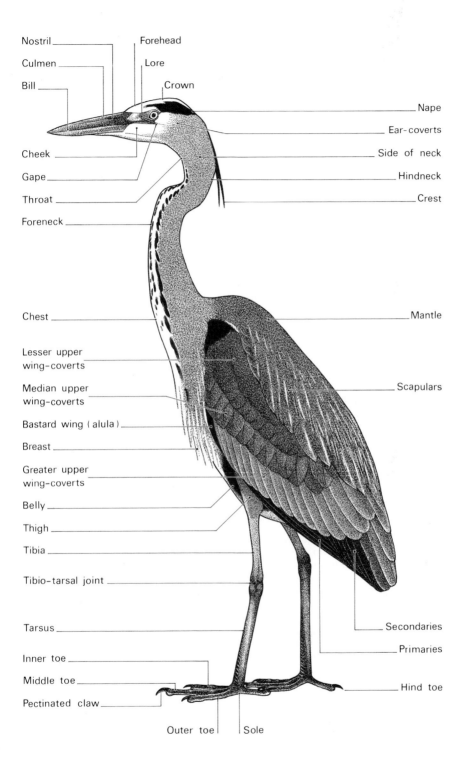

Nostril

Culmen

Bill

Cheek

Gape

Throat

Foreneck

Forehead

Lore

Crown

Nape

Ear-coverts

Side of neck

Hindneck

Crest

Chest

Lesser upper wing-coverts

Median upper wing-coverts

Bastard wing (alula)

Breast

Greater upper wing-coverts

Belly

Thigh

Tibia

Tibio-tarsal joint

Tarsus

Inner toe

Middle toe

Pectinated claw

Mantle

Scapulars

Secondaries

Primaries

Hind toe

Outer toe

Sole

Botaurus, Ixobrychus and *Nycticorax*, the scapular feathers are ordinary feathers which have not evolved into specialized plumes.

During the breeding season, the bare parts – lores, bill and legs – of herons become brightly coloured, usually red but sometimes other colours. Both powder down and feathers produce a fine powder which is composed of keratin particles approximately $1\,\mu m$ ($1/1000\,mm$) in diameter. In several families of birds, powder feathers or down occur either among the ordinary feathers, in distinct patches, or both in patches and mingled with ordinary feathers. The powder feathers sometimes grade into ordinary feathers, making it difficult to locate their exact position (Stettenheim 1972). Many families of birds, including most passerine families, lack powder down and powder feathers altogether. The herons, on the contrary, are characterized by their strongly differentiated powder down, which is found in well-delimited patches. The powder down does not shed but seems to grow and disintegrate continuously to produce the great amount of powder needed by these birds. The down consists of vestigial barbs directly attached to the calamus (they have no rachis) and modified barbules which produce the powder. The pattern of powder down patches is one of the morphological characters used to separate the families in the order Ciconiiformes. Neither the Ciconiidae, the Threskiornithidae or the Phoenocopteridae have any such patches. Among the heron family the number of powder down patches is one of the characters which separates the different subfamilies, and varies from two pairs in bitterns to three pairs in all other herons except the Boat-billed Heron and a few tiger herons which have four pairs. Breast-patches, which are generally the largest ones, and rump-patches, which are usually the second largest ones, are found in all herons. Inguinal patches are present in the subfamily Ardeinae where they form the smallest pair of patches. All species belonging to the subfamily Botaurinae lack inguinal patches. Back-patches are only found in the Boat-billed Heron and a few tiger herons. In a few specimens belonging to different species, the inguinal and rump-patches are more or less connected:

> It seems very possible that the primitive condition was a continuous tract from the upper breast, down along the ventral feather tract, about the rear of the leg and finally up along the spinal feather tract to about the region of the upper back. Evolutionary development may have consisted of a process of reduction and breaking up this continuous tract into smaller number of patches of definite location (Bock 1956).

A very good explanation of the function of this powder down has been given by Lord Percy, who has shown, with the help of an excellent series of pictures, how the powder is used to remove fish slime and oil from the feathers.

The oil glands (uropygial glands) are small in herons. A short tuft of feathers marks the openings of the glands which are localized on the dorsal caudal tract at the base of the tail feathers.

CHAPTER 5

Breeding behaviour and biology

SOLITARY AND GREGARIOUS BREEDERS

All grades of both colonial and solitary nesting are found among the European herons. Both species of bittern are typically solitary nesters. On the other hand, Cattle Egrets and Little Egrets are typically gregarious, usually nesting in large heronries. Purple Herons are intermediate and tend to nest in rather loose colonies. The other European species such as Grey Herons, Night Herons, Squacco Herons and Great White Egrets nest in colonies, but Grey Herons and Night Herons may sometimes establish solitary nests. When birds of the same species congregate in large numbers for pair formation, the activity of the group is assumed to stimulate individual birds to commence displaying. When the group is large enough and thus the stimulus strong enough, some birds start to display, hesitantly at first. The displaying birds are rapidly imitated by others, and within a few days all the birds are paired. It seems that a group of herons belonging to one or several species may induce the onset of courtship displays in a heron belonging to a totally different species. A very gregarious heron such as the Little Egret may establish only two nests (or even a single nest) in a Night Heron colony. The most surprising thing is that, in France where I have observed these birds, the Little Egrets

17

which migrate later than the Night Herons, come to the colony when nearly all the Night Herons are incubating. In this case, the stimulus to pair seems to be the presence of many herons incubating.

THREAT AND COURTSHIP DISPLAYS IN HERONS: THE USE OF THE "NUPTIAL PLUMES"

The first observers of heron behaviour believed that the elongated plumes were only used during courtship displays, probably because these feathers Grow just before pairing and are strikingly beautiful. These early observers never succeeded in properly understanding and explaining heron behaviour, since they started from an incorrect interpretation of the agonistic displays, mistaking them for courtship displays. Heron behaviour remained a mystery until the publication of Meyerriecks' (1960a) study, *Comparative Breeding Behaviour of Four Species of North American Herons*. Meyerriecks was the first to understand that most of the displays in which herons erected their plumes, called "nuptial plumes", were in fact threat displays. He described, as follows, the use of feathers by threatening herons (Full Forward Display):

- *Butorides virescens*: "erects crest, neck, back, breast and flank feathers to an extreme, and keeps them erected throughout the display. Erects scapular plumes in a fan-like manner."
- *Ardea herodias*: "erects all of its feathers, especially the back plumes, to an extreme degree."
- *Dichromanassa rufescens*: "the feathers of the head, neck, pectoral, and back regions are all erected to an extreme."
- *Leuchophoyx tula*: "erects its crest, pectoral and scapular plumes to an extreme, the tips of the scapulars almost touching the fanned plumes on the back of the head."

If one compares all the descriptions of agonistic displays of herons in this book, one will notice that during the typical threat display (Full Forward Display), all the feathers of the bird are erected to a maximum, especially the elongated plumes of the crown and the base of the neck, and that threat displays in all species are alike, with only small variations from species to species. These variations are caused by slight differences in posture, by new behavioural sequences added to the usual ones (such as Tail-flipping in the Green Heron *Butorides virescens*) and by conspicuous variations in the structure and colour of the plumes. Thus threatening birds look somewhat different depending on the species concerned. Despite this, all my observations of interspecific encounters show that threat behaviours are understood by all herons in a mixed-species colony. Other studies have shown that all Ciconiiformes and cormorants use threat displays that are closely related to those of herons.

Threat displays in herons are characterized by:

- the use of all erectile feathers, especially those of the crown and neck;

○ the fact that the bill of the displaying bird is pointed towards its opponent;
○ similar behaviours in males and females;
○ similar behaviours in all Ardeidae; and
○ behaviours similar enough in all Ardeidae, Threskiornithidae and cormorants to be understood by all members of these groups.

These fully erected plumes are the most characteristic features of threat display. They are hence important for reproduction but not, as first thought, only as beautiful ornaments during courtship, but also as conspicuous feathers used to emphasize the bird's aggressive mood to its neighbours. The smallest species nesting in large heronries in Europe and Africa is the Squacco Heron, which compensates for its size with the most conspicuous plumage during threat displays. The evolution of large ornamental plumes for agonistic display emphasizes the importance of these behaviours in heron society. Threat, expressed at various levels, is the common language of these birds.

On the contrary, courtship displays differ a good deal between genera and even between species. Some species have more numerous displays than others and a few have aerial displays as well. However, in the genera *Ardea* and *Egretta*, the Stretch Display – the principal courtship display – is common to all species studied to date. This display has not so far been observed in other genera such as *Nycticorax* or *Ardeola*, which have a quite different display, the Foot-lifting Display.

The feathers of the crown and neck, especially the elongated plumes, are not erected at all during the courtship of most species, including the Little Egret, the Great White Egret, the Night Heron, the Cattle Egret and the Green Heron. However, a few species erect the crown and neck feathers to various degrees during courtship displays. Such is the case in the Squacco Heron, the Reddish Egret and the Snowy Egret. On the contrary, the scapulars are erected to a maximum during all Stretch Displays. These feathers are also erected during the Foot-lifting display of the Squacco Heron, but not during the Foot-lifting Display of the Night Heron. In these last two species, the bright red-coloured feet are shown during courtship.

The calls given during courtship also differ from one species to another. A few, such as the Little Egret, have a very characteristic and loud courtship call given by the males. Courtship displays are therefore characterized by:

○ the use of only some of the erectile feathers (the scapulars) or, if all of them are used, only some are erected to a maximum, as during the typical threat display;
○ the fact that the bill of the displaying bird is never pointed towards the mate but is directed either upwards or downwards;
○ totally different behaviours in males and females; and
○ specific displays and calls for each species.

Courtship displays tend to be specific, and understood only by individuals of the same species, so preventing pairing between different species and thus avoiding hybrids (which can, however, be produced in captivity between many species of herons). The specificity of pairing displays maintains the very existence of the species, and is of great importance since the birds often nest together in both time and space.

Meyerriecks (1960) was also the first, while studying the Green Heron, to emphasize the use of the crest feathers as an indicator of the degree of intensity of a display. He wrote:

> The crest of the Green Heron is the most mobile of its feather units, and there is great variation in crest elevation. Green Herons show crest-raising in numerous situations. Moderate crest-raising, together with alternating erection and depression, is characteristic of conflict situations, while extreme erection is always an expression of high intensity attack tendencies. Full erection always accompanies the Full Forward display, and some degree of erection is shown by a bird assuming the Forward display.

Some years later, Blaker (1969a), when studying Cattle Egrets, gave the first clear explanation of the use of the crest feathers in this species: the position of the crest feathers indicates the fear and aggressive tendencies of the Cattle Egret at any moment during its life, except when it is involved in courtship displays.

This way of looking at the posture and behaviour of birds as a result of various tendencies (aggressive, sexual, fear), present in various degrees of intensity, is in my opinion generally the right way to understand bird behaviour.

The fact that a posture or a colour can act as a releaser while true for many behaviours, is far from the whole story. A heron may indicate to others, by its posture and behaviour, many tendencies present in various degrees. The posture and behaviour of a bird are not only the net result of a combination of various tendencies, but of the balance between their various levels of intensity. For that reason, for example, agonistic behaviour can be described as the result of a group of behaviours. The heron may threaten only slightly or very strongly when Forward displaying. The crest feathers of the Night Heron, including the long white plumes of the crest, are raised when they are aggressive, the more so the more aggressive they are. But the more they are afraid, the more they tend to be sleeked. The final position of the crest feathers thus depends on the intensity to which each of these components is present. Thus when agonistic displays are described by various observers, the crest feathers may be described as more or less raised. This has caused a lot of confusion in the past, and will continue to do so, as long as each posture of the bird is considered alone, and in isolation.

SOCIETY IN THE HERONRIES

A community of several hundreds or thousands of birds suggests a social organization. Observations of these large bird communities, composed of various species of Ciconiiformes, cormorants and anhingas nesting together have shown the total absence of any kind of hierarchy among the birds, such as exists, for example, in a flock of Jackdaws. The birds are so numerous that it is impossible for all of them to know each other individually and thus to establish a hierarchy. Society in the heronries seems, therefore, to be based upon the simple fact that a more aggressive bird dominates a less aggressive one. Thus, as in societies with a hierarchy, the heron society, though different, remains based upon aggression. In contrast to less primitive birds and mammals is the fact that the aggressiveness of an individual does not depend on its personality but on other quite strictly determined factors as we will see later on.

At every moment, the posture of a heron, the way it erects its feathers (in particular, the elongated plumes of the crown, those at the base of the neck and the scapulars) and its various vocalizations, clearly show the degree of its aggressive tendencies. When two birds face each other, the dominant one can be identified at a glance. Fights which may wound one of the birds (if not both) are thus useless and nearly always avoided in the heronry. However, the victory of the most aggressive bird demands that conflicts are restricted to contests between only a very few individuals. In fact, during all the years that I have studied these large heronries, I have never observed a flock of herons acting together in order to attack one isolated bird or to defend a bird in danger. Each heron attacks alone and defends itself alone except when defending its territory and nest, in which case its mate will help it.

Which factors are at the origin of aggressive tendencies in herons? Both internal and external factors seem to be involved. First, is an internal, hormonal factor, causing a great increase in aggressive tendencies on reaching sexual maturity. At the beginning of courtship, when the male chooses a territory and begins to display, he is particularly aggressive. His feathers are constantly more or less erected and he successfully drives away any bird that comes near him or his newly established territory. However, he is always dominated by other territory owners, males and females, while they stand in their own territories. Newcomers are thus unable to take the territory of previously established birds.

Secondly, the external factor is the position of the heron in the heronry. He might either be inside or outside his territory. If the heron is inside his territory, he behaves very aggressively and erects his feathers at the slightest threat, ready to fight. He dominates all the other birds in the heronry, even those belonging to the largest species.

If the heron is outside its territory and is a male at the beginning of the pairing season looking for a territory, he is dominated by all the established birds while they are on their territories, as shown above. However, if he or she is a breeder who is not on guard at its nest for the time being, or a bird unmated for various reasons (age or health, for example), he or she will be in the colony in order to sleep, rest, preen or collect sticks. This bird, male or female, is dominated by all territory owners when they are in their own territory and by all males in search of a territory at the beginning of the breeding season. These dominated birds do not tolerate other birds in the same situation coming too near to them. They defend an individual space – the space within reach of their bill.

The result of this social organization is the existence of small territories for each pair inside the greater heronry. No other heron is allowed by the pair to enter the territory where the nest is located. The existence of small territories is of great importance as any heron, either of the same species or not, is a danger to the young. This social organization enables the undisturbed growth of the young among a voracious multitude.

COMPARISONS BETWEEN THE VARIOUS DISPLAYS OF EUROPEAN HERONS

The study of the displays of these species is far from complete. Much of their behaviour is still undescribed, either because the displays are obscure or because no-one has yet had the opportunity to study them. Courtship displays are particularly difficult to observe. Herons display at the spot where they intend to nest, which is naturally a place where they feel quite secure. When a bird is aware of an observer's presence it does not usually feel so safe and thus does not display until the observer has left, or until it leaves itself to choose another nesting site. To see herons displaying, one must either be sufficiently far away or enjoy special circumstances. For example, birds which are used to people do not pay any attention to them. A hide is not usually useful for observing courtship displays, as its very appearance in the vicinity of the nest is enough to arouse the birds' mistrust. This is the reason why the courtship displays of the reed-nesting herons, which can only be observed at close hand, have not yet been recorded and remain a mystery Table 2).

Another difficulty in comparing heron displays often arises from the fact that observations have been made by different people. It is thus difficult to know if the displays described are homologous or actually different. More descriptions, photographs and films are needed before we can properly understand even the best known displays, such as the agonistic ones. Most of the agonistic displays, especially the Forward and the Full Forward, have proved common to all the colonial nesting species studied so far. On the other hand, solitary nesting Bitterns, in which the female raises the young alone, have a much less developed social life than the colonially nesting herons. Male Bitterns are known to fight fiercely, sometimes even to the death. These fights are probably due to the lack of a succession of well developed agonistic displays which clearly show the escalating threat of one of the birds so settling territorial conflicts without a fight. The absence of social interactions among solitary nesting Great Bitterns has probably prevented the development of more complex displays and the lack of social communication which seems characteristic of these birds may be a remnant of a more primitive type of heron behaviour.

The Bittern Stance is only performed by the three reed-dwelling species, whose cryptic plumage makes this behaviour particularly efficient in dense vegetation. The other escape strategies of the bitterns are particularly interesting and many more observations of them are needed.

It is particularly difficult to understand the meaning of the Snap Display observed in the Grey Heron and in the Great White Egret. Those who have studied the Grey Heron have differed, some classifying it as an agonistic behaviour, others as a sexual one. In the later chapter on the Grey Heron, this display is, after discussion, classified as an agonistic behaviour, though a sexual component remains obvious in it. To the various observers of the Great White Egret, the Snap Display in this species is a typical mate-attracting display. A major difference between the Snap Displays of the Grey Heron and Great White Egret is the appearance of the bird when the head, neck and scapular feathers are erect. In this posture, the raised head and neck feathers of the Grey Heron are very conspicuous, whereas the scapulars with their thin rachis cannot be raised very much. As a result, the aggressive message is probably enhanced. On the other hand, the scapulars are very conspicuous in the Great White Egret, whereas the head and neck feathers are so short that it is difficult to determine whether they are raised or not. In this case, therefore, the sexual nature of the display is emphasized. Thus homologous displays may not have exactly the same meaning in different species.

The most conspicuous and well-known courthip display is the Stretch Display. During courtship, it is only performed by unpaired males, though it may also be given by both males and females as a greeting display later in the breeding season. The Stretch Display seems characteristic of the genera *Ardea* and *Egretta*, confirming the close relationship between them. However, the Stretch Display is used as a greeting by *Ardea cinerea* and *Ardea purpurea*, but not by *Egretta garzetta*, *Egretta rufescens* or *Egretta thula*. When used as a greeting display, it is probably one of the characteristics of the genus *Ardea*.

Cattle Egrets belonging to the monospecific genus *Bubulcus* perform the Stretch Display both as courtship and greeting displays and seem, therefore, to be very close to the *Ardea–Egretta* group.

Nycticorax nycticorax and *Ardeola ralloides* perform quite different courtship displays, which I have called the Foot-lifting Displays. They are not identical in the two genera but have many aspects in common, in particular the exposure of the bright red feet.

LENGTH OF AVAILABLE FORAGING TIME FOR DIURNAL SPECIES IN TEMPERATE AND TROPICAL REGIONS

In the Camargue, as in the Djoudj (Sénégal), diurnal herons may forage from dawn to dusk. During the breeding season in the Camargue, the days are so long that the herons can forage for up to 17 hours each day (Voisin, 1976). In the Djoudj, however, they can only forage for 12½ hours each day (Voisin, 1983). Thus the diurnal herons in southern Europe have 4½ hours more each day to forage than those breeding in Sénégal. Though both areas enjoy high food availability, both Little Egrets and Great White Egrets cannot generally catch enough prey to rear all the young that hatch. Hence, in 1971, the Little Egrets in the Camargue reared an average of 2.4 fledglings per nesting pair, whereas in 1981 the Great White Egrets in the Djoudj reared 1.9 young per nesting pair, to an age of 20 days. Further studies are needed of herons in order to establish comparisons not only between closely related species but also within the same species. The length of time that can be devoted to foraging in spring and summer increases the farther north the birds breed. This is probably the main factor responsible for the often higher breeding success of birds nesting in temperate areas compared to those nesting in tropical areas.

PAIR FORMATION

In all herons studied to date, where both members of the pair rear the young, the male chooses one or several territories in which he displays to attract a female. The females fly from displaying male to displaying male to choose their mate. Usually, several females sit in the branches at some distance from the displaying male, looking at him. The displays are various, and described for each species later in this book. The bill of the displaying male is never pointed towards the surrounding females during these displays and in most species the feathers of the crown and neck are not erected. The surrounding females sleek their plumage in deference to their compromised situation: they want to approach the displaying male but have difficulty in doing so because the male does not accept strange birds in his territory. When one female approaches, the male usually stops displaying and begins to threaten instead (the frequent use of threat displays during pair formation has often contributed to the misunderstanding of heron behaviour). If the female does not escape fast enough, he attacks her. She must make several dangerous approaches and often suffers strong blows from the male's bill before succeeding in remaining on the territory where the male finally accepts her, sometimes at first for short periods only. No wonder, then, that she is nervous and initially adopts a very sleeked plumage. If she were alone, she would probably wait a long time before daring any movement towards the male, but she must act quickly before another female takes her place. Consequently, most attempts to approach the male are prompted by the arrival of a new female among the birds watching the displaying male. When the male at last becomes used to the presence of one female and ceases his attacks on her, the pair is formed. Since nesting herons are extremely territorial, pair formation is unduly difficult and may take 3–4 days to achieve. The newly formed pair does not copulate immediately. The birds must become accustomed to each other and several contact displays (breeding displays) are performed first. The first copulation generally occurs the next day. No particular display precedes copulation.

In order to succeed, pair formation must overcome the sexually mature male's urge to defend his territory against all intruders. It seems that this urge to defend a territory, which is necessary if the young are to survive, does not lessen during courtship. Rather, it adapts, leaving a little space for the sexual drive. The male learns progressively to accept the presence of one single female, his future mate, inside his territory.

PAIR BONDS AND PARENTAL CARE

There are significant behavioural and physiological differences between the great majority of heron species where the male stays with the female, helping her to build the nest, to incubate and to bring up the young and the few species where the male deserts the female immediately after copulation. Only the genus *Botaurus* exhibits this last pattern (although the behaviour of species belonging to the genus *Zonerodius*, *Zebrilus* and *Tigrisoma* is still unknown). Whereas pairs of herons, such as Grey Herons or Night Herons, have great difficulty in rearing their young, the females of the four species of great bitterns are able to build the nest, to incubate the eggs and to feed the young all by themselves. The eggs and young are left alone for long periods during which they are exposed to the cold and are vulnerable to predation. However, eggs and young usually survive. The young, at least, are probably specially adapted to enable a lowering of their body temperature and the female most likely forages close to the nest during the sensitive period when she incubates and when the young are newly hatched. These differences in behaviour, probably associated with differences in physiology, set the great bitterns very much apart from all the other heron species. Since the maintenance of the pair bond during the growth of the young is a complex process, and thus a more evolved behaviour than the raising of the young by the female alone, behavioural arguments are added to the others which argue for classification of the great bitterns as the most primitive heron group.

In all herons studied to date (except those in the genus *Botaurus*), one member of the pair remains at the nest continuously to defend the young against cold, rain and excessive sunshine, as well as against predation. For the first 4–5 days, the young are constantly brooded. Later, the adult often stays on the nest rim protecting them from predators. However, when it is cold or rainy the adult sits over the chicks, and in strong sunshine shelters them with its spread wings.

Adult herons never clean their nests, though the young often defecate inside the nest, especially when they are small. Their excreta, which is quite liquid, runs through the nest, and the loose sticks of the nest and the branches below rapidly become covered with a white layer. Prey items are rarely found in the nest as the young and adults, always hungry, eat all that can be eaten. On the contrary, dead chicks are often found in the nest. They are not removed by the adults but are left to rot or to dry. The parents never interfere when the young are fighting, and never try to defend the weakest one when it is picked upon by a stronger sibling. Adults recognize their young, at least when they are old enough to walk in the branches, and never seem to feed a chick from another nest if it comes begging for food. They peck at it and drive it away, even when feeding chicks outside the territory, which is often the case as they grow larger. The adults attack strange chicks coming into their territory in the same way as they attack strange adults. Thus chicks that have fallen from the nest accidentally find their attempts to return very hazardous, as they have to pick their way through strange territories and may only succeed in doing so when the owners are away foraging.

Heron chicks usually hatch in succession. At first, the adults take turns at the nest to prevent predation, but once the young are 10–20 days old, depending on the species, they are left alone and both parents forage simultaneously in order to feed them. At that age, the chick's thermoregulation is good enough to cope with unduly cold or hot weather and they are able to defend themselves against their voracious neighbours. They are, however, easily taken by birds of prey and probably also by large snakes. When an adult comes to feed its offspring, it lands in the vegetation some distance from the nest. As soon as the young are able to walk in the branches, they hurry to the spot, begging loudly and often fighting with each other on the way.

Once the young are able to fly, they begin to forage by themselves, most often in the water at the foot of the heronry. However, they fly back to the nest several times each day to be fed by their parents, often waiting for them at the nest but also returning to it on recognizing the landing calls of their parents. Young herons are thus fed for about 1 month, during which time they learn to forage. Since herons are predators, learning to feed is not easy for the young birds. They must learn what is edible and what is not, and how to capture prey that are often very swift and it takes time for them to acquire the skills necessary to survive on their own. If not fed by their parents during this period, they would die of hunger. Do the young, now able to feed themselves, stop returning to their nest, or do their parents abandon them at the end of the breeding season? It is probable that both occur. Pair and family bonds last as long as both parents and young frequent the nest. As soon as they no longer meet at the nest, the pair as well as the family cease to exist. Hence, pair bonds last about 3 months in small species and about 4 months in large ones. It would be interesting to use ringed birds to see if old herons tend to return to the same nest from year to year, and to pair with the same mate.

GROWTH OF THE YOUNG

Like most birds which hunt and capture their prey, herons are altricial birds or, to be more precise, semi-altricial, since they do not possess all the characteristics of true altricial species. Truly altricial birds, i.e.the Passerines, hatch naked, blind and unable to move, and are fed and attended by their parents. On the contrary, truly precocial birds, i.e. the Anatidae and the Charadriidae, hatch covered with down, open their eyes soon after hatching and are able to walk, run and feed themselves within a few hours after hatching. Herons are described as semi-altricial because they are not capable of much movement after hatching and are fed and attended by their parents, but are downy and not blind at hatching. Compared to precocial and semi-precocial birds, herons grow quickly, which is usually the case for altricial birds whose young are very vulnerable to predation at the nest. Many sea-birds breeding on oceanic islands have a slow growth rate although they are semi-altricial, a fact which may be explained by the difficulty faced by adults in even bringing up one offspring. The lack of predators on their breeding grounds has allowed evolution towards a slow growth rate. The growth rate of a species is innate and can only vary between very narrow limits from one individual to another, or change over a long period of evolution. Herons have a fast growth rate and chicks which do not grow fast enough are likely to die. There is a limit to the slowing down of their growth rate, below which they cannot survive and this is an inherited factor (Voisin 1983).

Herons begin to incubate as soon as the first egg is laid, and thus their chicks hatch one after the other, at 1- or 2-day intervals. (A possible exception is the Squacco Heron, which is said to begin incubating after all the eggs are laid.) A week may elapse between the hatching of the first chick and the last, with the result that the oldest chick may weigh about three times as much as the newborn. The differences among siblings are not always so great, but young herons of the same clutch are always of different sizes.

Because all birds in the heronry are predators, the small chicks cannot be left alone in the nest where they would be eaten by their voracious neighbours. The adults take turns to fish and guard the nest while the chicks are small, even though every study of herons has shown that the adults have great difficulties feeding their offspring. When a food shortage begins to be serious, and the whole brood is in danger, both parents go off to fish, leaving the young alone. This generally happens when the chicks are about one-third grown, have their maximum growth rate and hence a very large requirement for food. This sudden increase in the growth rate is easy to see as a sharp rise on growth curves, and requires the efforts of both parents to sustain it.

The adults always feed the one or two larger young first, these being the ones which beg the most forcefully. The smaller young are fed afterwards if there is any surplus food or if one of the larger chicks, being well fed, has not begged for food. Thus even when food is short, at least one or two chicks grow fast enough to survive. Comparisons with hand-reared birds show that the one or two older young follow the optimum growth curve very closely. The smaller ones survive if there is enough food to maintain their growth above the minimum level required; that is to say, if the feeding conditions are good and the adults are sufficiently experienced, or if one of their larger siblings becomes a victim of predation or meets with an accident.

Starting incubation as soon as the first egg is laid is probably a very old and primitive strategy, though it may be costly in energy terms, as one or several chicks usually starve to death in each brood. It has probably persisted because it allows the number of young reared to vary according to local conditions, which are highly variable in both temperate and tropical regions.

Table 2. Displays of European herons

	Grey Heron	Purple Heron	Great Bittern	Little Bittern	Night Heron	Squacco Heron	Little Egret	Great White Egret	Cattle Egret
Agonistic displays									
Full Forward and Forward Display	● ●				●	●	●	● ●	●
Aggressive Upright Display	● ●	● ●						●	
Snap Display (may also be a pairing display)			●	●					
Dancing-ground Display	● ●				●			●	● ●
Stab-and-counter-stab Display					● ●	●	● ●	● ● ● ●	● ●
Supplanting Run-and-flight								●	
Bill Duel									
Stab-crouch									
Courtship displays									
Aerial Stretch Display								●[a]	
Stretch Display	♂				♂	♂	♂	♂	♂
Foot-lifting Display	●				●		● ●	● ●	● ● ●
Courtship Flight					●		●	●	
Twig-shake									
Wing-spread								●	
Bowing Display								●	
Bow									
Breeding displays									
Feather-nibbling or Allopreening	● ●	●							
Billing	●				● ●				
Bill-clappering					●	●	● ●	●	
Back-biting					●	●	●		●

continued

Table 2. *Displays of European herons – continued*

	Grey Heron	Purple Heron	Great Bittern	Little Bittern	Night Heron	Squacco Heron	Little Egret	Great White Egret	Cattle Egret
Greeting displays									
Stretch Display	•	•							
Alighting Display	•	•							
Sway-and-bob Display		•							
Fear, alert and conflict displays									
Bittern Stance	•	•	•	•					
Alert Posture					•	•	•	•	•
Head-flick									•
Wing-touch					•		•	•	•
Upright Display									
Calls									
Advertising Call	♂		♂	♂			♂		
Alarm Call (typical)					•	•			
Coloured parts of the body shown during displays									
Feet						•			
Throat				•	•				

•, Display actually observed. If a display is not noted for a species, it usually means that it is not performed by it. However, it may exist but may not have been observed yet. ♂, Males only.

[a] Only observed in the subspecies *Egretta alba modesta*.

CHAPTER 6

Habitat, resource partitioning and species diversity

All the extant herons are wading birds whose early ancestors evolved slowly in extensive shallow-water areas in tropical and sub-tropical climates. The Ciconiiformes, among the oldest bird orders still living, occupied this habitat, favourable for predatory species, very early on, as soon as the end of the Secondary Era. The first Ciconiiformes would not have needed a high level of performance to survive; many of their prey were slow-moving and in tropical areas there would have been no need for long-distance migratory flights. The only flight requirement was to reach a perch for the night and to escape from predators. Thus the first Ciconiiformes evolved only slowly from generation to generation to utilize the extensive tropical marshes where fish, crustaceans and amphibians flourished as they sometimes still do today. In sub-tropical habitats, however, climatic conditions change seasonally and marshes and other shallow-water areas often dry up for a few months each year. Birds which are to become adapted to these habitats must be good flyers in order to switch foraging areas according to local conditions and the use of temporarily flooded areas could only be achieved by species which had evolved good powers of flight.

Since the Eocene, the ancestral herons have speciated in response to competition and environmental opportunities. While competition alone is not generally sufficient to promote speciation, competition during periods of food shortage is a most efficient promoter of species radiation.

Herons have specialized in their choice of habitat, in their methods of foraging, in the size of the prey which they hunt and in the time of day or night during which they hunt. All herons forage at least partially in aquatic biotopes and the density and height of the emergent aquatic vegetation is a factor of utmost importance. The structure of the biotope, and not the particular plant species, is the important ecological factor for these birds.

A few species forage in open habitat but tolerate some emergent aquatic vegetation, such as the Grey Heron and the Little Egret in Europe. Others, such as the Night Heron and the Squacco Heron, forage hidden in the vegetation. The densest biotope used by herons is reed bed where bitterns and Purple Herons are found. The habitat requirements for each species of heron are very precise and not many studies have yet been done on this subject, e.g. one on the Grey Heron by Geiger (1984b). The density of the emergent aquatic vegetation can be classified along a gradient from no vegetation at all (salt-water lagoons) to reed beds. Along this scale of increasing density, Grey Herons and Little Egrets are found in areas with no vegetation to areas with a medium density of emergent aquatic vegetation. Cattle Egrets occur where only a slight cover of vegetation exists. Night Herons, Squacco Herons and Purple Herons are found in areas with a medium to dense vegetation cover, though Night and Squacco Herons do not usually forage in reed beds where

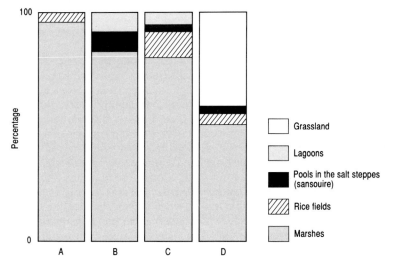

Percentage of the population of each species of heron foraging in various biotopes in the Camargue. A; Purple Heron (*Ardea purpurea*), B; Grey Heron (*Ardea cinerea*), C; Little Egret (*Egretta garzetta*), D; Cattle Egret (*Bubulcus ibis*). The percentage is calculated on a 67-km route through the Camargue that was covered 81 times from March to October during the years 1971 to 1977 (Voisin 1978).

only bitterns and Purple Herons are found. Terrestrial biotopes are also used by European herons. Cattle Egrets are commonly found on grazing land together with cattle, Grey Herons are found on open fields and pasture and Night Herons may hunt in tall grass beside streams. Marine habitats in Europe are only commonly used by Grey Herons, which fish mostly at low tide catching prey left behind in tidal pools. Wintering Little Egrets perhaps also use this habitat when all inland waters are frozen during cold spells, but up to now there are no observations to confirm this assumption.

The growth of emergent aquatic vegetation depends, in addition to climatic factors, and the nature of the soil, on two other limiting factors: the depth of the water and its salt concentration. Reeds are found in waters up to 1.5–2.0 m deep. Water deeper than 2.0 m are open. Most of the emergent aquatic plants are true freshwater species that do not grow in water with more than 1 g salt per litre. *Phragmites* and *Scirpus* tolerate the highest salt concentrations and grow in water with up to 6–7 g per litre. Waters with a salt concentration greater than 6–7 g per litre are open.

Vegetation is not the only important factor for herons; they must also be able to find sufficient prey. Fresh waters support a very rich and varied fauna. However, most freshwater fish and even a few amphibians such as *Rana ridibunda* or tadpoles of *Bufo calamita* can tolerate salinities of up to 3 g per litre. Many fish species are common in brackish waters which are hence good foraging areas for herons. A few marine fish species tolerate salt concentrations which are higher than those of the Mediterranean Sea (30 g per litre); among them are the atherines *Atherina boyeri* and the eels. No fish are found in lagoons with salt concentrations higher than 60 g per litre. Thus the two herons species which fish in lagoons, the Grey Heron and the Little Egret, are never found foraging in lagoons where the salt concentration exceeds this value.

The Little Egret is the most active fisher among the European Herons. They often forage together in considerable numbers, walking, Foot-stirring and sometimes running with open wings to catch their prey. Cattle Egrets also stalk their prey, usually walking together among grazing cattle. The Squacco Heron, which now and then uses a Stand-and-wait strategy, can often be seen slipping rapidly through dense vegetation in active search of food. In contrast, the Grey Heron, the Purple Heron, the Great White Egret, the Night Heron and the bitterns use Walk Slowly and Stand-and-wait strategies.

In Europe, the Night Heron is the only true nocturnal heron, foraging only after dark (except when feeding young, when it may also be seen during the day). The other European species often observed hunting by night is the Grey Heron. I think that this behaviour is a recent adaptation to human persecution, and that Grey Herons have altered their behaviour to survive, as have many species of surface-feeding ducks in recent times.

Herons have specialized not only in their fishing methods and the time at which they fish, but also in the size of the prey they catch. The largest, the Grey Heron, takes the largest prey. The Purple Heron and the Great White Egret take slightly smaller prey. The Bittern, the Night Heron and the Squacco Heron take still smaller prey, although ones which are large com-

A - Little egret

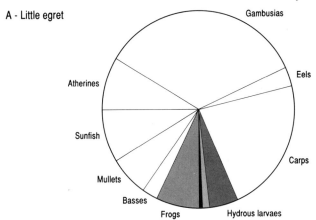

B - Night heron

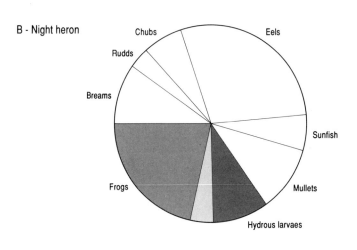

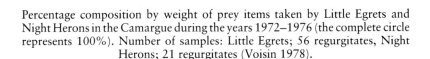

Percentage composition by weight of prey items taken by Little Egrets and Night Herons in the Camargue during the years 1972–1976 (the complete circle represents 100%). Number of samples: Little Egrets; 56 regurgitates, Night Herons; 21 regurgitates (Voisin 1978).

pared to their size. On the contrary, the Little Egret specializes in very small prey taken in large numbers. Since these items are often very swift, Little Egrets must be very active feeders to get enough food. Cattle Egrets often face the same situation when feeding only on insects. Competition for food among the various heron species is limited by the size of the prey taken by each. Large fish can only be swallowed by the larger species, which leave the small, unprofitable ones because if they wasted time catching them they would starve to death. However, medium-sized prey are taken by all species. Amphibians are a particularly important and a very nutritious source of food for all herons. In most cases, competition for food is more limited by habitat specialization than by the actual prey taken, although when food is short, competition still occurs between different species hunting in the same habitat.

All of the European habitats suitable for herons are shown in Fig. 4. Some heron species forage in many different habitats, whereas others use only a few. The only true generalist (Recher 1980) is the Grey Heron, which forages in all habitats: marine, inland aquatic (lagoons, lakes and river banks) and even terrestrial, mostly by day but by night as well. Their adaptation to marine habitats has allowed them to expand along the coasts of Europe to very high latitudes. As a generalist, Grey Herons should be numerous in Europe and this seems to be confirmed by the fact that as soon they were protected their numbers increased rapidly. Their patchy breeding distribution, which has much puzzled ornithologists, is probably due only to persecution by man. If this really proves to be the case, the protection should allow Grey Herons to nest everywhere in Western Europe where suitable habitats occur.

The second species that is not particularly specialized within its European range is the Night Heron. However, this species is never found in saltwater areas such as lagoons or along the coast because of the lack of vegetation in which to hide. This little heron, typically a bird of the mangrove forest, forages in marshes and along rivers and particularly thrives in gallery forests. It is the only survivor in Europe of the old and numerous genera of night fishing herons whose fossil ancestors seem to have been much larger birds.

Typical specialists among Western European herons are the Little Egrets and both bitterns. Little Egrets have evolved so as to enable a relatively large bird to live on very small prey not utilized by other herons. New foraging behaviours have appeared (Foot-stirring and Running-with-open-wings), together with special anatomical features. This slender bird is particularly swift and its long, thin bill is adapted to catch small items. Though very particular when fishing, Little Egrets are able to alter their usual choice of breeding site when the surrounding foraging areas are suitable for them. In the Camargue, they can thus be found breeding on pines growing on old sand dunes instead of breeding in trees in flooded areas. The bitterns have colonized the dense reed beds and are totally adapted to this habitat where they both breed and hunt. They have developed special anatomical features in order to move rapidly in dense reeds and have relatively short, strong legs and very long toes (see the Bittern). They are the only heron species totally dependent upon one habitat. While the Bittern can only live in extensive reed beds, the Little Bittern also colonizes small or very small ones. In both cases, the bird disappears if its only habitat is lost. The world distribution of the large bitterns confirms that these specialized birds belong to a very old genus, since different species are found in all the reed beds of the world, even those in remote parts of South America, Australia and Tasmania. Purple Herons have also colonized reed beds for breeding, and have developed at least one special feature for this, their long toes. However, they are much less specialized than the bitterns and still have the long legs characteristic of other herons. They

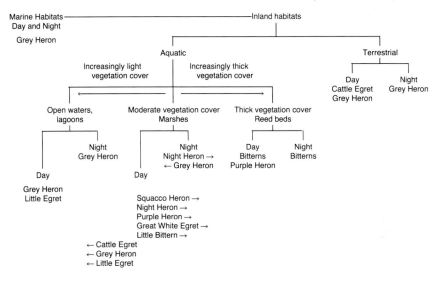

Figure 1   Habitat partition among foraging European herons.

may breed in very small reed beds, but can alter their choice of breeding habitat when no reeds are available but foraging conditions remain good. Purple Herons are thus found breeding in trees in western France together with other tree-nesting herons. They usually forage outside the reedy areas, in surrounding marshland.

The last three species do not really belong to western Europe and do not seem particularly adapted to its oceanic climate, needing much warmer summers. Such is the case with the Great White Egret, which is only found in eastern Europe and the Squacco Heron, always a rare bird in western Europe. The Cattle Egret is an African species which has never really invaded Europe properly. They are found locally in Spain and are still not breeding in Italy. Their invasion of France has been slow though they have established themselves in the Camargue and in the west of France. Compared to the explosive expansion of this species in America, this is indeed a very limited affair! I think that the summer months are not hot enough to provide the multitude of insects and amphibians which would be necessary to sustain a rapid increase in the European Cattle Egret population.

CHAPTER 7

Feeding behaviour

The most common feeding technique used by all the herons is a bill thrust in a downward or lateral strike involving a fast, directed movement of the head, neck and body. Some species, such as the Little Egret, often crouch and strike almost horizontal to the water, whereas others such as the Grey Heron and the Great White Egret tend to strike deeply and nearly vertically:

Strikes may be made with neck curled into an S shape or nearly extended and only slightly curved. The head may be lowered or extended towards a prey item, and the thrust made with the neck near full extension. A bill thrust may be accompanied by a body lunge, during which parts of the body submerge. Most bill thrusts are diagonal and must compensate for refraction. A strike is usually made with the bill slightly open. Small and thin fish are usually grasped; wide or large prey may be stabbed, more often with one than with both mandibles. Most prey are swallowed immediately. Large, hard or dangerous ones are battered, rubbed, shaken, dropped or stabbed. Often a prey item will be carried to an exposed place. Herons may or may not pause after prey capture. Pause time is generally longer with large prey. Swallowing in herons is often followed by head shaking and by dipping the bill in the water. The function of dipping is to ease the food passage (Kushlan 1978).

To facilitate the comparative study of feeding behaviours, J.A. Kushlan (1978) has established a standardized nomenclature of the various behaviours observed, based on his own previous work on the subject, as well as that of A.J. Meyerriecks (1960a). In the following list, behaviours added by myself are denoted*, and those from Meyerriecks (1960)[†] (see also Table 3).

1. *Ways of moving (standing, jumping, walking, swimming or flying)*

○ *Stand-and-wait*: stands in one place.
○ **Forward Throwing* of the body without losing grip with the feet: throws itself forwards and loses its balance but still grasps the branch with its feet. The bird catches its prey while falling upside down.
○ **Hanging Upside Down*: hangs upside down from a low branch just above the water surface to catch passing prey. The only heron observed to fish in this way is the Green Heron.
○ *Standing Flycatching*: while standing catches prey that are airborne.
○ *Jumping*: jumps from perch feet first.
○ **Jumping Upwards*: jumps upwards flapping once with the wings to get higher, in order to catch flying insects.
○ *Walking Slowly*: walks at slow speed.
○ *Gleaning*: catches prey located on an object (e.g. an emergent plant) above the water.
○ *Walking Quickly*: walks at a relatively fast speed.
○ *Running*: moves quickly.
○ *Hopping*: flies a short distance and alights.
○ *Leapfrog Feeding*: flies from the back of the feeding flock to the front.
○ *Swimming Feeding*: swims or floats on the surface of the water.
○ *Aerial Flycatching*: catches airborne prey while flying.
○ *Dipping*: puts head down and catches prey while flying.
○ *Plunging*: dives head first from the air.
○ *Hovering*: hovers over water or ground, picking up prey.
○ *Hovering Stirring*: hovers while patting, raking or stirring with the feet.
○ *Diving*: dives head first from a perch.
○ *Feet-first Diving*: alights on the water feet first.

2. *Movements of the bill, head and neck*

○ *Bill vibrating*: rapidly opens and closes its bill in water.
○ *Probing*: quickly and repeatedly moves its bill tip into and out of the water or substrate.
○ *Pecking*: picks up items from the substrate.
○ *Head-tilting*: turns its head and neck to one side.
○ *Head-swinging*: moves its bill from side to side in the water.
○ *Head-and-neck-swaying*: moves its head, neck and sometimes its body from side to side.

3. *Movements of the legs and feet*

○ *Foot-stirring*: vibrates a foot or leg.
○ *Foot-raking*: rakes the substrate with its foot.

○ *Foot-probing*: probes with its foot.
○ *Foot-paddling*: moves its feet up and down.
○ *Foot-dragging*: drags its toes or feet through the water while flying.

4. *Wing movements*

○ †*Wing-flicking*: moves forwards slowly or at a rapid pace, and then periodically extends and retracts its wings in a rapid flicking motion.
○ †*Open-wing Feeding*: runs forwards or dashes about wildly, both wings widespread, and then stabs to the right and to the left.
○ *Underwing Feeding*: places its head under its extended wing for the strike.
○ *Double-wing Feeding*: brings its wings forward and holds them over its head.
○ *Canopy Feeding*: brings its wings forward and holds them over its head to form a closed canopy.

5. *Hunting methods using elements other than the heron itself*

○ *Association with other birds, mammals or fire*: uses the presence of other birds, mammals or fire to improve its hunting results.
○ *Baiting*: places material that attracts prey in the water.
○ *Kleptoparasitism*: takes food items from other birds.

Each species has its own usual hunting behaviours, but in addition can use others in order to catch abundant or easily taken prey in a habitat which it does not normally frequent.

All herons use the Stand-and-wait method; many use it as their main technique, others only exceptionally. This behaviour is used while standing in the water, on a perch, on land or even on floating plants. Walking Slowly is also a foraging technique used by all heron species. The speed of walking differs and, when very slow, often merges imperceptibly with standing. Other common feeding techniques include the Disturb-and-chase hunt, where the herons walks quickly, runs or even flies for short distances, and alights again. However, herons do specialize. Those species which usually hunt using the Stand-and-wait method, do not use the Disturb-and-chase techniques, and those which do, only exceptionally Stand-and-wait for prey. Both large and small herons specialize in the Stand-and-wait or Walking Slowly methods. In contrast, medium-sized herons tend to use the Disturb-and-chase techniques. Large herons probably favour static techniques because of the considerable energy cost involved in fast motion, and small ones because their shorter legs prevent efficient wading. Small species are forced to forage perched over the water or at the water's edge, although they do walk and sometimes even run along the shore.

In addition to these hunting methods common to most herons, many species use specialized techniques that are characteristic of one or a few species only. These particular hunting methods are their preferred ones and have therefore been well observed and described. They involve various movements of the feet and wings, such as Foot-stirring, Foot-probing, Foot-paddling, Wing-flicking, Open-wing Feeding, Underwing Feeding, Double-wing Feeding, Canopy Feeding and Leapfrog Feeding. Canopy Feeding is a particularly spectacular hunting behaviour peculiar to the Black Heron *Egretta ardesiaca*. The bird raises its wings, fully spread, forward and downward until they meet in front and the tips of the primaries and secondaries touch the water, the tail droops and the elongated scapulars are erected. The shade created by the wings probably attracts swift-moving prey, such as small fish which usually seek shade under vegetation and overhanging river banks. Leapfrog Feeding, first described by Meyerriecks (1960) in Cattle Egrets, has since been observed in other species. Most observers interpret it as a case of cooperative feeding or communal beating. For Kushlan (1978), it is "rather a form of hopping in which a bird moves to the better, forward position of the group". Kushlan does not regard Leapfrog Feeding as communal beating since the birds "are in general well dispersed when feeding and maintain fairly large territories within the aggregation".

The choice of a particular technique from a species repertoire depends on the kind of prey being hunted. When a heron is seeking slow-moving prey, it only has to stand or walk slowly, picking them up, one after the other, without any hurry. When hunting for fast-moving prey, it arches its neck and has to use one of the more complicated behaviours described above. A few of the active fishing species use Neck-Swaying, which probably permits a still faster strike, the bird being already on the move before the strike is made.

Herons may also use unusual hunting behaviours to catch prey which suddenly become very numerous or easily accessible in a habitat not normally suitable for feeding, such as areas of deep water. On these occasions, behaviours such as Jumping, Dipping, Plunging, Hovering, Feet-first Diving, Diving, Aerial Flycatching and Swimming Feeding are observed. None of these is usually common, but most herons seem able to perform them when necessary or useful. As they occur seldom, they are of course only exceptionally observed, but fortunately observers usually report them in detail. Such notes are very useful, since a single observer, even if studying herons for many years, will only see a few of them personally. Reading the literature is thus the only way to obtain a thorough knowledge of the less common hunting behaviours, particularly those of European species which rarely resort to them.

It is interesting to compare the exceptional fishing techniques of Night Herons and Cattle Egrets. These two species have a very large range and have frequently been observed. The Night Heron, which often forages along river banks, uses many different techniques in order to catch prey in deep water, whereas the Cattle Egret, which forages mostly on grassland, has never been seen fishing in deep water. However, Cattle Egrets are probably able to Hover, to Jump into deep water or to Swim and Feed but do not have opportunities for these techniques in their normal habitat. The case of a Grey Heron observed probing in the mud to catch frogs is particularly interesting as this foraging technique had never been observed in other herons, although it is usual among closely related families such as storks, spoonbills and ibises. Clearly, the Grey Heron, which never normally uses this foraging behaviour, is in fact quite able to do so when it is particularly valuable in allowing the capture of large prey.

Herons not only increase their foraging success through new and more highly adapted techniques, but also use man-made or natural grass fires and the presence of other animals, mammals and birds, to improve their foraging rate. Like many other birds hunting on grassland, Cattle Egrets take advantage of grass fires which flush prey into view. They congregate in numbers whenever a fire occurs and hunt on either side of it, often coming very near to the flames. They also associate with large mammals which stir up numerous insects while grazing. Both strategies increase the number of prey taken per unit time compared to the catch of a lone bird in the same habitat without such help. Egrets tend to associate with other water-birds to increase their foraging success in a similar way. Little Egrets *Egretta garzetta* have thus been seen associating with spoonbills, ibises and cormorants (see the chapter on the Little Egret) and Snowy Egrets *Egretta thula* with mergansers.

> Each day in March 1968 in Florida near Sarasota, small groups of mergansers arrived in the bay about 15:00 and congregated into a large flock. After several periods of preening and regrouping the birds began fishing, swimming slowly, and frequently submerging the bill and eyes under the surface. The birds followed several predictable routes, zigzagging up the bay in a manner that forced a concentration of fish into shallow water. Four species of herons fed commonly in the area, the Common Egret *Egretta alba*, the Louisiana Heron *Egretta tricolor*, the Great Blue Heron *Ardea herodia* and the Snowy Egret *Egretta thula*. Three of these species seemed to benefit from the feeding tactics of the mergansers. The behaviour of Common Egrets and Louisiana Herons can best be described as follows: when mergansers drove fish toward where they were feeding, both their striking rate and capture rate increased predictably. More interesting was the behaviour of the Snowy Egrets. Each afternoon 10 to 15 individuals congregated on a narrow spit of land bordering the bay and engaged in various maintenance activities. Fishing behaviour was uncommon at this time, but as the flock of mergansers formed and began moving up the inlets, the egrets flew to the shorelines near or in front of the mergansers and actively followed the progression of the merganser flock. Additional egrets joined this progression, and not uncommonly as many as 20 egrets followed the feeding mergansers. When the mergansers swam in close to the shore the egrets moved out to meet them. At these times the feeding activity of the egrets was intense, and individual capture rates of five to eight small fish per minute were not uncommon. Intense feeding frenzies of this type seldom lasted more than a few minutes because mergansers normally changed course and moved toward another shore of the narrow bay. The egrets then also abandoned the area, flew across the bay, and waited as the mergansers approached the new shore. These observations seem to represent a clear-cut example of one species learning to exploit the normal feeding habits of a second, unrelated species (Emlen and Ambrose 1970).

This kind of relationship may involve a much greater number of species, such as described by D.W. Lamm (1975), where not only herons but also gulls, pelicans and a cormorant took advantage of a group of fishing mergansers. At Bahia de la Conception (*c.* 26°38′N, 111°50′W) on the Gulf of California, a group of

> about 40 Red-breasted Mergansers were seen swimming together with their heads often below the water, parallel to the rocky shoreline and ranging from 10 to 30 ft from the shore. Moving along the shore abreast of the ducks were 7 snowy Egrets, a Reddish Egret *Egretta rufescens*, 18 Heermann's Gulls *Larus*

heermanni and 3 Ring-billed Gulls *Larus delawarensis*. This assemblage was gradually augmented by another Reddish Egret, two Brown Pelicans *Pelecanus occidentalis* and a Double-crested Cormorant *Phalacrocorax auritus*. The pelicans and cormorant stayed on the open-water side of the ducks. When the mergansers found fish and commenced diving, the whole scene became one of frenzied activity. As the fish sought to escape, some fled toward the shore, and the herons moved into shallow water and darted about, snatching them up. The pelicans and cormorant fed on fish which moved towards deeper water. The Heermann's Gulls showed an interest in the mergansers but did not obtain any food from them; they did successfully harass the pelicans and both they and the Ring-billed Gulls robbed the Snowy Egrets. Both species of gulls also waded in to get food from the shallow water. After a few minutes, the school of fish was dissipated or moved to deeper water. The procession then moved on. Three such scenes of activity involving the same group of birds were observed in 40 min of observation.

A few bird species have been observed using tools. . . . This behaviour is not characteristic of the more highly evolved passerines. The Pied Kingfisher *Ceryle rudis* and the Black Kite *Milvus migrans* both use bait to lure prey and the Egyptian Vulture *Neophron percnopterus* breaks open Ostrich eggs by dropping stones on them. Recently, tool use in the form of bait has been observed in the Green Heron *Butorides striatus* and the Squacco Heron *Ardeola ralloides* by several observers (for the Squacco Heron, see the chapter on this bird).

At least nine observations of Green Herons using bait have been made both in Africa and in America. Walsh *et al.* (1985) wrote:

In May 1981 near Ouagadougou, Burkina Faso, we noticed beside a stretch of about 100 m of nearly stagnant water an adult Green Heron perched on an overhanging branch, about 80 cm above the water surface. This bird was poised, pointing down with its longitudinal axis at an angle of nearly 150°. It held a small pale object between the tips of its mandibles. It remained stationary for a minute or so, then slowly stretched itself so as to be nearer the water, adapting an almost vertical stance. After a few seconds the bird released the object from a height of about 20 cm, on the surface of the water. Very slowly the object drifted towards us and it proved to be a white and mauve flower.

Norris (1975) photographed a Green Heron that dropped a feather onto the water surface and thus caught a fish, clearly demonstrating the purpose of this behaviour. Lovell (1958) wrote:

On Lake Eola at Orlando, Florida many visitors feed the water birds during the winter with the result the birds become very tame. On April 16, 1957, a Green Heron was fishing from a low retaining wall on the edge of the lake. When we threw him a piece of bread, he picked it up and placed it in the water. At first we thought he was softening it before eating, but instead, he allowed the piece of bread to float slowly away. When it was almost out of reach, he picked it up and placed it close to the wall again. Suddenly the heron speared a fish which came up to nibble on the bread. We threw him another piece some distance back from the wall. The heron picked it up and ran back to the edge of the lake and again

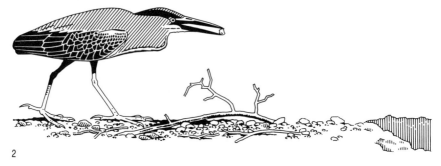

2

Figures 2–4   Green Heron fishing with a pellet as bait (after Sisson 1974);
2, the Green Heron brings the pellet to where it intends to fish.

starting fishing with the bread as bait. Several times when some American Coots *Fulica americana* swam in after the floating bread, the heron retrieved it and drove away the intruders with threatening strokes of his long bill. As soon as the coots were dispersed, he again placed the bread in the water near the wall and resumed his fishing.

At the Miami Seaquarium, a Green Heron was seen fishing with a pellet as bait. The whole sequence was photographed by Sisson (1974), who wrote:

The heron picks up a dry pellet from the island and carries it in his bill down to the edge of the water. Reaching the channel, he pauses and seems to survey the water for the best fishing spot. Then slowly his neck stretches out and out, as if made of elastic and ever so gently he drops the bait in the water. Now the fisherman in him really takes over. Hunkering down between two rocks, he stays as still as a statute; his eyes never leave the pellet as it bobs in the water.

This observation shows that even the sight of a motionless heron is enough to frighten a fish. The heron not only hunts using bait it has brought for this purpose, but it must also hide while watching the bait. The complexity of hunting behaviours among herons, catching such swift prey as small fish, is very clearly illustrated in this case.

Keenan (1981) further reported a Green Heron fishing with mayflies (Ephemeroptera) in South Carolina and Boswall (1977) reported two more instances of fishing with bait from Florida and one from Cuba. Some common elements emerge from these observations. Either, food items or inanimate objects may be used to lure prey. The bait may be taken some distance away, either by walking or flying, with the intention of using it as a lure. During a conflict with another bird, the heron seems to keep the object in its bill, not forgetting its purpose, and when it catches an insect, it does not swallow it immediately but keeps it to use as bait later. The habitat of the Green Heron favours such fishing techniques, as many fish in streams normally capture insects that fall on the water surface. These fish are usually

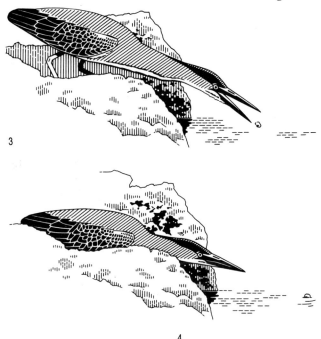

3, the Green Heron lets the pellet fall into the water 4, it hides while waiting for the bait to attract fish.

small and do not make up enough food for the Night Heron which also forages in the same type of habitat. The fact that a Squacco Heron was once seen to use bait in the same way as the Green Heron when far away from its range and where food was almost certainly scarce, shows that many herons are probably able to use this method of fishing if necessary. As already mentioned in the chapter on classification, Payne and Risley (1976) have, on anatomical grounds, proposed not to maintain the genus *Butorides* but to include it in the genus *Ardeola*. The fact that *Butorides* and *Ardeola* are the only herons which have been observed hunting with bait further suggests a close relationship between these genera. However, if as suggested above, this hunting technique is much more usual than previously thought, this opportunistic behaviour will not have much taxonomic value.

In conclusion, three kinds of tools are known to be used by birds: stones to drop, bait to attract prey, and twigs, spines and strips of wood as probes to catch insects. Some birds can even be said to make tools, as spines and twigs are modified to serve their purpose. The fact that several bird species use tools to forage, presents new perspectives when estimating the intellectual capabilities of birds. Their ability to innovate when catching prey is probably much greater than is commonly thought. The best way to reveal and study the intelligence of birds seems to be, therefore, to observe the opportunistic behaviours of foraging wild birds, strongly motivated by conditions of food shortages.

While a few species of heron nearly always forage in flocks, most usually forage alone. However, the behaviour of the various species is often very plastic in this respect also. The Grey Heron, for example, is particularly variable, probably because it winters in temperate latitudes where food is difficult to find. Grey Herons are very opportunistic and it appears that individuals, as they grow older and gain more experience, improve their foraging abilities. They may forage alone, sometimes defending territories and then, later, may form groups foraging in a relatively restricted area.

According to Kushlan (1978), the tendency for herons in an area to feed either in flocks or dispersed more widely depends a great deal on the degree of dispersion of the local food resources which may be clumped, highly dispersed or have an intermediate distribution. When food is dispersed, the defence of large territories is both possible and useful. The size of the territory depends on its ease of defence, indicated by the frequency of aggressive encounters. The energy cost of defence must be lower than the extra benefits of holding a territory defended. This relationship depends on the degree of dispersion of the food resources in the territory and also on the size of the heron population there. When birds are numerous, they tend to defend smaller territories. When food is abundant and very clumped, such as for example in a pool which is drying up, no territory is defendable; the herons all fish together, maintaining only their individual distances.

Herons have opportunistic feeding behaviours and among prey of the right size for a given species, they catch the easiest and most numerous ones in a given locality and season. How herons choose to switch foraging areas is not known. The Little Egrets in the Camargue (Voisin 1978) always choose to forage where the water levels are receding, avoiding places where it is stationary or rising. When the change in water level is not at all obvious to a human observer, how do the birds know if it is rising or falling?

The Ciconiiformes seem to be especially sensitive to small changes in water level. I have observed how a small lowering of the water level in a heron colony in the Djoudj, Senegal, caused the desertion of the entire colony during the incubation stage. The drying up of the area occurred too soon and the young would not have had enough food to survive by the end of the breeding season. Among Wood Stork colonies in the marshes of the Everglades, Kushlan (1978) observed that a rise in the water level equal to or greater than 3 cm during the first 2 months of the breeding season causes desertion of the colonies. Wood Storks forage during breeding by probing the mud in drying areas where prey become relatively concentrated. The Ciconiiformes, therefore, are not only sensitive to small changes in water level, but can also anticipate the results of this on their breeding success. The members of this ancient bird family, which evolved in this habitat of periodically flooded shallow-water areas, have, I believe, developed a special aptitude for evaluating changes in water level which has yet to be understood.

Whether or not roosts and colonies are used by herons as information centres, enabling them to learn the whereabouts of food from each other, has been a subject of much debate. In my opinion, numerous observations of birds leaving the heronry, clearly show that this is indeed the case. At dusk each day, Night Herons leave the heronry in groups. One, two or three birds fly off uttering their loud and characteristic Departure Call, and then circle over the colony one or several times, still crying loudly. After one or two such Circle Flights, the first Night Herons are joined by a few others that also perform Circle Flights, calling all the while. After perhaps one, but usually after a few such flights they fly away, often in several directions in small groups, still calling. The leading birds in one of these groups fly towards a good foraging area which they know, and are probably followed by one or two birds who will doubtless then explore the foraging areas around those where the leading birds land. Little Egrets leave the colony at dawn in numbers, each squadron heading straight in one definite direction. Of course, individuals which were foraging the previous evening in places where prey had become scarce will follow one of these determined squadrons to areas where the whole group can fish together in loose flocks. Colonial breeding and roosting are common in birds that utilize a patchy food distribution. Among herons, it appears that the roosts and colonies do act as information centres, enabling all the birds to find the best foraging grounds, particularly in situations where the progressive drying-up of pools and waterways leads to a patchy and constantly changing distribution of prey.

HOW YOUNG LEARN TO CATCH PREY

Young herons must learn to catch and to handle prey. During my study on the Little Egret (Voisin 1977), I observed that young birds which had begun to fly from branch to branch also soon flew down into the shallow water of the lagoon, which extended almost up to the foot of the trees in the heronry. Wading around, the young birds seized all kinds of floating objects such as bits of wood, leaves and feathers. At first, they only stayed in the water for short periods, soon flying back to the nest. As the days passed, they stayed in the lagoon longer each time, trying to catch prey. As long as they returned to the nests regularly, they were fed by their parents, that is to say for about 1 month. During that time, they learned to hunt sufficiently well to sustain themselves after leaving their parents.

B. Snow (1974) has observed the Plumbeous Heron of the Galapagos (*Butorides striatus sundevalli*). She wrote:

> I first saw juveniles walking about on the shore and among the shallow silty pools below the mangroves at an age of 27 to 30 days. At this age they seize and mandibulate in the tips of their bills all sorts of inanimate, usually elongated, objects such as rolled up leaves, leaf stipules, and bits of root. They also pick up and put down again hermit crabs lodged in the shells of gastropods. This exploratory mandibulating of inedible objects continues until they are at least 40 days old. I first saw juveniles catch prey between 33 and 35 days. One juvenile caught a small prawn and held it for about 20 seconds in the tip of its bill before swallowing it; another caught a small starfish that wrapped itself around the tip of the heron's bill where it remained for 20 minutes without either escaping or being swallowed. Four days later the same juvenile caught a small species of crab among the mangroves that, when caught, presses its legs tightly to its body so that it appears to have changed into a round pebble. The juvenile managed to swallow

the first two crabs it caught, but it seemed unable to shift the next one from its bill tip to its throat. After picking it up and putting it down about twenty times, it abandoned the attempt. Early efforts by juveniles to catch *Grapsus grapsus* were invariably unsuccessful, for the young herons clumsily hopped and ran after the crabs instead of stalking them. Between the ages of 64 and 81 days, juvenile D caught several species of crustaceans, including *Grapsus*, *Uca helleri*, *Uca galapagensis* and small prawns.

H.F. and J.A. Recher (1969) have compared the foraging efficiency of adult and immature Little Blue Herons *Florida caerula*. Field observations are easy in this species as the newly independent juveniles are quite distinct from their parents, being white, rather than dark coloured. This juvenile plumage is moulted during the birds' second summer, when they are at least 9 months old. During this moult, they sport a distinctive piebald plumage. These authors found differences in the success rate and weight of food obtained per minute foraging between juveniles and adults; the adults were more efficient than the juveniles, but not always significantly so. These slight differences were, in my opinion, due to the fact that first-winter birds, and certainly second-summer birds, have already foraged alone for some time and handle prey nearly as well as adults. B. Snow (1974) wrote about a juvenile heron in the Galapagos which she observed for 7 months following its independence: "I judged its fishing abilities when it was 81 days old, equal to an adult's." But, she also wrote: "It was always silent, furtive and inconspicuous; but even so, adults frequently chased it off."

The greater mortality of first-year birds may be caused by factors other than their fishing abilities. In the species which maintain foraging territories, the juveniles are subordinate and thus have to fish in the less favourable areas. Lacking the experience of adult birds, they are also at a disadvantage when foraging conditions change with the season. By trial and error, with all its consequent problems, they must learn how to avoid potentially disastrous habitats. Their subordinate status and lack of experience probably explain much of their higher mortality from accidents and starvation during their first year.

Observing the behaviour of others probably plays an important part in the spread of unusual foraging techniques. The Green Herons which used pellets as bait at the Miami Seaquarium probably learned from one another following a chance discovery by a single bird. Observations, and a few experiments, have shown that herons must learn what is edible and what is not. In the beginning, they catch all sorts of inanimate objects. Poisonous prey such as certain caterpillars, which are taken at first by young Cattle Egrets, are later carefully avoided (Bigot and Jouventin 1974).

One particularly interesting experiment, however, clearly demonstrates that avoidance of very dangerous prey can be based on an innate response and thus does not have to be learned by the bird:

For many piscivorous birds, one dangerous potential prey is *Pelamis platurus*, the yellow-bellied sea snake. It is the world's most widely distributed species of snake. *Pelamis* has a venom many times more toxic than that of rattlesnakes, cobras, or coral snakes. It has a brilliant yellow underside, black back, and a strikingly patterned black and yellow tail. *Pelamis platurus* occasionally washes up alive on the Pacific coast of Central America where herons and egrets regularly feed on fish and eels. Mistaking a sea snake for a harmless eel could be lethal for a heron; yet, passing up an item as nutritious and favored as an eel would be energetically inefficient. We therefore used 12 naive, hand-reared herons to determine whether or not they could distinguish between sea snakes and innocuous serpentine prey available to them in Panama. Two Great Egrets *Egretta alba*, four Snowy Egrets *Egretta thula*, and six Green-backed Herons *Butorides striatus* were taken from their nests at 2 days of age. . . . Each bird previously had attacked other novel prey such as dully coloured grasshoppers, mice, and skinks without hesitation. . . . The initial responses to the sea snakes were dramatic and in each case the same. The bird upon seeing the dead sea snake immediately backed away, with crest erect, to a distance of about 2 m and then flew erratically around the aviary, trying to escape by scratching at the gate with feet and bill. None of the birds had tried to escape from the aviary before. After 15 minutes of attempted escape both Great White Egrets approached with neck outstretched and body held as far as possible from the snake, jabbed hard at the back of the snake's head, and flew suddenly backwards. The Snowy Egrets and the Green-backed Herons during the same period maintained the farthest possible distance from the snake, staring at it. For the remainder of the hour all birds remained immobile except for feeble attempts to get out of the cage. After the snake was removed the birds kept their eyes fixed on the place the snake had been but resumed begging 5 minutes later. The live sea snake and the dead sea snake with tail removed produced reactions similar to those given in the initial encounters with the dead sea snake. Each bird fled to the far corner of the cage and remained immobile with eyes fixed on the snake for the remainder of the trial. Reactions to other serpentine stimuli were strikingly different. The birds characteristically begged and either approached or ignored the potential prey . . . . Interestingly, the sea snake is the only bright yellow and black potential prey in Panama available to herons and egrets. . . . The combination of low encounter probability and high prey toxicity would favor a genetically based rather than a learned response (Sullivan Caldwell and Wolff Rubinoff 1983).

It thus seems that at least one innate pattern of prey avoidance exists in certain heron species. It is well known that many toxic or venomous animals display strikingly variegated colour patterns which warn potential predators of their noxious qualities. These colour patterns generally involve black and yellow or black and red, particularly conspicuous combinations. Until now, it was believed that predators almost always had to learn their meaning. That some species may avoid prey with warning coloration as an innate response is a fairly new observation and opens new fields of research. Of course, innate recognition of colour patterns which act as behavioural stimuli in birds are already well known in other contexts. For example, the colour patterns of the bill and gape of adults and chicks often function as stimuli during feeding of the young.

Table 3. Feeding behaviours actually observed among the nine species of European herons

	Grey Heron	Purple Heron	Great Bittern	Little Bittern	Night Heron	Squacco Heron	Great White Egret	Little Egret	Cattle Egret
1. Ways of moving (standing, jumping, walking, running, swimming or flying)									
Stand-and-wait	●	●	●	●	●	●	●	●	●
Forward throwing of the body without losing grip					●				
Hanging Upside Down[a]									
Standing Flycatching					●				●
Jumping									
Jumping Upwards									
Walking Slowly[b]	●	●	●	●	●	●	●	●	●
Gleaning	●		●	●		●		●	●
Walking Quickly	●							●	●
Running								●	●
Hopping								●	●
Leapfrog Feeding					●				●
Swimming Feeding									
Aerial Flycatching									●
Dipping[a]									
Plunging					●				
Hovering					●			●	
Hovering Stirring[a]									
Diving[a]	●	●			●		●		
Feet-first Diving									
2. Movements of the bill, head and neck									
Bill-vibrating									
Probing	●				●				

Pecking[a]
Head-tilting
Head-swinging[a]
Head-and-neck-swaying

3. *Movements of the legs and feet*
Foot-stirring
Foot-raking[a]
Foot-probing[a]
Foot-paddling
Foot-dragging[a]

4. *Wing movements*
Wing-flicking[a]
Open-wing Feeding
Underwing Feeding
Double-wing Feeding[a]
Canopy Feeding[a]

5. *Hunting methods using elements other than the heron itself*
Association with other birds
Association with mammals
Association with fire
Baiting
Kleptoparasitism

●, Observed behaviour.
[a]Feeding behaviour not observed among European herons.
[b]Walking slowly is identical with Wade-or-walk-slowly.

CHAPTER 8

The food of herons

Herons may, on occasion, catch and eat any living prey which can be swallowed. However, each species has specialized in a few kinds of prey which are energetically profitable for them and to which their hunting techniques are adapted. For all European species, except the Cattle Egret, the most commonly taken prey are fish and amphibians. The Cattle Egret is the only European species able to live for long periods almost on insects alone. However, during breeding, even Cattle Egrets hunt for fish or amphibians, since insects cannot provide enough energy to feed the brood. As the prey captured by herons depends greatly on their availability, there is marked variability in space and time. For a given species, the main source of food for one or several days may be fish or amphibians, but can also be small mammals in the case of Grey Herons, birds (both adults and chicks) in the case of Night Herons, crustaceans, molluscs or worms in the case of Little Egrets, or insects in the case of Cattle Egrets. In addition to their main source of food, all herons take odd prey which they may encounter occasionally. A few species, such as the Night Heron and the Little Bittern, have also been seen to steal eggs.

It has often been stated that herons select their prey so as to give small ones to small chicks and larger ones to older chicks. My observations, as well as those of Kushlan (1978), do not support this opinion. The Night Herons as well as the Little Egrets which I have observed seem to give very digested food to small chicks rather than to select especially small prey for them. While brooding, one parent feeds the young nestlings several times during its turn on the nest. The prey given are so well digested that they seem reduced to a semi-liquid condition. As soon as the brooding period is over, the adult feeds the young immediately on its arrival at the nest, items being then only partially digested. It frequently happens that when the nestlings are still small the food items provided are too large to be handled by them. The food falls to the nest bottom and is usually swallowed again by the adult. As adults have difficulty enough in catching sufficient food to feed their offspring, mortality of the young would increase greatly if they had to be overly selective in choosing the size of nutritious prey by not taking those that are too large. Increasing the acceptability of prey by pre-digestion seems much more profitable for the birds than choosing prey by size alone. Further studies on herons which feed on particularly large, hard and difficult to swallow prey, such as crayfish, may well show that they avoid taking them when feeding young. According to Kushlan (1978), a few prey often eaten by adults are particularly avoided by them while foraging to feed their young. This is the case, for example, in fish containing high levels of thiaminase which cannot be given in great quantities to the growing young. Marabous, which are able to live on carrion for long periods, switch to catching fish and frogs to feed their young probably in order to provide the calcium needed by the growing chicks.

Surprisingly, very few studies have been done on the food requirements of piscivorous birds, either adults or young, since these studies are not very difficult to carry out with captive birds. Junor (1972) has hand-reared chicks of various piscivorous bird species from Lake Kyle in Zimbabwe. He estimated the daily food requirement of virtually adult piscivorous birds to be about 16% their body weight. According to Kushlan (1978), the few data that are available on the daily food requirements of wading birds, including those of Junor, show that these requirements increase with body weight following the regression $\log y = 0.961 \log x - 0.640$, where x is the body weight and y is the food requirement, in grams.

The digestion of herons is rapid and selective; fish and frogs being digested much faster than the chitinous insects. Pellets regurgitated by herons many hours after a meal contain only selected remains. A study by Vinokurov in 1960 on Purple Herons shows how rapid digestion is. Having fed five Purple Herons with fish, frogs and insects, he examined the digestive systems of birds killed in succession. One hour after the meal parts of the intestines of the fish were digested, the fish scales and heads were strongly attacked by the gastric juices, and bits of the gill covers were already loosened. Parts of the skin and head of the frogs were digested; the fingers being totally digested. The insects were only flattened. After 2 hours, the skeletons of the fish were falling apart, only the tail flukes remaining. The skeletons of the frogs were dislocated and the insects were crushed. After 3–4 hours, only a few fish bones, mostly vertebrae, and the small horned plates which are found in the gapes of Cyprinidae, remained. The frogs had totally disappeared. The heads and legs of insects were still found. After 7 hours, only small bits of chitinous parts and one horned plate were found.

CHAPTER 9

The Bittern *Botaurus stellaris*

GENERAL APPEARANCE AND FIELD CHARACTERS

The Bittern is a medium-sized heron, 70–80 cm high with a wing-span of 125–135 cm.

Plumage. The sexes are alike except that the females are usually smaller than the males.

Adult: the general colour of the adult plumage is golden-brown, the upperparts being mottled and barred with black and the underparts longitudinally streaked with dark brown and black. The loose texture of the feathers resembles the plumage of owls. The crown, nape and moustache are black. The chin and throat are creamy white with a central line of brown feathers slightly mottled with black. The elongated feathers on the crown, neck and chest can be erected at will.

Juvenile: the juvenile plumage is similar but paler, with many fine brown mottlings and vermiculations. The black crown is tinged with brown and the moustachial stripe is brown also.

Downy young: the nestlings have a reddish brown down, darker on the head, neck and back and lighter on the belly. They are creamy white on the chin and throat as well as around the eyes.

Bare parts

Adults and juvenile: the coloration of the bare parts is the same for both. The bill is yellowish green and the ridge of the culmen is brown, darker towards the tip. The bare skin of the face is green to pale blue. The iris is yellow or orange-red (the latter probably in breeding adults only). The legs and feet are mainly pale green; the tarsal joint, the back of the tarsus and the soles being yellow.

Nestling: at hatching, the nestlings have a horn-coloured bill that soon becomes blue-green. The iris is white. The legs and feet are blue-green.

Field characters.

The Bittern usually appears as a stocky, bulky, thick-necked heron flying low over the reeds. The colour of the plumage can be difficult to observe, since most of the time Bitterns fly at dawn or dusk. If the light is reasonable, the bird appears golden-brown with black markings and a black crown (or a brown crown more or less tinged with black if it is a juvenile). This shy and secretive bird is more often heard than seen. In spring, the males perform their characteristic booming, an unmistakable sound which, though not very loud, may carry for distances of up to 3–5 km.

The American Bittern, *Botaurus lentiginosus* (Montagu), is sometimes reported from western Europe, principally in Britain. This bird is smaller than the European Bittern. The plumage is paler and the crown is chestnut, not black, while the moustachial stripe is very conspicuous. In flight, the brown-grey flight feathers contrast sharply with the pale brown coverts.

The juvenile American Bittern is more difficult to distinguish from the European Bittern, since it has a more streaked, darker plumage than the adult, and lacks the black moustachial stripe during the first autumn.

Though quite different, juvenile Night Herons are sometimes mistaken for Bitterns. Night Herons are much smaller and during their first winter their brown plumage is mottled with white marks, not black, as in the Bittern. During their second year, their plumage begins to show a greyish tinge, very different from the golden-brown of the Bittern.

Measurements.

The measurements (mm) of adult and juvenile birds taken from skins are given below (Cramp and Simmons 1977). The number of skins and the sex are indicated. Standard deviations are given in parentheses. The sex differences are significant.

wing	21 ♂♂ 335–357 (6.67)	16 ♀♀ 296–327 (7.34)	
tail	11 ♂♂ 112–126 (4.40)	8 ♀♀ 96–110 (4.87)	
bill	20 ♂♂ 61–74 (3.24)	16 ♀♀ 60–68 (2.10)	
tarsus	11 ♂♂ 97–109 (3.53)	9 ♀♀ 87–95 (2.63)	
toe	20 ♂♂ 110–132 (5.04)	15 ♀♀ 98–119 (5.02)	

Bauer and Glutz (1966) give the following maximum measurements (mm) for adult ♂♂: wing 377, tail 131, bill 80, tarsus 125.

Bitterns seem subject to great weight variations and overwintering birds in central Europe may become very emaciated, as the following figures show:

○ fat birds, or those in normal condition (Bauer and Glutz 1966): ♂ 966–1940 g, ♀ 867–1150 g:
○ emaciated birds (Cramp and Simmons 1977): 12 ♂♂ 462–787 g, 16 ♀♀ 430–750 g.

DISTRIBUTION, MOVEMENTS AND HABITAT

DISTRIBUTION AND MOVEMENTS

Only two subspecies are recognized, *Botaurus stellaris stellaris* (Linnaeus) and *Botaurus stellaris capensis* (Schlegel). The breeding range of *B. s. stellaris* extends from southern England, Sweden and Finland, east to 57°N in the Urals and 59°–64°N in Siberia (where a still more northern population may breed along the coast), to Sakhalin and Hokkaido in Japan, south to northern Morocco, Algeria, Tunisia, Turkey, Iran, Afghanistan, Mongolia and northern China (Hopeh). This subspecies winters from western and central Europe to northern tropical Africa, the Black Sea, the Caspian Sea, Iran, Iraq, the east coast of Arabia, Pakistan, northern India, China and Japan. It has wandered farther south to southern India, Burma, the Malay Peninsula, Taiwan and the Philippines.

B. s. capensis forms a small, isolated and sedentary population in eastern South Africa.

Not all European Bitterns are migratory. The autumn migration begins with the first hard night frost in late September, and continues until December. The spring migration begins in February. In England, the Netherlands and western France, the bulk of the population is sedentary during even the hardest winters. Of 17 birds ringed in the Netherlands and recovered between 1924 and 1953, 13 were recorded in the Netherlands and only 4 abroad, 3 in western France in the autumn and 1 in northern Germany in the summer (Bannerman 1957). A study of recoveries made in central Europe (Zink 1958) shows a southward and westward trend in autumn and winter, and a northward and eastward trend in spring. In Finland and Sweden, the whole population migrates south in autumn, even though during unusually mild winters some individuals may stay in southern Sweden. Recoveries of Bitterns ringed in Sweden have been made along the west coast of Europe from Denmark to Spain (Broberg, in Curry-Lindahl 1959).

Thus wintering birds flying west and southwest come to Denmark, Germany, the Netherlands, England, Belgium and France, while others flying a more southerly route reach Greece, Italy and Spain. In all these countries, the migrating Bitterns meeet already well-established sedentary populations.

Birds wintering in Iran and Iraq are of unknown origin, as are those wintering on both sides of the eastern part of the Mediterranean Sea. Most probably, many of these birds come from the USSR. One bird ringed in Greece on 3 February 1968 was found in the USSR near Koursk on the 10 August 1968 (Paris Ringing Centre).

A spring migration has been observed in Tunisia and Morocco (Heim de Balzac and Mayaud 1962) and individuals have been observed at many oases in the Sahara (El Golea, Ouargla, Touggourt) (Moreau 1967, Heim de Balzac and Mayaud 1962). Wintering Bitterns have been reported from Nigeria, the Sudan, Abyssinia, Eritrea and northeast Zaïre (Cramp and Simmons 1977).

Post-fledging dispersal begins in July and occurs in all directions during the summer (Zink 1958).

The oldest ringed Bittern recovered was ringed in Estland in 1942 and recovered in the same locality 9 years later (Zink 1958). The longest migration flight of a ringed bird covered 2000 km from Sweden to the Biscay provinces in Spain (Bernis 1966).

HABITAT

During the breeding season, Bitterns are restricted to large reed beds growing on lowland swamps and along the shores of lakes usually below 200 m. Being very specialized, these herons require large, unbroken areas of favourable habitat. They avoid reed beds where the water level fluctuates markedly and where the water is too acid (below pH 4.5). They tolerate brackish water and are sometimes found in estuaries, but not on the sea coast itself. Shallow pools of standing water, scattered here and there among dense reed beds are necessary for foraging. Bitterns also use man-made ditches to hunt. When resting, Bitterns usually stand in the fringe of dense vegetation near shallow pools or along ditches. When moving, they often avoid the ground, which is usually very loose or covered with water, but climb in the reeds, gripping several stems between their toes at each step. When possible, they prefer new reeds to old ones, probably because they are sturdier and make less noise when climbed upon. Bitterns also like to stand near the top of the reeds to preen, to sunbathe and even to rest. These birds are so specialized for life in the reeds, that they usually avoid shrubs and trees entirely even when growing quite densely in the marsh. However, Etchécopar and Hüe (1964) have noticed that, quite exceptionally, nests have been found in low trees.

Even during winter, most Bitterns stay in the shelter of dense reed beds, though some may wander. Those migrating from northern and central Europe to western Europe, may occur in winter "at all sorts of rank waterside vegetation, at gravel pits, cress-beds, fish-farms, sewage farms, reservoirs, ditches and riversides" (Bibby 1981). In freezing weather, Bitterns have a hard time and venture out from the shelter of vegetation to seek open water. During such periods, weakened birds may be found in very unsuitable places near human habitation.

POPULATION SIZE AND TRENDS

Nowadays, the numbers of Bitterns are very much reduced, there being only some hundreds of birds in each country. This small population is, therefore, vulnerable, since it is subject to great variation in numbers.

In Sweden, the Bittern became extinct as a breeding species by the middle of the last century. A small population tried to establish itself during the First World War (some males were heard and a nest found in 1919), but too many birds were shot and Bitterns disappeared again. However, by the 1940s, Bitterns had succeeded in colonizing some of the most favourable places in southern Sweden (Curry-Lindahl 1959). By this time, breeding had started in Finland (Day 1981). In Sweden, two national censuses were undertaken in 1953 and 1969. In 1953, 120–130 booming males were heard, all in southern Sweden. By 1969, the number of booming males had increased to 150. The map shows the distribution of Bitterns in Sweden in 1969. There were very

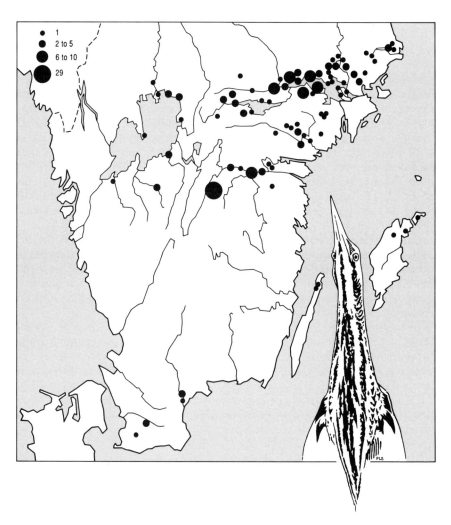

The distribution of Bitterns *Botaurus stellaris* in Sweden, 1969 (Broberg 1971).

few birds after the hard winter of 1962–1963, but their numbers had increased again by 1969, which seems to have been a moderately good year for them (Broberg 1971).

A census in the Netherlands during the period 1950–1953 showed that Bitterns bred in 280 localities. The number of breeding pairs was estimated at 300–330 (Braaksma 1958). During the last century, Bitterns also became extinct as breeding birds in Britain (Day and Wilson 1978), the last proof of breeding being in 1886 in Norfolk where downy young were observed. Although Bitterns continued to winter in Britain, it was not until 1900 that booming was heard again in Norfolk. However, nesting was not proved until 1911 when a nest was found at Sutton Broad. In the following years, the number of breeding pairs increased and in 1923, 23–25 pairs bred in Norfolk. That year the first breeding to take place outside Norfolk was observed at Thorpe Fen, Suffolk and the next 25 years saw a period of consolidation and a slow expansion of the breeding population. In 1954, there were 60 breeding pairs in Norfolk and 19–22 elsewhere.

During the 1950s and the 1960s, the Bittern's range continued to expand. A decline in Norfolk, which seems to have started in the late 1950s or early 1960s, was partly balanced by increases elsewhere in the country. The 1976 count of Bitterns showed a general decline, except in Lancashire where the number of boomers was stable and in Suffolk where it had increased. In 1978, the British population was reduced to 41 boomers. In 1979, the numbers were slightly up with increases in Norfolk and Kent (Day 1981) (see Table 4).

In France, breeders estimated by the number of booming males are also becoming less numerous. In 1974, M. Brosselin estimated that there were 400–500 breeding pairs in 36 departments. However, the 1983 census estimated that there were about 300 pairs in only 24 departments (Duhautois 1984).

A general count for Europe (except the USSR) was made in 1976 on behalf of the International Council for Bird Preservation (ICBP). An estimate of a breeding population of 2500–2700 pairs in 21 countries resulted, assuming that numbers in Greece, Turkey, Italy, Yugoslavia and the southern part of West Germany did not exceed 100 pairs in total (Day 1981; see Table 5). Estimates of the number of occupied nesting sites shows a general reduction. The population thus becomes more vulnerable. In England, 64% of all Bitterns breed in three sites only.

After the hard winter of 1978–1979, further enquiries were made in northwest Europe (Sweden, Denmark, Schleswig-Holstein and the Netherlands) which suggested a decline of 30–50% of the breeding population in 1979 compared with the previous year (Day 1981). In Britain, however, with less hard winters, cold weather does not usually seem to reduce the breeding population drastically. In some areas, such as Leighton Moss, the cold winter of 1962–1963 did not affect the number of Bitterns breeding the following spring and the cold winter of 1978–1979 did not affect the numbers breeding in Britain as a whole. That winter, 54 birds were reported found dead or dying (some were taken care of and released). Since this mortality did not affect breeding numbers the following spring, it must have been mostly migrating birds from the continent which fell victim to the cold. Not knowing

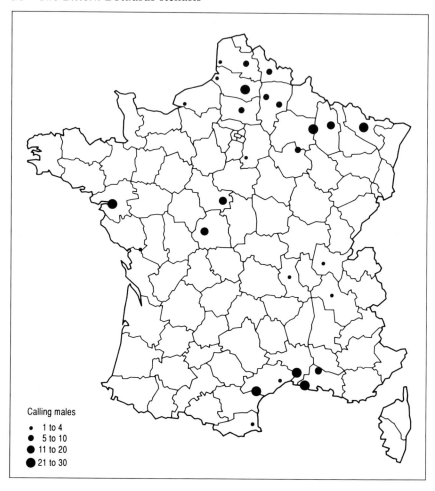

The number of calling male Bitterns *Botaurus stellaris* heard in France during
the spring of 1983 (Duhautois 1984).

their surroundings well, they could not easily find good hunting places and,
being always on the move, were more subject to accidents (Bibby 1981).

Numerous factors which may affect the numbers of Bitterns were studied
in Britain by Day and Wilson (1978). Although mortality is often high during
cold winters, studies suggest that reduced populations of Bitterns can recover
after a period of 5–10 years. At Hickling and Horsey, the population suffered
after the winter of 1962–1963, but had recovered by 1970. In Sweden,
booming males were few during the spring of 1963 but by the 1969 census the

The recoveries of Bitterns *Botaurus stellaris* ringed in two locations in Germany
(Zink 1958).

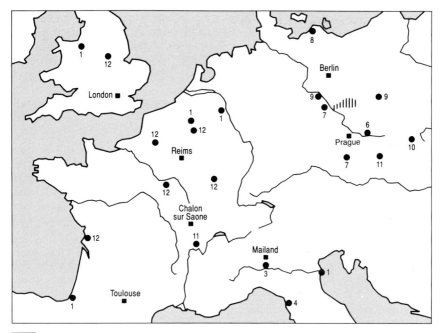

Ringing area   ● Recoveries (The number indicates the month of the recovery)

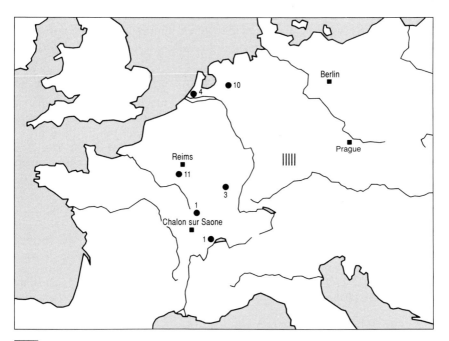

Ringing area   ● Recoveries (The number indicates the month of the recovery)

population had reached its normal level again. The winters of 1969–1970 to 1977–1978 were mild. The result was a high population of resident species normally affected by cold weather (Batten and Marchant 1976), but the Bittern population declined in England during this period; a decline which therefore cannot be explained by cold winters. The Coypu, *Myocastor coypus*, is a newcomer to the wild fauna of England, established on the Norfolk Broads in the early 1940s through escapes and releases from fur farms. Within a few years, these animals became very numerous: "At Hickling large areas of reed swamp were grazed – in some places to the point where open water was created – by hundreds of Coypus" (Beales, in Day and Wilson 1978). Despite this, the population of Bitterns remained stable at Hickling up to the winter of 1962–1963. Cutting and burning of reeds (if not done too late in the season) does not seem to harm Bitterns. They may even benefit as dykes and canals are maintained by the removal of the reed bundles. The maintenance of dykes slows down the silting-up of the marshes, and canals often provide the only open water areas available for hunting Bitterns. Cutting and burning also destroys scrub vegetation which tends to invade the less inundated parts of the marsh. Day and Wilson (1978) concluded: "On the Norfolk Broads, where the decline has been most marked, habitat deterioration caused mainly by pollution appears to be substantially responsible. Elsewhere, the reasons are unclear."

In France, many sites which are now deserted would still suit Bitterns, as they have changed little in recent years. It is possible that, if the Bittern population is in difficulty, for reasons not presently obvious, the smallest hunting pressure can be disastrous, especially at the end of the winter. As nearly all Bitterns in England breed in reserves, hunting cannot be considered as a limiting factor. On the continent, the situation is quite different. Bitterns winter in marshes which are often heavily hunted during the whole autumn and winter period. Of 42 Bitterns ringed between 1953 and 1961 (Gauckler and Kraus 1965), 12 were recovered by 1965. Among them, five had been shot and one mortally wounded by a harvesting machine. For the six others, the cause of death was not known. Thus at least 12% of all birds ringed were shot. Since 1975, Bitterns have been protected in France but it is difficult to appreciate how much the situation has improved. Careless or ignorant hunters are probably still shooting Bitterns now and then, especially when no legal quarry is available.

BEHAVIOUR AND BIOLOGY

MAINTENANCE ACTIVITIES

Lord Percy (1932) made a very detailed study of a female Bittern's use of its powder puffs, foot comb and oil gland:

> A quick movement and her head was buried beneath her shoulders, while the feathers at the base of the neck heaved and shook for ten to thirty-five seconds as she rubbed one side of her head up and down her 'powder-puffs'. As her head

emerged from the first application of the 'powder-puff', not only powder but the actual powder-down also, could be seen clinging to her forehead.

Repeated further application followed, first on one side and then on the other, her head becoming whiter and more dishevelled, and the feathers at the base of the neck protruding more and more after insertion of the head in the 'powder-puff'. These neck-feathers were always a signal by which the conclusion of her powdering could be foretold, for as soon as she was satisfied with it they relapsed into their normal position.

The toilet was not yet nearly complete. An interval must be allowed for the powder to do its work, before it could be brushed off, by a vigorous scratching first with one foot and then the other, leaving the head slightly ruffled but now nearly dry. During this interval she would divide her attention between her young and a general bill-preening of her own plumage. The average time occupied by the whole performance up to this stage was about forty-five minutes. . . . Now while her powder had effectually removed the oily eel-slime from the head and neck, it had as effectually relieved them of the natural oil necessary for water-proofing, and so, with tail-coverts vertically raised and oil-gland fully exposed, a most elaborate oiling of her head and neck was to form the spectacular final act, a fitting climax to this astounding toilet.

Leaving the nest, after a final shake out of her plumage, and climbing to the very summit of the reeds, it was her custom to perform this last act in this peculiar situation.

DISPLAYS AND CALLS

Agonistic displays

Forward and Full Forward Displays. Portielje (1926) has described two displays, a *Schreck-Stellung* and an *Imponier Stellung*. These displays are performed towards humans before a proper attack. They also seem to be used by males fighting each other (Palm 1962). As the *Schreck-Stellung* is the display adopted just before the attack, it is probably homologous to the Full Forward Display already described in many herons as the last display given before the actual attack. Good photographs taken by Portielje (1926) and Lord Percy (1951), and Portielje's own text make possible a description of this display:

○ The birds bends his legs, thus assuming a crouched position.
○ The extended neck is bent, so that the occipital region is directly over the upper part of the back the neck in an "S" shape. The open beak is pointed at the intruder.
○ The unfolded wings are largely drawn aside and may be bent slightly forwards.
○ The crest feathers are erected and form a large fan on the top of the head, perpendicular to the beak.
○ The neck feathers are erected and parted on each side of the neck forming a shield in front of the bird.
○ The scapulars and the two shoulder tufts are raised.

The *Imponier-Stellung* is a less extreme threat display and thus seems homologous to the Forward Display. The chief differences from the Full Forward Display are that the feathers are less raised and that the unfolded wings are only slightly drawn aside. The bird may turn slightly in either of these two positions in order to remain face on to the intruder.

Fear display. This is the well-known Bittern Stance, a typical display in some heron genera such as *Botaurus, Ixobrychus* and *Butorides*. It is seen in a much less developed form in other genera such as *Ardea*. Portielje (1926) has made a detailed study of this display (*Pfahlstellung*) and provided good photographic evidence. The Bittern Stance is characterized by:

○ Total immobility, except for a very slow turning of the whole body so as to remain facing the predator or intruder if it moves.

The threat display of a Bittern at nest against man (after Lord Percy 1951).

○ The legs are straightened.
○ The body is held vertically and the tail depressed. The head and neck are in line with the body, the bill pointing towards the sky, the neck slowly stretched to its maximum.
○ The feathers are sleeked.
○ The eyes bulge, both looking forwards, fixing the predator or intruder, thus giving binocular vision.

The bird adopts this position when it sees or hears something unusual or frightening such as the sudden appearance of a human being. The Green Heron, *Butorides striatus*, also takes up this position at the sudden sight of a Marsh Harrier or when hearing the alarm calls of nearby birds of other species (Meyerriecks 1962). Although not yet observed in Bitterns, it is most probable that they react in the same way. When the Bittern Stance is adopted, the bird does not change its position as long as the observer looks at it. Portielje has thus faced a Bittern for 45 minutes during which time the bird remained absolutely motionless. Ultimately, it was the observer who left first! During another such confrontation, Portielje pushed the bird slightly with a long (3.5 m) bamboo stick without provoking the slightest movement. Should the observer leave, but stop some distance away remaining motionless, he or she might see the bird give up the Bittern Stance and, turning very slowly, disappear among the reeds or suddenly fly away with a harsh cry. The Bittern Stance is also adopted by a bird sitting on its nest, either incubating or brooding the young. The bird remains sitting, only streching its neck and head vertically, bill pointing towards the sky, eyes bulged. Portielje has also described a Bittern taking up the Bittern Stance posture while swimming across a ditch! The bird took the posture horizontally, lying in the water, and at once looked like an old stick drifting in the water, pushed by the wind between the reed bed and the land. Lundevall (1953) observed that during the whole week he held a Bittern captive, the bird, probably feeling insecure, slept every night in the Bittern Stance posture.

Courtship displays

These displays have never been described in any of the four species of the bittern family. Bitterns have two tufts of shoulder plumes which are usually hidden by the folded wings (in the European Bittern they are brown in the centre with a large white border). They are exposed conspicuously in the American Bittern during the threat display of the male, during booming and prior to copulation (Palmer 1962). As the pairing displays of the European Bittern have not yet been observed, it is still possible that these shoulder tufts are exposed not only during threat displays but also during courtship.

Calls

The most characteristic call of the Bittern is Booming. The sound is a "deep, slow, resonant call not loud but of great carrying power, sometimes audible up to 3–5 km" (Cramp and Simmons 1977). It is repeated at 1- to 2-second intervals, usually 3–4 times but sometimes 5–6 times or more. As no other animal produces such a sound, the Booming of the male Bittern is unmistakable; it resembles the blowing of a distant fog horn. The Booming itself is often preceded by 2–3 short coughs, grunts, clicks or taps and also sometimes by Bill-clappering audible at a short distance (Cramp and Simmons 1977, Percy 1951). The Booming of the male Bittern is heard during the whole reproductive period, as much during the night as during the day, usually from the end of February (Percy, 1951, noted a male Booming as early as 25 January) to the beginning of July. However, it is most often heard in April–May at dusk (20.00–22.00 h). The Booming is uttered without any external help, such as plunging the beak into the water or by blowing in the stem of a reed as had long been thought.

Lundevall (1953) observed a Booming Bittern in captivity. The bird was kept outdoors during the day for a week, after having been found starving. When Booming, the bird bent its legs slightly, its body held at an angle of 60° to the horizontal, its neck stretched vertically, nearly as much as during the Bittern Stance. Its head and beak were pointing upwards but not vertically. Rosenberg (in Curry-Lindahl 1959) has also described the Booming behaviour. While it takes in air the bird keeps its neck short, its beak pointed forwards, its whole body vibrating. The first part of the call, "uh", is heard during the intake of air. The bird then points its beak upwards and blows air out producing the second part of the call, "booh". The difference between Lundevall's and Rosenberg's descriptions may be due to the fact that the captive Bittern did not feel secure and thus kept its neck in as nearly the Bittern Stance as possible. Lundevall's bird made only one single Booming call that was probably not very loud.

Bauer and Glutz (1966) wrote, "The bird stretches its neck and fills the oesophagus with air which is used as a sound box." Since these few descriptions differ substantially, further observations of this behaviour are clearly necessary. The physiological mechanism of Booming has never been studied in the case of the European Bittern. Chapin (1922) has looked at the Ameri-

An alarmed Bittern walking away.

can Bittern and observed physiological changes in both the oesophagus and the mouth, which probably occur also in the European Bittern. The Booming is rather hesitant at first and does not seem to acquire its full power until the breeding season progresses (Percy 1951). Booming is a territorial call. A Bittern flying over a marsh, giving the usual Flight Call, causes the "owner" of that part of the marsh to start or increase its Booming rate. It is also used to attract females. They answer with soft "wumph" noises and even with gentle Booming (Whitherby *et al.* 1939). The male sometimes builds a platform on which to stand while Booming.

The Flight Call of the Bittern resembles that of the Night Heron, both sounding somewhat like that of the Common Crow. The Flight Call seems to be a contact call and is used by both the male and female. It is heard mostly at dusk in the autumn before migration when the birds fly in a circle above the reed beds (Gauckler and Kraus 1965).

The Warning Call is a rapid, short, quiet call, "ko, ko, ko" (Cramp and Simmons 1977), which may turn into a high-pitched "zeez" if the bird leaves the nest in alarm (Turner 1911).

The Threat Call is used by the female, for example, when she hears the young whimper. It may also be given by her on returning to the nest, either in flight or on foot (Bauer and Glutz 1966).

The Excitement Call used by the female on the nest is a rapid succession of bi-syllabic calls "tschätä, schätä, schätä" uttered with a short break between each triplet (Bauer and Glutz 1966).

The young have a Food Call which is an incessant cackling. They may also whimper (when picked up) and utter bubbling noises (Turner 1911).

FIGHTING BEHAVIOUR

Bitterns will attack a human hand which comes too near with sharp blows of the bill. The bird may also seize the hand with its beak and pinch and scratch it (Lundevall 1953).

In order to attack, the Bitterns suddenly stretch their neck to its full extent, all feathers erect and give a strong blow with the beak. To reach a target it may jump forwards. After the sudden attack, the Bittern withdraws to its former position. Portielje (1926) wrote that a Bittern attacks the head of an intruder as soon as it comes within reach of his jump. If the bird strikes the intruder's eye, it is by accident, since it does not aim at the eyes deliberately. However, I would welcome further studies on this last point, since the eyes are moving and movement is a common attack releaser. Reptiles, a less developed group, are known to specifically target the eyes of an enemy.

Male Bitterns are known to fight fiercely. Lord Percy (1952) once found a dead Bittern: "The body, covered with punctured wounds and with both eyes blinded, lying amid the broken stems, bore eloquent witness to the fury of the duel in which he had lost his life" (it was a male in breeding condition). As both eyes were blinded, accidental striking of the eyes seems extremely unlikely. Lord Percy also reported that workers going home after having cut reeds, saw two Bitterns so engaged in their struggle that they did not take any notice of the men passing by.

Palm (1962) has observed a fight between two Bitterns (probably males) which ended with the flight of one of the antagonists; a conclusion more usual in the case of a territorial dispute. Palm described the flight in detail. For long periods, the birds just stood still. From time to time, they slowly walked around each other, or one circled the other as it stood still. Now and then one of the birds, head and neck feathers erected, extended its wings and flew up some metres into the air. Sometimes, standing on the ground, head and neck feathers erected, wings unfolded and lifted upwards, they pecked at each other's chest, without however, giving serious blows. Meanwhile, there were pauses, during which both birds, all their feathers smoothed down, seemed to take no interest in each other. Suddenly, after a bout of chest pecking, one of the birds flew up into the air, higher than before, and disappeared above the reeds.

PURSUIT FLIGHTS

These probably involve several behaviour patterns that are still not well understood, involving as they do both males and females, which are so alike in appearance. Observation is made more difficult because the birds are hidden among the reeds at the beginning and end of the interaction. A probable explanation, however, is that Pursuit Flights occuring in spring and early summer are related to reproductive behaviour. There seem to be several types of aerial display in the spring. A few of them involve the majority of the community. They are seldom observed and seem to occur only in good weather. This is Percy's (1951) description:

> an individual returning from the fishing grounds . . . suddenly alters course and begins circling low over the tree tops. As this first bird swings upward, loud yelps burst from it as if to summon the community to grande parade. One by one the birds on the nests sweep up to join it until at length the whole company is soaring in spirals on motionless wings like vultures far up in the blue vault of heaven. . . . While soaring the heads are drawn back on the bended necks in the usual manner of herons in flight, but finally, with necks outstretched to their full extent they 'peel off' by twos and threes in giddy, twisting, 'falling leaf' dives to the tree tops below.

Turner (1957) records:

> aerial displays of as many as 4–6 individuals, mostly males, in May and June. Birds circling round one another like soaring gulls, sometimes shooting rapidly upwards and planing down. Occasionally one or two females take part . . . participants in some cases coming from territories as much as 3 miles away.

The great majority of Pursuit Flights, however, involve only 2–3 birds, exceptionally 4. They occur at any time during spring and early summer. Such flights seem to involve fighting males, and males and females pursuing each other. Kérautret (1969) described two Pursuit Flights seen in May. Two Bitterns pursued each other for about 8 minutes, circling above a marsh, sometimes as high as the top of the surrounding poplars. The pursuing bird tried to attack the other. The first then turned round to face its antagonist which tried to give blows with its beak and scratch with its feet. After a few blows the pursuit started again. The observer, as they were flying over him, heard both birds uttering a succession of harsh cries, "krr, krr, krr". At last, after having landed once or twice briefly and pursued each other among a few willows, flying just above the reeds, they both landed among the reeds and disappeared.

During another observation, three Bitterns were seen flying up from the reeds. One immediately landed again but the other two kept flying at a height of about 50 m for about 10 minutes. The pursuing bird remained 10–20 m behind the other and called continuously before both birds landed together.

Jefferies and Pendlebury (1967) described another Pursuit Flight:

[Two Bitterns] were at a height which varied between about 40 feet and 80 feet above ground level and were flying in a rough circle with a diameter of approximately half a mile. One remained directly behind the other, and mostly three to five lengths away from it, throughout the seven minutes they were in sight. The Bittern in the rear made no effort to reach or overtake the first one and slowed to a glide each time the other did. Twice in the seven minutes the first bird almost stopped moving forward, lowered its legs, raised its crest feathers, turned its head and opened its bill as if to ward off its follower. On these occasions the two were almost in contact, but the rear bird also braked and then flew on in its former station when the first one started to fly forward again.

Axell (1967) had the chance to follow the activity of one of the birds after it had landed in the reeds:

I saw three Bitterns in a pursuit flight . . . when only two yards from me, the leading bird dropped into the reeds and mounted a fourth Bittern which had suddenly materialised and was crouching just inside the reeds by a path. While what appeared to be copulation was in progress, or being attempted, on broken reeds a foot from the ground, the other two Bitterns flapped around, grunting, at the level of the reed-tops just above the pair until, after a minute or two, they became aware of my presence and flew off together, now calling loudly. The upper bird of the apparently mating couple then rose clumsily through the reeds and flew off, while the apparent female, which was also smaller, had extraordinary difficulty in extricating itself from the reed debris and then flew off in a different direction until it eventually landed about 400 yards away.

Gauckler and Kraus (1965) reported the flight activity of 1–3 birds which they related to fishing. Sanden (in Gauckler and Kraus 1965) have reported early morning and late evening flights in late summer and autumn which could be related to pre-migratory flights.

REPRODUCTIVE BEHAVIOUR

The male Bittern is territorial from late February to June–July. When Booming, it advertises its ownership of a part of the marsh. The area of the territory depends to some extent on the density of Bitterns. A map drawn by Zimmermann (1931) shows nesting sites and calling stations. The territories cover a radius of *c*. 100 m around the nests. Each male has two or three habitual calling stations and sometimes builds platforms from which to call. They attack every other male Bittern intruding on to their territory. The Booming of the male also attracts females, who sometimes answer with a soft Booming reply.

Lord Percy (1951) stated that the male Bittern is "markedly polygamous". However, in England, Bitterns are so few and scattered that this is impossible to prove either way. Polygamous breeding has been verified in central Europe where the bird is more common. Searching for all the nests in a particular area, as done by Zimmermann (1931) and Kraus and Gauckler (1965), shows that if there is more than one nest, they are usually found quite close together in groups of between two and five. In the case of Kraus and Gauckler's (1965) study, the nests were often only 15–20 m apart, and less than 50 m from a calling station. Since male Bitterns are territorial, such a close grouping of several occupied nests in one territory proves that polygamy does occur.

If the courtship displays of the European Bittern have never been observed, copulation itself has been observed by Yeates (1940) and Percy (1951). But in both cases it appears to have been the rape of a nesting female by an intruder rather than the pairing of the female with its established partner, the owner of the territory. Forced extra-pair copulation also occurs among other heron species, such as *Egretta garzetta*. Lord Percy wrote:

> A few seconds later the female fled from her platform, followed by a yellowish brown streak as the male drove her straight towards me, and both were lost to view below the hide, the flimsy side of which was lashed by the wings of the struggling pair. A glance out of the back of the hide revealed the male mounted on the female within a few feet of my face. For a moment they appeared oblivious of my presence, and then, parting, sprang after each other with wings extended in great fifteen-foot bounds.

In Yeates' description, the male, his "mane" fluffed out and his wings outstretched, mounts and feeds the female simultaneously "pushing his beak well down into her wide open beak."

The nest is built by the female alone (Cramp and Simmons 1977), the male being busy with the defence of the territory (Booming and fighting) and with the courting of other females. The nest is to be found at water level in dense reed beds usually near some open water, a natural clearing or a man-made ditch (Bauer and Glutz 1966). It is constructed on broken reeds or on a tuft of aquatic vegetation, its greater part often under water. The nest material is taken from around the nesting site and mostly comprises old stems of *Phragmites, Typha* and *Cladium*. The nest itself is a platform, 35–40 cm wide, usually reaching 10–15 cm above the water surface, formed by a rather loose heap of dead reeds and bits of other vegetation (Zimmerman 1929). The females continue to build upon the nest until the young are well grown, so that at the end of the nesting period it might be as much as 90 cm wide and 50 cm high (Dementiev and Gladkov 1951).

Lord Percy (1951) has definitively established that the female incubates and brings up the young alone. He wrote:

> The ground of the statement that the male plays no part in the upbringing of his progeny is that neither during forty-five days spread over seven years at different

nests, nor during the eighty-seven days at one nest, did any male make the slightest contribution towards it.

In later years, with the idea of resolving any lingering doubts whether the existence of a hide could possibly deter the male from visiting the nest, observation of nests where no hide existed and no disturbance of any kind had been caused, was attempted from the vantage point of the top of an old disused windmill overlooking the marshes. As female bitterns feeding young generally walk away from the nest, but fly to and from their feeding grounds to its vicinity, a loose check on their movements can be kept, and the cock can be located by his repeated booming; but this attempt yielded no more than negative evidence.

Egg-laying commences at the end of March or very early in April (Gentz 1965, Percy 1951) in western and central Europe, whereas in Sweden the first eggs are laid mid-April and often not before the beginning of May (Broberg, in Curry-Lindahl 1959). The main egg-laying period in western and central Europe is April, May and the first half of June, although eggs are laid until the end of June and even the beginning of July (Cramp and Simmons 1977).

The eggs are blunt oval, matt olive-brown, sometimes with a fine spotting at the large end (Schönwetter 1967). A sample of 100 eggs measured by Schönwetter gave the following measurements (mean and range): length 53 mm (41–58 mm), width 39 mm (34–48 mm). A sample of 32 eggs measured by Bauer (in Niethammer 1938) gave a mean length of 53.2 mm and a mean width of 38.1 mm, and Zimmermann's (1925) sample of 22 eggs gave a mean length of 52 mm and a mean width of 39.2 mm.

According to Bauer and Glutz (1966), the mean weight of the eggs is 40.0 g (range: 35–48 g).

DEVELOPMENT AND CARE OF THE YOUNG

At hatching, the nestlings weight 30–32 g. After 8 days, they are already able to adopt the Bittern Stance (Bauer and Glutz 1966), and at 3 weeks of age they leave the nest. With the weather becoming hotter at that time of the year, they often use new nest-platforms built by the female in a more shaded location than the original nest (Percy 1951). At 4–5 weeks of age, the young wander about in the reeds at some distance from the nesting site (Bauer and Glutz 1966). After 7–8 weeks, they begin to fly (Cramp and Simmons 1977), but at 2½ months they are still fed by the female (Percy 1951) who provides food for them long after they are fully fledged, during the difficult period while they learn to fish for themselves. They breed in their first year, the following summer (Cramp and Simmons 1977).

The breeding success of Bitterns was studied in West Germany by Kraus and Gauckler (1965). Of 21 clutches, only 12 were successful (57%) most of the losses being caused by man. In 13 clutches with 66 eggs, 42 young hatched (36.4% of the eggs were lost before and during hatching, giving a mean number of 3.2 young per nest). After 14 days, 37 young could be counted at the nests (11.9% lost during the first 2 weeks, giving a mean number of 2.8 young per nest).

During the first days of life, the female feeds her young without her bill being grasped by them, letting the partially digested food fall from her bill into the open bills of the begging chicks. After a few days they begin to seize her bill crosswise when she regurgitates, and the food passes directly from her bill to that of the chick. When food falls onto the nest floor, the young are able to pick it up and eat it (Bauer and Glutz 1966).

The usual clutch size is 5–6 eggs, but it can vary from 3 to 7 (Bauer and Glutz 1966). In West Germany, in a sample of 13 full clutches, Kraus and Gauckler (1965) found 4–6 eggs, though usually there were 5 (mean clutch size, 5.08). Of 31 clutches in Denmark, Hermansen found 3 eggs in 3% of the nests, 4 in 10%, 5 in 48%, 6 in 36% and 7 in 3%. The mean clutch size was 5.25 (Hermansen in Cramp and Simmons 1977). The Bittern rears only one brood each year, but if the clutch is destroyed a further 3–6 eggs are laid – twice if need be (Zimmermann 1934). The eggs are laid at intervals of 1–3 days (Bauer and Glutz 1966). According to Bernhardt (1929) and Schuster (1928), the incubation period is 25–26 days, but Kraus and Gauckler (1965) noted that 22–24 days elapsed between the laying of the first egg to the hatching of the first young. The incubation period may be longer for the last egg. The young of any one nest hatch during a period of up to 7 days (Kraus and Gauckler 1965).

As long as the female Bittern has only herself to feed, she leaves her eggs for short periods only. But as Percy (1951) noted:

> the female bittern, laying her clutch of four or five eggs over a period of five to nine days, and incubating from the date of the laying of the first egg, is faced at the end of the incubation period of the first egg with the double task of feeding the young already hatched and incubating the remaining eggs.
>
> At a late nest in May, or in an exceptionally warm spring, performance of the double task may call for no excessive admiration, but to watch a bittern's nest hatching at any time in April when food is hard to come by, and the reedbeds are swept by squalls of icy rain or sleet, is to witness the most skilful preservation of a finely adjusted balance in the struggle to defend the young from the twin threats of starvation and death from exposure. The unhatched eggs may be left for periods of anything up to two or three hours with no other warmth than that which the bodies of those already hatched can supply. As one chilling shower succeeds another, the shivering young droop till the watcher becomes convinced that the last flicker of life has left the miserable fragile bodies that now lie apparently lifeless in the nest. As the old bird returns and settles down to brood, the young may be too weak even to raise their heads, and it seems she has nothing but sodden corpses to cover; yet half an hour later, when she stands up to feed them, the tawny down is standing erect and dry on the heads that weave uncertainly in the effort to connect with the beak that, with a few drops of half-digested matter, rekindles the flames of life in those bodies in which, for all their apparent fragility, the spark dies so hard.
>
> On such a day, one incautious visit by a human which keeps the female from her young for another twenty minutes, and that spark would be gone. In a letter to me, Jim Vincent once wrote: 'In my opinion there is not one of our marsh birds the mere finding of whose nest at that period is a greater threat to its successful outcome' – and his conclusion was founded on similar experiences.

The fact that the female manages to bring up her brood alone is quite unusual among herons. In other European herons, one pair always has great difficulties in bringing up their young and even though there are two adults to nourish them, their numbers are greatly limited by the difficulties in finding enough food. How then is the female Bittern, alone, able to bring up a brood with a number of young apparently quite normal for a heron?

According to Lord Percy's (1951) observations, Bitterns are active during the day when they normally fish and feed the young. Like the Grey Heron, but even less frequently, they occasionally fish and feed the young at night, when necessary. To avoid persecution when moving from one marsh to another, Bitterns frequently move at night. That Bitterns are normally active during the day and sleep during the night is confirmed by observations on captive birds. The Bittern kept for a few days by Lundevall (1953) slept during the night from about 20.00 to 04.00 h and was active during the day.

When fishing, Bitterns often use the Stand-and-wait method (Meyerrieck's 1960). One Bittern observed by Sermont (1980) stood at the fringe of a reed bed with water up to its belly, its body and neck (not stretched) held horizontally just above the water, head slightly tilted, its eye at water level and its beak partly in the water. Just before each catch, the bird tramped a few times in the water stirring up the mud. Then it stretched its beak forwards, its head disappearing in the water, and caught a small fish between its mandibles. The fish was rapidly turned head first and swallowed. During the 50 minutes of observation the Bittern took 42 small fish. This tramping of the Bittern probably frightened the fish, perhaps even making them swim upwards, and in fleeing, they were doubtless less aware of the heron's bill. An alternative interpretation is that the tramping of the heron causes small clouds of mud in the water, such as are usually caused by small prey moving about on the bottom. The fish are attracted by these mud clouds and swim towards them to catch the imagined prey. They thus come within reach of the heron's bill and are easily caught. In this case, the heron creates a bait, the mud cloud, to attract its prey, the fish.

Percy (1951) observed Bitterns "walking up" their prey on dry land or in shallow pools. Bitterns "though generally feeding in dense cover, may on rare occasions be seen running with feverish activity over a bare reed bed which has been recently cut and picking up small objects – presumably fish fry or tadpoles – as fast as any hungry hen picks up grain."

Sometimes, when not fishing, the Bittern observed by Sermont (1980) moved across the pond, body kept horizontally above the water, tarsus and foot lifted to the horizontal at each large step. Lundevall has described two modes of walking by a captive Bittern. When it fled, the body was held horizontally or at an angle of 30° above the horizontal, neck and head kept high. When the bird felt secure, or had something to hide behind, it went head and neck horizontal. As one food was put down using all its width, the other was lifted up to the chest. Sermont's bird walked with bent toes, Lundevall's with stretched toes.

The food taken by Bitterns is mainly fish (pike *Esox*, carp *Cyprinus*, roach

A Bittern foraging.

Rutilus, dace *Leuciscus*, eel *Anguilla*, tench *Tinca*, perch *Perca*), amphibians (*Rana, Triton, Bombina, Pelobates*) and insects (Hemiptera: *Notonecta* and *Naucoris*; Coleoptera: Dytiscidae and Hydrophilidae; Orthoptera; Odonata). However, worms, leeches, molluscs, crustaceans, spiders, lizards, small mammals (water-vole *Arvicola*, vole *Microtus*, and shrew *Neomys*) and small birds (wren *Troglodytes*, tit *Panurus*) are also eaten (Cramp and Simmons 1977).

Moltoni (1948) examined the contents of 17 Bittern stomachs from Italy. He found frogs (*Rana esculenta*) in six, parts of various aquatic insects (*Hydrous, Dytiscus, Notonecta*) in five and fish (*Esox lucius*, one 30 cm, and *Eupomotis gibbosus*) in four. One contained a grass snake (*Natrix natrix*) 73 cm long, one a water-vole (*Arvicola*) and one 2 earthworms (*Lumbricus*). Vasvàri (1938) examined 51 stomachs from Hungary and found that they contained mostly amphibians (frogs and *Triton*), aquatic and terrestrial insects, and only some fish and small mammals. Madon (1935) examined nine stomachs from France and found that they contained mostly fish [loaches *Cobitis*, 5–7 cm in length, dace *Leuciscus* (no measures) and eels *Anguilla*, about 25 cm in length] and frogs (*Rana esculenta*). But a few mammals (shrew *Neomys*) and aquatic insects had also been eaten.

The young are fed with fish and frogs. Regurgitated prey found in nests by Gauckler and Kraus (1965) belonged to the following species: tench (length 5–13 cm), carp (8–12 cm), perch (7–10 cm), pike (10 cm) and frogs (only small ones, hatched the previous year). If the diet of the Bittern varies very much with locality and seasons, the main part of the food is always based on either fish or amphibians.

The Bittern captured by Lundevall (1953) was, at the time of its capture, very weak due to lack of food. It weighed only 710 g. To save the bird, Lundevall gave it as many small herrings as it could eat over a 6-day period. During this time, the bird ate 1245 g of fish and retained 965 g. When released, it weighed 870 g. The mean weight increase per day during its captivity was 27 g, the total weight gain during the whole period being 23% of its weight when captured.

INTERACTIONS WITH OTHER BIRDS

When flying from the nest to the fishing grounds, Bitterns avoid Marsh Harriers and land in the reeds to hide should they meet one. But when a Marsh Harrier comes near a nest, it is immediately attacked by the owner. The female might even get some help from the male if he is near by, as was observed by Percy (1951): "The male rose from some distance away and joined the female as she sprang from a nestful of young when a Marsh Harrier sailed at reed-head height over the nest; together the two Bitterns escorted it on each side, uttering a series of piercing yelps." Another fight was observed by E.L. Turner (in Bannerman 1957), who wrote: "Suddenly a Bittern shot up from the reed-bed, and the Harrier only avoided being impaled on the point of the adversary's beak by a dextrous twist. . . . The Harrier sheered off, closely pursued by the Bitterns."

Bitterns also seem to attack birds which present no danger to them. Thus a Kingfisher which had just landed on a perching post near a Bittern was killed, the Bittern leaving the dead Kingfisher in the water. E. Hosking and J. Vincent saw a Bittern in full chase after a White-fronted Goose, which flew out of sight across the marshes (Bannerman 1957).

There are very few observations of predation on Bitterns. Uttendörfer (in Gentz 1965) found Bittern feathers in a Goshawk nest and the remains of a Bittern taken by an Eagle Owl. Peregrines are also said to take Bitterns occasionally (Gentz 1965).

Table 4.   The number of breeding pairs of Bitterns in Britain in the census years 1954, 1970 and 1976 (Day and Wilson 1978)

	1954	1970	1976
Norfolk	60	27	10
Suffolk	14–15	16–17	21–22
Kent	1–2	3–4	0
Lancashire	1–2	10	1–2
Lincolnshire	1	5–6	1–2
North Wales	1–2	5	2
Somerset	1(?)	1–2	1
South Wales	0	1	0
Total	78–83	68–72	45–47

Table 5.   *Places where the number of breeding pairs of Bitterns exceeding 100 in 1976 (Day 1981)*

	No. of breeding pairs
Netherlands	500
East Germany	400
France	<400
Sweden	200–250
Hungary	215–218
Schleswig-Holstein (West Germany)	130–140
Romania	100
Poland	85–100

CHAPTER 10

The Little Bittern *Ixobrychus minutus*

GENERAL APPEARANCE AND FIELD CHARACTERS

The Little Bittern is the smallest of the European herons, 33–38 cm high with a wing-span of 52–58 cm.

Plumage. The male and female have different patterns, without a particular breeding plumage. Both sexes posess elongated hindcrown and chest feathers. The hindneck is bare but hidden by the feathers of the sides of the neck.

Adult male: the crown, mantle scapulars, back, rump, tail and innermost secondaries are black with a greenish gloss. The feathers of the sides of the head and neck are grey, washed with a light vinaceous tinge. The chin and throat are white on the sides and ochreous-buff in the centre. The foreneck and chest are ochreous-buff, faintly streaked deeper buff, as is the belly, which is usually somewhat lighter in colour. The feathers of the foreneck, chest and belly are white at their basal part. Most individuals possess some feathers with brown shafts on their flanks and belly, giving the plumage there thin, brown streaks. The feathers of the shoulders and breast are blackish with buff margins. The alula, primary coverts and their quills are black. The lesser upperwing-coverts are ochreous-buff, the marginals are darker. The upper median and greater wing-coverts are grey (the innermost feather has a glossy black inner web). The underwing-coverts and axillaries are white as are the undertail-coverts.

Adult female: the crown is black and less glossy than in the male. The feathers of the mantle, scapulars, back and innermost secondaries are brown, more or less tinged with rufous and edged with ochreous-buff. The sides of the head are grey-buff. The feathers of the sides of the neck are buff with a tinge of grey and strongly washed with red-brown on their distal parts. The chin and throat are white on the sides and ochreous-buff streaked with brown in the centre. From the foreneck to the belly, the bird is ochreous-buff to whitish, distinctly streaked with brown (the central parts and shafts of some feathers are brown). The feathers of the shoulders and of the breast are dark brown edged with ochreous-buff, as are those of the back. The wing pattern is the same as in the male but the colours are somewhat different. The alula, primary coverts and their quills are dark brown. The lesser upperwing-coverts are ochreous-buff, the marginals are darker. The upper median and greater wing-coverts are grey, washed with ochreous-buff. The innermost wing-coverts are brown, edged with ochreous-buff. The rump is brown, the tail black. The underwing-coverts and axillaries are white, as are the undertail-coverts.

Juvenile: the young resemble the female but some juveniles are more red-brown on the upperparts. The wing-coverts are ochreous-buff. The young are more heavily streaked on the underparts.

Adult male, first year: like the adult male but not so grey on the head and neck. The underparts are still streaked. The upperwing pattern is less striking, since the upperwing-coverts are duller and the quills not so black with sometimes one or two red-brown secondaries remaining.

Downy young: these have a short, dense, ochreous-yellow down, darker above. The hindneck is bare.

Bare parts

Adult: the eyes are yellow. The legs and feet are green, yellowish on the hindlegs and under the toes. The bill is yellow or green-yellow, darker along the culmen. The lores are yellow with a narrow dusky line from the eye to the nostril. The base of the bill and the lores becomes temporarily red during the breeding season. In a study of *Ixobrychus minutus payesii* from Africa, C.H. Langley (1983) gives a description of the reddening of the bare parts during breeding:

> Bill colour changes as follows. During the breeding season the bill and lores of both sexes are yellow or greenish yellow, but rapidly flush reddish to bright red for varying periods during courtship, copulation, and nest-relief. The colour is more intense in males, especially during courtship. Flushing extends from the naked skin at the base of the bill to at least half the length of both upper and lower jaws.

Wackernagel (1950) has also noticed these brief colour changes in *I. m. minutus* in Europe and Asia and has described them briefly. He thought, as I do, that they were caused by a dilation of the capillaries. Such a short-lived colour change of the bill and lores has not so far been recorded in any other heron species. The red colour and other bright colours which are characteristic during breeding, are permanent during the whole pair-formation and egg-laying period in other herons, though the intensity of the colours may vary. They usually appear to brighten in males during courtship displays. Also unusual is the fact that the light-coloured parts of the legs and feet do not seem to redden.

Field characters. The Little bittern is a very small heron. In the field it is usually encountered singly, flying low over the reeds. The male is easy to recognize since the light patches on the upperwing contrast sharply with the rest of the black upperparts of the bird. In the females, and especially in the juveniles, the contrast is less strong but the crown, quills and tail are always darker than the rest of the plumage. Its flight is very rapid for a heron, with shallow wing-beats. They may, as Cramp and Simmons (1977) pointed out, be taken for a small duck or a Corncrake when seen in flight at a distance. They land in dense cover, usually reeds, with a characteristic glide followed by a sudden bank. When rising from the reeds, before gathering speed, the bird lets its feet trail, appearing to be in difficulty. This stealthy little heron is usually not to be seen when in the dense vegetation in which it lives. When in danger, it adopts the Upright Posture and can hardly be noticed among the reeds. When the danger lessens, perhaps when the observer has moved away a few steps, it prefers to creep rapidly away through the reeds, instead of flying directly off.

Some rare vagrants of Schrenck's Bittern *Ixobrychus eurhythmus* from Asia and of the Least Bittern *Ixobrychus exilis* from America have been reported in the western Palearctic. Two Schrenck's Bitterns have been caught, one in Germany and one in Italy, and five observations made of the Least Bittern, four in the Azores and one in Iceland.

The male Schrenck's Bittern is dark chestnut on the upper part of the body where the Little Bittern is black. The female and juvenile are brightly spotted. The Least Bittern is also much more chestnut-coloured, in fact, chestnut-red, especially on the sides of the face, on the long feathers of the side of the neck which cover the hindneck, and on the upper greater wing-coverts. The pattern of the Least Bittern is otherwise very similar to that of the Little Bittern. A pair of thin, white lines, however, border the scapulars at all ages and are often visible both at rest and in flight.

Measurements. The measurements (mm) of adult birds taken from skins are given below. The number of skins and the sex are indicated. Standard deviations are given in parentheses. The sex differences are significant, except for the tail (Cramp and Simmons 1977).

wing	15♂♂	149–157 (2.47)		12♀♀	142–153 (3.42)
tail	14♂♂	47–53 (1.65)		10♀♀	47–51 (1.57)
bill	14♂♂	46–53 (1.91)		11♀♀	44–49 (1.75)
tarsus	12♂♂	43–52 (2.79)		8♀♀	41–47 (2.00)
toe	12♂♂	50–54 (1.48)		8♀♀	48–53 (2.00)

The weight of breeding adults (Cramp and Simmons 1977): 11♂♂ 145–150 g (mean 149 g), 7♀♀ 140–150 g (mean 146 g).

The extreme range of full-grown birds (Bauer and Glutz 1966): 64–170 g.

DISTRIBUTION, MOVEMENTS AND HABITAT

GEOGRAPHICAL VARIATION

There are four subspecies. *Ixobrychus minutus minutus* (Linnaeus) has already been described. *I. m. payesii* (Hartlaub) is smaller than the nominate subspecies and more red-brown on the side of the head, neck and breast. Its wings are shorter: the wing-length of 7 males measured 135–142 mm and of 5 females 141–150 mm (Chapin 1932). The wing formula is different in these two subspecies. In *I. m. minutus* the primaries P10 and P9 are the longest. Occasionally, one of these feathers is up to 2 mm longer than the other. In *I. m. payesii*, P10 is distinctively shorter than P9. *I. m. podiceps* (Bonaparte) is still smaller than both *I. m. minutus* and *I. m. payesii* and is red-brown on the foreneck, breast and belly. *I. m. novaezelandiae* (Potts) has red-brown wing-coverts.

BREEDING AND WINTERING AREAS

The breeding range of *I. m. minutus* extends from Western Europe (except Britain and Denmark) and southern Europe to western Siberia (about 80°E). Its northern limit is generally around 56°N, but in the vicinity of Kirov it reaches nearly 59°N. Eastwards, the breeding range of *I. m. minutus* extends on a broad belt from the Near East, Iraq, Iran, Pakistan, northern India and southern Russia to western Sinkiang. In Africa, *I. m. minutus* breeds in Morocco, Tunisia, Egypt and at least in one area in southern Africa (Curry-Lindahl 1981). *I. m. minutus* winters in Africa, south to the Cape Province, and in Iraq, Iran, Pakistan and northern India (to about 25°N). It has wandered to Iceland, the Faeroes, Britain, Scandinavia, Finland, the Azores, Madeira and the Canaries. *I. m. payesii* breeds and winters in Africa south of the Sahara. *I. m. podiceps* in confined to Madagascar. *I. m. novaezelandiae* is found in eastern and southern Australia. Rare stragglers have been recorded from islands such as New Guinea and New Zealand.

MOVEMENTS

The post-fledging dispersal of Little Bitterns occurs from July to early September. The autumn migration begins in August and continues until October. Only a few individuals, mainly juveniles, are to be found in southern Europe in the late autumn and winter (Zink 1961). The western Palearctic breeders winter mostly in east Africa, south to the Transvaal and the eastern Cape Province but some are to be found in west Africa. Breeders from the

USSR and Iran are believed to winter in east Africa too, thus accounting for the passage observed over Arabia (Cramp and Simmons 1977). The return migration begins in March but most individuals migrate in April. The most northerly breeding areas are occupied only at the end of April and during the first week of May. Little Bitterns are able to cross the desert in one flight, but often land in oases where they rest hidden in the vegetation during the day. They fly up at dusk singly or in small flocks to continue migration by night.

HABITAT

Little Bitterns usually occur in lowland habitats below 200 m. However, in mountain areas such as the Alps, they commonly nest up to 500 m and sometimes even higher, as at Amsoldinger See near Berne where a nest was found at a height of 641 m (Bauer and Glutz 1966). Little Bitterns occupy a wide range of freshwater habitats such as marshes, swamps, and inundated areas along rivers, the fringes of lakes and pools. They hunt and breed in reed-beds but they do not require large unbroken areas of suitable habitat as Bitterns do. Quite small areas, with reeds and other similar vegetation, may be inhabited even near human settlements – three nests have been found in an area of only 1800 m^2 (Bauer and Glutz 1966).

The presence of shrub and tree vegetation, mostly willows and alders, favours the establishment of Little Bitterns. They are markedly arboreal and climb easily and rapidly through the dense vegetation where they live. They rarely venture onto the ground, which is usually inundated. Little Bitterns commonly feed and breed in the same area, not leaving it until time for dispersal and migration. However, during courtship, and when the foraging area is some distance away, they may commonly be seen flying low over the reeds. Little Bitterns are silent birds except during the breeding season. During May and June and sometimes even during July, the so-called "Spring Song" is heard mostly during late afternoon and evening. However, males call both by day and night (Bauer and Glutz 1966). Hearing these calls is a convenient indication of the presence of this secretive and inconspicuous bird.

POPULATION SIZE AND TRENDS

Very little is known about the actual numbers of this elusive little heron, which is not a colonial breeder and which often uses quite small areas of reeds and willows to nest, and few authors have ventured to try to estimate the number of breeding pairs in their country. Brosselin (1974) estimated the total population in France at 1050–2000 pairs. Lippens and Wille (1972) estimated that before 1960 about 100–200 pairs nested in Belgium. This number has since diminished to about 60 pairs. Braaksma (1968) estimated that about 170 pairs normally bred in the Netherlands between 1961 and 1967, with peaks of 200–275 pairs. In Baden-Würtenberg, the number was estimated at about 250–300 pairs (Hölzinger 1970). Their numbers may therefore be estimated at only a few thousands in the whole western European part of their range.

BEHAVIOUR AND BIOLOGY

DAILY ROUTINE

Although Little Bitterns are usually solitary feeders, in favourable localities a number may feed together (Witherby 1939). Individuals "have favoured feeding areas at the fringes of reeds above water or at the edge of channels where suitable cover exists, to which they return" (Langley 1983). If, in Europe, *I. m. minutus* shows some activity during the day, it is active mostly at dawn and towards evening, and in some localities European Little Bitterns have even been observed flying to their favourite feeding places at dusk (Witherby 1939). C.H. Langley (1983), using an automatic nest-visit recorder, showed that *I. m. payesii* is a diurnal bird in South Africa, at least during breeding, with a peak of activity around midday (see Fig. 5). Does the difference in behaviour observed between these two subspecies reflect a genuine subspecific difference, or is the European subspecies active at twilight and at night merely to escape human persecution? This is often the case with normally diurnal ducks and is probably so for this species also.

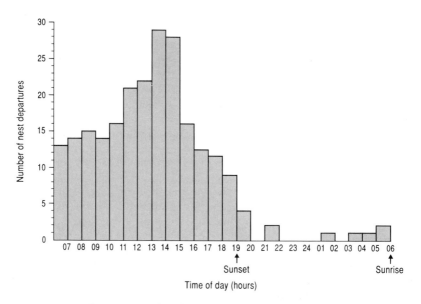

Figure 5   Little Bittern *Ixobrychus minutus* activity based on the number of nest departures per hour (Langley 1983).

The behaviour of the Little Bittern is the least well known of the European heron species. Nobody has succeeded in observing its courtship displays and observations concerning its agonistic displays are fragmentary. Only the famous Bittern Stance has frequently been observed.

Agonistic displays towards men

A photograph taken by Böhmer (Falke 1959, cover of part 2) shows a Little Bittern in a threat posture. This posture was called *Schreck-Stellung* (or Fear Posture) by Portielje (1926) when he described its performance by the Bittern. Though it is the last display before an attack, it does not seem to represent a true Full Forward Display since the fear component is an important part of it. Thus the crest feathers are depressed and the feathers at the base of the neck are not raised, as is certainly the case in the true Full Forward Display. This display of the Little Bittern may be called the Threat and Fear Display and is very like the *Schreck-Stellung* of the Bittern. It includes the following components:

○ The bird bends its legs, thus assuming a crouched position.
○ The neck is bent in an "S" curve, the open beak pointing towards the aggressor.
○ The unfolded wings are largely drawn aside.
○ The scapulars are held erect.
○ The crest feathers are depressed and the feathers at the base of the neck not erected.

According to some authors (Gentz 1959), the Little Bittern displays side-on to its enemy, the unfolded wing facing the aggressor being lifted and the other one lowered, the beak pointed at the enemy. This form is probably adopted when the bird has insufficient time to face the intruder head on. As the crest and neck feathers are not raised, the fear component seems more obvious than in the case of the Bittern, which holds them raised when performing this display.

Agonistic displays towards conspecifics

The first part of the nest-relief behaviour described by Gentz (1959) as *Drohen* (Threatening), is composed of forward displays of various degrees.

When a Little Bittern sitting on its nest hears a conspecific approaching, it raises its head obliquely and opens its bill. According to Gentz's drawing, all the feathers of the bird are sleeked, indicating a significant fear component. Soon after, facing the approaching intruder or mate, the bird stretches its neck slightly and opens its bill, showing the bright red throat (the colour of the throat does not redden in other European herons). It then claps its bill

A male Little Bittern on its nest. (Left) The beginning of a threat display with an important fear component. (Right) Forward Display giving in threat (after Gentz 1959).

several times. The neck feathers, and to some extent the back feathers also, are raised. The crown feathers are alternatively raised and sleeked. At higher levels of threat, the bird raises itself from the nest, neck held in an "S" curve, the bill open. All the feathers are raised, those of the neck and crown most so.

Fear display

This is the well-known Bittern Stance, and seems identical to that of the Bittern.

The Bittern Stance is characterized by:

○ Total immobility, except for a very slow turning of the whole body so as to remain facing the predator or intruder if it moves.
○ The legs are straightened.
○ The body is held vertically and the tail depressed. The head and neck are in line with the body, the beak pointing towards the sky, the neck slowly stretched to its maximum.
○ The feathers are sleeked.
○ The eyes bulge, both looking forwards, fixing the predator or intruder, thus giving binocular vision.

The Little Bittern adopts the Bittern Stance at the nest, which it is unwilling to leave. It reacts to the alarm calls of other bird species and adopts this posture on the arrival of a human or an animal predator. When away from the nest, it adopts this posture when it does not have time to sneak away unseen. When in the Bittern Stance, it may remain motionless for long periods, as long as the intruder is in sight. Indeed, Little Bitterns have been taken by hand while steadfastly keeping this position (Witherby 1947).

A female Little Bittern in the Bittern Stance.

The Bittern Stance is taken up by young at the nest when they are only a few days old. Usually, the youngest do not try to stand but adopt the posture while crouching on the nest floor. Only the neck, head and beak are stretched upwards. When in the Bittern Stance, young have been observed to sway slowly from side to side like reeds in a light wind (Noll 1924).

There is an old but very interesting observation concerning one of the escape behaviours of the Little Bittern. R.B. Lodge (in Witherby 1947) recorded a Little Bittern "laying flat on the water in a shape-less lump" apparently to escape a hawk. It would be very interesting to have more observations concerning this behaviour, since one observation by Portielje (1926) mentions the Bittern as using a similar but somewhat different technique to escape unseen. This kind of behaviour has never been described in any other heron genus, but may in fact be common among other poorly known species which have a cryptic plumage.

Calls

Little Bitterns have a characteristic Advertising Call or "Spring Song" that is given by the males on their territory to attract females. It is a "low-pitched, short, far carrying 'högh,' 'rru' or 'woof', described as croaking, froglike or resembling a deep bark of a dog, muffled and repressed; repeated at roughly two seconds intervals" (Cramp and Simmons 1977). Little Bitterns also have a Flight Call, an Alarm Call and Nest-relief Calls. Small chicks have a special Begging Call, though when they are older they give harsh calls when fed.

REPRODUCTIVE BEHAVIOUR

Breeding season

In the western Palearctic, the "Spring Song" of male *I. m. minutus* is commonly heard from the middle of May to June, and sometimes in July. The eggs are usually laid from the second half of May to the end of July (a few being laid at the beginning of August). In the Cape Province, *I. m. payesii* lays most commonly from August to February, but a few eggs are laid as early as June and July. Thus in Europe, which has a temperate climate with a cold autumn, winter and early spring, the laying period covers 3 months, whereas in the Cape Province, which has a Mediterranean climate with no cold periods, it extends over a period of 9 months.

Pair formation

Little Bitterns, including the subspecies *I. m. minutus* and *payesii*, are territorial during the breeding season (Gentz 1959, Bauer and Glutz 1966, Langley 1983), the male maintaining a territory from which all other males are chased. In his territory, the male begins to build a nest and most probably displays so as to attract a female. These sexual displays, as previously emphasized, have never been observed, since they take place in such dense vegetation and probably only when the bird feels totally secure. Only the Courtship Call of the male can usually be heard from the depths of the reedbeds. However, a few recent observations of interactions between a male and female perched on the top of the reeds, or flying over the reedbed, have been made by H.C. Langley (1983):

On the first occasion, a male with bill flushed red, alighted on top of tall reeds and began calling the courtship call. After about 3 min of continous calling, a female with red-flushed bill (but not as bright as that of the male) emerged about 2 m from the calling male, which immediately stopped calling and flew to her. They then both stretched their necks toward each other and crossed bills with raised crests. The female then flew off followed by the male, possibly having been disturbed by the observer.

On the second occasion, an unseen bird was giving the courtship call from dense reeds in the nesting area. After about 5 min of continuous calling, a female with yellow bill flew into view and perched on the reed tops in the vicinity of the calling bird, whereupon her bill flushed red. After about 50 s she flew out of view, followed by a male with red-flushed bill, that had emerged from where she had been perched. They then reappeared and flew into the reeds from where the male was originally heard calling. A nest with a single egg was found in the area four days later.

During both these observations, the male when in flight, flew with its neck slightly extended and head held below its body. This particular flight posture was observed only during courtship activities.

An old observation of what could be Advertising Flights of the Little Bittern has recently been published by B. King (1981), who visited a locality

A male Little Bittern on a branch.

in Somerset, England in July 1958, where a male and a female Little Bittern had been seen. The male

> suddenly rose from the reeds and circled the marsh in a clockwise direction, only a metre or two from the ground. By noting the time when he first appeared and continuing to record each flight throughout the day, I found that the intervals between flights varied from seven minutes to one hour and 40 minutes. The bittern never varied his flight behaviour, always emerging from the same spot and returning to it.

King does not mention hearing any Advertising Calls during the whole day he stayed watching and he did not find a nest later, so the behaviour sequence was perhaps not quite normal. The female should probably have been present. However, Advertising Flights seem to be a part of the sexual behaviour of the Little Bittern, as do some of the circling flights of Bitterns.

Once a male is paired and nest construction well advanced, it becomes possible for another male to establish its territory in the vicinity of the first one and, some days later, when the second male is also well established, a third male may defend a territory near the first two. The paired birds, which are less aggressive than the displaying male, seem to defend only the nest and its immediate surroundings against intruders. Hence, when the area is favourable, nests may be only 3–10 m apart. Older males are the first to become established in the spring; the younger ones, nesting later in the season, settle down in the places that are left (Braschler *et al.* 1961).

Nest site and nest building

In Europe, where new reeds grow late in the spring, *I. m. minutus* seems to prefer breeding in old reeds and thus uncut areas are very important for this species. In Yugoslavia, in a marsh where the reeds had not been cut for 8 years, 68 nests were found. The next year, after the reeds had been cut, only 8–10 nests were found in the same area (Szlivka 1958). At Rondevlei, in Cape Province, where breeding occurs in established areas of aquatic vegetation, Little Bitterns were found nesting exclusively in growing stands of bulrush (*Typha latifolia*) with open water beneath them (Langley 1983). The nests of both subspecies are generally built near clearings, channels or other areas of open water.

The male, after having chosen the nest site, begins to build the nest alone (Gentz 1959, Langley 1983). This differs from normal heron behaviour, where the nest is not constructed until the pair is formed. Once paired, the female helps to finish building the nest. According to Langley's (1983) observations on *I. m. payesii*, the female also helps to gather nest material (22% of the nest material was gathered by females). This is quite unusual among herons. In all European species except the Bittern, only the male collects nest material. When constructing a nest among reeds, the male Little Bittern begins by bending reeds to make a good base for the nest, a behaviour first described by Ali and Ripley in 1968. The bent reed stems are visible in a photograph of a nest published by Wackernagel in 1950. Loose reed stems are then laid in a pile on top of the bent ones. The nest is always built of old, mostly wet reeds, even when constructed among growing young reeds. Sticks are used when the nest is constructed in close proximity to or on a tree or a bush. A varying amount of flexible aquatic vegetation is also usually incorporated into the nest.

The whole nest may comprise 250–300 dead reed stems, generally 10–20 cm long (though the longest may be about 50 cm long) and a varying amount of reed leaves (up to 300) (Wackernagel 1950). The nest is finally lined with finer stems, leaves and even grass. This last task is done mostly by the female. The diameter of the finished nest is 18–35 cm, and its height varies from 8 to 30 cm. The cup is shallow (2–4 cm) with a diameter of 12–20 cm (Bauer and Glutz 1966).

In Europe, the nests of *I. m. minutus* are about 10–50 cm above water level or damp ground. The depth of water under the nest is generally 0–1 m. In the Cape Province, 22 *I. m. payesii* nests studied were situated 23–135 cm above the water level (mean 69.7 cm), the water beneath being 40–120 cm deep. In Europe, the nests are sometimes protected by bent reeds above the nest (Braschler *et al.* 1961), although, in my opinion, these may just be reeds that had been bent too high to later be used as a support for the nest. Occasionally, nests can be found in the lowest branches of bushes and trees (up to 3 m) that grow among reeds and other similar aquatic vegetation (Steinfatt 1955). Nests do not normally lie floating on the water, but this may occur after a badly constructed nest has slid down, or more likely when the water level has risen after nest construction.

Copulation

Wackernagel (1950) has observed the copulation of *I. m. minutus*. The male mounts the female without any previous display. During copulation, both birds unfold their wings to maintain their balance, and, in Wackernagel's drawing, the male holds them upwards like the Grey Heron. The male did not grasp the female's neck or neck feathers on this occasion.

Langley (1983) has observed the behaviour of paired birds before and after copulation, and a case of forced copulation, or rape:

Copulation was seen five times. One was a case of rape, in which an incubating female was raped by a colour-ringed male that was not her mate. In the other four cases, copulation took place on nests while females were incubating complete clutches, the last egg having been laid from one to six days previously.

Behaviour of birds during copulation, except for the single rape case, was basically the same. The male approached the nest and incubating female with bill flushed red and crest partially raised. The female raised and lowered her crest and body feathers and appeared to threaten the approaching male with open bill. When the male was near or on the edge of the nest, the female partially opened and closed her bill very rapidly (bill quivering) and might also peck or nibble at the nest lining, which appeared to be a form of displacement behaviour. By this stage the female's bill had flushed red. The male might then nibble the female's breast and neck feathers (two observations), while the female adopted a submissive posture, crouching down with flattened crest and body feathers raised. Once a male mounted and copulated at this stage, but on the other three occasions, females behaved as if begging for food, crouched down with head turned upwards towards the male, with bill open and emitting a soft twittering call like that of nestlings. The male then mounted and copulated for 7–20 s after which it quickly left the nest.

In the rape incident, a colour-ringed male which had a nest containing three young 8 m from the nest being observed, suddenly appeared and mounted an incubating female. She immediately grasped the male's head in her bill so that the point of her upper mandible appeared to be in his eye. Efforts by the male to break the female's hold failed. He then turned the female partially on her side using his feet and claws and then copulated for about 10 s, his head being held fast throughout by the female. He then again attempted to free himself, succeeding only after a struggle which resulted in his falling from the nest. Throughout this incident, the male's bill did not flush red as in normal copulatory behaviour.

Egg-laying and clutch size

The eggs are blunt oval, usually chalky white (occasionally greenish) with no gloss. Langley (1983) has noticed that "newly laid eggs have a pinkish tinge and are slightly translucent, becoming opaque white about an hour after laying". A sample of 250 eggs measured by Schönwetter (1967) gave the following measurements (mean and range): length 36 mm (32–39 mm), width 26 mm (24–28 mm).

According to Bauer and Glutz (1966), the weight of full eggs (size of sample not given) is 10.40–14.38 g and the weight of eggshells 0.57–0.83 g.

Clutches of 5–6 eggs are most common for *I. m. minutus*. A total of 25 clutches from Saxony comprised the following number of eggs: 3 eggs had 4 eggs, 8 had 5, 10 had 6 and 4 had 7 (mean clutch size 5.6 eggs). The data for 73 clutches in Switzerland are given in Table 6.

A total of 14 *I. m. payesii* nests yielded clutches of 3 or 4 eggs (mean 3.5) (Langley 1983). It is interesting to note that this subspecies, which lives at lower latitudes, has smaller clutches. The egg loss before hatching at these nests was 37%.

Nest relief

The nest-relief behaviour of *I. m. minutus* has been described by Gentz (1959), who distinguished two phases:

1. Threat displays against the incoming bird by the bird at the nest (see *Agonistic displays*).
2. Appeasement displays by the incoming bird so as to gain admittance to the nest. These displays are as follows:

○ To touch or cross bills with the bird at the nest.
○ To nibble its feathers.

○ To bring nest material which is deposited on the nest rim (this has only been observed in the case of incoming males).

○ To tread quietly on the bird at the nest. This, in my opinion, is not a display, but shows that the incoming bird intends to incubate or brood. The bird at nest has certainly recognized its mate and therefore does not attack.

According to Gentz's observations, the feathers of the incoming bird are sleeked.

C.H. Langley (1983) has observed the following behaviour during nest relief in *I. m. payesii*.

Allopreening: On four occasions females preened the breast feathers of relieving males with a nibbling action before leaving the nest. Once a male nibbled a female's back feathers after mutual bill crossing.

Bill-pecking or nibbling: Mutual nibbling or pecking at each other's bills took place five times when relieving birds arrived at the edge of the nest. Crest and neck feathers of both birds were raised during this activity.

Bill-quivering: Females often slightly opened and closed their bills very rapidly while facing toward oncoming males or when approaching incubating males.

Neck-crossing: This activity was seen twice, when an incubating female was being relieved. The male stood next to the sitting female and crossed his neck over hers; she immediately pulled her head back and extended her neck over his. This action was repeated two or three times on both occasions, before the female left the nest.

Fixed-stare: On eight occasions, before the relieving bird occupied the nest, both birds faced each other with bills almost touching and stared fixedly at each other for a few seconds. On four of these occasions, the female accompanied this behaviour with bill-quivering.

At no stage during nest relief did either sex make any discernible sound. During this study no nest material was seen to be added to nests during nest relief, although twice a male returned to the nest within seconds of being relieved and added material to the nest without disturbing the female.

Incubation and hatching

The incubation period of 23 *I. m. minutus* eggs was as follows: 17 days for 2 eggs, 18 days for 4 eggs, 19 days for 12 eggs, 20 days for 4 eggs and 24 days for 1 egg (K. Braschler, in Bauer and Glutz 1966). The incubation period of 21 marked eggs of the subspecies *I. m. payesii* was as follows; 18 days for 2 eggs, 19 days for 17 eggs and 20 days for 2 eggs (Langley 1983). The most common incubation period for both subspecies is thus 19 days. In 10 clutches studied by Langley (1983), 7 were incubated from the laying of the first egg, 2 from the second egg and 1 from the third and last egg.

Both the male and female incubate. In the subspecies *I. m. payesii*, the male and female generally share incubation equally (mean incubation shifts: 128 minutes for males, 138 minutes for females). The longest incubation shift recorded was 540 minutes by a female, and the shortest was 61 minutes by a male. Either parent sometimes incubates throughout the night without being relieved.

Where incubation begins with the first egg laid, hatching occurs at 24-hour intervals. If incubation begins with the second or third egg, the eggs hatch at intervals of 5–35 minutes. The eggs usually hatch in the order in which they were laid, though not always (Langley 1983).

DEVELOPMENT AND CARE OF THE YOUNG

Development

Information on the development of the European Little Bittern is scarce. The chicks are able to leave the nest after 5–6 days to climb in the surrounding reeds. At 8–10 days of age, they can move rapidly thorugh the reeds. They are able to fly at the age of 25–30 days (Bauer and Glutz 1966). The weight of recently hatched chicks is 10–11 g. One chick, measured in the wild, increased in weight from 13–123 g in 11 days (Wackernagel 1950). The development of the young of *I. m. minutus* may be very similar to that of *I. m. payesii*, which is much better known due to the recent study of Langley (1983).

The average weight of the chicks of *I. m. payesii* at hatching is 7.9 g, with a range of 7–9 g. At 20 days old, the chicks weigh about 120 g and are thus nearly fully grown (adult weight: 140–150 g). The legs and feet of the chicks develop rapidly and at 15 days they are nearly fully grown. The development of the culmen is slower. At 4 days of age, the pin feathers begin to replace the down and by 7 days the feathers begin to break through their sheaths.

When the chicks are less than 2 days old, they do not react to the approach of an intruder. At 2 days, they attempt to take up the Bittern Stance and are able to perform it fully at 5 days. During that period, they will peck at a human intruder if he or she tries to catch them. At the age of 6 days, they begin to flee from the nest to escape both man and other predators. They often regurgitate food so as to be able to move faster. At an age of 15 days, they can move so quickly that it is almost impossible to catch them.

After 8 days, the chicks normally leave the nest to seek shade in the surrounding reeds. When younger, they stay in the nest and often gullar flutter. At about 15 days (14–16 days for the oldest chicks), they leave the nest completely, returning only to be fed by their parents. They are able to fly short distances by 23 days of age when frightened, and fly normally at the age of 27 days (Langley 1983).

Feeding and care

The chicks of both subspecies are fed by regurgitation. During the first 48 hours after hatching, adults deposit food on the nest floor, guiding the chick's bill to the food with their own. They swallow any food not eaten by the chicks and regurgitate it again later. At 3 days and older, the chicks grasp the adult's bill and the regurgitated food falls directly into their open mouths. Both adults feed the chicks, the feeding rates of males and females being the same. The parents feed only two chicks at a time, although a third may receive some scraps of food, the first getting the greatest proportion. However, sibling rivalry was low in the nest studied by Langley (1983), since the chicks were fed so often that the two which had been previously fed did not usually beg for food the next time around. The average interval between feeds for individual chicks was 149 minutes (range 45–240 minutes). The chicks were mostly fed with fish, 3–8 cm long, but frogs, lizards and insects were also given. They were brooded constantly by one of the parents until the oldest chick was 8–10 days old. At this stage, nest-relief occurred more frequently and with less display than during incubation: "After about eight days from hatching, the adults leave the chicks unattended while they both hunt for food. They do, however, occasionally brood chicks or remain near nests for short periods after feeding the young" (Langley 1983).

Adult Little Bitterns may carry their young to a safe place when in danger. K. Braschler (in Bauer and Glutz 1966) observed a Little Bittern successively carry away three young (aged 2, 3 and 4 days) in its bill, from a damaged nest to another one 3 m away.

Breeding success, additional broods and replacement clutches

There are no data concerning the breeding success of *I. m. minutus*. Of 33 chicks of the subspecies *payesii*, 30 left the nest at the age of 14–16 days. This high breeding success indicates that there was enough food available to bring up the small clutches observed in this case.

The breeding period in Europe is short and the subspecies *minutus* lays only one clutch each year. The longer breeding season of *payesii* in the Cape Province allows two broods, and an attempt to rear a third one has been observed. The first eggs of second broods were laid on average 16.8 days (range 12–22 days) after the previous broods had flown (Langley 1983). One instance of a replacement clutch was observed. A pair of *I. m. payesii* laid their eggs a few days after the loss of their first clutch, in a nest 2 m from the abandoned one.

FEEDING BEHAVIOUR AND FOOD

Little Bitterns almost exclusively use the Stand-and-wait method (Meyerriecks 1960) for hunting. As the Little Bittern is a very small heron, the water may easily be too deep for it. They therefore usually hunt from a perched position on the lowest branch of a shrub or a tree. In the reedbed, they often use an old nest as a platform for hunting. Little Bitterns also like to fish at the edges of pools, lakes, channels and small streams where they remain under cover. Sometimes, however, they use the Wade and Walk Slowly method (Meyerriecks 1960) to hunt, slipping between standing stems of aquatic vegetation. When hunting in this way, they may even venture out into more open habitat for short periods.

An opportunistic foraging behaviour was observed by Wackernagel (1950), a Little Bittern regularly taking fish refuse thrown into the water.

The Little Bittern's most common prey are fish and frogs. Insects are also often taken but their small size makes them less important in the diet. Molluscs, crustaceans, spiders, worms, small mammals and even the eggs and young of marsh-nesting birds are also taken. The fish prey, usually 6–10 cm long, are mostly bleak *Alburnus*, dace *Leuciscus*, carp *Cyprinus*, perch *Perca*, pike *Esox*, gudgeon *Gobio* and sunfish *Eupomotis*. The insects most commonly taken are water-boatmen *Notonecta*, *Naucoris*, mole-cricket *Gryllotalpa*, water-beetle *Dytiscus* and dragonflies *Libellula* and *Aeschna* (Cramp and Simmons 1977).

In 53 stomachs of Little Bitterns from Hungary, Vasvàri (1929) found 13 fish, 7 frogs, 1 salamander, 24 aquatic hemipterans, 16 terrestrial Coleoptera, 14 larvae of aquatic Coleoptera, 6 aquatic Coleoptera, 5 dragonflies, 4 dragonflies' larvae, 2 spiders, and some remains of small mammals, lizards and crustaceans. In the stomachs of Italian birds, Moltoni (1948) found an abundance of insects (Coleoptera, Libellulidae and aquatic Hemiptera), fish (mostly sunfish *Eupomotis* and gudgeon *Gobio*) and amphibians (*Rana*). Eight stomachs of birds from central Africa contained fish, frogs, spiders, shrimps, mole-crickets and other insects (Chapin 1932).

PREDATION

Langley (1983) observed a Purple Gallinule, *Porphyrio porphyrio*, which most probably had taken three eggs from a Little Bittern nest: "A visit to this nest was prompted on hearing bittern and gallinule alarm calls accompanied by much thrashing about in the nest's vicinity. A gallinule with egg yolk on its bill was seen close to the nest and all three eggs had been broken open." The only mammalian predator suspected of taking eggs and young in the area observed by Langley (1983) was the Brown Rat, *Rattus norvegicus*, which inhabits abandoned Masked Weaver and Red Bishop nests in the vicinity.

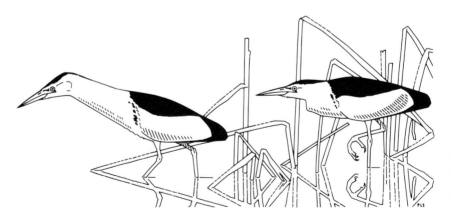

Two Little Bittern males foraging.

Birds of prey must certainly take a few Little Bitterns when they venture out from the reeds, but there have been no observations to confirm this. There is one record of a snake taking a Little Bittern. A cobra, *Naja naja*, was found "lying dead on the bank of river Tawi (Kashmir), with a little Bittern stuck in its throat. Examination confirmed that the snake had died in the struggle to swallow the Little Bittern" (Sharma 1981).

Table 6.   Frequency of I. m. minutus clutch size in Switzerland[a]

	No. of eggs							Sample size
	3	4	5	6	7	8	9	
May		2	8	4	2		1	17
June	2	3	7	24	5			41
July		3	8	2	2			15

[a] After Bauer and Glutz (1966).

CHAPTER 11

The Black-crowned Night Heron
Nycticorax nycticorax

GENERAL APPEARANCE AND FIELD CHARACTERS

The Black-crowned Night Heron is 58–65 cm high with a wing-span of 105–112 cm.

Plumage. The sexes are alike, and the general colour of the adult plumage is grey, white and black, glossed dark green or dark blue.

Adult: the crown, mantle and upper scapulars are black, with a strong dark green gloss in the winter plumage and a more steel-blue gloss in the breeding season. During breeding, the birds also have a few – usually two or three – elongated white plumes on the nape, which are up to 24 cm long in males and slightly shorter in females. The ear-coverts, the sides and back of the neck, the sides of the chest and breast, lower scapulars, back, rump, uppertail-coverts and wing-coverts are ash-grey grading to pale grey on the chest, breast, flanks, underwing-coverts and axillaries. The forehead, a narrow line above the lores and eyes, the chin, cheeks, middle of the throat, belly and thighs are white. The tail feathers and quills are dark grey, the secondaries showing a slight tinge of dull green and the primaries often a tinge of brown.

Juvenile: these are quite different from the adults, having a brown plumage, heavily spotted with buff-white. The crown, mantle, scapulars, wings and tail are dark brown. The crown feathers are finely streaked with buff. The neck, mantle, scapulars and upperwing-coverts have wider buff streaks, mostly V-shaped at the tip of the feathers. The dark brown primaries, secondaries and tail feathers are tipped with buff-white. The underparts are white, heavily streaked dark brown, except for the area around the vent and the undertail-coverts, which are both white.

Immature: during the winter of the second calendar year, juveniles acquire the immature plumage which has much less contrast than the juvenile one. They may breed as soon as the next spring in immature plumage, though the pattern of this plumage is very different from that of the adult bird and particularly lacks the long white crown feathers. The crown, mantle and scapulars have dark brown feathers often with a slight purple gloss. The wings (secondaries and primaries often still tipped white), tail, back and rump are brown. The sides of the head, neck and breast are streaked brown. The chin and throat are white. The flanks, belly and undertail-coverts are pale grey, more or less streaked with buff. In the summer and autumn of the second calendar year, the immatures moult into a plumage more resembling the adult one, but still not quite like it. The crown, mantle and upper scapulars become uniformly dark brown with a slight green gloss. The rest of the plumage, which is grey and white in the adult, is tinged brown. Do these birds moult the following winter to acquire full adult plumage? It seems that they do not. They sometimes nest in this plumage during their second year (third calendar year) without the long white feathers on the crown, attaining full adult plumage only during the following summer and autumn.

Nestling: the nestlings have brown down on both their upperparts and underparts, except on the abdomen where they are white. On the crown the long hair-like down is dark brown on its basal half, the outer half being buff-white.

Bare parts

Non-breeding adult: the bill is green-black, sometimes with some yellow on the lower mandible, especially on the cutting edges. The lores are dark grey-green or yellow-green. The iris is red. The legs and feet are pale yellow.

Breeding adult: the bill is black. The lores are dark red. The iris is deep red. The legs and feet are bright red.

Nestling at hatching: the bare skin, bill, legs and feet are pale flesh-coloured. The iris is pale yellow.

Juvenile: the bill is green-brown, darker along the culmen. The iris is yellow, becoming orange in the autumn. The lores are grey-green. The bare skin is greenish grey. The legs are pale green becoming yellowish green.

Immature: the bare parts are as in the adults except for the pale yellow legs and feet which seem sometimes to have a green or red wash, the latter probably during pair-formation.

The very detailed descriptions of Gross (1923) and McVaugh (1972) show that the coloration of both feathers and soft parts change in small, successive stages and that a short description is always an oversimplification.

Field characters. The adult Night Heron is easily recognized since no other bird resembles this stocky little heron with its black crown, mantle and scapulars, grey wings and white underparts. The two or three long white crown feathers are very conspicuous, as is the black bill and yellow legs and feet which redden during pair-formation. Adult Night Herons are active during the day only when feeding their young. During this period, they may be observed fishing, either waiting or walking slowly among dense vegetation usually at the edge of a pool, in a marsh or along a small stream. Nearly all my observations of Night Herons fishing or flying by day were made in June. However, they are also seen, though less often, in late May and in July.

During the rest of the year, Night Herons are only seen at dawn and at dusk when flying – usually singly – to and from their foraging grounds. Their silhouette is very characteristic when flying at dusk, low over the vegetation. The neck is retracted, the wings are short and rounded and the toes extend only slightly beyond the tail and are often not visible. Now and then, as it flies, the Night Heron utters a typical "kwak" call, resembling that of a Raven. This has given the bird its Latin name, *Nycticorax*, which means Night Raven.

Juvenile and immature Night Herons may be confused with Bitterns *Botaurus stellaris*. However, Bitterns are larger birds whose plumage is golden-rufous, whereas the plumage of juvenile Night Herons is mottled white and that of immature Night Herons is dull grey-brown. The American Bittern *B. lentiginosus* – both adults and immature – has a much paler plumage than the European species, but has a very conspicuous moustachial stripe, which both European Bitterns and Night Herons lack.

The young Little Bittern *Ixobrychus minutus*, which is straw-coloured with brown streaks, and the young Green-backed Heron *Butorides virescens*, which is mottled white, are too small to be confused with Night Herons, being about half their size. These two species also have comparatively long bills.

Measurements. The measurements (mm) of adult birds taken from skins are given below (Cramp and Simmons 1977). The number of skins and the sex are indicated. Standard deviations are given in parentheses. The sex differences are not significant, although males are often slightly larger than females.

wing	27 ♂♀	278–308	(7.79)
tail	9 ♂♀	102–112	(3.71)
bill	27 ♂♀	64–78	(3.54)
tarsus	10 ♂♀	68–84	(4.74)
toe	6 ♂♀	71–85	(5.00)

In Italy, Moltoni (1936) weighed 23 Night Herons (range and mean): 12 ♂♂ 600–800 g (66.8 g), 11 ♀♀ 525–690 g (49.9 g). In the Camargue, a total of 127 adults weighed an average 532 g and 197 juveniles 514 g (Bauer and Glutz 1966).

The wing-beat rate of Night Herons was found to be an average 154 wing-beats per minute by Voisin (unpublished). Blake (1948) reported an average 2.6 wing-beats per second and Maxwell and Putnam (1968) 2.8 wing-beats per second. Maxwell and Putnam (1968) also reported flight speed to be approximately 20 miles per hour.

One Night Heron lived for 22–23 years in a zoological garden (Blaszkiewitz 1981).

DISTRIBUTION, MOVEMENTS AND HABITAT

GEOGRAPHICAL VARIATION

The Black-crowned Night Heron *N. nycticorax* is certainly one of the most cosmopolitan heron species. It is found in Europe, Asia, Africa and both North and South America. The species is only absent from Australasia where the Nankeen Night Heron, *N. caledonicus* (Gmelin) replaces it. These two species are largely allopatric despite some range overlap in Indonesia and the Philippines, and are often considered to form a superspecies (Hancock and Elliott 1978). On the whole, the separation between the two species follows Wallace's Line – the boundary between the Oriental and the Australasian regions. There are four recognized subspecies of the Black-crowned Night Herons. The first, *N. n. nycticorax* (Linnaeus) has already been described. *N. n. hoactli* (Gmelin) is on average larger than the nominate subspecies and the white streak above the eye is narrower or interrupted. It also seems to differ slightly from the nominate subspecies in the coloration of the bare parts. During breeding, the lores are deep blue-black and the legs and feet flush salmon-pink rather than bright red. *N. n. obscurus* (Bonaparte) is easily distinguished from the two previously described subspecies since the whole of its underparts, except for the throat, are tinged smoky-brown. Finally, *N. n. falklandicus* (Hartert) is intermediate between *hoactli* and *obscurus*.

BREEDING AND WINTERING AREAS

N. n. nycticorax breeds in scattered localities, in western Europe up to 50°N, in the USSR up to 53°N and from the Near and Middle East, eastwards south of the Himalayas to China, Japan and Taiwan and southwards to Indonesia. This subspecies also breeds in Africa north of the Sahara in Morocco, Algeria and Egypt, and in scattered localities in the whole of Africa south of the Sahara and in Madagascar. *N. n. nycticorax* does not usually winter in Europe; it winters in its southern range. In Africa, the birds are mostly found wintering south of the Sahara, except for a population that commonly winters in Egypt along the River Nile. In Asia, the birds winter from the Near and Middle East to south China, the Philippines and Indonesia. *N. n. hoactli* breeds in North America from southern Canada (up to 52°N) to the southern USA, in Central America, in the West Indies, on the Hawaiian Islands and, finally, in South America from Peru and northern

Chile to northeastern Argentina north of Mendoza and the Rio Negro. The North American birds winter in their southern range; that is to say in the coastal states of the USA, where a few winter as far north as southern Oregon and Long Island. They avoid the northern central states but winter in the southern ones. They are also found wintering in Central America and in South America. *N. n. obscurus* breeds south of a line from the Atacama Desert in Chile to Mendoza and the Rio Negro in Argentina. This subspecies is found as far south as Tierra del Fuego (53°S). The birds also winter in the breeding range. Local movements are unknown and should be studied. *N. n. falklandicus* breeds and winters on the Falkland Islands (Wood 1975).

MOVEMENTS

In July and August in Europe, juveniles disperse in all directions: many juveniles (up to 70% in France) fly north and northeast and are found within a radius of 800 km from their nesting site. One was found 1200 km northeast: ringed at Maringues (Allier, France) on 29 May 1960, but was found dead at Mecklenburg (Eastern Germany) on 7 August 1960. This dispersal merges into the autumn migration, which in Europe lasts through late August, September and October. A few individuals are still found in north Africa in December, while some rare stragglers stay in Europe. For example, one juvenile remained in the heronry in the Allier where it was born, throughout the winter of 1971–1972 (Voisin, unpublished). In 1977–1978, a flock of 20 Night Herons (adults and immatures) overwintered in the Po River valley and was noted twice each month from November to March. Two other groups of wintering Night Herons were also observed that winter in northern Italy (Tosi *et al.* 1979). I suppose that this dangerous habit of wintering near the breeding area in these northern latitudes was abandoned during the very cold winters of the 1980s. Apart from such exceptions, the whole European Night Heron population is migratory.

The large numbers of recoveries of birds ringed in France, Spain, Portugal and Italy during the autumn migration, combined with the absence of recoveries in coastal areas along the Mediterranean Sea, in Morocco and Algeria, indicates that Night Herons do not cross the Mediterranean during this migration but rather fly over Spain and Italy, and to a lesser extent Portugal. There is no evidence for the Corsican–Sardinian route proposed by Lippens: there has not been a single recovery in Corsica or Sardinia of a Night Heron ringed in France (Voisin, unpublished). Those Night Herons that have been recovered in Sardinia have probably come from Italy.

Night Herons do not only leave Europe but also north Africa (Morocco, Algeria and Tunisia), cross the desert where there have been many recoveries at oases (Colomb-Bechar and Ahaggar, Aïr, Bilma, Fezzan, Ghat, El Goléa, Kufra and Aoufous; Moreau 1972, Lippens and Wille 1969, CRBPO ringing centre). A migratory route towards east Africa along the Nile River is probably also used by the eastern populations of European Night Herons and by the ones from the Near East. A few Night Herons that reach tropical Africa stay there even while they should be breeding in Europe. One bird ringed in

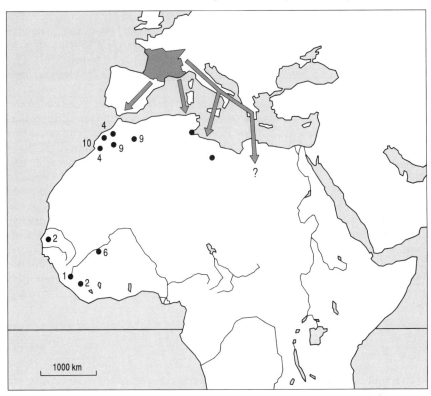

Recoveries of Night Herons *Nycticorax nycticorax* in Africa that were ringed in France (the month at which each recovery occurred is indicated (Lippens *et al.* 1969).

the Camargue on 19 July 1961 was recovered near Bamako (Mali) on 24 June 1964 (CRBPO). Night Herons ringed in Europe are found in tropical Africa and even in equatorial Africa. One bird ringed at the Volga Delta was recovered near Yaunde, Cameroon (Cramp and Simmons 1977) and one ringed in Krasnodar, USSR on 4 July 1958 was found 45 km upstream of Impfondo on the Oubangui River (Congo) on 18 February 1959 (CRBPO). One Night Heron ringed at the Volga Delta and another in Hungary were recovered in Nigeria. Hungarian and Czechoslovakian Night Herons were recovered in Guinea (Cramp and Simmons 1977). Night Herons from France were recovered in Sierra Leone, the Gambia and Mali (Lippens and Wille 1969). One bird ringed in Spain was recovered in Senegal. The migration routes between Europe and Africa go in a southwesterly direction. One bird ringed in Azerbydzhan was recovered in eastern Sudan (Cramp and Simmons 1977). Only the most eastern populations of Night Herons seem to winter in east Africa.

In North America, the beginning of the breeding season extends from

February to April. On Shamrock Island in Texas the birds begin to breed in early February (Chapman *et al.* 1981). At Long Island, New York, the first Night Herons appeared in late March (Allen and Mangels 1940) and in St Clair County, Michigan only during the first days of April (Henny 1972). The autuman migration begins in September and goes on into October and November.

Night Herons (of indeterminate subspecies) have been reported far to the north, on Newfoundland. They have also been observed on various islands in the Pacific such as the Galapagos Islands and Wake Island (Hancock and Elliott 1978). The return migration begins at the end of February, the birds coming back to Europe in March and during the first half of April. A few individuals arrive as late as the second half of April and probably even in May. Either in spring when "overshooting" or in autumn during the post-breeding dispersal, Night Herons have been observed as accidentals in the following countries: Britain, Ireland, Iceland, the Faeroes, Norway, Denmark, Sweden, Finland, the Azores and Madeira. Observations of accidentals in Britain are quite common. Many of these birds probably come from a little, self-sustaining colony established at Edinburgh Zoo in 1950, the birds being free to roam as they wish. Unfortunately, these birds, imported from Canada, belong to the American subspecies *N. n. hoactli* (Dorward 1957).

Habitat

In temperate climates, Night Herons of the subspecies *N. n. nycticorax* are found in freshwater areas: along streams and rivers, at the margins of lakes and pools, in marshes and exceptionally on dry or inundated grasslands. They forage also in man-made sites such as reservoirs, canal banks, ditches, rice fields and even small ornamental waters. They always remain hidden in dense vegetation whether on the breeding sites or the foraging grounds. In temperate Europe and Asia, this type of habitat only occurs in freshwater areas. In tropical and subtropical areas, Night Herons both breed and forage – often in great numbers – in the dense mangroves which grow along the coasts in both brackish and saltwater areas. This subspecies is found mostly in lowlands but small parties are established up to 2000 m. It breeds farther north (up to Orel in the USSR) in dry continental climates than in oceanic ones (Hancock and Elliott 1978). They nest mostly in mixed heronries but may also be found in more or less sizeable heronries of their own. The nests are usually built high up in tall trees, such as alders (*Alnus*) and poplars (*Populus*) where they will not be disturbed. In fact, all sorts of deciduous trees are used and sometimes conifers too (one heronry in the Camargue, now deserted, was in pine trees *Pinus*). In areas with no high trees, Night Herons use small ones such as willows (*Salix*) and tamarisk (*Tamarix*). They may even nest in reedbeds when neither trees nor bushes are available.

The American subspecies *N. n. hoactli* breeds and forages in the same kind of habitats as those used by the Palearctic and African subspecies. They nest in trees throughout eastern North America and on the west coast, but mainly in marshes in the Great Plains states and the prairie provinces (Bent 1926). They breed further north in dry continental climates (up to Saskatchewan in Canada) than in oceanic ones, as do their European counterparts.

A surprising change in the habitats used by part of the Night Heron population of South America is of interest and needs further study. *N. n. hoactli* seems to have established itself high up in the Andean mountains of Peru and northern Chile and along the arid coast of northern Chile. These are the traditional habitats of *N. n. obscurus* and I would not be surprised if both subspecies interbreed in southern Peru and northern Chile. A.W. Johnson (1965) found a colony of *N. n. hoactli* on a rocky islet in Lake Cotacotani in northeastern Chile at a height of 4800 m and this subspecies is apparently also found along the arid coast and in a few oases of the Atacama Desert up to Antofagasta. The subspecies *N. n. obscurus* lives and breeds from the Atacama Desert to Tierra del Fuego, and along the coast, in a marine habitat and in the highest lakes in the Andes (Johnson 1965).

N. n. falklandicus is endemic to the Falkland Islands where they remain all the year round. They fish along small streams, on the beaches and, at low tide, in rocky pools. They also stay on kelp beds up to 500 yards from the shore, where they appear to capture small fish. Their heronries are very small (the largest not more than 24 pairs) and single pairs also breed alone. The nests are built on steep cliffs near the shore on clumps of vegetation, often tussock grass. They also nest among rushes. During the cold period, they roost in dense cypress trees near human habitation or in hulks. A study of their mortality during this difficult time of year would certainly provide interesting observations.

POPULATION SIZE AND TRENDS

From the Middle Ages to the beginning of the eighteenth century, Black-crowned Night Herons bred commonly in western Europe as far north as the Netherlands and Germany. Destruction of their habitat and the widespread collecting and hunting of their young drastically reduced the population during the eighteenth and nineteenth centuries. Night Herons, as other heron species, were commonly eaten. In 1357, near Gouda in the Netherlands, 2000 young Night Herons and 564 young Grey Herons were sold and eaten (G.A. Brouwer, in Lippens and Wille 1969). With the destruction of extensive wetlands in the eighteenth and nineteenth centuries, the remaining birds became more accessible so that there were probably no areas left undisturbed where heronries could act as population reserves. Nowadays, tziganes and other nomads still collect and eat young herons when they encounter an unguarded heronry. Today, a few nests are found here and there in western Germany, Austria and Switzerland. No Night Herons nest in Belgium. Two small heronries numbering a few nests were found in the Netherlands in recent years (Cramp and Simmons 1977). In France in 1849, Night Herons still bred as far north as the vicinity of Strasbourg. Before the Second World War, they bred commonly only in the Dombes area and in the Camargue. A few nests were occasionally observed in western France (Brosselin 1974).

During the war, the Night Heron population expanded rapidly into roughly the same areas as today. However, the size of the population was unknown until the first national census, undertaken by M. Brosselin in 1968 (Lippens and Wille 1969) (see Table 7). About 2200 nests were counted. A new census was carried out in 1974, also by Brosselin (1974), but only 1550 breeding pairs were found. The Night Heron population in France had diminished and several old heronries were deserted. According to Brosselin, until herons were completely protected in October 1975, the destruction of heronries by fishermen was the most important factor limiting or even decreasing the Night Heron population in France. Another factor was the shooting of many young at the onset of waterbird hunting in August each year. The severe drought in the Sahel which began during the summer of 1968 and lasted through the 1970s seems also to have greatly affected the Night Heron population, especially during 1968, viz. the decrease of the Night Heron population in the Camargue between June 1968 and June 1969. A third census was undertaken in 1981 by Duhautois and Marion (1981) and Night Herons were found breeding in 35 heronries, the two largest numbering 352 and 649 nests. Both these heronries were in western France, one in Moissac and the other near Toulouse. The total number of breeding pairs had increased to about 3500, apparently due to the total protection of the species since the last census. The birds also seem to have adjusted to the drought conditions in the Sahel, probably migrating farther south to overwinter. The population has increased most markedly in the western part of the country. In the area along the Adour and Garonne rivers, 355 breeding pairs were counted in 1974 and 1186 in 1981. In 1981, the Camarguan Night Heron population had still not recovered from 1968, and since 1983 has begun to fall again. In my opinion, this recent diminution is due to the increased salinity of most of the water in the area following the reduction of rice cultivation there. This change in salinity affects the vegetation, especially the dense marshes where Night Herons thrive and is also responsible for a decrease in the number of frogs which form an important part of their diet (See Table 8).

In Italy, the first national census of Night Herons was undertaken by M. Fasola in 1981 (Fasola *et al.* 1981). There were 17300 breeding pairs in 45 heronries, all in northern Italy (see Table 9). Two-thirds of the Italian Night Heron population is concentrated in a *c.* 6000-km^2 area where there is intensive rice cultivation.

In Spain, M. Fernandez-Cruz (1975) counted 1270 breeding pairs in 11 heronries, during the years 1972–1974. The numbers of Night Herons breeding in each heronry were not usually very numerous, numbering from a few nests to about 100. Only three heronries contained more than 100 nests: "La Rocina" (Huelva), 100–200 nests in 1973 (Ree 1973), "La Albufera" (Valencia), 170 nests in 1972 and a heronry on the Rio Tajo near Caleras y Chozas (Toledo), 235–240 nests in 1973 (Fernandez-Cruz 1975). A new heronry established in reedbeds was discovered in 1977 on the Ebro Delta. In 1978, 25 pairs of Night Herons bred there among numerous other heron species (Martinez and Martinez 1983).

In Portugal, Night Herons have bred regularly in at least one heronry northeast of Lisbon since 1935–1940, the heronry of "Paul de Boquilobo" at

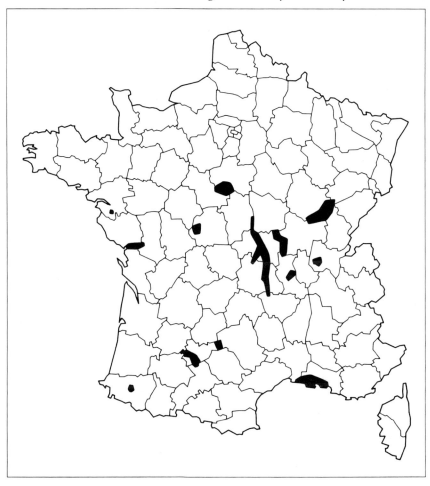

The breeding locations of Night Herons *Nycticorax nycticorax* in France in
1968 (Lippens *et al.* 1969).

Golega (Londot 1971), although a census is yet to be undertaken to determine
the number of birds breeding there.

In Greece, 1500–1600 pairs nested in 1973 (Cramp and Simmons 1977),
but only 492–591 in 1985–1986 (Crivelli *et al.* 1988). In the USSR, according to Dementiev and Gladkov (1951), a few heronries contained up to 2500
pairs of Night Herons. In the Volga Delta, 720 pairs nested in 1951 and only
19 pairs in 1958 (Lugovoy in Cramp and Simmons 1977). In Hungary, 652
pairs were counted in the 1950s and in Czechoslovakia 100–200 pairs in the
1960s. In Turkey, in the delta of the River Meric, 600–700 nests were
counted in 1967, and at Lake Manyas Gölü, 500 pairs (Cramp and Simmons
1977). In Yugoslavia, 225–796 nests were counted between 1954 and 1970

in the Kopacevski area (Majić and Mikuska 1972). In Morocco, Night Herons nest in a colony near Allal Tazi in very varying numbers from no nests at all to about 400 nests. They nest also near Oued Smir between Ceuta and Tetuan, where about 500 adults and young were seen at the end of the nesting period (Haas 1969, Vernon 1973).

The mortality rates of Night Herons from ringing data have been studied only in the subspecies *N. n. hoactli*. First-year birds had a mortality rate of 63.6%, whereas birds older than 1 year had a mortality rate of 25.8% (Cramp and Simmons 1977).

BEHAVIOUR AND BIOLOGY

DAILY ROUTINE

Night Herons differ from all other European herons in their nocturnal behaviour. Outside the breeding season, they sleep on a branch at the roost during the day remaining hidden in the dense vegetation. Light intensity determines the arrival and departure of birds at the roost and varies greatly from day to day according to the weather conditions. Unfortunately, outside the breeding season the light intensity at departure time from the roost or heronry is too low to be measured with ordinary photoelectric instruments. In spring in France (Allier), at the end of March and the beginning of April, Night Herons leave the heronry after sunset and return next morning just before sunrise. The birds leave and return in the space of about 30 minutes. Siegfried (1966) recorded the mean departure time of Night Herons roosting in two different roosts in Cape Province, expressed as minutes after sunset, on moonless evenings free from cloud, mist and wind. The mean departure time from a roost situated in a valley was 11 ($\pm$ 2.6) minutes after sunset and from a second roost situated along the coast, 21 ($\pm$ 5.6) minutes after sunset (the difference being due to the sheltered position of the first roost). According to M. Fasola (1984), Night Herons leave the heronry on average 19 minutes after sunset and return on average 17 minutes before sunrise. In the evening, Night Herons often first emerge from the dense vegetation and perch quietly in an exposed position before flying off. When leaving for the foraging grounds, a few individuals often circle once or twice uttering their characteristic call – a loud "kraa". Two or three perched Night Herons then usually fly off to join them. When flying alone or in small parties towards the foraging grounds, now and then they utter a loud "kraa", and since it is dark or nearly so, they are more easily heard than seen. This nocturnal way of life changes abruptly when the birds begin to breed. Night Herons display during the day at the heronry but still leave at dusk each evening to forage during the night, returning only at dawn. It seems unlikely that Night Herons display during the night since they need all of the time available to them to forage. Using a light intensifier during incubation, M. Fasola (1984) observed that Night Herons commonly change over during the night. The birds tend to leave earlier in the evening and return later in the morning than during the pre-egg period. Later, when feeding young, Night Herons greatly increase the time spent foraging, not only during the night but also during a great part of the day. In May and June, while many Night Herons return to the heronry at dawn, between 03.00 and 03.30 h, arrivals are observed as late as 08.00–09.00 h. Adults also leave the heronry for the foraging grounds throughout the morning. In the evening, they return mostly between 17.00 and 19.00 h. They may leave the heronry at any time during the evening, but most depart at about 19.00 h. During May and June, Night Herons quite commonly forage by day and are easily observed on the feeding grounds, though most often early in the morning or in the evening. Night Herons feed their young during the morning, the late afternoon and also throughout the night.

ARRIVAL AT THE HERONY IN THE SPRING

When Night Herons which migrate in small parties arrive at the heronry by day, they fly around above the trees of the heronry for some time before landing (Brosselin, pers. comm.). In Allier, France at the end of March, the vegetation is still as it was during the winter: the trees and bushes are leafless, the old reeds are yellow and the emergent aquatic vegetation has not yet grown up. Although the birds left the heronry in luxuriant vegetation the previous August or September, they are still able to recognize the spot. In spring, the snow on the mountains of the Massif Central has not yet melted and the wind is still very cold. In both 1968 and 1969, some snow fell during my observations at the heronry, though it did not settle. The temperature fell to $-6°C$ in 1968 and $-5°C$ in 1969. The Night Herons that had just arrived from Africa spent the days sleeping in a small tree which, unlike the ones in which the birds would later nest, had many low branches just above the water. They could not hide, since there were no leaves at all. As long as the cold weather lasted they remained inactive, sleeping during the day and leaving at dusk to forage. The first day on which the sun shone, giving some warmth, they flew up into the high trees and a few males began to display. These attempts to breed ceased as soon as the weather became cold and windy again a few hours later, but many birds remained in the high trees of the heronry sleeping or preening. As the days passed, other small groups of Night Herons came to the heronry. In both 1968 and in 1969, the first juveniles were seen some days later than the first adults. The first adults came to the heronry between 24 and 28 March in 1968 and on 24 March 1969; the first juveniles, on the other hand, were seen on 4 April 1968 and 12 April 1969. Displays really started at the herony on the first warm and sunny spring day with no wind. The courtship period is short, and male Night Herons need only display for a few days before pairs are formed.

MAINTENANCE BEHAVIOUR

Resting Night Herons adopt the typical heron posture (see chapter on the Grey Heron). At the heronry, Night Herons spend much time preening, proceeding very much like Little Egrets (see chapter on the Little Egret). They

Neck-preening.

rub their heads against the powder-down patches. They nibble and stroke their feathers, usually beginning with the lower neck and breast feathers and going on to the belly and wing feathers. To clean the head and upper neck feathers, which they cannot reach with the bill, they raise them and scratch them thoroughly with one of their pectinated claws. They scratch the head and neck directly by bringing the leg straight up while lowering the head. According to V. Piette (1986), they bend their necks backwards, along the back, to rub their heads against the oil gland. Night Herons also shake, stretch and yawn.

Shaking was observed at the end of a preening bout, or as an isolated activity. The Night Heron leans forward slightly, erects most of the contour feathers and shakes vigorously while rapidly moving the wings in and out. The length of a shaking session is from 5 to 10 seconds. Shaking apparently places the feathers in order. Stretching usually occurs during the preening bout, but was also observed as an isolated incident. The heron shifts his weight to the right (or left) leg. The left leg is lifted until the tibiotarsus is parallel to the abdominal wall and the tarsometatarsus hangs vertically. Extension of the left wing down and out is followed by an outward extension of the left leg. The same but opposite procedure is followed for the right wing stretch. Yawning occurred irregularly while the herons rested. The Night Heron remains in the perched position; the bill is opened wide and the eyes are open and bulging slightly. It did not appear to be associated with sleeping and no external factors were observed influencing the yawn (Maxwell and Putnam 1968).

Night Herons sometimes bathe to cool down when they are too hot. They walk out into the water until it reaches up to their belly or even to their shoulders. They stand or walk slowly, feathers slightly raised. Now and then, they plunge briefly like feeding ducks and raise their tails vertically while their heads are under the water. On coming out of the water they body-shake. When it is hot at the nest, they gullar flutter (Piette 1986, Voisin 1975). Night Herons apparently also sunbathe and Piette (1986) has observed this twice in captivity. The bird stood vertically, feathers slightly raised, neck retracted, bill pointing downwards, wing half unfolded sideways and downwards, and remained motionless in this position in full sunshine for about 10 minutes.

DISPLAYS AND CALLS

The Night Heron's displays were among the first heron displays to be studied (Lorenz 1934, Allen 1940). At that time, courtship displays interested scientists much more than agonistic displays, which were quite neglected. In addition, the significance of Crest-raising in Night Herons was misinterpreted. Twenty years later, a new framework for understanding heron behaviour was introduced by J. Meyerriecks (1960) and D. Blaker (1969). Meyerriecks studied several species of North American herons (*Butorides virescens, Egretta rufescens, E. thula* and *Ardea herodias*) and Blaker the Cattle Egret *Bubulcus ibis*. Since then, the various displays of the Night Heron have been studied by myself in 1970, by M. Fasola in 1975 (whose observations largely agree with my own) and, finally, by V. Piette who studied captive birds in 1986. When not otherwise stated, the following descriptions are written from my own study (Voisin 1970) and a film also made by me.

All the agonistic displays and the Fear Display are performed by both sexes. The threat and alarm calls seem to be the same for both males and females. On the other hand, the typical sexual display, the Foot-Lifting Display, is only performed by males and is accompanied by a typical call.

Agonistic behaviours

The Forward Displays represent a succession of increasingly intense threat displays and are used at the heronry to maintain individual distances and to defend the nest territory.

Full Forward Display. The Full Forward Display of Night Herons is very like that of the other heron species. The bird assumes the following position when facing an intruder:

- body in a nearly horizontal position;
- legs slightly bent;
- wings partly spread;
- neck curved backwards in an "S" shape, bill pointed forwards, ready to strike.

All the feathers are held erect, particularly on the breast, neck, crown and nape, and loud threat calls are given. In the Full Forward Display, Night Herons may either stand or walk towards their opponent. In the second case, their relatively short neck is generally not curved backwards in the "S" shape, but stretched upwards, the head and bill directed towards the opponent. During this display, the aggressive component is at its maximum and no other feeling has any place, the fear component being totally eclipsed. From this extreme situation, in which aggression is at its most intense, the bird may assume postures in which the aggressive component becomes less and less strong. Thus while in many situations the aggressive component may dominate, the fear component may also be present and more or less strongly expressed.

The following agonistic displays represent characteristic graduations, arbitrarily chosen, along this continuous succession of postures.

The Forward Display (after photographs by D. Robert).

Forward Display. In the Forward Display, the aggressive urge is less than in the Full Forward Display, the fear component sometimes being present. The bird assumes the following position when facing an opponent:

○ body in a nearly horizontal position;
○ legs slightly bent, but less than when in the Full Forward Display;
○ wings partly spread, but less than in the Full Forward Display;
○ neck in various positions, stretched upwards or towards the opponent or even completely retracted.

All the feathers are held erect, but particularly those of the breast and neck. The crown and nape feathers are more or less erect, depending on the relative strength of the aggressive and fear components, the long nape feathers ranging from completely to only half erect. Threat calls of variable intensity are given.

I consider Night Herons to be among the most aggressive herons. In contrast with Little Egrets, which display with much walking in the branches, Night Herons often attack after only a short threat display, flying straight at the opponent and delivering strong blows with the bill. An intruder suffering such an attack always leaves rapidly! A bird at the nest is dominant and will not be attacked. The fact that Night Herons attack readily perhaps explains why the fear component seems to be more often present in threatening Night Herons, than among say, threatening Little Egrets.

A very common threat display of Night Herons at the nest is the following version of the Forward Display:

○ The bird remains sitting on its nest.
○ Its feathers, mostly those of the crown, nape, breast and neck, are held erect. However, the crown and nape feathers are held more or less erect depending on the strength of the aggressive and fear components, the long crown and nape feathers ranging from being totally to only half erect.
○ The neck is slowly extended horizontally to a maximum, and then withdrawn as slowly, while the bird utters loud threat calls.

Upright Threat Display. This has been described as a low-intensity threat display by Palmer (1962), who wrote:

> Threat displays include 'upright threat' in which bird extends head and neck fully upward and slightly forward; slight to moderate erection of crown, neck and back feathers; erection of long plumes rare; typically no vocal component, but rarely bird may utter one or more harsh ok-ok or rok-rok calls; wings typically closed but may be extended slightly.

Stab-and counter-stab. When two nests are very close to each other, as soon as some change occurs in one of the nests, as for example the arrival of a mate, the bird in the other nest commences a Forward Display while remaining in its nest. The bird in the first nest answers with a threat display. The behaviour is the same as described above but the two birds remain in their nests and extend and withdraw their necks alternatively. If one of the mates is present, it often also joins in this behaviour, but remains on the nest rim and does not stretch the neck as much. When only slightly irritated, the Night Heron only raises its crest feathers a little.

Snap Display. This display has also been described by Palmer (1962):

> Ritualized 'snap' display is seen only during nesting season: bird moves slowly about branches of tree in a low crouch, suddenly extends head and neck fully forward and slightly down, erects crown, neck and back feathers moderately, but plumes if erected, only slightly; eyes appear to bulge from head; at moment when head and neck are fully out and down, bird either snaps mandibles together, or, more typically momentarily seizes a twig.

Fasola (1975) has also briefly described this behaviour: "the bird stretched its neck obliquely downward, clapping its mandibles. A feeble 'tac' was heard."

Direct Attack. This behaviour is seldom observed. It occurs mostly during courtship when a Night Heron, either a male or a female, approaches too close to a displaying male. The Direct Attack is very sudden. The bird does not give a preliminary threat display. Its feathers only slightly raised (or possibly not at all), it crouches down and flies off, straight at the intruder, to deliver sharp blows with the bill. The intruder always flees.

Supplanting Run. Night Herons on the foraging grounds threaten others using the Supplanting Run, which is exactly the same as that described for the Little Egret (see chapter on the Little Egret).

Fear and conflict displays

Alert Posture. Night Herons take up this posture when afraid of humans or animal predators. They stand with legs, body and neck nearly vertical, the head and bill pointing towards the danger. All the feathers are sleeked against the body. Birds threatened by others in the heronry do not adopt this posture but try to flee with sleeked plumage, either rapidly slipping through the branches of flying away. Night Herons do not perform the Bittern Stance.

Alarm Call. Night Herons have a loud, typical heron call which they use when danger approaches.

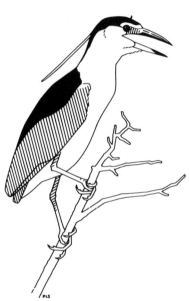

A Night Heron on a branch calling.

Wing-touch. This is a typical conflict display among both unmated males and females when in the presence of a bird of the opposite sex. The movement is exactly the same as in Cattle Egrets (see chapter on the Cattle Egrets).

Courtship displays

The Foot-lifting Display. This display, which I have called *danse* in French (Voisin 1975), is only performed by unmated males. It is used as often, and in the same situation, as the Stretch Display among Grey Herons, Little Egrets and Cattle Egrets. It is clearly homologous to the Stretch Display but, since it is so different in form, and is the most common sexual display of male Night Herons, it clearly merits a special name. In the Foot-lifting Display:

○ The Night Heron stands almost horizontal, legs slightly apart (position 1).
○ The legs are stretched and the shoulders are raised, while the tip of the bill and tail, now pointing downwards, remain almost in the same position (position 2).
○ Once in position 2, the Night Heron lifts one leg (positions 3 and 4), and the big, bright red foot is exhibited. The leg and foot is then placed again in position 5 which is the same as position 2.
○ The Night Heron bends its legs and lowers its shoulders, coming back to position 6 which is the same as position 1.

Usually, the bird lifts its feet alternately 3–4 times. Sometimes, it lifts the same foot one or several times and then the other foot once or several times in succession. The feathers are not raised during this display. The nape feathers with their long white plumes are kept lowered and thus not exhibited.

Allen and Mangels (1940) report a characteristic call given during this display and Piette (1986), studying captive birds, heard it also when the displaying male was in positions 2 and 3. It resembled the muted sound produced by a vibrating wire fence – "zzzdong".

Bowing Display. This display is performed by unmated males as an altern-ative to the more common Foot-lifting Display. Before displaying, the Night Heron looks around, often with a stick in its bill (position 1). When display-ing, he stands up almost vertical, body and legs motionless (position 2). He then bends down, head along the belly, and lifts it again several times, the bill pointing downwards (position 3). All sorts of sticks are used, from very long ones to quite small ones hardly visible at a distance. When the male displays with a long stick, the intention to construct a nest may be signalled. When it has only a very small one, or none at all, the movement seems pointless, or at least only symbolic. Later, the Bowing Display is also performed at the nest during its construction by males arriving with a stick, before giving it to the female. The Bowing Display thus functions both as a courtship display and a greeting display between paired birds.

Stretch Display. A Stretch Display has been described briefly by Piette (1986). After a Foot-lifting Display, the Night Heron stretched itself upwards as far as possible, bill pointing towards the sky. As soon as the bird had stretched himself to the maximum, it relaxed, adopting the resting position again. Though taken for a Stretch Display, this was probably just an ordinary body stretch.

Twig-shake. This is a common courtship behaviour in male Night Herons. The male stretches the neck and seizes a twig between its mandibles, then shakes the head horizontally while not pulling at the twig (Piette 1986). This behaviour has not been reported after pair formation.

Breeding or appeasement displays

Bill-clappering. The Night Heron stands on the nest in a horizontal posi-tion, the neck outstretched, all its feathers raised. First, a low call is heard: "og, og, og". As the neck is lowered, the bill is moved rapidly and with a small amplitude from side to side. A slight clappering of the mandibles is heard during this movement (Piette 1986).

Billing. The two birds at the nest, all their feathers raised, gently peck at each other's bill. Their necks are sometimes in a "S" curve, but most often one of the birds stretches its neck and raises itself while the other, neck retracted, squats down low. Continuously pecking at each other's bill, the two birds swap their positions, the high one sinking down while the lower bird raises itself (Piette 1986).

Back-biting. This occurs often in newly formed pairs. As in Billing, the birds are in physical contact with each other. The crown and nape feathers are

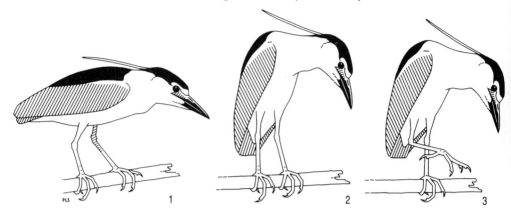

Successive postures during the Foot-lifting Display.

partly raised, the displaying bird standing beside its mate. It runs its partly open bill through the feathers of the back, head or even sides of its mate, moving its head with rapid movements of low amplitude from side to side. At the same time, it rapidly opens and closes its bill.

REPRODUCTIVE BEHAVIOUR

Pair-formation

Pair-formation in Night Herons easily passes unseen. The males have no Advertising Call and they choose only one territory, usually well hidden,

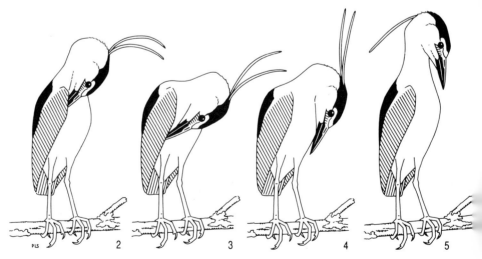

Successive postures during the Wing-touch Display.

where they display and where they will nest at a later date. As the males always remain on their territory when they are not foraging, no pursuit flights have ever been observed.

The onset of pair formation has been described by Fasola (1975). A male Night Heron displayed on a branch. Another bird, probably a female, was a few metres away, jumping from branch to branch. When a third Night Heron landed on a branch nearby, the displaying male stopped his display, raised all his feathers and after a short threat attacked the intruder, giving loud threat calls. The intruder rapidly fled. However, after a short period of time, the same or another intruder returned. Occasionally, the female would drive off intruders also, even though this female and the displaying male were not yet paired. She tried to enter his territory three times, edging very slowly towards

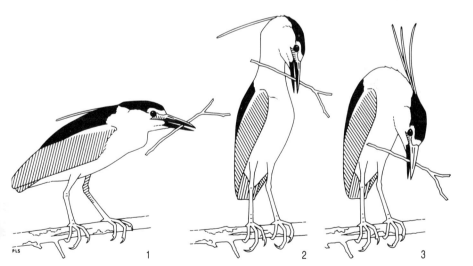

Successive postures during the Bowing Display.

him along the branches. Each time, when both birds were quite near each other, they raised their feathers and the male attacked the female who flew away for the time being.

The chief difficulty seems to be for the female to remain on the male's territory without being attacked by him. As long as he attacks her, the pair cannot be formed. After a few unsuccessful attempts, the male's aggressive tendencies usually decrease and he accepts the female's company.

Another example of pair formation was observed by me on 10 April 1968. Three birds were present. One of them was standing on an old nest Bowing with a twig in its bill, while the other two watched him. A fourth bird landed on a branch nearby and was immediately attacked by one of the spectators (a female as I confirmed later), who gave him several sharp blows with her bill. The bird rapidly fled. Having chased the intruder, the female then tried to approach the displaying male. She jumped from branch to branch around the old nest, at each jump coming nearer to him. Now and then she stopped and made a few Wing-touches. The male continued Bowing without interruption. Suddenly, the female jumped onto the old nest. The male did not react at all but continued Bowing. Neither of the birds had raised feathers. Facing the male, the female tried to take the twig but without success at first. She then performed a few Wing-touches and at last succeeded in getting the twig. She placed it in the old nest, with much time and effort, during which time the male, remaining on the nest, made a few Wing-touches. Once the twig had been placed in the nest, the two birds began Back-biting, their feathers slightly raised. After a short period of time, the male left to fetch a stick which he gave to the female on his return to the old nest. The pair had been formed, the entire performance lasting some 40 minutes.

Copulation

Copulation does not occur as soon as the pair is formed, but later during nest construction. Copulations are numerous at the beginning of the nest construction period (up to 2 to 3 times during one afternoon), but become much less frequent after only a few days and cease when the eggs are laid. The pair copulates at the nest or on a nearby branch.

As the following observations show, no display precedes copulation. On the 20 April 1967, the male came to the nest, bringing a stick. After a mutual greeting, the female took the stick from the male and placed it in the nest and then crouched on the nest. The male, unfolding his wings to keep his balance, jumped on her back. To steady himself, he grasped her back and the base of her wings with his long toes, before lowering his rump sideways. Cloacal contact was only brief. The male then left the female to land on a nearby branch, while she shook herself thoroughly, probably to bring her feathers into order again. After a moment, the pair resumed nest building.

On the 26 April 1967, the male brought sticks to the female, who placed them in the nest for at least an hour. The male then took over nest building while the female stood inactive on a branch close to the nest. After a short period of time, the male started gently Back-biting her. She returned to the nest and both birds began Billing, feathers somewhat erect. Calming down, they stopped Billing and remained inactive for a moment. The female then crouched down. The male tried to copulate but did not succeed; either he slipped or the female moved. Both birds stayed still for some time and then copulated successfully.

Piette (1986), who has observed these birds at very close quarters, reports that the red colour of the legs and feet, especially those of the male, becomes a deeper red just before copulation. No calls were heard during copulation.

Greeting Behaviour

The Night Heron is often already calling on returning to the nest, as it flies over the heronry before landing. The returning bird does not land directly on the nest, but on a branch, usually the same one each time, a few metres from the nest. It then walks slowly towards the nest with bent legs, body held horizontal, neck in an "S" curve and all its feathers held fully erect, the long white crest feathers often falling forwards. This posture is identical to that of the Full Forward Display except for the position of the bill, which according to Piette (1986), is pointed slightly downwards and not directed towards the other bird. The significant difference from the agonistic displays is that the calls given by the incoming heron as it nears the nest, are not harsh threat calls but soft greeting calls. The bird at the nest, if sitting on it, raises itself and stands with bent legs, body held horizontal, neck in an "S" curve and all its feathers held fully erect and gives soft greeting calls, either the same ones as the incoming bird, or as part of a duet. These calls enable the mated pair to recognize each other and are thus the most important part of the Greeting Display. The posture adopted is, in my opinion, just a threat posture, perhaps slightly modified, both the bird at the nest and the incoming bird being ready to fight should they meet an intruder inside the territory rather than their mate. As Night Herons are very aggressive birds, it is no wonder that they hold their feathers more erect than most herons during the Greeting Display. They probably have difficulty in calming down after they have recognized each other and therefore often indulge in appeasement displays after Greeting such as Bowing, Billing and Back-biting. At the beginning of the nest construction period, the male usually brings a stick with him when returning to the nest, and begins Bowing with the stick in his bill. The feathers of the female sleek as she watches him display, and after a moment she takes up the stick and places it in the nest.

When the incoming bird has no stick, the pair usually begins Billing and then Back-biting. According to Piette (1986), Bill-clappering also occurs. When both birds have stopped displaying, they often stand inactive for a moment, side by side, feathers in a neutral, resting position. After a moment, the bird that was at the nest usually leaves, moving slowly away along the branches before taking flight.

Greeting followed by much Bowing, Billing, and Back-biting is characteristic of the early part of the breeding season. The importance of these appease-ment displays also varies with the situation. The birds display a lot when they meet again after a fight against an intruder. In contrast, there is hardly any Greeting and no appeasement displays at all when the male brings sticks at short intervals during nest construction. As time passes, the pair spend less time Bowing and Back-biting and, after hatching, only Billing can be observed.

Nest building

Nest building begins as soon as the pair is formed. Old nests from the previous year are consolidated and used again. When no more old nests are available, the newly formed pair builds a new one. The nests are constructed in a tree fork usually against the trunk, the branches protruding from the trunk being included in the nest. Observations of copulation during nest building show that only males gather sticks, bringing them one at a time to the female. At the beginning of the nest building period, they often gather sticks from old nests. They also gather sticks from the ground. These often come from old nests which have blown down during the winter. They also try to plunder other herons' nests if they are not well guarded. However, most sticks gathered are twigs that are still growing on branches. The bird takes a twig between its mandibles and pulls 3–4 times. He then loosens his grip and rests a moment, before trying 3–4 times again. He pulls harder each time, often using all his weight. When at last the twig breaks free, he often loses his balance and falls backwards. Like the Little Egret, he does not loosen his grip on the branch and with a few wing-beats comes upright again. He then rests a few seconds before flying back to the nest. After the Greeting Display and the male's Bowing Display, the female takes the twig and places it in the nest. Thus the male brings the sticks and the female builds the nest. However, if she is away foraging, of if she does not take the stick after a few bows, the male places it in the nest himself. When placing the sticks, Night Herons use the same behaviour patterns as Little Egrets, that is to say the Tremble-shove (Lorenz 1955) and the Push-pull (Blaker 1968) (see chapter on the Little Egret).

The male often stands at the nest while the female places the twig in the nest. When this is done, both birds may begin Billing and Back-biting again before the male leaves to gather more sticks. When the female at the nest has no new stick to place, she often pulls at the nest material and rearranges it. The first sticks seem to remain stuck in the tree fork mostly by chance and nest building in the beginning is slow. Once the first sticks are well fastened, those following are much easier to put into place and nest building proceeds rapidly until the first egg is laid 2–5 days later (Moltoni 1936). Night Herons continue bringing sticks, but only occasionally, to the nest during the entire incubation period. Finally, the nests may reach 30–45 cm in diameter and 20–30 cm in height.

The nests are usually well secured in the branches and often remain throughout the winter to be used again the following spring. However, I once observed a nest that was only fastened on one side, the other side having slipped free from the branch during a thunderstorm. The three young were clinging to the inside of the nest, so as not to fall out. The adult remained, with unfolded wings, on the fixed side of the nest, trying to keep it as horizontal as possible and to protect the young against the rain. With each gust of wind, it seemed that the nest must be blown to the ground. This continued for hours until night fell. Miraculously, the nest was still in place the following morning; it had been consolidated after the storm and the three young were still alive.

Egg-laying and clutch size

The eggs of the Night Heron are elongated ovals, matt green-blue often becoming discoloured with time. A sample of 300 eggs measured by Schönwetter (1967) gave the following measurements (mean and range): length 50 mm (44–56 mm), width 36 mm (32–38 mm). A sample of 377 eggs of the subspecies *N. n. hoactli* measured by Wolford (1966) gave the follow-

Nest-building. The male on the branch has just given the female on the nest a twig.

ing measurements: length 52.4 mm (41–62 mm), width 37.7 mm (35–47 mm). Schönwetter measured mostly – if not only – eggs of the European subspecies *N. n. nycticorax*. The eggs of the American subspecies thus appear to be larger than those of the European subspecies.

According to Moltoni (1936), the mean weight of full eggs is 34 g (range 32–36 g). Bauer and Glutz (1966) found the mean weight of eggshell to be 2.20 g.

In temperate areas, egg-laying occurs in the spring, whereas in the tropics, it occurs at the end of the main rainy season. In the Camargue in France, the first eggs are laid at the end of March, with most eggs being laid in April. Egg-laying continues at a lower level throughout May and June and into the first half of July (Voisin 1979). In eastern Europe, Night Herons begin to lay later in the spring.

Clutches of 2–4 eggs have been found in Italy. In 1973, 11 nests contained 3 eggs and 8 nests 4 eggs. In 1974, 1 nest had 2 eggs, 10 had 3 and 39 had 4. The mean clutch size in both 1973 and 1974 was 3.6 eggs (Fasola and Barbieri 1975). During 1970–1972 in the Camargue, Night Herons laid clutches of 2–6 eggs (mean clutch size 3.6 eggs) (Hafner 1977). In Alberta, Canada, clutches of 1–6 eggs were laid. Here, the mean clutch size of first clutches was 4.0 and 3.2 eggs in 1964 and 1965 respectively; that of replacement clutches was 3.7 and 2.5 respectively. In 1979 in New England and North Carolina, USA, clutches of 2–5 eggs were reported by Custer *et al.* (1983), with a mean clutch size of 3.63 eggs. Clutches of 7 or 8 eggs have been reported, but the pattern in which the eggs were laid suggests that two or more females were involved. Eggs are usually laid at 48-hour intervals, however, according to Wolford and Boag (1971), 5% of eggs are laid 72-hours after the previous one.

Incubation and hatching

Incubation lasts for about 21 days (Allen and Mangels 1940). The eggs within a clutch hatch asynchronously. According to Wolford (1966), 11 eggs in Alberta hatched after 21–28 days of incubation (mean incubation 23.6 days). Both adults incubate, with change-over occurring mostly in the early morning and late afternoon, the nests never being left unguarded. The incubating bird sometimes leaves immediately on the arrival of its mate. Often, however, it remains on the eggs showing no inclination to leave. The incoming bird places itself beside the incubating bird and starts gently to push it away. After slight resistance, the incubating bird stands up, steps aside and takes off. According to Piette (1986), the incoming bird sometimes also pushes the incubating bird with its head, or tries to creep under it. It often even steps on the incubating bird in order to take its place on the eggs.

Egg losses can be very high if research observations are not made with great care. Only short nest visits during good weather (with no rain or wind, and when it is neither too hot nor too cold) should be made, so as not to significantly increase natural mortality. In the Camargue, Hafner (1977) reported that 86.6% of eggs hatched successfully (5.2% did not hatch, 3.8%

were lost during incubation, 4.4% were lost during hatching and during the first 4 days of life). In New England and North Carolina, USA, 77.2% of eggs hatched successfully, and in Georgia, USA, 91.7% (Custer *et al.* 1983, Teal 1965). At hatching, young of the American subspecies averaged 30.7 g in weight (Chapman *et al.* 1981).

DEVELOPMENT AND CARE OF THE YOUNG

The guardian period

During the first 4–5 days of life, the chicks are brooded constantly. One of the parents remains at the nest until the oldest chick reaches 10–14 days of age. It protects the young against bad weather (excess heat or cold, rain and strong winds) and predators. Within 10 days, the young are transformed from near-naked, uncoordinated hatchlings into nestlings able to move about in the nest. The replacement of natal down by juvenile plumage begins with feather sheath emergence on day 4, although the body covering remains sparse until about 10 days of age. The flight feather sheaths begin to emerge at about 10 days (Chapman *et al.* 1981).

The post-guardian period

The young are left on their own at the nest during the day since both parents are away foraging, returning to the nest only to rapidly feed them. Within 10 days, young Night Herons are able to leave the nest and disappear into the dense vegetation at the slightest disturbance. By 15 days, they wander frequently in the immediate vicinity of the nest and climb about in the branches, using the bill as a climbing tool. At that age, the young are covered with juvenile plumage with only some down feathers remaining on the head, neck and upper back. After 18 days, it becomes impossible to capture the young without considerable disturbance to the colony. At this stage, although the young run easily in the branches, the young of one nest do not approach when the young of another nest are being fed. They defend their nest against intrusion and the adults also drive away young from other nests. This aggressive behaviour – of both young and adults – makes it very difficult for those young which have fallen from their nest to return to it.

Chapman *et al.* (1981) found that nestling Night Herons were able to maintain a temperature above ambient from a very early age, although nestlings younger than 6 days were not subjected to temperature studies for fear of nest desertion by the parents (see Fig. 6). The temperatures of the young were taken for an hour following 15 minutes rest. Their body temperature never declined more than 2°C and actually increased in several nestlings, particularly the older ones.

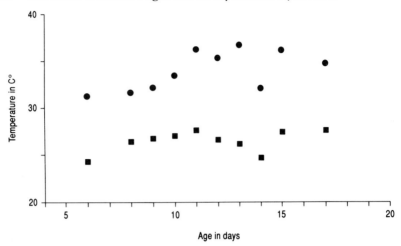

Figure 6   The average temperature ambient (■) at the time of measurement of nestlings temperature (●) plotted against nestling age (Chapman *et al.* 1981).

The fledgling period

Towards the end of the post-guardian period, the young often climb to the tops of the trees where they remain, flapping their wings. When about 1 month old, they begin to fly. At first, they lift about 50 cm up into the air before slowly gliding down to the branches again. The following day, they are able to glide from branch to branch. The fledging stage lasts about 1 month and ends when the young, able to fly and fish for themselves, leave the heronry.

Feeding the young

Both parents feed the young. During the guardian period, they are fed by the adult on guard at the nest. It is hardly possible to see the newly hatched chicks although their begging calls are very soon heard. A small head sometimes emerges from the breast feathers of the brooding adult as it feeds one of the chicks. At a few days old, the chicks, lifting their heads higher than before, peck at the bill of the adult, which usually regurgitates a small amount of quite digested food directly into the open bill of the chicks. Any food that falls onto the nest floor is swallowed again by the adult and probably also eaten by the chicks later. At about 6 days old, they grip the adult's bill crosswise. As soon as they are able to stand, they beg with great energy; keeping their bodies horizontal and flapping their wings, they move the head and neck up and down while calling loudly. When food is scarce, feeding becomes dramatic, even when the young are only about 1 week old. They quarrel and struggle in the nest to grip the adult's bill.

At 2 weeks of age, they begin to walk out onto the branches to meet the incoming adult which lands some distance from the nest. The oldest ones are fed in the branches. The young, keeping their balance with difficulty, fight and push each other. Quite often one may fall off. It usually manages to grip a branch before falling to the ground, but it takes so much time for it to climb up again that it has no chance of being fed on that occasion. The first of the young to reach the adult tries to grip its bill, but the adult is usually not ready to regurgitate at once. It takes quite a time for Night Herons to regurgitate, perhaps becuase their prey are usually large. The adult gives a Full Forward Display and holds its bill very high, out of reach of the young, who, trying eagerly to reach it, find great difficulty in keeping their balance. When the chicks are older, the adult may give real blows. At last the adult lets the nearest young seize its bill crosswise and regurgitates directly into the young's opened bill. The bill of the adult is most often seized crosswise. Sometimes, however, being in a great hurry and struggling, the chick only succeeds in seizing the tip of the adult's bill, although this is good enough to ensure that the food falls directly into the young bird's throat. The adult regurgitates once or twice before flying off to feed one or two other young near or at the nest. Often, one or several young in the brood are not fed. These birds try to grip the bills of those who have been fed to force them to regurgitate. I have never seen this ploy succeed, but suppose it may if one sibling has been fed a lot.

In the Allier in France, I observed the following sequence, which shows how fierce the fight for food may be among young Night Herons. There were only two chicks in the brood, and both climbed out onto a branch to meet the adult. The first was rapidly fed. The second, just behind the first, had not received any food and when the first young turned to get back to the nest, both young faced each other. They immediately began to fight, pecking violently at each other, and trying to seize each other's bill. They succeeded after a while, but the chick who had not been fed lost its balance and fell. He did not, however, lose his grip on the branch and remained hanging upside down. Flapping his wings he tried to right himself, but the first young pecked him on the head and body. However, he managed to regain his perch and returned to the nest. The adult remained totally unconcerned by the fight and flew up and landed at the nest to feed the second chick before leaving. Both chicks pecked at each other's bill for a long time after that. Piette (1986) has not observed much aggression between siblings in captivity fed by their parents, tending to show that the aggression is probably caused by a lack of food.

Once the young are able to fly, they follow the adult who leaves them. When the adult lands on a nearby branch, the young land beside the adult and beg violently. The adult then flees towards the low branches of the heronry. During the fledging stage, a few adults can be seen foraging in the pool surrounding the heronry and along the ditches in the vicinity where no adults were seen earlier. It is probably while following the adults, that fledgling Night Herons first land in the water. However, the adults do not allow any young to come nearby while they forage. The young learn to fish by themselves while at the same time continuing to be dependent on food brought to the nest by their parents.

Growth and mortality of nestlings

A growth study of young Night Herons has been undertaken in Texas by Chapman *et al.* (1981). The young were weighed from the age of 1–18 days, it being impossible to capture young older than 18 days. Particularly rapid growth occurred between days 5 and 10; during this period, the surface-to-volume ratio decreased rapidly and the dorsal plumage developed.

Great care is necessary when mortality studies are undertaken. Teal (1965) wrote: "The regular visits to the nests were timed so that the eggs were exposed only a few minutes early in the day." In Georgia, USA, of eight nests studied by Teal (1965), seven were successful. In three nests, there was no loss of either eggs or young. A total of 71% of the eggs laid and 77% of the young hatched reached the fledging stage. Those nestlings deaths that occurred were caused either by starvation – in a nest from which the parents had disappeared – or accidents. In the Camargue in France, the smallest young (sometimes the two smallest) very often die of starvation between the ages of 5 and 10 days. In the heronries studied in the Camargue during 1970–1972, 13.4% of the eggs and nestlings younger than 5 days were lost. About 19% of the young died between the age of 5 and 24 days. The mean number of young fledged per nest was 2.2 (Hafner 1977). In New England and North Carolina, USA, 91.4% of the chicks survived to 15 days of age. In five heronries studied in 1979, the mean number of young per nest which reached the age of 15 days varied between 1.89 and 2.65 (Custer *et al.* 1983). Henny (1972) estimated that 2.0–2.1 young Night Herons had to be fledged per nesting pair to maintain the population at a stable level.

A study of the effects of organochlorine contaminants (DDE and PCB) on clutch size and reproductive success of Atlantic coast Night Herons showed that their impact was minimal (Custer *et al.* 1983).

FEEDING BEHAVIOUR AND FOOD

Night Herons usually fish in shallow water among dense vegetation, the water coming up to their tibias and sometimes to their bellies. They also fish in deep water, usually perched on a low branch, and may hunt on land though never far away from water.

Usual methods of foraging

Night herons commonly use the Stand-and-wait and Wade or Walk Slowly foraging methods (Meyerriecks 1960). When using the Stand-and-wait method, the bird stands absolutely motionless, waiting until its prey is within reach before stretching out its neck rapidly to seize the prey. I have seen a Night Heron standing on floating vegetation among *Typhas* catching dragonflies in this way. Night Herons often perch on a low branch just above the water. When prey comes within reach they rapidly seize it. Sometimes, if the prey is a little too far away, the Night Heron throws itself forwards and loses its balance. When this happens, the bird maintains its grip on the branch while seizing the prey between its mandibles. It then manages, with some wing-beats, to return again to the branch where it swallows the prey.

When Wading, the Night Heron slowly slips between the long stalks of the dense aquatic vegetation, often along the border of some open water. It walks with its body held horizontal or nearly horizontal, neck withdrawn between its shoulders and bill pointing forwards. If it sees a prey it stretches its neck slightly to get a better view of it. It then moves slowly with great care towards the prey and suddenly stretching out its neck catches the prey between its mandibles.

During the night, the percentage of time spent in Standing feeding is greater than in Wading feeding. At dawn, Wading is used more often and by day both feeding techniques are used almost equally. Using the Stand-and-wait method, Night Herons catch 1.8 large prey and 6.8 small prey per hour. Using the Wade or Walk Slowly method, they catch 1.8 large prey and 9.9 small prey per hour. The food intake is greatest at dawn between 03.00 and 05.00 h. (Fasola 1984).

Unusual methods of foraging

Running. Observed in the Allier in France, when Night Herons hunted on dry land. The birds (about eight individuals) ran forward a few steps before catching their prey, which were frogs. They were foraging early in the morning, in the high grass of a meadow, near and along a ditch (Voisin 1978).

Bill-vibrating. The Night Heron stands in shallow water while rapidly vibrating its bill at the surface to attract prey. This behaviour has been observed by Stone in Kushlan (1973) and by Drinkwater (1958).

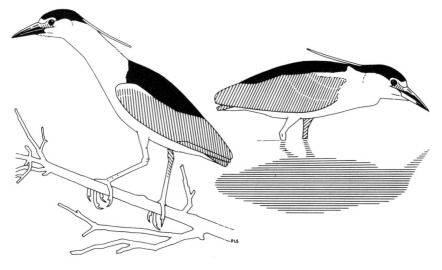

Night Herons foraging.

Hovering-flight. The Night Heron flies above the surface and catches prey without landing on the water. This behaviour is mentioned but not described by Meyerriecks (1960).

Feet-first Diving and Swimming-feeding. Observed in the Allier in France, the Night Heron was perched on a low branch waiting for prey. It suddenly saw a fish (*Silurus* sp.) that was in poor condition about 3 metres away (the bottom of the pool was deprived of oxygen). The Night Heron, stretching its neck, looked for a long moment at the fish which had come up to the surface. Suddenly, the bird jumped from the branch and landed feet first in the water. It seized the fish, which was swallowed head first while the bird was still swimming. Seeing another fish a few metres away, the Night Heron flew up from the water and landed again in exactly the same way. It seized and swallowed this second fish before flying back to its perch. This method of feeding has been observed by several authors (Wetmore 1920, Dean 1975, Voisin 1978).

This habit of catching dying fish may turn out to be fatal for Night Herons if the cause of such incapacitation is due to the chemical pollution of the water, although this has yet to be reported.

Plunging. Observed in Florida in the USA, several Night Herons "flew out to the centre of the pond, which was free from emergent plants, and dove into the water head-first with wings held slightly away from the body. The birds submerged up to their chest and then surfaced and remained there floating or swimming. Fish caught by this method were either swallowed at the surface or carried back to a perch" (Kushlan 1973).

Under-wing feeding. This behaviour has been observed only once:

In northeast Eritrea, I observed an immature Night Heron at dusk by a shallow stream, feeding on tadpoles, small frogs and toads. On one occasion when it was standing by the water's edge and peering into the water, it raised and spread one wing; it maintained this position for several seconds and then lunged forward to take a prey item. This seemingly deliberate behaviour in no way resembled wing-stretching, where the wing is spread outwards and not raised over the head (Tyler 1979).

Foraging rhythm and food intake of adults during the breeding period

"During the course of the breeding cycle the time spent in feeding, flight and other activities outside the colony increased from 45.7% (prelaying) via 47.6% (incubation) to 79.2% during the nestling period" (Fasola 1982). In the Camargue, the food intake of Night Herons is greater by night than by day, since the large prey – fish longer than 6 cm – are caught mostly by night. In contrast, in the rice fields of Italy, the intake of food by Night Herons is greater by day. Both in Italy and in the Camargue, the number of prey captured is greater by day than by night, but most prey taken by day are smaller, such as tadpoles (Watmough 1978, Fasaola 1982). In the rice field area of Italy, the daily food intake of an adult Night Heron feeding young is about 147 g dry weight per 24 hours; the food intake during the night is about 67 g dry weight, which is roughly the amount needed by the adult for maintenance. Thus foraging by day is a necessity when feeding young (Fasola 1982).

Food

Night Herons catch mostly fish and amphibians but also insects, crustaceans and small mammals. To a lesser extent, birds, reptiles, molluscs, worms and spiders are also taken. The size of prey varies from very small items 1 cm in length, to larger items 21 cm in length and in the case of eels 35 cm in length. There have been numerous studies of the food of Night Herons. As this species is commonly protected nowadays, the most usual way to study prey taken is to collect food regurgitated by the young at the nest. However, studies of stomach contents have also been made.

In Europe, the first study was published by Moltoni in 1936, to be followed by Vasvàri (1948–1951), Valverde (1956), Skokova (1960), Hafner (1977), Voisin (1978) and Fasola *et al.* (1981). The prey of Night Herons in Europe is, in the main, the same over their whole range. The following is a list of the most commonly taken items:

○ Spiders: not determined.
○ Insects: Odonate larvae and adults, beetles (Hydrophilidae): *Hydrous* larvae, Dytiscidae) and flies (larvae and adults).
○ Crustaceans: *Triops cancriformis.*
○ Fish: pike *Esox lucius*, carp *Cyprinus carpio*, Crucian carp *Carassius carassius*, roach *Rutilus rutilus* and *Rutilus rubilio*, rudd *Scardinus erythrophtalmus*, chub *Leuciscus cephalus*, eel *Anguilla anguilla*, gambusia *Gambusia affinis*, silverside *Atherina boyeri*, sunfish *Lepomis gibbosus*, mullet *Liza* sp., bleak *Alburnus alburnus*, tench *Tinca tinca*, loach *Gobitis taenia.*
○ Amphibians: adults and tadpoles of *Rana* sp.
○ Mammals: water-voles *Arvicola.*

Comparative studies of the weight of the prey taken shows that both in Italy and France, Night Herons live mostly on fish and to a lesser extent on amphibians. Mammals, insects and crustaceans make up only a small part of the diet. In Hungary, while fish and amphibians are the main food, insects seem to be much more important as a food resource (Vasvàri 1935, 1938). Terrestrial prey are also more numerous: snakes, urodeles and beetles. In the Volga Delta, fish are the main food. The results of Skokova's (1960) study are given as a percentage of the total number of prey: molluscs 0.2%, aquatic arthropods 15.2%, land arthropods 3.8%, fish 76.6%, amphibians 5.2%, reptiles 0% and mammals 0%.

In India (West Bengal), the main source of food (by weight) of Night

Herons is composed of amphibians (*Rana* sp.), molluscs (*Lymnea* sp.) and crustaceans (crabs and shrimps). A common prey of Night Herons in this area is aquatic snakes (Colubridae and Hydrophidae) (Mukherjee 1971). In Japan, in a rice field area, Kosugi (1960) found that Night Herons took mostly fish and amphibians. A prey not reported from elsewhere was crayfish (*Procambarus clarki*).

Night Herons in America also catch mostly fish and amphibians. The great difference from Europe and Asia is that they commonly take eggs and young birds, not as an exception. Several observers have found young egrets, ibises, ducks, terns and stilts among the Night Heron's prey (Beckett 1964, Kale 1965, Collins 1970, Hunter and Morris 1976, Andrew 1981). The food habits of Night Herons were thoroughly studied in southern Alberta by Wolford *et al.* (1971). The heronry was in an area where fish were unavailable until the end of May or beginning of June. The fish entered the irrigation canals when they opened in mid-May and invaded extended shallow marshes. However, numerous Franklin's Gulls (*Larus pipixcan*) and blackbirds (*Xanthocephalus xanthocephalus* and *Agelaius phoeniceus*) nested a little later than the Night Herons in the area. The Night Herons fed their young almost exclusively on eggs and young birds in May. From June they captured fish, mostly minnows *Pimephales promelas* and brook sticklebacks *Culaea inconstans*, but nestlings remained the principal food of the Night Herons until the end of July. The Night Herons were able to nest in the area only because gulls and blackbirds nested there. The often observed tendency of Night Herons to take a nestling now and then when they get the opportunity, permitted them to completely change their main source of food and feed almost exclusively on birds. However, this unusual feeding habit was artificial in that it occurred in a man-made habitat.

Night Herons established in a heronry at Long Island, New York were seen feeding on crabs (*Callinectes sapidus* and *Uca* sp.) and on molluscs (*Venus mercenaria* and *Mytilus edulis*) in addition to fish and small mammals (Allen 1937).

The variation in the spring and summer diet of nestling Night Herons was studied by Fasola *et al.* (1981). The categories of prey found in regurgitates of nestling Night Herons during the period May–August shows that the fluctuation in percentages of amphibians and fish are small and inversely correlated except in May and the beginning of June when crustaceans are often an abundant but irregular source of food. Fasola also noticed that an increased presence of each prey in the diet coincided with periods of increased abundance in the aquatic habitat. It seems that as soon as a prey of suitable size becomes abundant, the Night Herons feed mostly on it. Thus the food of Night Herons changes greatly with local and seasonal conditions: they are highly opportunistic feeders.

PREDATION

When foraging and at the heronry, Night Herons are probably preyed upon by nocturnal raptors but there are no recorded observations of this. In

North America, an Osprey was seen carrying away a freshly caught Night Heron (Green 1981).

Table 7.   The number of Night Herons breeding in France[a]

	1968	1974	1981
No. of breeding pairs	2200	1550	3500
Total no. of heronries	31	28	35
No. of heronries with:			
1–10 breeding pairs	7	7	7
11–50 breeding pairs	12	11	14
51–100 breeding pairs	3	4	8
101–350 breeding pairs	9	6	4
351–650 breeding pairs	0	0	2

[a] After Brosselin (1974) and Duhautois and Marion (1981).

Table 8.   The number of breeding pairs of Night Herons in the Camargue[a]

Year	No. of pairs	Year	No. of pairs
1968	830	1977	565
1969	325	1978	488
1970	387	1979	642
1971	368	1980	604
1972	357	1981	531
1973	341	1982	697
1974	455	1983	390
1975	531	1984	253
1976	617	1985	277

[a] After Hafner (1987) and Voisin (1977)

Table 9.   The sizes of the Night Heron colonies in Italy[a]

No. of breeding pairs	No. of heronries
1–10	0
11–50	5
51–100	4
101–350	17
351–650	11
651–1000	6
1001–1400	2

[a] After Fasola *et al.* (1981).

CHAPTER 12

The Squacco Heron *Ardeola ralloides*

GENERAL APPEARANCE AND FIELD CHARACTERS

The Squacco Heron is 44–47 cm high with a wing-span of 80–92 cm.

Plumage. The sexes are alike, and the general colour of the adult plumage is golden-buff and white when breeding and brown and white when not breeding.

Adult breeding: the feathers of the mantle, the innermost secondaries and the elongated scapulars are golden-buff with a deep vinous tinge on the mantle and scapulars. These feathers more or less cover the entire back; the wings and the tail are white, as is the belly. There is a golden tinge on the wing-coverts, which is not visible at a distance. The chin and throat are white. The neck and the elongated chest feathers are golden-buff. Some of these feathers, situated on the sides of the neck and on the hindneck, have black longitudinal streaks. The crown feathers are straw-coloured and bordered with black and are slightly elongated (1–5 cm). On the hindcrown, some very elongated feathers (13–14 cm) are white bordered with black.

Adult non-breeding: the plumage is dull. Out of the breeding season, the Squacco Heron lacks the long black and white feathers of the hindcrown. The

128

crown, chest and scapular feathers are shorter. The mantle, scapulars and innermost secondaries are earth-brown. The neck and chest are straw-coloured, streaked with black. The back, wings and belly remain white.

Juvenile: as for the adult in winter, but the primaries have a brown tinge and in very young birds the distal part of the tail feathers is also washed with brown. The shafts of the primaries are brown and not white as in the adult.

Older young at the nest: the plumage is very like that of juveniles but there is much more brown on the primaries. The wing-coverts are white and straw-coloured, streaked with brown.

Downy young: the down is long on the crown, where it stands erect, and on the upperparts and flanks. On the crown, it is brown, lighter in colour on the distal part. It is dark grey on the mantle and neck and white on the belly and back, where it is washed slightly with grey and even with some buff on the back.

Bare parts

Adult breeding: the distal half (*c.* 3 cm) of the bill is black and the basal part bright blue. The lores are either green or blue. The eyes are yellow. The legs and feet are bright red, becoming pink when the bird is paired.

Adult non-breeding: the bill, except the black tip, becomes dull greenish yellow, as do the lores, legs and feet. The eyes remain yellow.

Juvenile: as for non-breeding adults, though the bill and legs are slightly more yellow and the bill pattern is less marked.

Downy young: the skin is olive-green with the exception of the head, where it is yellowish pink. The yellow colour appears also on the back of the legs. The bill is horn-coloured. The eyes are light yellow (Valverde 1958, Cramp and Simmons 1977, Voisin 1980).

Field characters. The Squacco Heron is easily recognized and can hardly be taken for any other bird. When fishing, this small heron has a brownish buff appearance. It either stands motionless among the dense vegetation bordering a pond or a ditch or, walking very crouched, slips rapidly among the stems of plants growing at the water's edge. When it takes off, the bright white of the wings, rump, tail and belly appears suddenly as a white flash against the darker marsh vegetation.

In flight, the dark head, neck, chest, mantle and scapulars contrast sharply with the bright white of the wings, rump, tail and belly. This contrast, which is obvious even in juveniles, makes the bird easy to recognize. The feathers of the Squacco Heron appear brighter than those of the Little Egret, probably due to the lack of contrast in the case of the Little Egret which is a wholly white bird. Little Egrets are larger and more slender birds with a long, thin black bill. Cattle Egrets are the only birds that may sometimes be confused with the Squacco Heron. Cattle Egrets are usually found in groups, but are sometimes encountered singly as is usually the case for Squacco Herons. Squacco Herons are smaller, but this is not always obvious in the field. They are also much darker than Cattle Egrets, which are wholly white with only a few rufous feathers. The difference in bill colour between the two species is a sure and obvious sign. The bill of the Squacco Heron, with its dark tip, always appears dark in contrast to that of the Cattle Egret, which is lightly-coloured, yellow, orange or bright red.

It is possible to detect the presence of a few Squacco Herons in a mixed colony quite rapidly, since when alarmed, they have a very particular call. This call had not been noticed until recently, being unlike the usual harsh cries of herons. In fact, it resembles nothing so much as the discreet cooing of a pigeon! The alarmed Squacco utters this call occasionally, while on its nest. In order to produce this very special call, the bird stretches its neck and flutters the gular region slightly (Voisin 1980).

In a mixed colony, the young of the Squacco Heron are the smallest and most cryptic, and are thus the most difficult to find. The contrast between the white and the heavily streaked parts of their plumage breaks up their outlines, their white bellies often appearing to be sun-patches. The rest of the plumage is not visible in the dark shade of the foliage.

Measurements. The measurements (mm) of adult birds taken from skins are given below (Cramp and Simmons 1977). The number of skins and the sex are indicated. Standard deviations are given in parentheses. The sex differences are significant for the wing, tail and bill.

wing	9 ♂♂	208–234 (7.95)	9 ♀♀	209–228	(7.73)
tail	8 ♂♂	73–84 (4.42)	9 ♀♀	66–84	(5.27)
bill	8 ♂♂	62–70 (2.49)	9 ♀♀	58–65	(2.49)
tarsus	9 ♂♂	51–62 (3.57)	9 ♀♀	54–59	(1.86)
toe	9 ♂♂	62–72 (3.00)	5 ♀♀	64–68	(1.79)

The weights of very few Squacco Herons have been recorded. However, Moltoni (1936) gives the following: breeding adults, ♂♂ 230–350 g, ♀♀ 250–370 g; fledglings, ♂♂ 225–300 g, ♀♀ 206–250 g.

The wing-beat rate of the Squacco Heron averages 146 wing-beats per minute (Voisin, unpublished).

DISTRIBUTION, MOVEMENTS AND HABITAT

BREEDING AND WINTERING AREAS

In western Europe, Squacco Herons breed only in the southern half of the Iberian Peninsula, in France (the Camargue and the Dombes) and in northern Italy. Breeding sites are more numerous in eastern Europe where the species breeds in Hungary, Romania, Bulgaria, Yugoslavia and Greece. The Squacco Heron has its most northerly breeding site in the USSR along the Dnêpr River, at almost 50°N. The species breeds in the southern USSR, along rivers and around the Black, Caspian and Aral seas. The most easterly breeding sites are along the Syr Darya River and perhaps also along the Amu Darya River near the Afghanistan border. Squacco Herons also breed in Turkey and in Israel. They are numerous in summer in southern Iraq, and probably also breed there. In north Africa, Squacco Herons seem nowadays only to breed in

Morocco. However, there is an important breeding population south of the Sahara, where the species breeds in scattered localities in West, East and South Africa, and even in Madagascar (Curry-Lindahl 1981). In Europe, the species is completely migratory. Some birds winter in North Africa from Morocco to Egypt, but most seem to cross the desert on a broad front to winter south of the Sahara although there is no evidence that they cross the tropics for wintering areas further south. Wintering Squacco Herons belonging to the African populations are to be found in any favourable area south of the desert. Some birds from Asia cross the Red Sea to winter in Africa, while others winter in Iran and Iraq (Cramp and Simmons 1977).

TIMING OF BREEDING AND MOVEMENTS

In the Palearctic, Squacco Herons begin to breed in spring, at the end of April, and in May and June. Sterbetz (1962) wrote: "In general we may state that our bird appears in Hungarian territory . . . when the temperature sets lastingly at 20°C, and the permanently warm weather coming from the Balkans and South West Europe has become stable in these territories."

After breeding, Squacco Herons disperse, the first as soon as July. The autumn migration begins in August and continues through September. In southern countries, some passages are noted as late as October. The spring migration occurs in March, April and May. Migrating birds, both in the autumn and spring, are found throughout the Mediterranean region both on the mainland and on the various islands. Autumn and spring passages are recorded from numerous oases in the Sahara. Squacco Herons also cross Arabia regularly in September–October and March–April. There have only been seven recoveries south of the Sahara of birds from Europe: two from the Camargue were found in Guinea and Sierra Leone, and three from Yugoslavia and two from Bulgaria were found in Nigeria. In spring, some birds fly too far to the north, and in autumn some disperse northwards. Squacco Herons have thus been found as accidentals in Iceland, Britain, Ireland, Belgium, the Netherlands, Denmark, Sweden, Finland, eastern and western Germany, Poland, Austria, Switzerland, the Azores, Madeira, the Canary and the Cape Verde Islands (Cramp and Simmons 1977).

Information regarding the breeding season and migration of the African population is very scarce. Along the Senegal River, Squacco Herons begin to breed at the end of the rainy season, during the flooding of the river; that is to say, at the end of August or in September. They only breed if the water level is sufficiently high and they will abandon the heronry if the water level falls rapidly.

In Madagascar, Squacco Herons breed at the beginning of the rainy season in November and winter in East Africa (Werding 1970).

HABITAT

In their northern range, Squacco Herons prefer a dry continental climate with dry summers to an oceanic one. In their more southerly range, they accept a Mediterranean climate as well as subtropical and tropical ones. They usually frequent lowlands, river margins, inundated floodplains and deltas. However, in their eastern range, they have been found nesting in high mountain valleys up to 2000 m (Cramp and Simmons 1977).

Squacco Herons breed in mixed colonies with other tree-nesting herons, mostly Little Egrets and Night Herons. They seem to choose heronries situated in dense vegetation; for example, in the Camargue, in poplars, ashes and alders with an abundant undergrowth of cornel trees, privets and brambles. Tamarisks are often present at the edge of such woods. In the Camargue, their nests are only to be found in heronries whose foraging grounds are almost exclusively in freshwater areas. There are no Squacco Herons in heronries depending on brackish water, such as lagoons and saltpans. Although usually nesting in trees or bushes, they may nest in reedbeds when nothing else is available.

Squacco Herons prefer permanently inundated areas where they can hide and fish in dense vegetation. They are solitary feeders and usually hunt and fish at the water's edge catching prey both on land and in the water. They either walk or stand motionless waiting for prey to come within reach, in marshes and along rivers and pools in places overgrown by aquatic vegetation with some trees or at least some bushes nearby. They also use man-made habitats and often fish along ditches, irrigation and drainage canals and in rice fields. Their avoidance of brackish water is probably because of the lack of aquatic vegetation in this habitat. However, brackish and coastal waters are frequented when the birds are migrating (Hancock and Elliot 1978).

POPULATION SIZE AND TRENDS

A drastic decrease in the number of Squacco Herons at the end of the last century was caused mainly by the depredations of plumage hunters. Following the end of the plumage trade, the still unprotected Squacco Herons continued to decrease in numbers until the Second World War. During the second half of the twentieth century, a more or less important increase in the population has been possible mainly due to the establishment of reserves, and in more recent times by the protection of the bird itself.

Squacco Herons, which have never been numerous in western Europe in recent times, are nowadays very few. In a mixed heronry, usually only about 1–3% of the nests belong to Squacco Herons (Sterbetz 1962). During a census of heronries in Spain in 1975, the number of breeding Squaccos was estimated at only a few hundred (Fernandez-Cruz 1975). In Italy, Fasola *et al.* (1981) counted 270 breeding pairs during a national census of heronries. In Greece, the number of breeding pairs was estimated to be over 1000 in the 1970s and only 201–377 during the years 1985 and 1986 (Crivelli *et al.* 1988). The fact that the small number of breeding Squacco Herons is subject to important variations from year to year is shown by the counts undertaken in the Camargue in France by Hafner *et al.* (1982), where the number of nesting Squacco Herons varied from 115 pairs in 1972 to 47 pairs in 1978.

Being typical of areas with warm and dry summers, the population of this species is much more important in eastern Europe and in the Middle East than it is in western Europe. In mixed heronries in these countries, 10–30% of the nests may belong to Squacco Herons (Sterbetz 1962). In 1953, Kumerloewe estimated that 200–300 Squacco Herons fished regularly near Muradbasi along the northern river of Lake Amik Golu (near Antakya in Turkey). Such a concentration cannot be found anywhere in western Europe. There were about 5500–6000 breeding pairs in 46 sites in the middle Danube area during the second half of the nineteenth century, falling to only 1000–1200 pairs during the first half of the twentieth century. There has been a slight increase in numbers since 1960. The population of the Danube Delta and the north of the Black Sea seems to have suffered less persecution than that of the middle Danube area, at least until the 1950s. There were 3800–4200 breeding pairs in 31 sites during the second half of the nineteenth century. This population decreased rapidly to half its size but had recovered again by the 1950s, when it was estimated at 4500–4800 breeding pairs (Jósefik 1969–1970). However, since then, their numbers have probably greatly decreased again.

In Hungary, Squacco Herons are very few. There are counts from only two colonies: Kis-Balaton which numbered 7–14 pairs in 1968–1972 and Horto-bágy with 30 pairs in 1967 (Cramp and Simmons 1977). In Yugoslavia (Kopaĉeviski Reserve), the number of breeding pairs varied from 478 in 1954 to 139 in 1968 during the period 1954–1970 (showing an overall tendency to decrease) (Majić *et al.* 1972). Squacco Herons are relatively numerous in Turkey where 800–1000 pairs were counted recently in four colonies (Cramp and Simmons 1977). There are no estimates of the number of breeding pairs in Iran, Iraq and the USSR east of the Black Sea.

BEHAVIOUR AND BIOLOGY

DISPLAYS AND CALLS

The most important displays and commonest calls have been studied by the author (Voisin 1980). Though not exhaustive, this study appears to be the only one ever published on the subject.

Agonistic behaviours

Full Forward Display. The bird assumes the following position when facing an opponent:

○ The bird, body held nearly horizontal, bends its legs, thus assuming a crouched position.
○ The folded wings are drawn slightly aside.
○ The extended neck is bent, so that the occipital region is directly over the upper part of the back, the neck in an "S" shape. The open beak is pointed at the intruder.

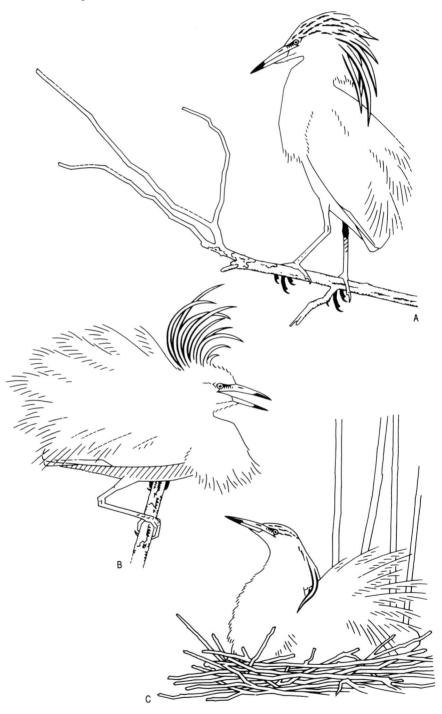

A

B

C

o All of the feathers are held erect, the long black and white crown feathers standing straight up with their distal parts falling forwards. The erected chest feathers are held nearly horizontal and the raised scapulars form a light golden-buff cloud above the bird.

During the Full Forward Display, the apparent increase in size of the Squacco Heron is proportionally larger than in most other herons, due to the length, number and the bright colours of the crown, chest and scapular feathers in the breeding season.

Forward Display. As in the other herons, there is a progression in the aggressive displays from the resting position to the Full Forward Display, in which the bird progressively raises the crown feathers slightly, then the neck feathers. However, there are fewer stages in this series in the Squacco Heron, which rapidly and readily adopts the Full Forward version. This is probably because this little heron is the smallest and thus must be very aggressive to defend its nest and to maintain its territory in a mixed heronry.

Stab-and-counter-stab. This display is a particular form of the Forward Display first described by Blaker (1969) for the Cattle Egret, which enables birds to establish and maintain very small territories. Stab-and-counter-stab occurs when a new nest is constructed near a previously established one or after a change of an incubating or brooding adult in a nest very near another one. The two birds, each on its own nest, threaten each other, with the neck in the "S" shape, beaks open and all the feathers raised. They "lunge at each other a few times, each bird drawing back as the other stabs and vice versa" (Blaker 1969), without leaving their nests. In the case of Squacco Herons, the blows are given slowly, and although they are often near enough to deliver each other real blows to the head and neck, they do not do so. After a short period of time, one of the birds stops lunging, the other also calms down, and finally both birds stop threatening each other completely.

Fear behaviour

Alarm. The Squacco Heron adopts this posture when frightened by the presence of humans or predators in the colony. It stands with legs, body, neck and head nearly vertical, the bill pointing upwards, the feathers sleeked against the body. The bird, which now appears very thin, easily goes unnoticed. A true Bittern Stance (see the chapter on the Bittern) has never been observed in Squacco Herons.

The threat displays of the Squacco Heron. A, Forward Display; B, Full Forward Display; C, changing from threat to alarm. The crown feathers are already sleeked, whereas the nape and neck feathers and scapulars remain slightly to fully erect.

Successive postures during the Foot-lifting Display of the male.

Courtship displays

The Foot-lifting Display. I have called this the "Stretch Display" (Voisin 1980) as it is clearly homologous with the "Stretch Display" performed by several heron species belonging to the genera *Ardea* and *Egretta*. However, since the display given by the male Squacco Heron is very different from the usual Stretch Display and is somewhat like that of the male Night Heron, I propose here to give it the same name, i.e. the Foot-lifting Display. I have only been able to observe this display in Squacco Herons a few times. There is no photographic or film evidence of it, so further observations of this unusual display would be useful.

The Squacco Heron perches on a branch, its feet parted and performs the following movements of the legs and feet. The bird bends slightly, firmly grasping the branch with one foot. At the same time, it loosens its grip with the other foot, which it lifts with extended toes. It then grasps the branch again and bends that leg, while the other foot is lifted with all the toes extended. Meanwhile, the bird sways slowly from side to side in a short "dance". Only 3–6 successive swaying motions have been observed followed by resting periods when the bird looks around.

During this "dance", the positions of the body, wings, head and neck are variable, the feathers held more or less erect. The bird may perform the display at varying levels of intensity:

○ At full intensity, the Squacco Heron leans forwards and stretches its neck downwards, until the point of its bill is level with its feet and the branch. The wings are slightly drawn aside and the scapular feathers are completely raised. The neck and crown feathers are raised and the long crown feathers fall forwards.

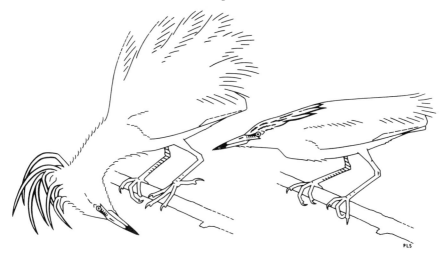

○ At low intensity, the heron does not lean forwards and the wings are not
drawn aside. The neck is not stretched downwards, but has a variable
position more or less stretched as the bird looks around. The bird may even
keep its head between its shoulders while swaying slowly. During this
display, the scapulars are either not raised, or only slightly erected, in
which case the feathers of the neck and head are not erected.

The common Stretch Display, observed in many heron species, when the
bird crouches down, head and neck stretched upwards and bill held vertical,
has not been observed among Squacco Herons.

Back-biting. Newly paired birds at the nest often perform Back-biting. This
behaviour, being the only one with a tactile element, strengthens the pair-
bond. It is performed in exactly the same way by Squacco Herons as it is by
Night Herons and Cattle Egrets (see the chapters on these species for a full
description). However, I have never seen a Squacco Heron grasp its mate's
neck as Cattle Egrets sometimes do.

Billing. The two birds peck gently at each other's bill (see the chapter on
Night Herons).

Calls

The characteristic call of an alarmed Squacco Heron on its nest has already
been described in the section on Field characters. The threat calls of Squacco
Herons are very like those of the other small heron species. However, the
greeting calls are very different from those of other species, and are thus easily
recognized in a mixed colony.

REPRODUCTIVE BEHAVIOUR

Pair formation

I have observed the pair formation of Squacco Herons in the Djoudj, Sénégal. The males establish and defend small territories in the trees of the heronry where they display and where they will later build nests. In the mixed heronries of western Europe and Sénégal, Squacco Herons arrive late when there are usually no old nests still available to them. On his territory, the male rests, preens and begins nest-building activities, though with little real nest-building (he pulls on the sticks in the branches around him and may try to place some in the tree forks). Most important of all, he displays, using the Foot-lifting Display to attract females. His alert look, the position of his feathers – always slightly erected – the red colour of his legs and feet and the bright blue of his lores and bill, show clearly – even when he is not displaying – that he is a male ready to breed. The females move about in the heronry, landing here and there, but always at some distance from the displaying males. When an interested female is present on a nearby branch, looking with stretched neck and sleeked plumage at the male, he displays with much more intensity than when he is alone. But if the female comes too near, the newly established male threatens her, using the Full Forward Display. If the female does not flee, the male attacks her. The displaying male reacts very strongly to the arrival of another male in full breeding plumage. He soon threatens using the Full Forward Display and immediately advances to attack. Sadly, I did not manage to observe the moment when, after several days and many unsuccessful attempts, the female was finally accepted by the male on his territory and the pair was actually formed.

Copulation

Copulation occurs on a branch in the territory some hours after pair formation and during nest construction. Indeed, as soon as the nest is begun, copulation occurs on it. I have never observed any display preceding copulation, which usually occurs when both birds are at the nest resting. Sometimes the male, resting on a nearby branch, returns to the female whom he has left at the nest some minutes before, and copulates. During copulation, the male needs only to draw his wings aside very slightly to keep his balance.

Nest building

I have observed several pairs of Squacco Herons building their nests in the Camargue in France and the Djoudj in Sénégal. Both the male and female help to build the nest. Since copulation occurs during nest building, the birds are often in a hurry to finish nest construction before the eggs are laid. When both birds are present, the male collects the sticks and the female works them into the structure. The method used in building is exactly the same as that used by other heron species; that is, tremble-shove and push-pull (see the chapter on the Cattle Egret). When the female is away hunting, the male both collects material and builds the nest. When the female is alone, she stays at nest, working on the fine details, pulling and pushing the sticks to place them better. The sticks collected by the male are usually several tens of centimetres long, but he sometimes brings sticks that are only 3–4 cm long and which, though of very little use, are taken and placed in the nest by the female. Squacco Herons may pick living branches from the trees, despite the difficulty of collecting them. However, they usually take dead sticks, found laying, or floating, at the base of trees. Squacco Herons do not only collect sticks as nest material, but they also collect more flexible material such as aquatic plants in the Djoudj and ivy in the Camargue (Voisin 1980). This behaviour has never been observed in Cattle Egrets, Night Herons or Little Egrets. When Squacco Herons nest in reedbeds, the reeds are used as a nest material. The nest is usually completed within 6–8 days, but extra nest material is added after egg laying. The completed nest is a platform 17–27 cm in diameter, of either substantial or flimsy construction (Sterbetz 1962).

Squacco Herons usually build low in the tree. In the Djoudj, where the heronry was in an inundated area, they often nested only 75–100 cm above the water surface in tamarisk trees. Squacco Herons were the lowest nesting herons in the Camargue, often, but not always, building their nests only 2 m above the water in small trees and bushes on the periphery of the heronry. Some nests, however, were high up in the trees. In the Sasér Reserve in Hungary, the situation is entirely different and Squacco Herons build their nests in the central part of the heronry above the other herons' nests at a height of 10–20 m.

Greeting Behaviour

Both the male and female incubate and brood the chicks while they are small. When one member of the pair returns from a foraging trip to take its turn on the nest, Greeting Calls and a Greeting Ceremony are necessary for both members of the pair to recognize each other and accept their presence at the nest. The returning bird lands in the branches at some distance from the nest, usually at the same place. Even before landing, the bird utters Greeting Calls. With all feathers erect, it then slips rapidly towards the nest, still calling. The bird at the nest, its feathers also erect, answers with similar Greeting Calls. The birds meet in the threatening Forward Display, but the aggression soon fades and their feathers are slowly lowered.

If the nest is still being built, the male often brings a stick which he presents to the female. Both birds often perform Billing and Back-biting when there is no stick to give. Only during Back-biting do the birds relax completely. The bird at the nest usually leaves immediately to allow its partner to brood or incubate. Sometimes, however, the incoming bird has gently to push its partner off the nest so as to take its place. After having left, the departing bird often lands on a nearby branch and begins to preen.

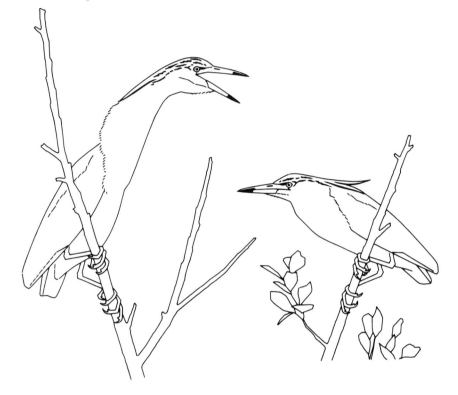

A Squacco Heron (left) regurgitating and (right) sitting on a branch (after photographs by J. Delpech).

Egg-laying, incubation and hatching

The eggs of the Squacco Heron are oval, pointed at both ends and green-blue in colour. A sample of 160 eggs measured by Schönwetter (1967) gave the following measurements (mean and range): 39 × 28 mm (35–42 × 27–32 mm). According to Moltoni (1936), the eggs weigh 15–17 g.

In Europe, clutches of 4–6 eggs are usual, though 7 eggs have been found. These are usually laid at 24-hour intervals, though occasionally at 48-hour intervals (Cramp and Simmons 1977). In southern Africa and Madagascar, the clutches are of 3–4 eggs, though nests have been found with only 2 eggs. The incubation period was found to be 22–24 days in Hungary (Sterbetz 1962), but only 18 days in Madagascar (Milon *et al.* 1973).

According to Cramp and Simmons (1977) and Hancock and Elliot (1978), incubation only commences when the clutch is complete. Thus hatching is synchronous. The Malagasay Pond Heron *Ardeola idae* is also noted as having synchronous hatching (Hancock and Elliot 1978), though the situation in other *Ardeola* species is not known. In all other European herons, hatching is asynchronous. This difference is quite surprising and needs further investigation. Perhaps synchronous hatching is more common among the truly tropical species than among palearctic and nearctic species.

DEVELOPMENT AND CARE OF THE YOUNG

Both parents feed the young. First, there is a guardian period, when one of the adults stays at the nest constantly protecting the chicks, followed by a post-guardian period, when the chicks are left alone at the nest while both parents go off to hunt. At this later stage, the chicks are able to leave the nest and often hide in the thick foliage of the surrounding branches. While the chicks are still very small and being brooded constantly, the adult at the nest regurgitates predigested food directly into their open bills several times during its guard duty. When the chicks grow older, they grab the bill of the adult firmly at the base and the regurgitated food is passed directly to the begging young. When the chick loosens its grip to swallow, another chick takes its place. Several, but not all, of the chicks are thus fed at each visit by an adult. Once the chicks are able to move about in the branches, they run towards the incoming adult as soon as it lands in the trees, begging eagerly. There are no data concerning fledging success in this species.

FEEDING BEHAVIOUR AND FOOD

Usual methods

To hunt, Squacco Herons either stand motionless or wade and walk, usually rather rapidly, in a crouched position between the dense vegetation, stopping now and then to peer into the water or at the river bank (Voisin

A Squacco Heron foraging.

1978). This last method is very effective in catching frogs which are the major prey items of Squacco Herons. They are generally solitary feeders. However, when an area is very rich in prey, many individuals may fish only a few metres apart. Their foraging success seems to be greater when they hunt alone (Hafner *et al.* 1982). Squacco Herons have been reported fishing from a perched position (Bauer and Glutz 1966), but no detailed descriptions of this behaviour have been published.

According to one study, the mean number of prey taken per minute by Squacco Herons feeding in marshes is 0.21 (±0.03) and in rice fields 0.45 (±0.11). The mean dry weight per peck in marshes is 0.36 g (±0.07) and in rice fields 0.16 g (±0.03) (Hafner *et al.* 1982). Thus Squacco Herons appear to take fewer, but larger prey in marshes than in rice fields. In the Camargue, they seem to leave the marshes for the rice fields only when the latter are able to provide as much food as the marshes; this is usually only the case for short periods.

Although Squacco Herons may be active all day, they are most active at dawn and in the evening, often long after sunset (Voisin 1978). Sterbetz (1962) noted that during breeding, the Squacco Heron is most active from 05.00–07.00 h and from 18.00–19.00 h.

Unusual methods

A vagrant Squacco Heron was observed hunting on the Isles of Scilly (southern England) on 1 May 1970 in "fairly long grass in a small dry field".

Sheep droppings were carefully inspected by the Squacco Heron which extracted small worms from the droppings . . . and other unidentified edible matter . . . in addition, the heron also obtained dozens of very small snails from the grass stalks by slowly extending its neck and head and gently picking them off.

A Squacco Heron foraging.

A Squacco Heron (probably the same one) was later observed fishing in a pool for small eels which it battered and then swallowed (King 1975).

It seems possible that Squacco Herons use insects as bait, viz. the following observation:

> During 20 minutes . . . I saw the heron jab and catch 18 flying or settled insects. Immediately afterwards each one was placed carefully on the surface of the water and then the area was watched, or hunted, for a while. . . . This behaviour suggests that the Squacco Heron was actually attempting to lure fish within striking distance. It did catch one small fish during this 20 minute session (Prytherch 1980).

Food

The prey taken by Squacco Herons are small, up to about 10 cm in length and mostly comprise amphibians, fish and insects, varying in proportion depending on the food available. The proportion of insects increases when the birds fish in rice fields. For the same hunting effort, insects provide less food value than fish and amphibians (see the chapter on the Cattle Egret).

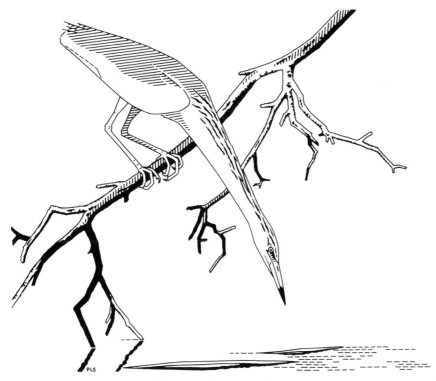

A Squacco Heron foraging.

The stomach contents of 108 Squacco Herons were studied by Vasvàri (1938–1939) in Hungary. They contained (by frequency) insects and their larvae – *Naucoris, Notonecta* 67.5%, *Dytiscus, Cybister* and *Hydrous* 55.5%, terrestrial beetles 37.9% (some probably via frog stomachs), *Gryllotalpa* 36.1% – small fish, chiefly rudd *Scardinus*, bleak *Alburnus* and Crucian carp *Carassius* 31.6% and amphibians 26.8%. As insects weigh very little compared to fish and amphibians, the Squacco Herons studied by Vasvàri lived mostly on fish and amphibians.

Moltoni (1936) analysed the stomach contents of 92 Squacco Herons from Italy. The birds had eaten, by frequency, 83.3% insects (chiefly *Noctonecta, Naucoris, Hydrous, Dytiscus* and *Gryllotalpa*), 40% amphibians (*Rana esculenta*) and 5.5% fish (sunfish *Eupomotis gibbosus* and tench *Tinca tinca*). In the USSR, the diet was composed chiefly of insects (especially grasshoppers), spiders and small frogs (Dementiev and Gladkov 1951). The importance of grasshoppers in the diet was also recorded by Stronach (1968), who noted the abundance of grasshoppers regurgitated by Squacco Heron chicks in a large heronry in Tanzania.

PREDATION

According to Sterbetz (1962), Peregrines and Saker Falcons living in his study area during the summer pose a threat to adult Squacco Herons. Stoats, weasels and foxes capture young, inexperienced Squacco Herons when they begin to hunt on the ground.

CHAPTER 13

The Cattle Egret *Bubulcus ibis*

GENERAL APPEARANCE AND FIELD CHARACTERS

The Cattle Egret is 48–53 cm high with a wing-span of 90–96 cm.

Plumage. The sexes are generally alike with the general colour being white tinged with rufous-buff.

Adult non-breeding: the plumage is entirely white, with a slight buff colour to the crown feathers. In males, the feathers of the chest and centre of the mantle are tingled cream-buff and slightly elongated; in females, they are white and of normal structure.

Adult breeding: in the breeding season, longer, hair-like rufous-buff feathers develop on the crown, nape, foreneck and chest. The scapular feathers of the same colour and structure become much longer than previously, and in some individuals extend 1–2 cm beyond the tip of the tail. In the Asian subspecies *B. i. coromandus*, the colour of the feathers which develop during the breeding season is not rufous-buff but varies from deep gold to dark cinnamon and extends upwards from the foreneck to the throat and cheeks (Hancock and Elliot 1978). The other parts remain entirely white.

Juvenile: entirely white with no elongated feathers.

Nestling: the down is white and the chicks remain downy for about 2 weeks. The flight feathers are white and fully grown at about 8 weeks. However, young birds are capable of flying short distances from about 6 weeks of age.

Moult: the annual post-nuptial moult is quite drastic. The sequence of replacement of individual remiges and rectrices in adult birds appears to be irregular with no real obvious pattern. The first moult begins at 6 months of age and replaces the body plumage. The last juvenile contour feathers are lost at 9 months of age. The young bird's plumage is not totally replaced when entering the first breeding season. Sometimes, young females breed with no scapular plumes and very reduced pectoral plumes (Siegfried 1971).

Bare parts

Adult non-breeding: the iris and lores are pale yellow. The bill is yellow, paler at the base. The legs and feet are dark green, and seem black at a distance. In many individuals, the tibia, the sole of the feet and sometimes the upper tarsus are yellowish in colour.

Adult breeding: the colour of the bare parts seems to differ slightly in different populations. Generally, during pair formation, the dark green colour of the legs and feet changes to pale yellow in most populations. However, in some individuals, the dark green colour seems only to fade slightly. The colour of the legs and feet then becomes more or less yellowish green (e.g. in the African Cape population). In some populations, it seems that the dark green colour does not fade at all.

For a very short period before mating, the legs and feet turn bright red where they were yellowish before, but only dusky red where they were still more or less green. In Sénégal, I have seen an individual with bright red legs and dark green feet. Thus, it seems possible that in some cases the dark green colour may remain during pair-formation. Further investigation is, however, necessary on this subject.

In all Cattle Egrets, the bill and iris become bright red in colour before mating. The lores are usually also bright red but are described as ruby-magenta for the Cape population (Blaker 1969). Displaying males always have the brightest red colour on the bare parts. For both males and females, this red colour disappears rapidly after mating. The redness of the bill recedes towards the base, and in the eyes towards the perimeter of the iris over a period of 5–10 days. The redness of the legs and feet becomes paler every day. After about 10 days, the red colour has usually totally disappeared and the legs and feet become pale yellow or yellowish green again.

Nestling: at hatching, the bill is horn-coloured, the iris pale yellow and the skin olive-green. By about 6 days of age, the bill is already black and during the second and third month gradually becomes yellow. The legs and feet, which are olive-green at hatching, take on a more or less definite yellowish tinge. Before flying, they became gradually dark green (appearing black at a distance).

Field characters. In the field, Cattle Egrets appear as small white, rather stocky herons, with short legs and stout bills. In the breeding season, the buff colour of the head, chest, and scapular feathers is easily seen. When flying, usually in groups, the bright white colour of the wings and body flashes in the sun as the birds change direction. They forage mostly in flocks on flooded grasslands and fields where they follow wild and domestic herds of grazing mammals. They are the only herons which forage around the heads and legs of grazing animals and perch on their backs.

Measurements. The measurements (mm) of 20 ♂♂ and 20 ♀♀ of each subspecies has been given by C. Vaurie (1963) (range and mean):

Bulbulcus ibis ibis

wing	♂♂	241–266	(253.0)	♀♀ 240–258	(247.6)
tail	♂♂	79–93	(87.5)	♀♀ 74–93	(86.0)
bill from skull	♂♂	61–71	(66.3)	♀♀ 60–70	(65.5)
tarsus	♂♂	70–85	(77.0)	♀♀ 70–81	(76.1)
bare tibia	♂♂	19–34	(25.3)	♀♀ 16–38	(29.0)

Bulbulcus ibis comorandus

wing	♂♂	243–260	(253.8)	♀♀ 230–256	(264.4)
tail	♂♂	76–98	(85.6)	♀♀ 76–92	(83.7)
bill from skull	♂♂	66–77	(71.1)	♀♀ 62–73	(68.5)
tarsus	♂♂	80–91	(85.0)	♀♀ 78–87	(82.3)
bare tibia	♂♂	27–52	(38.0)	♀♀ 23–52	(38.6)

Three captive-reared chicks reached a weight of 350 g by the age of 40 days (Siegfried 1972b). Four birds captured in the USA ranged in weight between 300 and 400 g (Palmer 1962). Seven captive Cattle Egrets from Florida, USA weighed between 233 and 432 g (mean weight 338 g) (Woolfenden *et al.* 1976).

There are only three observations available of the wing-beat rate of Cattle Egrets (Voisin, unpublished): 130, 180 and 192 beats per minute.

DISTRIBUTION, MOVEMENTS AND HABITAT

Geographical variations

There are three subspecies of Cattle Egret, two of which are well established: the nominate *B. i. ibis* (Linnaeus 1758), type locality Egypt, and *B. i. coromandus* (Boddaert 1783), type locality Coromandel coast. The differences between these two subspecies are treated in the previous sections on Plumage and Measurements. A third subspecies, *B. i. seychellarum* (Salomonsen 1934), from the Seychelles, requires further study as only one specimen in breeding plumage has been described.

BREEDING AREAS

B. i ibis breeds in southern Europe (only in the Iberian Peninsula and the Camargue), in the USSR and Iran (along the west coast of the Caspian Sea and the bottom of the Persian Gulf), in Israel and the Yemen. In Africa, it breeds in Egypt, Algeria, Morocco and on the whole continent south of the Sahara. It also breeds in Madagascar, Sâo Tomé, the Cape Verde Islands, Comoro Islands, Aldabra and Mauritius. In the New World, *B. i. ibis* breeds northwards from the Guianas, where they first became established, to Colombia, the West Indies, Mexico, California, the east coast of the USA and southeastern Canada. Southwards they breed in the deltas of the Amazon in Uruguay and Argentina. They have been introduced to Hawaii where they now also breed.

The subspecies *B. i. coromandus* breeds on the Asian continent from Pakistan and India to eastern China, South Korea and southern Japan. It breeds also on various islands around India: the Laccadive Islands, the Maldive Islands, Sri Lanka, the Andaman Islands and the Nicobar Islands. Farther east they breed on Hainan and recently became established in northern and northeastern Australia.

MOVEMENTS

Some individuals, probably young ones, are highly erratic and cover great distances. However, many are sedentary as long as the food supply and weather conditions are sufficiently good.

In temperate areas, Cattle Egrets nest during the warm summer months in flooded or irrigated localities. In Europe, particularly in the Camargue, they arrive in spring (May) to nest. Many leave in the autumn, but a sizeable part of the population generally stays throughout the winter. Their numbers, which are lowest in January, are already increasing by February (Voisin 1979, Hafner *et al.* 1982). In the USSR, Cattle Egrets are summer visitors to Azerbaijan and the Volga Delta (Dementiev and Gladkov 1951).

A significant part of the Spanish population migrates to North Africa and birds on passage have been observed at Gibraltar. In North Africa, they move from place to place according to the food supply, only exceptionally crossing the Sahara (Heim de Balzac and Mayaud 1962).

In the tropics, this species, which is very dependent on water, nests during the rainy season. They seem to be migratory in tropical Africa (Curry-Lindahl 1981), although their movements have not yet been sufficiently well studied to be known in detail. In the Djoudj, northern Sénégal, Cattle Egrets arrive at the beginning of the rainy season in August. They begin to nest only if the water conditions are adequate and leave as soon as the area dries up (Voisin 1983). In Nigeria, they nest in the north from May to October, flying southwards to winter (Elgood *et al.* 1973).

In Cape Province, with its Mediterranean climate, Cattle Egrets are present during the whole year. A large part of the population nests during the rainy season from October to November, but many birds seem to come only to winter during the dry season, foraging on irrigated meadows and fields. However, some birds hatched in the area leave during this time. Young ringed at Cape Province colonies have been found in tropical areas northwards from Mozambique to Zaïre (Curry-Lindahl 1981).

In North America, Cattle Egrets leave for the south when the weather and water conditions deteriorate in their northern territories.

The migratory movements of *B. i. coromandus* in tropical Asia are not known in any detail. After the breeding season, birds nesting in the northernmost parts of their breeding range, in Pakistan, India, China and Japan, migrate southwards. Wintering – but not breeding – Cattle Egrets are to be found on the islands of Indonesia, the Philippines, New Guinea and Taiwan. In Australia, Cattle Egrets are present throughout the year, breeding in the north and northeast. A part of the population winters from April to November, in the south. Central Australia has not been colonized by Cattle Egrets (Cramp and Simmons 1977). In New Zealand, the bird is becoming more and more common, especially as a winter visitor, but has not been reported nesting as yet (Falla *et al.* 1979).

The fact that Cattle Egrets are very erratic and may fly great distances, particularly over the sea, is demonstrated by numerous observations made on remote islands such as Tristan da Cunha (Elliot 1957), St Paul's Rock (Bowen and Nicholls 1968), Gough Island (Voisin 1979), Marion Island (Newton *et al.* 1983) and the Falklands (Strange 1979).

Habitat

Cattle Egrets usually nest in heronries with other herons and water-birds. Their colonies and roosts are established in trees and bushes often over water but also on dry land. Deciduous trees are preferred, but conifers are also used. Exceptionally, reedbeds and stands of bamboo are colonized. Cattle Egrets often nest close to human habitation, near farms, in villages and even in small towns.

The ancient breeding range of the Cattle Egret seems to have been restricted to the tropics of the Old World, in freshwater wetlands. The birds' natural habitats were and still are the annually inundated floodplains which dry up slowly and the short-grass margins of lakes, marshes and wide rivers (Siegfried 1978). A characteristic of the floodplains in Africa is the huge herds of buffalo (*Syncerus caffer*) which seldom occur far from open water. Living in exactly the same habitat as the buffalo for hundreds and probably thousands of years, Cattle Egrets have evolved their curious and well-known habit of using grazing mammals to forage more efficiently. Even nowadays the African buffalo is still the preferred companion of Cattle Egrets.

Living betwen terrestrial and aquatic habitats, this species feeds on both terrestrial (e.g. grasshoppers) and semi-aquatic prey (e.g. frogs). Amphibians are a much richer source of food than insects. By nesting during the rainy season in the tropics, they are able to utilize the relatively rich food source provided by frogs and the like.

Observations from many authors as well as my own show that where both freshwater and saltwater biotopes are available, Cattle Egrets always choose the freshwater areas, not only in their original range but even in the new territories more recently colonized. Thus Cattle Egrets have expanded over a great part of the world without changing their foraging habits. In the Camargue, the freshwater and saltwater wetlands are very distinct due to the use of saltwater areas by industry (Salins) and freshwater areas by agriculture. Here Cattle Egrets avoid salt-marshes and lagoons. During our 10-year study in the Camargue, we did not see a single Cattle Egret in the salt-marshes and lagoons belonging to the Salin, nor did the species nest in heronries established in this habitat (Voisin and Voisin 1975, 1976).

In the Seychelles, Cattle Egrets frequent open grassy areas, often feeding around cattle. They are not usually encountered on the shore except for occasional flocks gathered at sewage outfalls or rubbish dumps. On Aldabra, they are most common by inland pools or among the giant tortoises, which they follow as they do cattle elsewhere (Penny 1974). In the Caribbean at St Croix (Virgin Islands), the first flock noted by local observers was foraging on a small pasture among a herd of cattle (Seaman 1955). In Trinidad, where they are reported nesting in saltwater mangrove stands with other herons, "they feed themselves and young on food obtainable only in freshwater areas, and every meal for the young has to be transported back to the saltwater area" (French 1966).

BEHAVIOUR AND BIOLOGY

DAILY ROUTINE

Cattle Egrets are gregarious throughout the year, sleeping in roosts or colonies, numbering from some 20 birds to many thousands. They roost and nest in trees, or in bushes if no trees are available. At dawn, the birds leave the colonies and roosts in groups in search of herds of grazing animals. Foraging flocks are of varying size: 1–200 birds in Cape Province (Blaker 1968) and 1–100 birds in Djoudj, Sénégal (Voisin, unpublished). In the Camargue, where this species is not yet numerous, flocks seen between 1974 and 1978 were of 1–15 birds. Although large flocks are sometimes seen in the Djoudj, as in Cape Province, small flocks are more common. In the Djoudj, 70% of the Egrets observed which were not associated with cattle were either single birds or groups of 2–3 birds. Flocks associated with cattle are larger, usually 20–30 birds. In contrast, in Cape Province, the average flock size for unassociated birds is 7.99 and for associated birds only 4.24. This difference may be in response to the size of the grazing herds; large in the Djoudj, small in Cape Province.

The greatest recorded distance between the nearest roost and feeding Cattle Egrets is 22 km (Blaker 1968). Skead (1966) and Craufurd (1966) have observed feeding Cattle Egrets 12 miles from their roost.

During midday, the birds often rest near their feeding grounds; Vincent (1947) pointed out that these midday rest periods are to a certain extent a consequence of the inactivity of cattle at that time. About 1 hour before sunset, Cattle Egrets begin to fly towards their roost or colony. Observations by Blaker in the Cape Province, and by myself in Andalusia, Spain, show that birds seldom fly directly from their feeding grounds to their roost or colony. Usually, they congregate at gathering points 1–10 km from the colony before flying home in bigger flocks. These colony- or roost-bound flights tend to follow water-courses (Craufurd 1966).

DISPLAYS AND CALLS

One of the best behavioural studies made on herons was carried out in 1969 by Blaker. Thanks to his observations, the behaviour of Cattle Egrets is one of the best known among the Ardeidae, and is summarized in the following section.

The position of the crest feathers indicates the opposing alarm and aggressive tendencies of a Cattle Egret except when it is involved in courtship displays. Blaker drew a distinction between the movement of the proximal

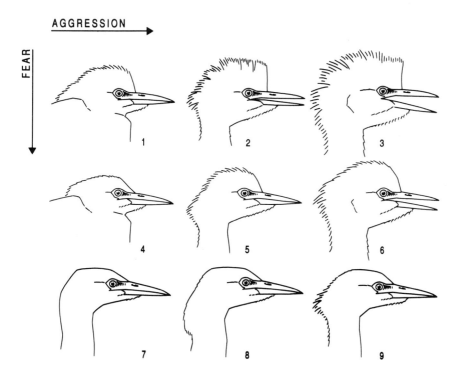

Crest positions of the Cattle Egret. From left to right, increasing aggression; from top down, increasing alarm. Anger tends to raise the crown and nape feathers, whereas fear tends to sleek them. Fear has more of an effect on the crown feathers than on the nape feathers (after Blaker 1969).

crest feathers and the distal ones. Position 1 (see figure) is characteristic of a bird totally relaxed and inactive. From that position, increasing alarm causes a flattening of the anterior crest feathers and tends to prevent the erection of the posterior crest feathers. Increasing aggressive tendencies cause the progressive erection of the posterior crest feathers and inhibit the sleekening effect of alarm on the anterior crest feathers. The nine positions of the crest feathers illustrated are observed during different situations, e.g. full intensity threat, position 3; a bird remaining on its nest despite the proximity of a predator, position 8; intense mutual threatening, position 9.

Agonistic displays

Forward Displays. The Forward Display is a threat display and tends to increase the distance between individuals. The releaser is usually another bird trespassing on the territorial bounds of a nesting site. It also serves to maintain individual distance between birds in the colony or at the roost.

When the bird displays, the crest feathers are erected (positions 2, 3, 5, 6 or 9). The neck, pectoral and scapular feathers are partly or fully raised. The neck, extended forwards and upwards assumes an "S" shape. A more retracted and posterior neck position indicates a higher fear component. The bill is directed slightly downwards and is opened at higher intensities. The bird stabs at its opponent (contact is only rarely made). Simultaneously, the bird gives a brief, harsh "raa" call. Prior to pair formation, this is replaced by a

Forward Display.

Withdrawn Crouch.

short "thonk" (Skead 1966). The wings are partly spread and one forward and downward beat is made.

The Forward Displaying bird sometimes remains on its territory threatening its opponent with frequent stabs. In most cases, however, it walks towards its opponent who then flies away. If the intruder is a much larger heron, the Cattle Egret usually stops some metres from it and continues to threaten from a distance. Such threats are quite ineffective, the larger bird ignoring the smaller Cattle Egret until it is very near the nest where the attack might be carried out in earnest. The threatened Cattle Egret may on rare occasions perform a Withdrawn Crouch, although Blaker states that this display is only given in response to a Forward Display by a bird immediately above it. The bird peforming this display "suddenly crouches, with body horizontal, fully flexed legs, slightly raised scapulars, neck retracted and crest positions 7, 8 or 9". A particular form of Forward Display occurs when two birds on nearby nests threaten each other. Blaker calls this display the Stab-and-counter-stab. The birds "rapidly lunge at each other a few times, each bird drawing back as the other stabs and vice versa". The crest feathers are raised. Like Blaker and Skead, I have observed that the birds do not actually strike each other, although they could do so if they were to stab simultaneously.

Direct Attack. This happens very rarely and Lancaster (1970) is the only author to have documented it. One bird flies up to meet the attacker and both birds fight all the way down to the ground. Such aerial fighting leads to bloodied heads, faces and bills. Lancaster has not given any detailed interpretation of the conditions leading to this aerial fighting, saying only that pair formation and nest ownership were involved.

Supplanting Run. This display is performed only on the ground, by resting or feeding birds, and replaces the Forward Display. "With neck retracted . . .

Stab-and-counter-stab (after Blaker 1969).

the displaying bird runs at another with stiff-legged strides". The crest feathers are more or less erected while the rest of the plumage is sleeked. If the attacking bird does not chase the other away, both birds fight briefly, though this is uncommon.

Fear and conflict displays

Alert Posture. The Alert Posture has a practical function, permitting the bird to see further. This display seems also to act as an alarm signal. It is given in the presence of humans or predators in the colony. The Alert Posture is "characterised by upright stance, erect neck, fully sleek plumage and bill tilted above the horizontal".

Head-flick. The bird Head-flicks when it is confused. This display is prompted by conflict situations such as when predators are near the nest, or the bird having threatened but failed to dislodge a trespasser, or when

Supplanting Run (after Blaker 1969).

watching a fight, or in the case of males, after having attempted to mount an unreceptive female. The display consists of "rapid, small-amplitude head-flicks in a horizontal plane, given with the beak closed. It may be peformed once or twice per second."

Wing-touch. This is a typical displacement activity given in conflict situations, and is essentially a display of unmated males, and to a lesser degree unmated females due to the presence of a bird of the opposite sex. After pairing, this display is rarely observed. When displaying, the bird "turns its head to one side and runs its slightly opened beak downward along the leading edge of the folded wing. The carpal joint is always held slightly away from the body while the wing is being touched. The crest position is 2, 3, and 5."

Courtship displays

Stretch Display. In unpaired birds, this display is performed only by males to attract females. In paired birds, the display is given by males or females in response to the mate's approach. The Stretch Display is the chief distance-reducing display. Blaker considered that since it is quite inconspicuous in Cattle Egrets, it may not have an important advertising effect. When display-ing, the bird

> stretches head and neck vertically upwards, with legs partly flexed and body at an angle of about 45° to the horizontal. Crest fully depressed, scapular plumes almost fully depressed. After half a second in this position the bird suddenly retracts its neck slightly and flexes its legs, the body is moving forward and downward. The scapular plumes are fully raised. The beak remains at an angle above the horizontal. Some unmated males but not all give one or more 'ow' notes at the apex of the stretch movement, then a short 'roo' call on the main downward movement.

Females seldom perform the display at full intensity. Normally, a paired female "performs a brief downward-squatting movement with neck retrac-ted, head and beak pointing upwards, crest flattened, scapulars raised and rarely with a 'roo' call".

Flap-flight. Because it is so noisy and easy to see, the Flap-flight is probably the chief advertising display of Cattle Egrets. It is characteristic of unmated birds of both sexes, and disappears some hours after pairing. Site ownership tendencies are present in this display, since the male, some metres before landing on his territory, often changes from normal flight to Flap-flight. The aggressive component also seems important, flap-flights often being used in supplanting approaches.

In this display,

> the wing beats are deep and exaggerated which produce loud sounds. The body axis is at about 45° to the horizontal and the neck is partly extended. The legs

Stretch Display. The end of the movement.

dangle. The beak is often open. Crest, pectoral and scapular plumes are partly raised in flight. All plumes are raised further on the instant of landing.

Twig-shake. This display, characteristic of unpaired males, seems to have an important advertising function. It contains elements of nest building. The crest feathers of the bird are raised and a twig is violently shaken in the bill. As in the flap-flight display, aggressive tendencies appear to be strong. When displaying,

> the perched bird stretches out its neck almost to full extension, grasps a leaf or a twig in its beak and shakes its with sideways head movements for one to three seconds. Back-and-forth jerking movements of the head are also present while the twig is being shaken and in a few cases may predominate over sideways components. The crest is fully erected while scapulars and pectoral plumes are partly raised.

The bird is generally silent, but this display may be accompanied by a nasal chatter.

Wing-spread. This display still serves its original function as a balancing action but probably also has an advertising function, since it is one of the most characteristic activities of unpaired males. It is often adopted immediately after a Flap-flight Display, or before a Forward Display while walking towards another individual or while walking down to the nest immediately after landing on a nearby branch: "The wings are almost fully spread downward for one to five seconds, usually with rocking movements exactly as if balancing the walking bird. All plumes are partly or fully erect. The neck is never more than half-extended, beak always pointed downward."

Breeding display

Back-biting. This display is the only one in which the birds are in physical contact with one another. It reinforces the bonds between paired birds and occurs in newly formed pairs, mostly during the Greeting Ceremony. The displaying bird, crest partly raised,

> stands beside its mate and rapidly runs its partly open beak to and fro through its mate's back and/or neck feathers, with sideways headshaking movements. Quivering open–close beak movements are always present, although the maxilla and mandible never actually clatter together. At higher intensities the mate's neck may actually be grasped and shaken.

Calls

Rick-rack. This harsh double croak is the Cattle Egret's most common call. It is more muffled and hoarse in red-beaked individuals.

Chatter. Blaker distinguishes many forms of Chatter: Nasal Chatter (only in unmated males), Soft Chatter (in recently mated red-beaked birds of both sexes), Harsh Chatter (in yellow-beaked birds of both sexes during Greeting Ceremonies).

Kok. This is a light alarm call given singly or in series.

Kaah. This is the loud alarm call given, for instance, when a predator comes towards the nest.

REPRODUCTIVE BEHAVIOUR

Pair formation

Cattle Egrets commonly breed during their first year (Siegfried 1966c). The following description is based on the studies of Blaker (1969) and Lancaster (1970).

The territory of a displaying male usually extends some metres around an old nest, though if no nest is available the bird frequently adopts a horizontal branch and its immediate surroundings as its territory. As soon as an unmated male begins to display, females start to appear. They perch on nearby branches, usually slightly above the male's territory and in a radius of about 5 m. The females adopt "a highly characteristic long neck, peering attitude, with crest feathers partly erected and neck almost fully extended" (Blaker). Lancaster counted as many as 10 females in the vicinity of a displaying male. Females fly from one displaying male to another, spending anything from a few minutes to several hours near each one. At this stage, the males invariably respond aggressively to the approaching females and threaten them with high-intensity Forward Displays. A frontal approach by a female never succeeds, and landing beside the male is not much better. Both Blaker and Lancaster have observed that the female usually tries to land on the male's back from behind, whereupon the male tries to dislodge her. Lancaster has observed females directing real blows at a male's head; Blaker has only observed Back-biting. If the male fails to dislodge the female, he generally submits and crouches slightly, and the female often remains for several minutes on the male's back. At this stage, Back-biting occurs and Lancaster has observed that the female also rubs her bill against the side of the male's neck and face. Once the two birds have remained together for some hours, the pair is formed and remains stable. Blaker has observed that the new pair often leave the territory first adopted by the male for a new one, where they build their nest.

Greeting Behaviour

The incoming bird begins the Rick-rack Call while still in flight. On hearing its mate, the bird at the nest calls in answer, and then points its head downwards and gives a harsh "roo" call. The flying bird lands some distance from the nest and then walks towards it, sometimes stopping to perform a low-intensity Stretch Display. When both birds are on the nest, the loud Rick-rack Call is replaced by harsh Chattering. Back-biting occurs if the pair is still newly formed. During the Greeting Ceremony, the crest feathers of both birds are completely flat and the scapulars partly to fully raised.

Copulation

Copulation occurs without any preparatory display. It always occurs at the nest or within 50 cm of the nest rim. The female sits on her tarsi, with wings slightly spread. The male steps onto her back, grasps the humerus region of each wing in his feet, and begins rhythmic treading movements, before lowering his tail to make cloacal contact, flapping his wings to maintain his balance. During copulation, the male often nibbles and then grasps the female's head or neck feathers. "Extramarital" copulations are frequent and mostly occur after egg-laying. At this stage, the male is more often away from the nest and the aggressiveness of the female has much decreased. Since they seldom fertilize eggs, "extramarital" copulations do not significantly affect paternity of the brood (Fujioka and Yamagishi 1981).

Nest-building

The following description is based on the accounts of Blaker (1969) and Siegfried (1971). Nearly all nest material is brought by the male to the female, who builds the nest. In normal conditions, the nest is constantly guarded to avoid plundering by other nest builders. An abandoned nest disappears within a few days. The male collects sticks usually 1–30 cm in length. He takes mostly dry sticks found on the ground, but may also break off growing twigs from nearby trees. Only two behaviour patterns are used in nest-building. The most important is Tremble-shove (Lorenz 1955). The bird grasps a stick and pushes it slowly downwards, while shaking its head with short lateral movements. The other pattern, Push-pull, is used to remove an unwanted twig. The bird grasps it in its beak and "violently jerks it back and forth". At the time that the female is ready to lay, the nest contains on average 196 sticks (range 110–280). Nest-building continues until the eggs hatch, with a fully built nest being composed of up to 400 sticks. The average diameter of the nest is 36.3 cm (range 29–44 cm) with a cup 5.0 cm (range 2–8 cm) deep. It is of a platform type with a fairly loose structure that may cause some egg losses, but it drains easily; this is important for those birds which nest during the rainy season in some countries.

Egg-laying and clutch size

The eggs of the Cattle Egret are whitish (Lancaster 1970), light blue (Weber 1975) or light blue-green (Voisin, unpublished). Table 10 lists some data regarding the size of Cattle Egret eggs.

According to Weber (1975), the mean weight of the eggs is 24 g (range 19.0–24.4 g). Observations regarding mean clutch size from a number of studies are shown in Table 11.

The average interval between pair formation and egg-laying is 7.3 days (range 5–10 days) (Blaker 1969). The birds spend an average of 6.6 ± 0.37 days (range 3–11 days) building their nests before laying the first egg (Jenni 1970). According to Weber (1975) and Jenni (1969), the interval between the laying of successive eggs is 2 days. Blaker (1969) reported slightly different times: an interval of 2 days in 13 cases, 3 days in 10 cases and 1 day in one case.

Incubation and hatching

Incubation begins as soon as the first egg is laid and both sexes incubate. Normally, one bird sits from 09.00 to 16.00 h and the other from 16.00 to 09.00 h (Blaker 1969). The eggs are never left unguarded. According to Blaker (1969), the mean incubation period is 23.7 days (range 22–26 days). Weber (1970) reported a mean of 24 days (range 23–25 days) and Jenni (1969) 22.9 ± 0.04 days (range 22–23 days). Observations regarding hatching success from a number of studies are summarized in Table 12.

Blaker (1969) noted that the eggs of the Cattle Egret usually hatch at intervals of 1 day (12 cases), though in one case it was 2 days. Jenni (1969) observed that of the second egg in each brood, about half hatched 1 day after the first egg and about half 2 days later. After the second egg, all of the eggs hatched on alternate days. According to Siegfried (1972c), the mean weight of Cattle Egrets at hatching is 23.7 g (range 22–26 g; 28 chicks, first of each brood); Weber (1975) found 20.7 g (range 16.1–25.8 g; 41 chicks) and Voisin (unpublished) 23 g (range 22–25 g; 3 chicks).

DEVELOPMENT AND CARE OF THE YOUNG

Feeding the young

Both parents feed the young. During their first week, the chicks peck at and try to grab their parent's beaks without success, being still too weak and poorly co-ordinated. The adults, standing in a hunched position, beak pointed downwards, let the food boluses fall into the chicks' open mouths or onto the nest floor where it can be picked up by them. As the chicks become older, they succeed in grabbing the adults beak firmly at the base and the food can be passed directly to them. The chicks leave the nest when they are about 15 days old, balancing on nearby branches. They go to meet the incoming adult as it advances slowly along the branches towards the nest. When the adult leaves, the young do not pursue it more than a few metres from the nest. When the adults are not yet ready to regurgitate, they stretch their necks and lift their heads out of reach of the young. Adults are completely indifferent as to which chick is fed. Since the chicks hatch in succession, the oldest receives the most food. Being the largest and strongest it is the first to grab the parent's bill or to run along the branches to meet them. When food is scarce, as it usually is (see later), the fourth, the third and sometimes even the second chick will starve.

Growth and mortality of nestlings

All who have studied the growth of Cattle Egrets have noticed the difficulties that the parents have in raising the whole brood. They almost never succeed in bringing up more than two chicks, occasionally three and, only exceptionally, four. The younger chicks of a brood generally starve to death. Blaker (1969) noted that "starvation was the chief cause of mortality in *Ardeola ibis* chicks, the great majority of third – and fourth – hatched chicks dying before they are 15 days old". He observed 12 nests with 3 chicks from a hide in which one of the first-hatched and one of the second-hatched chicks died, while 11 of the 12 youngest chicks died 7–17 days after hatching.

Siegfried (1972c) has also emphasized that starvation is the major cause of chick mortality and is "heaviest when the chicks are around 10 days of age". Having reared chicks in captivity, Siegfried estimated that during its second week of life, a chick needs 95 g of fresh food daily. Each parent needs 74 g for itself; therefore, to raise a brood of three chicks an adult must catch about 216 g of food. Since an average grasshopper weights 0.125 g, each adult must catch 1728 grasshoppers daily. It is easy to understand why Cattle Egrets are more successful raising broods when amphibians are available. Fledging success differs from place to place according to food availability. Other studies are summarized in Table 13.

The chicks soon develop the ability to climb, probably as a means to avoid predators. As soon as they cease to be brooded (after 9–10 days), they start to climb in the branches around the nest. The first flight is usually made at 25–30 days and all the brood are able to fly by 30–35 days (Blaker 1969).

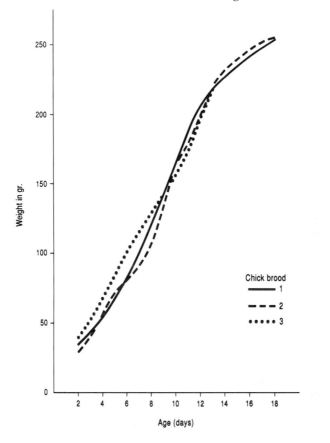

Figure 7   The average growth in body weight of first-hatched Cattle Egret chicks in broods of 1, 2 and 3. The data are based on 37 chicks (curves smoothed) (Siegfried 1972).

Some data relating to growth weight are shown in Fig. 7. The weight of the first-hatched chick at 18 days of age is the same regardless of the initial brood size, indicating the efficiency of the brood reduction system in maintaining the healthy growth of at least one chick in the face of a variable food supply.

FEEDING BEHAVIOUR AND FOOD

Feeding behaviour

Usually, Cattle Egrets feed near large grazing animals, such as cattle or horses, but may also follow goats and sheep as I have observed in Sénégal. However, they generally prefer large mammals. Blaker (1969) noted an average 0.285 Cattle Egrets per horse or donkey, 0.183 per cow and only

0.0084 per sheep. This preference for large mammals also applies to wild species: buffaloes and elephants are usually followed in their habitats. Since settling in the Camargue at the beginning of the 1970s, Cattle Egrets have followed the white horses and black cattle there as they graze, often on very wet grassland.

A few birds are always to be seen perched on the back of grazing animals. The rest of the flock hunts close to their heads and legs from a few centimetres to some metres distant. The Cattle Egrets move slowly, heads and necks withdrawn, then pulled forwards at each step. When a prey item is spotted, they stretch their necks rapidly to catch it. They will even run to catch an interesting prey. Heatwole (1965) has quantified the biological advantage of this association with cattle. Egrets feeding within 1 m of grazing animals obtain 1.25–1.50 times as much food, and take 33% fewer steps to get it, compared with Egrets further away. Dinsmore (1973) found that Cattle Egrets foraging within 3 m of a cow, took 1.25 times as much food and took only 0.74 times as many steps per unit time than birds further away.

Burger and Gochfeld (1982) observed that these birds got the most prey when taking 10–30 steps per minute, and chose, when possible, grazing species which best allow them to maintain that step rate. Cows, buffaloes, and wildebeest move at a particularly favourable speed. Among the animals of one herd, Egrets follow those moving at the optimum speed for their foraging success. If they slow down, or begin to move faster, the Egrets switch to another host.

I have never seen any other heron species associate with cattle or horses. Even the Little Egret does not forage at their feet or perch on their backs; though in the Camargue, they very often hunt in the vicinity of grazing herds.

Cattle Egrets are not shy birds and willingly associate with motor vehicles. They often forage behind tractors, and Reynolds (1965) has seen them catch insects and frogs that had jumped away from the wheels of his slow-moving Land Rover. Cattle Egrets will also make use of fire. In Florida, Smallwood *et al.* (1982) observed that Cattle Egrets congregated both at controlled and naturally occurring grass fires: "Cattle Egrets flew through the smoke and foraged on the ground within 1 metre of the flames on both windward and leeward edges of the fires." They captured small prey on the ground that did not fly away, but were jumping or running to escape the fire.

When many insects are available but no herd is present, Cattle Egrets use a hunting technique which Meyerriecks (1960) calls Leap-frog Feeding:

> A dozen Egrets land in an empty pasture. One or two birds at the edge of the group begin to peer carefully at the stubble. One runs forward, snaps up a grasshopper, stirring up other insects. A second bird follows his example. The flock begins to mill about, and a bird from the rear flies up and over the foraging Egrets to catch its own insects, disturbed by its landing. Two more fly from the flock, and up over to the front; then peer, and strike their prey. The remaining birds in the flock then fly up and over to the front, leaving those who began to forage first at the rear; soon to repeat the leap-frog pattern. Thus the birds act as a team, each one taking a turn as beater, forager and feeder.

In Cape Province, as in Sénégal, it is not unusual to see Cattle Egrets hunting alone. The Stand-and-wait method (Meyerriecks 1960) is sometimes adopted by these birds, as they stand motionless, usually peering into the water. If a prey comes within reach, the bird lunges and grasps it. However, when hunting in groups or alone, Cattle Egrets usually walk, though they may sometimes make short runs or even flights to catch their prey.

When walking slowly alone, a bird may begin "Neck-swaying" Ried 1955, Blaker 1969): "The bird extends and weaves its head and neck from side to side as it slowly approaches a prey item. The oscillations gradually subtend a smaller and smaller angle until the bird pounces forward and strikes the prey" (Dinsmore 1973). Blaker (1969) suggests that "Neck-swaying" might be used "chiefly on prey animals which the birds recognise as active and likely to escape".

Goodwin (1948) and Blaker (1969) have noted that larger prey such as big insects, frogs and lizards are dipped in water several times before being swallowed whole. Sometimes, the prey are pecked to death (Skead 1956, Valentine 1958). Venomous prey, such as some caterpillars, are avoided, but it seems that young birds must learn which prey are inedible by trial-and-error (Bigot and Jouventin 1974).

Food

The first studies of the diet of Cattle Egrets were made by Chapin (1932), and some years later by Kadry (1942). They showed that the birds capture mainly

A Cattle Egret foraging. The bird spots an item of prey and then runs to catch it.

grasshoppers. More recently, the food of Cattle Egrets has been studied in Cape Province, South Africa by Siegfried (1966d, 1969, 1971a, b, 1972a, b, c), in Florida, USA by Jenni (1969, 1973) and Fogarty and Hetrick (1973), in the Camargue, France by Hafner (1977) and in Japan by Kosugi (1960).

Siegfried, Jenni and Hafner have studied the diet of nestling Cattle Egrets from boluses of undigested food regurgitated by nestlings in response to their intrusion into the colonies. In 200 boluses in Florida, Jenny found 59.4% orthopterans, 1.3% other insects, 3.4% spiders, 34.4% amphibians and 1.7% snakes (by percentage volume of total diet). In a study based on 98 food samples, Siegfried found (by percentage weight of total diet) 36.1% orthopterans, 41.2% other insects, 0.4% arachnida, 12.7% amphibians, 3.0% reptiles and 3.8% birds. In 62 boluses, Hafner found 6 worms, 21 crustacea (triops), 71 spiders, 375 orthopterans, 354 other insects, 146 amphibians, 4 fishes and 2 snakes. Fogarty and Hetrick examined the stomach contents of 841 adult Cattle Egrets shot at different roosts in Florida in June and July 1969. Orthopterans represented 80.5% of the total food volume, other insects 3.1% and spiders 4.7%. Other invertebrates identified were earthworms, centipedes, crawfish and free-living flatworms. Of the vertebrates, 7.4% were amphibians, but there were some reptiles and mammals (mainly field mice).

Siegfried examined the stomach contents taken from 250 birds shot from December to September over a period of 3 years (October–November being the nesting period when none was shot). Insects formed 57% of the total diet by weight. The major insect groups in order of importance were lepidoptera (caterpillars), orthoptera, coleoptera and diptera. Earthworms (*Annelida-Lumbricus* sp.) were second in importance and accounted for 33% of the total diet. The remainder was made up of 8.3% vertebrate and 1.7% arachnid, chilopod, mollusc and isopod items (see Fig. 8). The most obvious seasonal variation in diet involved earthworms. These accounted for 60% by weight of the total food taken during the rainy season (April to the end of September) but were absent from the stomach contents at other times of the year. A study made in Japan by Kosugi (1960), on the food of Cattle Egrets foraging in rice fields, showed that the birds had eaten mostly insects. In six stomachs he found 436 insects (77 locustids and 186 dytiscids), 16 arachnids, 3 amphibians (*Rana*) and 2 reptiles (*Takydromus* sp.). Kosugi's study shows that even in an aquatic environment, Cattle Egrets live on insects, amphibians and reptiles.

The importance of insects in the diet of such a large bird as a heron is quite unusual and does not seem well suited to rearing young, as described earlier on. In fact, the number of chicks raised in each brood depends greatly on the availability of larger prey, generally amphibians, but also other vertebrates. Siegfried showed that vertebrates count for 19.5% (by weight) of the total diet of nestlings and for only 8.3% of the diet of adults during the non-breeding period. The situation in Florida seems better than in the Cape Province. There, vertebrates account for 36.1% of the volume of the nestling diet. The average size of the broods is 1.83 at the end of the third week in the Cape Province and 2.9 ± 0.11 at the end of the second week in Florida. The significant proportion of amphibians and other vertebrates in the diet of

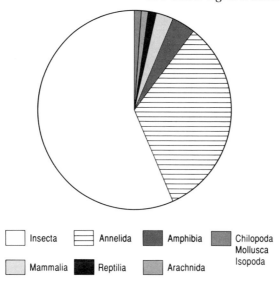

Figure 8   The percentage composition by weight of the major food items in the diet of Cattle Egrets. The complete circle represents 100% (Siegfried 1971b).

Camargue nestlings (see above) is probably responsible for the large broods raised there (mean 3 young per nest during their fourth week).

Unusual foods. Cattle Egrets occasionally take flies when perching on grazing cattle or horses (Halley and Wayne 1978) or when they are attracted by rotting fish or carcasses (Reynolds 1965). Wan Ee (1973) observed Cattle Egrets preying on nesting Quelea near Bloemfontein, South Africa. About 1000 Egrets congregated at the Quelea colony which comprised about 6000 nests. They used their bills and feet to tear open the nests and expose the young which were gulped down. About 70% of the Quelea nestlings were taken. Cattle Egrets may prey on adult birds too if they catch them by chance (Taylor 1979) or if they are starving and no other prey is available, as in a study on the Dry Tortugas, Florida (Cunningham 1955).

Pellets. Cattle Egrets regurgitate pellets; "A regurgitated pellet is about 50 × 25 mm in size, oval in shape, well compressed, and damp and soft when first expelled" (Skead 1956). The frequency at which these pellets are regurgitated depends entirely on the food taken. Pellets can be found where the birds congregate and at the heronry.

PREDATION

Not many animals have been reported as predators of Cattle Egrets. In all observations but one, where the predator was a monkey, the hunter was a diurnal bird of prey. Nocturnal birds of prey probably sometimes also kill Cattle Egrets in colonies and roosts, since in temperate areas other herons are sometimes killed by these birds.

Predation at the colonies

Monkeys were observed taking Cattle Egret eggs in South Africa. A very cold spring prevented fruit from ripening and hungry Vervet Monkeys, *Cercopithecus aethiops*, began to prey on eggs, causing the desertion of the colony. Having no more Cattle Egret eggs to eat, the monkeys went on to take the smaller eggs of the Masked Weaver (Skinner and Skinner 1975).

In Guiana, an unidentified hawk was seen eating the eggs of one of the uppermost Cattle Egret nests. The owner of the nest pecked at the hawk but was knocked away by flaps from its long tail. Later in the season, a Brazilian Hawk Eagle took up residence near the colony and killed many young herons (Lowe-McConnell 1967).

Predation on the foraging grounds

A New Zealand Falcon was reported to have killed a Cattle Egret by Fox (1975). Unfortunately, no details about the event were given other than noting surprise that the prey was a Cattle Egret. Apparently, it is not uncommon for a female falcon to take prey as large as the White-faced Heron, a bird rather larger than the Cattle Egret.

In Florida, a Red-tailed Hawk was seen in close pursuit of a flock of 6–7 Egrets. The hawk struck the last bird in the flock at a height of about 2 m and both birds fell to the ground. After a short period of time, the hawk carried the dead bird to a fence post and rested there for some minutes before flying up into a tree with its prey (Courser and Dinsmore 1971).

In the same region, a Peregrine Falcon trained to kill cotton rats, *Sigmodon hispidus*, took a Cattle Egret. Whenever the falcon approached, the Egrets hid under the cattle with whom they were foraging. Unfortunately, one of them which did not have time to hide was eventually caught (Carr, in Courser and Dinsmore 1971).

Table 10.   *Dimensions of Cattle Egret eggs (mm)*

Width		Length		Reference
Mean	Range	Mean	Range	
33.4	30.0–34.5	43.4	40.0–49.0	Weber (1975)
—	30.8–35.1	—	41.3–49.0	Dusi (1966)
33.7	31.5–38.2	46.6	42.0–52.0	Bowen (1962)

Table 11.   Hatching success of Cattle Egrets

% eggs which have disappeared	% eggs failing to hatch	Total egg mortality (%)	% mortality during hatching	% mortality during incubation and hatching	Reference
17.80	17.60	35.40	—	—	Blaker (1969)
13.14	17.40	30.54	—	—	Siegfried (1970)
—	—	12.50	—	—	Weber (1975)
4.00	6.10	—	4.90	11.00	Hafner (1977)
—	—	—	6.90	10.90	Jenni (1969)
—	—	—	—	85.20	Dusi and Dusi (1970)
—	—	—	—	32.10	Goering (1977)
—	—	—	—	42.00	Morel and Morel (1961)
—	—	—	—	38.00	Bowen (1962)

Table 12.   *Clutch size of Cattle Egrets*

Mean clutch size	No. of eggs per nest	Location	Latitude	Reference
4.60	3–7	Camargue, France	43°30'N	Hafner (1977)
3.40	—	New Jersey, USA	39°23'N	Burger (1978)
2.86	2–5	Cape Province, South Africa	33°60'S	Blaker (1969)
2.97 (outer)				
3.00 (inner)	1–6	Cape Province, South Africa	33°60'S	Siegfried (1970)
3.15 (central)				
2.42	—	Alabama, USA	31°12'N	Dusi and Dusi (1970)
3.50	1–6	Florida, USA	29°37'N	Jenni (1969)
2.90 and 2.78	—	Texas, USA	29°19'N	Goering (1977)
2.86	2–5	Florida, USA	27°00'N	Weber (1975)
3.00	1–5	Sénégal	16°00'N	Morel and Morel (1961)
2.60	1–5	Ghana	6°00'N	Bowen (1962)

Table 13. *Fledging success of Cattle Egrets*

Mean no. of fledglings ready to leave each nest	Location	Latitude	Reference
3.40 in 1975 3.80 in 1976	Camargue, France	43°30'N	Hafner (1977)
2.40 ± 0.90 at 2 weeks	New Jersey, USA	39°23'N	Burger (1978)
1.12	Cape Province, South Africa	33°60'S	Siegfried (1970)
0.36	Alabama, USA	31°12'N	Dusi and Dusi (1970)
3.20 ± 0.09	Florida, USA	29°37'N	Jenni (1969)
1.92	Texas, USA	29°19'N	Goering (1977)
1.80	Florida, USA	27°00'N	Weber (1975)
1.27	Ghana	6°00'N	Bowen (1962)

CHAPTER 14

The worldwide extension in the range of the Cattle Egret

The expansion in the distribution of the Cattle Egret is one of the first events of this type which it has been possible to study as it happened. The explosive phase of this process occurred principally between 1950 and 1970, but continues today albeit more slowly. However, the first stages of the expansion began in the last century. Cattle Egrets are very conspicuous birds and no experienced birdwatcher can possibly miss them for long. There are therefore reliable observations from the last century as well as the beginning of this century which enable us to reconstruct this extension in the range of the Cattle Egret from the very beginning.

The interest of this event lies in the fact that it is both a natural and a successful expansion. Usually, zoologists are only able to relate the decreasing ranges of different species, as habitats and resources deteriorate. In addition, this extension is most surprising since it has occurred in a particularly ancient family, whose native habitat has generally declined in quantity and quality.

THE SPREAD OF CATTLE EGRETS IN EUROPE

The extension in the range of the Cattle Egret in Europe has been slow. Some areas which seem quite favourable have yet to be colonized, such as the rice-growing areas of the Po valley in Italy. However, Cattle Egrets are not newcomers to Europe as they are to America. As long as there have been records, Cattle Egrets have been reported nesting in Andalucia. Since the mid-1960s, the only newly colonized areas have been in central and eastern Spain and the Camargue in France.

In Europe, Cattle Egret colonies are usually quite small and their population growth is slow, probably due to habitats made up of a patchwork of small areas of variable composition; the marshes are not very extended, the grazing herds not very large, and suitable hunting areas rather small.

SPAIN

During the last century, Cattle Egrets were certainly common in Andalucia. They fed among cattle on wet marshy grounds and migrated over the Strait of Gibraltar (Irby 1875). At that time, Cattle Egrets were also seen in southern Portugal (Rey 1872, Paulino d'Oliveira 1896).

In 1944, W.H. Riddell noted that Andalucia was the only part of Europe where Cattle Egrets were common and resident. He discovered a new colony of 2000–3000 nests established on tamarisks in an inundated area along a recently built irrigation dam and estimated the total number of colonies in Andalucia to be three, perhaps four.

In 1961, no change in the breeding range of Cattle Egrets was noted by F. Bernis, but observations of vagrant Cattle Egrets were becoming more and more frequent in Spain and Portugal. There was at that time, one big colony in Andalucia at Doñana, Huelva (in 1963, 2300 pairs of Cattle Egrets nested there) and 4–5 much smaller ones situated not far from the coast (Fernandez-Cruz 1975).

In August 1961, F. Bernis discovered a roosting place used by 175 Cattle Egrets near Merida in the province of Badajoz, which had been in use for 4–5 years. Some years later, the provinces of Badajoz and Cáceres were colonized by breeding Cattle Egrets. A colony discovered in the province of Cáceres in 1966 numbered 111 pairs (Fernandez-Cruz 1975). Another, discovered in the province of Badajoz in 1967 by J.L.P. Chiscano, numbered 35–40 nests.

In 1972, the number of colonies was about the same in Andalucia as 10 years previously, with one large colony and four smaller ones. The large colony at that time was "La Rocina" Almonte, Huelva (Voisin and Voisin, unpublished). V. Ree (1973) estimated the number of breeding pairs of Cattle Egrets at "La Rocina" to be about 2000 in 1971. They nested in a mixed colony with Little Egrets, Night Herons and Squacco Herons.

From 1971 to 1974, Cattle Egrets became well established in the province of Badajoz. J. L. P. Chiscano discovered three new colonies with 8 225 and 651 nests. Cattle Egrets were also well established in the province of Cáceres in

1974, with three colonies of 462, 260 and 818 pairs. Cattle Egrets also began to colonize the province of Toledo where 20–25 pairs nested in 1973 in a mixed colony with Little Egrets and Night Herons (Fernandez-Cruz 1975).

In the province of Valencia, an important colony of Little Egrets and Night Herons had been established for some years in the Lagoon of La Albufera. In 1972, a precise census there, revealed the presence of 550 Cattle Egret nests.

In 1973, two pairs of Cattle Egrets seem to have nested in a mixed colony in the province of Gerona in the northeast of Spain (Boada 1975).

In the delta of the Ebro, two colonies were found in 1977 and 1978 by Martinez and Martinez (1983). The colony of Alfacada is a mixed colony established on *Phragmites australis*. In 1978, it had 650 pairs of Cattle Egrets, 100 pairs of Squacco Herons, 50 pairs of Purple Herons and 12 pairs of Little Egrets. The colony of Isla de San Antonio contained about 300 pairs of Cattle Egrets (Ruiz *et al.* 1981). The nesting of Cattle Egrets in the delta had not been noticed before and seems to be a recent event. Since the mid-1960s, rice culture has developed rapidly with the consequence that the freshwater areas have steadily increased in extent. This change in the environment is particularly favourable to Cattle Egrets.

PORTUGAL

The fact that Cattle Egrets nested in Portugal, long since suspected by F. Bernis, was finally established in 1962, when a mixed colony of Little Egrets and Cattle Egrets was discovered south of Porto, near Aveiro. This colony contained about 288 Cattle Egret nests in 1965.

In 1968, an important mixed heronry comprising Little Egrets, Night Herons, Squacco Herons and Cattle Egrets was discovered near Colegà, northeast of Lisbon. Local people said that the colony had existed for many years; it seems to have been established between 1935 and 1940.

FRANCE

Since 1957, several unsuccessful nesting attempts by one or two pairs of Cattle Egrets have been observed in the Camargue. In 1966, two pairs bred successfully for the first time and raised nine young, and by 1970 a small population was nesting there. A total of 22 nests were recorded in three colonies and about 74 young were raised (Hafner 1970).

The Cattle Egret population continued to grow slowly until 1980. Then, in 1981, a marked reduction was noted (see Table 14). Because many Cattle Egrets remain in the Camargue during the winter, was it the cold winter of 1980–1981 that caused this reduction? Certainly about 30 dead birds were found during that winter (Hafner *et al.* 1982).

In about 1950, rice culture was developed in the Carmargue and rapidly gained in importance, with a maximum of 33000 hectares in production by 1961. These thousands of hectares of freshwater crops with their numerous irrigation ditches totally changed the nature of the Camargue which, since the dykes along the Rhône were constructed in 1869, had been a very salty and often dry area. Since 1973, rice culture has declined and the central lagoon (Vaccarès) has become more salty again, but the large irrigation system is still used for various crops (mostly wheat) and to inundate extensive shallow marshes which waterfowl hunters use in the autumn and winter. Horses and cattle are abundant in these areas. Here, as in many other places in the world, colonization by Cattle Egrets followed an important man-made change to the local environment (Voisin 1978). During the spring of 1981, seven observations of Cattle Egrets were made in the west of France and for the first time that spring two pairs nested successfully in Lac de Grand Lieu (Loire Atlantique). At least three young were raised (Marion 1982). Two years later, in 1983, 2–4 pairs nested successfully in Charente-Maritime (Bredin 1985). Did these birds come from the Camargue (vagrant Cattle Egrets have been observed in the Rhône valley) or from Spain, or were they released birds (or descendents of released birds) from Alsace?

The expansion of Cattle Egrets in Europe is not easy to follow as some heronries are artificial, like the fairly ancient one in Vienna (Bauer and Glutz 1966) and one or two in Alsace where about 100 birds were released, mostly at Kintsheim in 1970 and the years following (Marion 1982). In England, a few birds have escaped from captivity (Sharrock 1972). Cattle Egrets are accidental in Iceland, England, Belgium, the Netherlands, Denmark, Sweden, Hungary, Switzerland, Yugoslavia, Greece, Bulgaria, Romania, Malta, the Azores, Madeira and the Canary Islands (Cramp and Simmons 1977).

THE SPREAD OF CATTLE EGRETS IN SOUTH AFRICA

The Cattle Egret is not new to this country, but a very important extension in range and increase in population has occurred there and has been thoroughly studied by Skead (1952) and Siegfried (1965, 1966b).

Before 1875, Cattle Egrets were apparently permanent residents in the tropical and subtropical, high-rainfall areas. However, at about the turn of the century, a few widely scattered permanent colonies existed in the temperate regions along rivers and other waters. The most significant increase and spread of Cattle Egrets occurred between 1920 and 1940. The main factors causing this extension seem to have been the clearing of bush and woodlands leading to their conversion to grassland, and the ever increasing development of water conservation dams and irrigation systems.

The total adult Cattle Egret population counted at both nesting sites and roosts in the Cape Province during the nesting season of 1963–1964 was 102 200 birds (Siegfried 1966a).

THE SPREAD OF CATTLE EGRETS IN THE AMERICAS

Arrival

Never before in modern history has a bird appeared in the New World and become established without man's assistance. Why has this colonization occurred now and not before? There seem to be two main possible causes for such an event: the dispersal power of the Cattle Egret may have changed and/or the new environment colonized by the bird is more favourable than the ancient one. It seems unlikely that the behaviour of Cattle Egrets has changed in recent times.

The latest expansion of Cattle Egrets to the Falklands and Galapagos Islands, and the numerous observations from boats of Cattle Egrets over the Atlantic and Pacific Oceans, show that at least some individuals may fly out over the open sea without heading for any known destination. After breeding, Ardeidae are very erratic, especially the young ones. They often undertake quite significant dispersals in all directions before starting their autumn migration. Is the tendency to sometimes venture out over the open sea a new behaviour? There is no reason to think so. It is true that many Cattle Egrets have recently been reported from remote islands, but there are many reasons for this other than a change in their habits. As this species is now spread worldwide, there are always some individuals not so far from the remotest places and Cattle Egrets are certainly the most common heron today. As the population increases, the opportunities to observe the bird also increase. One important question arises: is it possible for Cattle Egrets to cross the Atlantic Ocean between Africa and the Americas? The journey has certainly been made by a Little Egret, a bird of comparable size, ringed in Spain and found later in Trinidad. In 1953, Haverschmidt wrote that "there is in my opinion no reason to doubt that the spread is a natural one". There had not been any introductions and there were not any zoos keeping these birds from which individuals could escape. Judging by the actual observations of Cattle Egrets in good condition on St Paul's Rock, Tristan da Cunha and Gough Island, it seems very likely that a group may have flown an even greater distance than to these islands, provided that wind conditions were favourable. The dominant winds just happen to blow from Morocco and Mauritania to the northern part of South America where Cattle Egrets were first seen in the Americas.

The earliest reports of Cattle Egrets in South America were made by Sir Everard im Thurn (report seen by J. Long, now lost) who observed them between 1877 and 1882 on the Dutch side of the Courantyne River (which forms the boundary between Surinam, formerly Dutch Guiana, and Guiana, formerly British Guiana), and by A.B.W. Long who had found them some years later (1911–1912) on the Essequibo coast, Guiana (V. Roth, in Bond 1957). Long reported that their number had built up in the backlands behind the coast, although even in 1925 they were scarce. A letter to Mr Phelps from a plantation owner on the Demerara River said that he had observed flocks of Cattle Egrets since 1930 (Lowe-McConnell 1967).

If the journey was possible once, it must certainly have been possible before. I think that now and then since ancient times some Cattle Egrets have made this flight. If this is the case, why did the birds not become established before? Of course, newcomers must not only survive, they must also breed successfully. Any population starting from only a few individuals must grow rapidly if it is not to be wiped out after only a few years. Siegfried has described the ancestral and most favourable habitat for Cattle Egrets and points out the importance to them of moist pastures along rivers where they follow grazing African buffaloes. No such biotope exists naturally in the Guianas, which are mostly covered with forest, deep swamps and coastal mangroves. Besides, the total absence of their favourite symbiont – large grazing mammals – increases the difficulty of them establishing themselves. In ancient times, Cattle Egrets could not have thrived in the Guianas. When the Dutch and English arrived there, they cleared the land, cut the forest down and developed a drainage system for their crops and pastures. This was carried out along the rivers first, on a very small scale. The small group of Cattle Egrets which happened to cross the ocean at the end of the eighteenth century found a suitable place to breed successfully and a small population became established, foraging on land cleared by the Dutch in Surinam and the English in Guiana. The importance of stock farming and crops such as rice for Cattle Egrets is well demonstrated by Haverschmidt's (1950) observations many years later:

> Now that I knew that this egret was numerous in the cultivated area on the right bank of the Surinam river I went searching for them in other places. It was found that the birds were equally common in the open fields on the left bank of the Surinam river, wherever there were cattle. . . . It became clear that *Bulbucus ibis* was in fact the most numerous heron in all cultivated areas between the Surinam and Saramaca rivers. It also occurs in other districts of the coastal region. . . . On May 5, 1947, there were at least 100 birds in the rice fields on the right bank of the Corantyjne river at Nieuw Nickerie.

Cattle Egrets seem to have spread quite rapidly, not only in the Guianas but also to other parts of South America.

During the World War, an Englishman, I.R.B. Cunninghame Graham, travelled through Colombia to undertake a survey of the cattle industry in connection with a projected meat-packing plant. In 1970 Graham published a book describing his journey. When riding along the lower Rio San Jorge en route from San Benito to Jégua, he noted:

> Sometimes the road ran on a narrow causeway between deep swamps where alligators basked in the sun. . . . At other times the trail passed shallower swamps on which fed cattle, standing up to their hocks in water and in mud. White ibises sat on the cattle's backs swaying to keep their balance, as a sailor sways upon a deck.

A. Wetmore (1963), who has brought this passage to the knowledge of ornithologists, is certain that the "White ibises" are Cattle Egrets, and indeed no other large white bird behaves in this way. The political events in Graham's book place the observation either in 1916 or 1917. However, at the end of last century, Cattle Egrets, though established in the Guianas, must have been very few and localized, as they had escaped the attention of important collectors such as the three Penard brothers, who collected birds in Surinam with the help of numerous assistants.

SOUTH AMERICA

The first specimen collected in the New World was taken by E. Blake in 1937 near Buxton on the coast of British Guiana (Blake 1939). This bird was not in the company of other Cattle Egrets but was feeding among Snowy Egrets, Tricolored and Little Blue Herons in a partially submerged rice field. In 1943, a specimen was collected in the state of Guarico, Venezuela. This bird was with three others on a prairie along the Apure River, many hundreds of miles from the coast.

By 1957, the range of the Cattle Egret almost covered the whole of Columbia (Lehmann 1959). Two colonies were discovered containing 300–350 and *c.* 500 nests. The biotope used by these Egrets is described as follows by Lehmann: "in Colombia these birds prefer dry country and recently planted rice paddies to marshy areas. The two colonies of breeding birds are found on solid ground with no marshes for several miles around, but both colonies are located above small artificial water supply channels". Here, as in Africa, Cattle Egrets are not shy. A group of 60 individuals is reported to have come to roost every night in the tallest trees of the main plaza of a small town called Popayan. On 3 December 1953, a Cattle Egret was shot near Irupana, Bolivia, on the east side of the Andean cordilliera at an altitude of 1950 m (Niethammer 1955).

Cattle Egrets were first reported from Peru by K. Slott, who saw four individuals in the company of feeding cattle on 22 October 1956 on the River Itaya near Iquitos in northeastern Peru. By 1964 in Peru, they had been recorded in the northern and southern jungle areas, on the central and southern high Andean plateau up to 4000 m and on the north and central coasts (Frazier 1964). Here, as in other countries, Cattle Egrets are usually found together with cattle. Frazier saw a flock of about 60 in March 1964 at Laguna de Pacca near Jauja in central Peru at an altitude of 3550 m. These birds were feeding on grassland among cattle and on swampy lake shores. However, their presence at such a high altitude seems to be sporadic (McFarlane 1975).

Some years later, Cattle Egrets were already numerous along the coast of Peru in the Atacama Desert. They reached the southern part of that area in 1968, when some individuals were seen at Mollendo, 17°S. The Atacama Desert of Peru and Chile extends for 23,000 miles. More than 40 rivers cross the desert in Peru and these, "with their associated irrigated farmlands, provide the only lowland habitat for herons and egrets" (McFarlane 1975). The fact that Cattle Egrets appeared inland in Bolivia and Peru, near Irupana and Iquitos, before being observed along the coastal lowlands, shows that they probably reached these countries by following the rivers of the Amazon basin.

The first report from Chile came from the coastal town of Antofagasta in January 1969. One bird was on the shore with a pair of Snowy Egrets (Post

1970). In 1972 and 1973, however, McFarlane could not find a single Cattle Egret in Chile. He looked for them chiefly in the Atacama Desert, in the Taracapa area and in the mountains. The southward progression of Cattle Egrets seems thus to have been halted in southern Peru. The Taracapa area in northern Chile is the driest part of the Atacama and a number of species do not cross this region but reach their southern distributional limits in south-western Peru. It might thus take some time for Cattle Egrets to expand to the other side of this natural barrier.

Cattle Egrets have also spread southwards along the east coast of South America. In Brazil, they nest in the Amazon Delta (Cramp and Simmons 1977). H. Sick saw Cattle Egrets near Brasilia in 1971 (Sick, in Belton 1974). On 16 September 1973, W. Belton (1974) observed a flock of Cattle Egrets feeding with a small herd of cattle in a rice field and cattle grazing area, lying between Camaqua, Rio Grande do Sul and the Lagoa dos Patos (31°06'S, 51°41'W).

In Argentina, the first Cattle Egrets were observed by M.A.E. Rumboll on the 2 August 1969 on the Rio Salado near Firmat (33°29'S, 61°29'W), in the province of Santa Fé (Rumboll and Canevari 1975). A few months later, in April 1970, some individuals were seen at Trenque Leuquén (35°56'S, 62°43'W), in the province of Buenos Aires. During December 1972, the first Cattle Egret nests were discovered by S. Narosky (1973) in a mixed colony near the town of Azul, in the province of Buenos Aires. There were three nests in a colony of Snowy Egrets, Great White Egrets, White-faced Ibis and Roseate Spoonbill at "la Laguna de Burgos".

In 1973 and 1974, there were numerous observations of Cattle Egrets in the provinces of Santa Fé and Buenos Aires and a few in the province of Cordoba. The birds were mostly seen between September and October and between February and April, but there were observations from all seasons. By 1974, records commonly concerned many hundreds of birds at a time. On 26 February 1974, P.J. Canevari counted 1000 Cattle Egrets between Nueve de Julio and Las Flores (Buenos Aires province) and it is most likely that Cattle Egrets already nested there in some numbers. In July 1973, two birds were seen in the province of Corrientes (northeast of the province of Santa Fé) and in October 1974 a group of 60 birds was observed there.

The provinces in Argentina where Cattle Egrets have so far established themselves – Corrientes, Santa Fé, East Cordoba and Buenos Aires – have warm, rainy summers and not very cold winters; but the hard climate of Patagonia is not far away, with its dry, cold weather and strong winds. It begins in the Chubut and extends southwards to Tierra del Fuego. Despite this harsh climate, Cattle Egrets have spread southwards into Patagonia. In 1974, small groups were seen by Rumboll and Shaw in April and May at Wiedma, Rio Negro, at Punta Tumbo, Chubut, at Rio Gallego, Santa Cruz and at Rio Grande, Tierra del Fuego.

In the Falkland Islands, Cattle Egrets were recorded for the first time on 29 April 1976 (Strange 1979) when three birds were seen feeding along the shoreline at Stanley. In 1977, eight birds were seen; in 1978, 75–100 and in 1979, 250 birds. They were mostly in good condition but some were not and died shortly after their arrival. A surprising fact is that all the observations of

Cattle Egrets here were during the autumn migration, from March to July. Perhaps the birds arriving in the Falkland Islands are those trying to escape the hard winter in Patagonia. Some perhaps fly northwards from Patagonia to winter, but others seem to fly eastwards. Do they survive? I.J. Strange wrote: "On the night of 28 April 1977 a severe snow storm hit Stanley, after which there were no further sightings of Cattle Egrets that year" and "1 July 1978: one bird was living about a settlement until this date, when a very severe snow storm hit Falklands. Not seen since." In 1979, one Cattle Egret was seen on King George Island, South Shetland (*c.* 62°S), a little more than 1000 km south of the Falklands by R.P. Schlatter (1980).

NORTH AMERICA

In Florida, an important change in stock management seems to have occurred during the decade prior to the arrival of the first Cattle Egrets. A. Carr (in Siegfried 1966) noted:

> In the early thirties of this century it was still about the same; the beef was lank and fatless and the herons were in the ponds. Then all at once the land began to change. A new sort of ranching grew up, with fences and pure-bred stock and planted pastures . . . and pretty soon all over northern Florida, fat cows were being gentled on a new kind of tented lawn.

Favourable foraging areas were thus created before the arrival of the Cattle Egrets, which appeared first in small numbers and remained unnoticed for many years.

The first time Cattle Egrets were seen in the USA was during the summer of 1941 or 1942. Two individuals were observed feeding in a marshy pasture near Clewiston, Florida by W.E. Dilly. Thinking that the birds were escapees, he did not report his sighting (Sprunt 1954). It seems that from 1946 or 1947 up to 1949, a group of Cattle Egrets was often seen feeding in an area south of Lake Okeechobee, but they disappeared from the area after a hurricane. S.A. Grimes got this information in 1954 during a Cattle Egret population survey (Sprunt 1954). In 1951, a single individual was seen in New Jersey.

In 1952, near Lake Okeechobee, R. Borden photographed what he thought were Snowy Egrets, but were later correctly identified as Cattle Egrets. From that summer onwards, ornithologists began to look in particular for Cattle Egrets and there were many observations in Florida that year. During the autumn of 1952, an individual was taken aboard a fishing boat off the Grand Banks of Newfoundland (Sprunt 1956) and two others were seen – and one taken – in Massachusetts that same year.

During 1953, the number of reports of Cattle Egrets observed in Florida grew. The first nests were found by S. A. Grimes and G. Chandler (Sprunt 1954) in May in a heronry on King's Bar, an island in Lake Okeechobee. Four birds were observed feeding on mudflats along the coast of Key West. Not at all shy, these birds occasionally crossed the street to drink in a freshwater pond. During that year, the species was observed in Virginia in May, in

Bermuda in November and in Maine in December (the last bird was surely starving as it was taken by a farmer while "disturbing" chickens).

In 1954, Cattle Egrets nested for the first time at Lake Alice on the campus of the University of Florida in Gainesville (Rice 1956). An initial population of seven birds hatched 3–4 broods of young in a large mixed heron and ibis colony.

In 1956, Cattle Egrets were for the first time reported breeding outside Florida, in North Carolina, South Carolina and Louisiana. New sight records were reported from New Hampshire, Rhode Island, New York, Maryland, Texas and Illinois (Sprunt 1956), and the species was also reported from Ontario in that year (Devitt 1962). In 1957, a specimen was taken in Alabama and in 1960 three birds were taken in Mississippi (Williams 1961). In 1962, several nests were found in Ontario (Baillie 1963, Buerkle and Mansell 1963).

A total of 110 pairs of Cattle Egrets nested in Florida in 1956, and only a few pairs bred in North and South Carolina and Louisiana. Ten years later, in 1966, 10 000 pairs nested in the eastern states, from Florida to New Jersey (Schûz and Kuhl 1972). In 1959, 10 pairs were reported nesting in Texas, and by 1966 there were 20 000 pairs breeding in that state. In 1963, they began to breed in Oklahoma (Crosby 1972).

It took some years before the birds extended their breeding range into the central part of the USA and Canada. In 1976, they began to breed in North Dakota (Serr 1976), in 1978 they were nesting in Idaho (Rodgers 1978) and in 1981 in Saskatchewan at Old Wives Lake (Gollop 1981). Further northwards, Cattle Egrets were seen, and one bird taken, in the Northwest Territories in May 1972 (Kuyt 1972).

The species reached the west coat of the USA in 1964. On 7 March, two immature females were seen feeding among cattle at Imperial Beach, San Diego (McCaskie 1965). In 1977, 5000 pairs bred at Salton Sea and in 1978 they established one more colony further north. In 1980, Cattle Egrets were vagrant in Oregon, Washington, British Colombia and Vancouver Island (Roberson 1982).

In 1983, in the USA and Canada, Cattle Egrets bred locally in California, southern Idaho, northern Utah, Colorado, North Dakota, southern Saskatchewan, Minnesota, Wisconsin, southern Ontario, northern Ohio and Maine through Middle America, the Gulf and Atlantic states. The birds bred primarily in coastal lowlands, being very scattered in inland localities (American Ornithologists' Union 1983).

In 1959, Cattle Egrets were introduced to Hawaii from Florida to control flies (Breese 1959). A total of 105 birds were released on the main islands (40 on Oahu, 25 on Kauai and between 12 and 32 on the other islands). From this original stock and other, smaller releases in 1960 and 1961, the population grew rapidly on Oahu, which has a particularly large human population, a large breeding stock and much agriculture, but grew more slowly on the other islands. On Kauai, fewer than 25 birds were counted during each census up to the winter of 1975 when 296 were observed. Birds move between islands in Hawaii, so it may have been migrants from the Oahu population that initiated this onset of population growth on Kauai, where Cattle Egrets nest in mixed colonies with Redfooted Boobies (Byrd *et al.* 1980).

CENTRAL AMERICA AND THE WEST INDIES

This species appeared in Central America in 1954 when two birds were seen in the company of cattle in the Panama Canal Zone (Eisenmann 1955). Some other birds were seen later that year in the same area during the autumn migration. On 3 December 1954, the species was observed for the first time in Costa Rica, at a cattle ranch in the province of Guanacaste (Slud 1957). The northward movement through Central America continued with specimens taken in 1958 in both Guatemala (Land 1963) and southern Mexico (Dickerman 1964). According to Wolfe (1961), Cattle Egrets seem to have become well established in Mexico by the early 1960s. They had been sighted from as far as Teapa (Andrle and Axtell 1961) and Villahermosa (Wolfe 1961) in the south to Tampico in the north (Wolfe 1961). The first nest was found near Minatitlan, Veracruz, in May 1963 by Dickerman (1964). By that time, the species had become widespread in southern Mexico and along the Gulf's coastal lowlands, and was dispersing inland.

It had reached the west coast of Mexico, possibly by the Isthmus of Tchuantepec, by 10 April 1964 when Edwards (1965) photographed it there. The first specimen from the Pacific coast was taken in 1965 in Chiapas, Mexico (Hubbard 1966). As early as 2 November 1964, the first Cattle Egret was observed by M. Castro in new farmland on one of the Galapagos Islands. Later, 2–3 birds were seen on 11, 12 and 20 November 1964 (Lévêque *et al.* 1966).

In 1971 and 1972, Zimmermann (1973) reported numerous sightings in northern and western Mexico. The two first records from Baja California are a sight record made by A.J. Sloan in 1964 and a newspaper photograph which showed a lone Cattle Egret on board a sport fishing boat near Punta San Isidoro in 1967 (Hubbs 1968).

Cattle Egrets were not reported in the West Indies until 21 February 1955 when G.A. Seaman observed a flock of 26 birds in a pasture with cattle at Sprat Hall, St Croix, Virgin Islands, where an immature male specimen was taken (Seaman 1955). In November 1956, 20 Cattle Egrets were found feeding with steers in Jamaica (Bond 1957). During that same year, the species also appeared on Haiti (Owre 1959). In 1957, the birds were nesting on St Croix where four nests were reported (Seaman 1958). They also nested on Cuba that year and 50 nests were observed to be under construction (Smith 1958). In 1966, they nested in numbers on Trinidad. Unfortunately, French (1966) did not know when they began to nest on the island. On Guadeloupe, one Cattle Egret was seen among goats in 1969 (Guth 1971).

DISPERSAL PATTERNS: NEW MIGRATION ROUTES IN THE AMERICAS

Between 1877 and 1943, Cattle Egrets colonized and built up a large population in Surinam, British Guiana, Colombia and Venezuela. Lowe-

PLATE 1
Top: Little Bittern. Bottom: Bittern.

PLATE 2
Top: Night Heron. Centre: Squacco Heron. Bottom: Cattle Egret.

PLATE 3
Top: Great White Egret. Bottom: Little Egret (left in breeding plumage, right in juvenile plumage).

PLATE 4
Top: Grey Heron. Bottom: Purple Heron.

McConnell (1967) has pointed out that heron populations grew more rapidly in wet years and she noted that during the 1940s and the beginning of the 1950s, the largest cycle of wet years was recorded since the start of meteorological observations in Guiana in 1880. It thus seems that Cattle Egrets were very abundant in the Guianas coincident with their rapid spread throughout the Americas.

Between 1952 and 1955, they colonized Florida. Their most important range extension occurred between 1954 and 1958, when they appeared along the western coast of South America, in Central America, the West Indies and along the eastern coast of the USA reaching Canada. Since the invasion of Florida occurred earlier than that of Mexico, the birds do not seem to have come from Mexico but rather in direct flights from South America to Florida over the Caribbean Sea.

During 1959 and 1960, the states of the Gulf, Mississippi and Texas, were colonized. Did the birds come from Mexico, from Florida or from both places? In 1964, Cattle Egrets appeared on the western coast of Mexico, probably by flying over the Isthmus of Tehuantepec. That same year they were seen in Baja California and the Galapagos. In the 1970s, Brazil, Argentina and the Falklands were occupied in South America and the central states in North America. In the 1980s, Cattle Egrets began to appear along the western coast, north of California.

Post-nuptial wandering in young Ardeidae is a well-known phenomenon. It is useful for the young birds to disperse away from the often overcrowded foraging areas around the colony. Most birds move only 50–100 km away from the colony, but some fly long distances in a direction that is the opposite of the migration route. If they find a place suitable for wintering, they may stay there and, if numerous, nest in the area the following spring. Usually, however, particularly if the distance is great, the number of Cattle Egrets is not great and colonization does not occur so quickly. If the site is not suitable for wintering, the birds must subsequently migrate. Such places can only be colonized by birds seeking new nesting territories in the spring. Are they following other heron species on their migration route? This is most probable. Cattle Egrets have, for example, often been observed foraging with Snowy Egrets. Do they remember locations visited during their post-nuptial wandering and return in the spring to suitable spots, followed perhaps by other Cattle Egrets? This seems most likely, since before a place is colonized, a number of individuals have usually been observed there in previous years. In this way, it is probable that post-nuptial wandering is a useful means of establishing colonies in new areas.

However, many birds that leave the colony in the autumn to wander, may find the conditions too harsh to survive. This seems to be the case for those birds appearing on the Falkland Islands. All of the observations of Cattle Egrets made there have been during the autumn from March to July. The birds which leave the Falklands during good weather before the snowstorms, probably continue on their way eastwards; however, there is no land in that direction! The last sighting each year of Cattle Egrets seems to be just prior to the first Antarctic snowstorm. As the snowstorms arrive, the birds that leave have to follow the wind. Are they able to survive the storm? Do they alter their flight to a westwardly direction, flying back to South America when the storm has blown out? It is doubtful that there are any survivors.

A report by F. Williams (in Browder 1973) suggests that among the rapidly expanding Cattle Egret population, quite a number perish at sea while exploring new migration routes:

> Two research vessels were touring an area of the eastern tropical Pacific in November and December of 1971 when 11 separate sightings of Cattle Egrets, each involving from 1 to 24 birds, were made. Totalling 106 individuals, they were sighted in an area between 6° and 13°N and 115° and 121°W, at least 1100 miles from the nearest mainland (southern California). The nearest land mass, Clipperton Island, was several hundred miles away. Many emaciated birds landed on the ships. Directions of two permanent departures of birds from the ships were noted. A flock of 15 left around midnight of 12 November, disappearing toward the south. One egret, leaving 26 November, flew toward the west-northwest.

The new migration route over the Caribbean Sea has been studied in detail at the Dry Tortugas, a group of small coral islands on the northern edge of the Florida Strait (24°30′N, 83°W). Cattle Egrets that do not remain in Florida during the winter migrate south over the Caribbean Sea, some stopping at the Dry Tortugas. The first known observation of Cattle Egrets on these islands was in 1958 (Abramson 1960). The new migration route over the Dry Tortugas was clearly established by Browder (1973) and Harrington and Dinsmore (1975). Browder stated that "Flights of Cattle Egrets have been observed entering the Dry Tortugas from the north and departing toward the southwest in the fall", while Harrington and Dinsmore observed the spring migration:

> All the egret flocks we have seen arriving at the Tortugas were in the afternoon and were coming from the west or southwest. Spring movement away from the atoll is almost always toward the east. The times of arrival, the apparent weakness of some birds, and the direction of flight all suggest that many of the egrets that stop at Dry Tortugas may be arriving on flight from Central America.

In 1962, R.L. Cunningham (1965) noted the unusual behaviour of Cattle Egrets on the Dry Tortugas. They were capturing small birds such as Blackpoll Warblers and Myrtle Warblers. All of the birds were in fact starving, and the larger Cattle Egrets were unable to catch sufficient numbers of warblers to prevent starvation. Some years later, Browder (1973) weighed 16 dead Cattle Egrets, all obviously emaciated. The birds weighed from 156.8 to 201.1 g (cf. normal weight of 360 g). Browder thought that the islands probably acted as "an energy sink": the birds getting more and more emaciated each day they stayed there and becoming at last too weak to leave at all. Harrington and Dinsmore's (1975) observations seem to confirm this assumption:

> The daily counts show that many egrets stopping at the Tortugas remain there for only brief periods, and sightings of travelling birds showed that some do not stop

at all. We believe but cannot prove, that most of the mortality that occurred was in birds that remained at the islands for several days during which time they slowly starved.

However, the highly opportunistic Cattle Egrets learned to utilize new food supplies available during the end of May and the beginning of June. In 1968, J.J. Dinsmore did not observe any predation of Sooty Tern chicks by Cattle Egrets on Bush Key, but in 1970 Cattle Egrets were feeding largely on them.

THE SPREAD OF CATTLE EGRETS IN AUSTRALIA AND NEW ZEALAND

Cattle Egrets first invaded the north of Australia, coming probably as wintering birds from China or Japan, perhaps with a stopover in New Guinea where Cattle Egrets were reported by Mayr (1941) as a rare winter visitor.

The Northern Territory has a small human population and the habitats in which breeding Cattle Egrets establish themselves during the wet season are difficult to investigate. Frith and Davies wrote (1961): "Swamps develop in the wet season on large areas of subcoastal plains, which are inundated for several months each season." The rivers are bordered by monsoon forest with "dense, broadleaved, often deciduous trees comprising several layers . . . lianas are numerous." Here as in the Guianas, Cattle Egrets could begin to nest unnoticed.

In 1950, J.M. Hewitt (1960) tried to discover when Cattle Egrets were first seen in the Northern Territory. O. Herbert, who lived in Koolpinyah near Darwin, remembered "white birds with brown markings that used to feed among cattle, and perch on their backs as long ago as 1907", the year he came to Koolpinyan.

In fact, this northernmost part of Australia, with its mangrove forests and deep swamps during the wet season and lack of extensive wet grasslands and big grazing herds, did not really suit Cattle Egrets. However, as early as the 1840s, the first buffaloes were introduced to Port Essington near Darwin (Serventy and Wittell 1962). As farmers began to breed cattle, they had to clear suitable grazing areas. The open grassland was maintained in a very wet, even slightly inundated state for most of the year to best suit the buffaloes. The period in the year when rich and inundated grassland was available was thus increased. As in the Guianas, man changed the landscape, creating the most suitable habitats for Cattle Egrets – shallow inundated grasslands with grazing herds of buffaloes. It is not exactly clear when Cattle Egrets began to breed in the area, though it seems probable that it was at the end of the nineteenth century.

In 1933, 18 Cattle Egrets of the Asian subspecies *B. i. coromandus* were introduced near Derby, Western Australia. After liberation, the birds "gradually disappeared" from the locality where they had been released (Serventy and Wittell 1962). Did some of them find the Cattle Egrets of Darwin 1000 km to the northeast? The introduced birds were so few and the subspecies apparently already so well established in the north, that if they disappeared without breeding or if some joined the birds in the Northern Territory it cannot have had any real influence on the spread of the species in Australia.

When first reported by a scientist, Cattle Egrets were already numerous. It was in 1948, H.G. Deignan of the National Geographic-Smithsonian Institution Arnhem Land Expedition saw hundreds in the Oenpelli District (Deignan 1964). Knowing that large numbers of Cattle Egrets had been seen in 1948, Frith and Davies (1961) sought-out a colony during the wet season of 1957 from a low-flying aircraft. They found large rookeries on the Adelaide and Mary Rivers. The big Adelaide River colony numbered 10,000 nests, most with incubating birds. No other species of bird was present in the colony at that time, though later several thousand Pied Herons, Little Egrets and White Egrets also nested there. A few nests of Plumed Egrets, ibises and cormorants were also observed.

The first nesting Cattle Egrets to be reported in Australia were not the ones nesting on the Adelaide River, but six breeding pairs found in a mixed heronry (300 White Egrets, Little Pied Cormorants and Little Black Cormorants) in 1954 at the Ulmarra Swamps some 8 miles east of Grafton on the Clarence River in northeastern New South Wales (Goddard 1955).

In 1979, there were five colonies in New South Wales with a total of 2300 breeding pairs (Morris, in Pratt 1979). At that time, a number of colonies were also established in southeastern Queensland, especially in the Brisbane area (Pratt 1979). Nowadays, Cattle Egrets breed in the Northern Territory, in Queensland and in New South Wales.

Vagrant individuals were observed from a very early date in Victoria. The first Cattle Egret was reported to have been seen in 1949 at Cororooke, near Lake Colac (Brown 1949). Also that year, one bird was seen in Western Australia, in a horse paddock at Millstream Station on the Fortescus River. One bird was observed at Three Springs in 1952 and one in the Perth area in 1954 (Serventy and Wittell 1962). As early as 1959, a conspicuous irruption of Cattle Egrets in eclipse plumage occurred in the southwest of Western Australia (Jenkins 1960). Nowadays, Cattle Egrets are regular winter visitors to the coastal areas of Australia, arriving in April–May and departing in early November.

The first Cattle Egret to be seen in New Zealand was sighted near Belfast on a dairy farm on 29 September 1963 (Turbot *et al.* 1963). However, some vagrant birds were probably present on the islands before that time. B. Brown (1980) reported that Mr C. and Mrs M. Hamann told her of "seeing a small flock of about five white herons with cattle near Nelson in the early 1950s". These birds reminded them of the Cattle Egrets they knew so well from South Africa.

National counts were undertaken in late August between 1977 and 1980. The number of Cattle Egrets wintering in New Zealand were: 293 in 1977, 266 in 1978, 624 in 1979 and 771 in 1980.

The birds have a regular pattern of arrival (mainly April–May) and departure (mainly October–November) coinciding with movements in eastern Australia:

Arrival especially being prominent, widespread on the west, and in places where the birds do not stay, including some unexpected places such as far to the south of

New Zealand. A bird with a bright metal band was seen for several days in Southland in early April 1981 and no birds have been banded in New Zealand. Several were beach-wrecked on the western coasts in the arrival period, including one that had been banded as a chick in New South Wales 4 months earlier. The birds then assembled in traditional wintering places, where they remained for 4 months. Although most had gone by mid-November, a surprising number stayed through to December, and some oversummered in New Zealand each year. Breeding in New Zealand is not known and there is no evidence to suggest that it has occurred (Heather 1982).

In March 1980, shortly after leaving Sydney, seven Cattle Egrets were noted following a ship. They stayed with it intermittently landing on board until 4 March when they left it a few miles from Farewell Spit, New Zealand (Jenkins 1981).

The unusual feeding behaviour of Cattle Egrets in New Zealand described by Heather (1982) – loose association with cattle, searching for food near grain silos and in newly opened hay bales – suggests that they have difficulty finding enough food, and it is perhaps this factor that prevents their nesting there.

Table 14. *The number of Cattle Egret nests in the Camargue, France*

Year	No. of nests	Year	No. of nests
1969	2	1977	308
1970	22	1978	319
1971	26	1979	314
1972	56	1980	464
1973	52	1981	283
1974	98	1982	468
1975	128	1983	407
1976	172		

After Résèrve Nationale de Camargue (1987).

CHAPTER 15

The Grey Heron *Ardea cinerea*

GENERAL APPEARANCE AND FIELD CHARACTERS

The Grey Heron is the largest European heron, standing 90–98 cm high with a wing-span of 175–195 cm.

Plumage. The sexes are alike, and the general colour of the plumage is grey, white and black.

Adult: the head is white marked by a line of black loose feathers on the side of the crown, which goes from over each eye to the back of the crown, which is also black. Two to three black feathers on the hindcrown are elongated during the breeding season. They are 80–120 mm long but are often not full grown even by March or April. The forehead and the centre of the crown are white with feathers (often 60–70 mm long) that cover the middle part of the black feathers of the hindcrown. The chin and throat are white. The neck is pale grey except for the central part of the foreneck, which is white with heavy black streaks on each side, caused by grey and white feathers which have a black patch on the distal part of each inner web. On the chest, these feathers and the white median ones are elongated, particularly during breeding. The primaries, primary coverts, alula and most of the secondaries are black; the

e blue-grey. The upperwing-coverts are blue-grey. The
marginal coverts and some of the lesser coverts at the carpal joint are white.
The underwing is grey. The mantle, back, rump and tail are blue-grey. The
whitish grey feathers of the mantle and of the scapulars are elongated, each
feather being split into several lanceolated points. These feathers are more
developed during breeding. On each side of the white breast, the Grey Heron
has a conspicuous black shoulder-patch. A black line separates the grey flanks
from the white abdomen. The undertail-coverts and thighs are white.

Juvenile: more uniformly grey than the adult with a brownish tinge. The
forehead and crown are dark grey. Only the feathers of the back of the crown
are black. The sides of the head and neck (except the middle of the foreneck)
are grey. The chin, throat and the middle of the foreneck are white. The
foreneck and chest have dark brown streaks, broader than those of the adult
such that the bird appears more mottled. The white elbows are marked with
brown. A buff morph sometimes occurs which may be confused with the
juvenile Purple Heron (Cramp and Simmons 1977). The primaries, primary
coverts and alula are black as in the adult bird. The underparts are whitish
grey.

After a partial moult in September–December, the upper parts become
more grey and the underparts more white, the brown coloration tending to
disappear. After a new moult in May–June, the juvenile becomes more like
the adult, the streaks on the foreneck and chest
becoming black. But it is only at 2 years of age
that the Grey Heron acquires the black
shoulder-patches, the black lines along the
flanks and the elongated feathers, though fewer
and shorter than those of older birds. The forehead and middle of the crown of 2-year-olds
are often still whitish grey and not pure white
as they will become later (Curry-Lindahl 1957,
Bauer and Glutz 1966).

Downy young: the down is long on the
crown where it stands erect, and on the
upperparts and flanks. It is brown-grey with
white and silver-grey ends on the upperparts,
and whitish on the underparts. At 14 days, the
quills are plainly visible and by about 17 days
they are breaking out. At 20 days, the pattern
of the plumage emerges. The neck markings are
visible and the primary quills have nearly an
inch of web.

Bare parts

Adult: the bill and iris are yellow. The legs
and feet are dull brown with a variable amount
of yellow on the back of the tarsus and tibia.
The lores are yellow, tinged with green around
the eyes. The bill, iris and lores become pale to

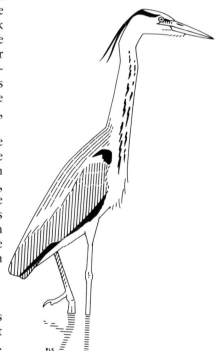

A Grey Heron walking.

deep red during pair-formation. The legs and feet also redden at this time where they are not too darkly coloured.

Juvenile: the iris is yellow. The upper mandible is slate-coloured, becoming yellow as the bird grows older. The lower mandible is yellow. The legs are dark grey, "paler and with yellow green tinge at joint and on bare part of tibia. In spring of the 2nd calendar year red tinges may appear as in the adult, often more pronounced in male than in females" (Cramp and Simmons 1977).

Downy young: the skin is grey-green and, according to Lowe (1954), the throat is orange-yellow. At 10 days, the orange-yellow area on the throat is down-covered. The iris is grey-green (Voisin, unpublished) or white, becoming pale yellow (Lowe 1954). The upper mandible is horn-coloured becoming pale yellow. At 20 days, the upper mandible is still slate-coloured and the lower mandible yellow (Lowe 1954).

Field characters. In the field, the Grey Heron is a very easy bird to recognize. The adult, standing at the edge of a lake or wading slowly in the water, shows a sharp contrast between the white, grey and black coloration of the plumage. The total absence of rufous tones distinguishes it from the Purple Heron *Ardea purpurea* as well as from the Great Blue Heron *Ardea herodias*. The juvenile Grey Heron has a much duller plumage, in which grey predominates, the white and black areas being much less extended, and with dark brown marks on the foreneck and belly. The white elbows are marked with, and are even sometimes entirely, rufous. It is important to remember that albino or discoloured adults and juveniles are relatively frequent in this species and may confuse inexperienced observers. The flight silhouette of the Grey Heron is characterized, as in all herons, by a retracted head and an "S"-shaped neck creating a bulge. Storks, Cranes and Flamingoes fly with extended necks.

In flight, at dusk or in bad weather, the Grey Heron may be confused with the Purple Heron, though it is a larger bird with a more massive body and longer wings. Seen from underneath, as is usual, the Purple Heron appears as a wholly dark bird, while the lighter-coloured Grey Heron shows a contrast between the grey wings and the white neck and belly. However, this contrast is usually not sharp, the white colour appearing rather dull in poor light.

Immature Grey Herons appear less brown than immature Purple Herons. The Great Blue Heron from North America has never yet been observed in Europe. If one were to appear as a vagrant, both adults and immatures are easy to distinguish from the Grey Heron by their cinnamon-coloured thighs. They also have a more or less prominent rufous tinge on the neck, belly and front edges of the wings. In Europe, there is no certain record of the Black-headed Heron, *Ardea melanocephala*, from tropical Africa. If such vagrancy occurs, it must be very exceptional, since this bird must first cross the desert and then the Mediterranean Sea to reach Europe. The Black-headed Heron appears slimmer than the Grey Heron and its narrow head, nearly as thin as its neck, gives the bird a slightly reptilian look. In adults, the black of the forehead and neck is very distinctive as are, in flight, the white underwing-coverts. The immature has a brownish grey neck like the Grey Heron but lacks the dark streaking on the foreneck and breast. The underwing-coverts are white as in adult birds.

Measurements. The measurements (mm) of adult birds taken from skins are given below. The number of skins and the sex are indicated. Standard deviations are given in parentheses. The sex differences are significant (Cramp and Simmons 1977).

wing	20 ♂♂ 440–485 (12.20)	12 ♀♀ 428–463 (9.77)
tail	20 ♂♂ 161–187 (7.21)	12 ♀♀ 157–174 (4.89)
bill	26 ♂♂ 110–131 (5.76)	19 ♀♀ 101–123 (5.06)
tarsus	23 ♂♂ 136–172 (8.14)	16 ♀♀ 132–153 (5.74)
toe	8 ♂♂ 101–116 (5.44)	5 ♀♀ 96–104 (3.56)

Witherby *et al.* (1939) recorded smaller minimum lengths for the wing (♂ 430, ♀ 425) and bill (♂ 100, ♀ 100). These measurements were probably taken from juveniles. However, the differences between juveniles and adults are not generally great. Though most juveniles are similar in size to adults, occasionally particularly small juveniles are found which are smaller than the smallest adult (Bauer and Glutz 1966). In a more eastern population, Spangenberg (in Dementiev and Gladkov 1951) recorded larger birds: longest wing, ♂ 490 mm, ♀ 475 mm.

The weight of Grey Herons is subject to great variations depending on the availability of food. Cramp and Simmons (1977) weighed adult birds in the Netherlands (range and mean): 17 ♂♂ 1071–2073 g (1505 g), 13 ♀♀ 1020–1785 g (1361 g). In Italy, Moltoni (1936) weighed breeding birds: 7 ♂♂ 1650–1890 g, 6 ♀♀ 1380–1700 g. A very emaciated bird may weigh only 810 g and a particularly fat male 2300 g (Bauer and Glutz 1966).

The mean wing-beat rate of the Grey Heron has been calculated as 142 wing-beats per minute by Cooper (1971).

DISTRIBUTION, MOVEMENTS AND HABITAT

GEOGRAPHICAL VARIATION

There are four recognized subspecies. *A. c. cinerea* Linnaeus has been described above. *A. c. jouyi* Clark is paler on the neck and the upperwing-coverts than the nominate subspecies, and it has a population that is probably clinal with many populations in Asia intermediate in colour between *A. c. cinerea* and *A. c. jouyi* (Vaurie 1965). *A. c. monicae* Jouanin and Roux is very pale, the sides of the neck being pure white, the black on the breast and chest much reduced, and the upperwing-coverts pale grey to white (Jouanin and Roux 1963). Finally, *A. c. firasa* Hartert is quite like *A. c. cinerea*, but has a heavier and longer bill and a longer tarsus.

BREEDING AND WINTERING AREAS

A. c. cinerea breeds from the British Isles, Norway (to 69°N), the southern third of Sweden, and south Finland, east across the USSR to Ussuriland and

Sakhalin, and south to Spain, France, Italy, the Balkans, Egypt, Turkey, Iran, Russian Turkestan, India and Sri Lanka. It also breeds in scattered localities in Africa; in north Africa, Nigeria, Uganda, southeastern and southern Africa (Curry-Lindahl 1981). The breeding areas are more numerous in east and southern Africa than in west Africa where there are very few. It winters from the British Isles and central Europe south to Africa, and east to Iran, Baluchistan and India. It has been reported in Iceland, the Faeroes, Spitsbergen, Greenland and on Ascension Island, and has even wandered as far afield as Martinique, the Lesser Antilles, Trinidad and Brazil.

A. c. jouyi breeds from Mongolia, northern China, Korea and Japan in the north, south to southern China and Thailand. There are breeding colonies in the Malay Peninsula and Indonesia. The birds winter in the southern part of this area, in Indochina, the Philippines and Taiwan. There are three records from Australia and one from New Zealand.

A. c. monicae is restricted to the Banc d'Arguin off Mauritania where it breeds and from where some individuals may wander into Sénégal.

A. c. firasa is restricted to Madagascar. The population of Grey Herons on Aldabra Island seems intermediate between *firasa* and *cinerea* (Benson and Penny 1971).

MOVEMENTS

A great many ringed recoveries have provided data on the rather complex movements of the various Grey Heron populations. Before their true migration, Grey Herons – especially young ones – disperse in all directions, southwest usually prevailing. In June, recoveries are most frequent within 150 km of the colony, in July within 200 km, in August within 250 km and in September within 300 km (Rydzewski 1956). However, these distances are highly variable, since there are great differences between both individuals and populations. During this nomadic dispersal, the birds avoid the open sea as well as mountains over 1000 m.

The autumn migration begins in early September and lasts until late October. Local cold-weather movements often occur later. The great majority of the population winters in Europe, only a few individuals moving further south to Africa. Grey Herons migrate on a broad front, but show some tendency to follow coasts and rivers. During migration proper, they may cross both seas and mountains, though often hesitate when leaving land to fly out over the open sea, flying in circles or in a zig-zag formation for some time before proceeding on their way (Suchantke 1960).

Apart from a few exceptions, Grey Herons breeding in Scotland, northern and central England, and Ireland do not migrate. In winter, they stay, even during cold spells, within a radius of 200 km of their natal colony. Among those breeding in southern England some do migrate, crossing the channel to winter in western France. Some also fly to Belgium, the Netherlands and, exceptionally, to Spain (Rydzewski 1956).

The great majority of the Norwegian population migrates to Scotland, England and Ireland (although a few recoveries have been made in Iceland), but a small number migrate to western continental Europe. The Norwegian population is particularly maritime, the birds breeding along the coast and foraging at sea during the spring and summer, before migrating in the autumn and early spring mostly over the open sea. However, they also often winter inland.

The other European populations migrate chiefly in a southwesterly direction; over 70% of the Swedish and Danish birds, 50–60% of those from other maritime countries (from France to Prussia) and 25–45% of those from central and eastern Europe follow this trend (Rydzewski 1956).

The most easterly and northerly populations are totally migratory, since the climate would not permit them to survive in winter on the breeding grounds. These birds are also those that migrate the farthest. Thus the average dispersal distance for December recoveries in different European countries is: Switzerland 250 km, southern Germany 330 km, France 430 km, the Netherlands 470 km, Poland 800 km, Denmark 920 km, Sweden 950 km, east Germany 980 km and from the Soviet Baltic 1120 km (Rydzewski 1956).

A more or less significant part of the Grey Heron populations of central, western and southern Europe is non-migratory and just disperses around the breeding area. However, these birds often move south and southwest during cold spells.

Some European birds cross the desert. There have been recoveries from the middle of September in Sénégal, Guinea and Sierra Leone of birds from France, the Netherlands, Switzerland and Russia; in Mali and Upper Volta from Sweden, the Netherlands, Hungary, Czechoslovakia, Poland and Russia; in Togo and Nigeria from Germany, Hungary, Czechoslovakia, Poland and Russia; in southern Egypt from Russia; and in Kenya from northern Caspia (Volga Delta) (Cramp and Simmons 1977).

There have also been recoveries of western European Grey Herons in the Azores, the Canary Islands, Madeira and the Cape Verde Islands. All of the birds recovered except one were juveniles (Rydzewski 1956).

Five birds ringed in France have been recovered in the West Indies: two in Martinique in 1962 and 1968, one in Montserrat in 1959, one in Trinidad in 1958 and one off the Bermudas in September 1961. This last bird, which was exhausted, landed on a ship and died soon afterwards. A sixth bird was recovered near Belem in Brazil in 1973. All these birds, except the one taken in Martinique in 1962, were juveniles. Whether they were blown out over the open sea by strong easterly winds or flew out of their own volition remains an open question.

The return journey from the winter quarters begins in February, and the colonies are usually reoccupied in March. Some young stay in the south during their first year. Like the autumn migration, the spring journey proceeds on a broad front, the birds flying chiefly northeast. There is some evidence that birds coming from Africa fly predominantly over Italy (Rydzewski 1956). Many birds return to their natal colony; however, some go to nearby ones and others to colonies far away. Older birds are more attached to their home than juveniles (Rydzewski 1956). Grey Herons usually migrate in small parties and may form flocks with other Ardeidae. The migration is principally, but not exclusively, nocturnal (Suchantke 1960).

HABITAT

Grey Herons are most common in the middle latitudes and are not numerous in northern Europe. Along the Norwegian coast, which is ice-free, they breed up to 69°N, but inland and along the Baltic Sea they do not breed north of 63°N. The length of the ice-free period probably limits the extent of northward breeding. Southwards, Grey Herons become more scattered in the Mediterranean, subtropical and tropical zones. They are mainly lowland birds, but are found locally in mountain regions up to 1000 m, and on occasion at higher altitudes.

In order to fish, a Grey Heron usually stands motionless or walks slowly in shallow water, along broad rivers and narrow streams (where the current is not too strong), in lakes, marshes, lagoons, estuaries and along sea-coasts. Man-made stretches of water are also used, such as reservoirs and barrage lakes, saltpans, ditches, dykes, canals, sewage-farms and fishponds. In fact, the Grey Heron fishes equally often in fresh, brackish and salt, or very salt water. The most important consideration seems to be the structure of the landscape, Grey Herons typically preferring an open landscape. In the Camargue in France, they avoid foraging in all biotopes with dense vegetation, such as rice fields, freshwater ditches and freshwater marshes where the vegetation has become abundant. They fish in the open areas of the marshes, in lagoons and saltpans.

The distribution of Grey Herons fishing along a river has been studied in Switzerland by Geiger (1984). The importance of the different sections of the river for fishing depends on the shape of the river banks (the presence of steep or gentle slopes down to the water) and the density of the vegetation, not only of that growing on the banks but also of that growing some distance away, such as groves and thickets on the upperparts of the river banks and in the nearby fields (see Fig. 9).

Grey Herons also fish at sea, along sandy and rocky coasts alike. They follow the tide or fish in the shallows uncovered at low tide. This marine habitat is used especially in the northern and southern part of their range.

In winter, Grey Herons are often found on open grasslands and on ploughed fields where they hunt mostly rodents. They also roost in fields, where they stand motionless in small parties at the same particular place each day.

Grey Herons nest in a wide range of biotopes and a few examples from France will show the variety of nesting sites used in both inland and coastal habitats. First, a heronry of medium size (52 nests in 1974) was established for many years in three enormous poplars isolated in the middle of a meadow. Another very ancient heronry (about 30 nests in the 1970s) was established in the park of a castle in old trees (oaks, poplars and ashes). This is a common situation, since during times of persecution, the species was saved as a breeding bird in Europe by a few landowners, the colonies established on such sites being very stable from year to year. Finally, a heronry of 20 nests was discovered in 1974 in firs and spruces on a slope above a lake.

Grey Herons prefer nesting sites in high trees, in quiet and commanding places. They also use other habitats such as gallery forests as was the case for an important heronry of about 70 nests in the 1970s, which was established

Figure 9   Where do Grey Herons like to forage? The size of the silhouette indicates the relative preference of a number of habitats: a little stream with steep banks covered with forest; a stream without steep banks but bordered with trees and bushes; the same stream with bushes and trees nearby but not bordering the water; a canal with gently sloping banks surrounded by an open landscape without trees; and a canal with vertical banks in the centre of town (after Geiger 1984).

in poplars and elms with an abundant undergrowth of willows, in an inundated gallery forest along the River Allier in France. Grey Herons nested there in company with Night Herons and Little Egrets. This habitat is quite seldom used, probably because trees in gallery forests are cut too often. They also nest in reedbeds, a common habitat in eastern Europe. They may even nest on the ground, in rough herbage near water. In western Europe, the only place where Grey Herons nest commonly in reedbeds is the Camargue in France. Elsewhere, they are seldom used and the colonies in them are small, as for example a colony of seven nests found in willows and reeds at the end of a small lake in central France, where Grey Herons nested in association with Purple Herons. Single pairs may use old raptor nests, as was observed in Sweden (Curry-Lindahl 1957). In places where the food supply is good but old trees, gallery forests and reedbeds are lacking, Grey Herons have adapted to more unusual nesting sites. In Norway, heron nests are often established on the steep cliffs flanking fjords, small bushes and trees often providing anchorage for the nests. Colonies in trees are usually found on small, isolated islands. These northern colonies are usually small in size and change site very often (Roalkvam 1984). In a similar biotope in Great Peter's Bay, south of Vladivostok, Grey Herons also nest directly on the ground, on steep and rocky islands, with gulls and cormorants nesting in close proximity (Litvinenko 1982). In southern Sweden, nests may be found on flat rocks near the sea. Three nests found on such a site (Carlson 1978) were as sturdily built as usual, but were very near the water level. On the islands of the Banc d'Arguin (Mauritania), where there are no trees, Grey Herons nest on the ground using stones, some vegetation and bones (mostly Pelican bones) to make their nests (Jouanin and Roux 1963).

The three most important colonies in France are situated in regions with extensive suitable foraging areas. The largest in France, and probably in western Europe, is at Charente-Maritime (southwestern France). Being well protected by a local association for nature protection, it has expanded greatly in recent years. In 1981, the colony numbered 1100 Grey Heron and 150 Little Egret nests. The herons nest in tall trees (oak, ash and elm) 20–30 m high. The nesting area, situated at the foot of the hills along the border of an extensive marsh, is usually inundated. An abundant undergrowth of willows and blackthorns grows between the deep ditches which drain the area. The size of this colony reflects the importance of the foraging areas round about which are formed from marshes extending down to the coast, which are now drained by numerous canals and are used as grazing lands. In addition, there are small water pools separated by dams and connected to each other, and to the sea, by numerous ditches, used for mussel growing. Lastly, there are extensive mudflats that are uncovered at low tide along the coast.

The colony of Lac de Grand-Lieu (4000 ha in summer and 6300 in winter) in the Loire Atlantique is situated in an environment which has practically disappeared from Europe today. This colony numbered 840 nests in 1981 (Marion 1979). The lake, which is crossed by the River Bologne, is situated in an old peat bog and has open water only in its central part. It is surrounded by marshes which dry up each year. Between the marshes and the open water, there is an extensive area of floating aquatic plants and huge reedbeds. Trees, mostly willows, but also alders, emerge here and there above this aquatic vegetation. As they are loosely rooted in the mud, the wind blows them down once they grow above about 10 m. Once fallen, the trees do not die, but go on growing in a horizontal position and become entwined with other vegetation. Deep holes, cut in the loose mud, are created where the roots of the trees are lifted. Whole sections of such aquatic forest sometimes become separated and drift away, leaving deep pools. The Grey Herons nest and thrive in this chaotic forest. The whole structure is very unstable and the heron colony, which in fact consists of 2–5 smaller units, changes shape every year. It is within easy reach of the coastal marshes and of the estuary of the Loire River (Marion 1979).

The third French colony of importance is to be found in an extensive reedbed in the western Camargue, and numbered 350 nests in 1981. Here

Grey Herons nest in association with Purple Herons. Important foraging areas in the vicinity include the freshwater marshes, saltpans and lagoons.

POPULATION SIZE, TRENDS AND DYNAMICS

THE SIZE OF THE BREEDING POPULATION OF GREY HERONS IN EUROPE

The first national census of breeding Grey Herons in Britain was organized in 1928 by M. Nicholson (1929) and sample counts were carried out under his direction up until 1938. Others have subsequently succeeded him, among them J.F. Burton (1956), J. Stafford (1969, 1971) and C.M. Reynolds (1974, 1979). This inquiry provides the longest continuous series of population counts available for any European breeding bird. Since 1928, the English and Welsh population has varied between 2250 breeding pairs in 1963 and 5400 in 1977. The mean number of breeding pairs is 4000 (see Fig. 10). In 1954, 1100 nests were counted in Scotland and 396 in Northern Ireland (Burton 1956).

The last complete national census was undertaken in 1985. The total number of breeding pairs was estimated at 5790 in England and Wales, 2950 in Scotland and 490 in Northern Ireland (Anonymous 1986). The winters of 1984–1985, 1985–1986 and 1986–1987 were very cold. The winter of 1984–1985 did not seem to have much impact on the population. The next winter, however, included a particularly cold February, followed by a stormy spring. The total breeding population in 1986 in England and Wales was then estimated at 5100 pairs. A downward trend was also observed in Scotland and Northern Ireland. However, as many nests were blown down, the number of adult pairs are probably higher than the number of nests occupied (Anonymous 1987a).

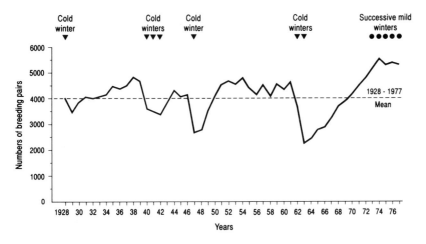

Figure 10   The level of the Grey Heron population in England and Wales, 1928–1977 (after Reynolds 1979).

A very incomplete count in France in 1928 estimated a breeding population of about 350 pairs. Of these, 200 pairs bred in two colonies of 100 nests each. During the Second World War, the number of Grey Herons increased, probably because of the very limited opportunities for hunting (J. Berlioz, in Lowe 1954). In 1962, a general census of breeding Grey Herons was carried out in France for the first time. The total number of breeding pairs was estimated at between 2500 and 2700. During the census of 1967, only 1900 were counted. But the number of breeding birds increased subsequently. A total of 2032 pairs were counted in 1968, 3363 in 1974 (Brosselin 1974) and 9313 in 1981 (Duhautois and Marion 1981).

The French Grey Herons nest principally in western and eastern France but have recently begun to colonize the Camargue, first nesting there in 1964 (Blondel 1965). The number of birds breeding in the Camargue has increased rapidly since, with 57 pairs in 1974 and 515 in 1981. All these nests are in reedbeds.

In Belgium, the number of breeding pairs has been estimated since 1900, when there were between 230 and 480 breeding pairs. Their number seems to have increased slowly up to 1925, but may be the result of a better knowledge of the nesting sites. After a slight decrease before the Second World War (450 nests in 1939) and perhaps at the beginnng of it, the number of breeding pairs increased to 652 in 1952. A rapid decrease occurred during the following period and in 1966 there were only 178 breeding pairs (Verheyen 1966). Protection saved the species as a breeding bird in Belgium. A total of 297 nests were counted in 1969 (Lippens and Wille 1972) and 1309 nests in 1981 (Van Vessem *et al.* 1982).

In the Netherlands, 6500–7000 pairs bred in 1925, 8000–8500 in 1935, 4500–5000 in 1949, 6000–7000 in 1962, 3500–4000 following the very cold winter of 1962–1963, and 3250–3750 in 1964; the population not having recovered and the estimate for 1963 being probably too high (Van der Ven 1962, 1964). In 1974, there were 8000 breeding pairs in the Netherlands and in 1975 over 10,000 pairs (Blok and Ross 1977).

In 1900, the breeding population in Switzerland was reduced to about 50 pairs by human persecution and the species was near to extinction as a breeding bird in that country when it was protected in 1925. Once protected, the number of breeding pairs increased slowly. In 1953, there were 500–750 breeding pairs (Géroudet 1955). In 1970, the population had fallen again to 350–400 breeding pairs (W. Thönen, in Cramp and Simmons 1977). The cause of this decrease is unknown, but the recovery from the hard winter of 1962–1963 was probably very slow. During the 1970s, the numbers of breeding Grey Herons improved and 1036 breeding pairs were counted in 1981 and 880 pairs in 1982 (Geiger 1984).

An almost complete census performed in West Germany in 1961 (Krämer 1962) gave a total number of 4625 breeding pairs: 2260 nests were in Niedersachsen, 790 in Schleswig-Holstein, 30 in Hamburg, 395 in Westfalen, 190 in Nordrhein, 30 in Rheinland-Pfalz, 250 in Hessen, 380 in Baden-Würtenberg and 300–450 in Bayern. During the 1960s, there was a considerable fall in numbers. In Baden-Würtenberg, there were still 363 pairs in 1968 but only 277 in 1972. In the Rheinland, 197 pairs nested in 1961 but only 50 in 1971; in Hanover, 282 pairs nested in 1958 but only 156 in 1967; in Hessen, 250 pairs nested in 1961 but only 75 in 1969 (Hölzinger 1973, Cramp and Simmons 1977).

In Bayern, the number of breeding pairs has been estimated each year since 1960. There were 527 breeding pairs in 1960 and only 287 after the severe winter of 1963. The number increased slowly to 562 in 1967. Thereafter, the numbers of breeding Grey Herons fell again. In 1972, the species was totally protected and from 433 pairs their number increased to 1224 in 1980. In 1981, hunting in the vicinity of fish farms was allowed again with the result that there was again a slight fall in the breeding population, with only 1142 breeding pairs (Utschick 1983). However, the mild winters of the 1970s, in conjunction with protection, have permitted a significant increase in the number of Grey Herons in Bayern. In 1960, there were 2064–2135 breeding pairs in East Germany (Creutz and Schlegel 1961). In 1978, 4000–4100 nests were counted, an increase due mostly to the increased protection of the species (Rutschke 1982) (see Table 15).

The first census of heronries in Denmark was undertaken as early as 1910 by Weibüll (1912), who also published results from 1880 when 1280 pairs nested. In 1910, there were 1450 pairs. Other national censuses were also carried out: 1450 pairs nested in 1927 (Holstein 1927), 2000 pairs in 1945 (Krüger 1946), 2037 pairs in 1953, 1883 pairs in 1968 (Dybbro 1970) and 2673 pairs in 1978. From 1968 to 1978, the total breeding population had increased by 42% (Møller and Olesen 1980).

The first, incomplete, heron census in Sweden was undertaken by N. Dahlbeck (1946) in 1943. The total number of breeding pairs was estimated at 600. By the census of 1972, the number had risen to 1800. In Sweden, there are vast areas of forests and lakes and small colonies may be easily over-looked. S. Swenson (1976) estimated the total number of breeding pairs to be about 2500. The increase of the Swedish population between 1945 and 1976 is probably not as great as it seems, since the census of 1943 was not complete and researchers are now better acquainted with the terrain.

Grey Herons are very scarce in Finland and in 1958 only 5–10 pairs bred (Merikallio, in Cramp and Simmons 1977).

In Austria, there is no complete census available before 1968. In 1951, 180 pairs bred at the Neusiedler See (Bauer *et al.* 1955) but in 1975 there were only 20 pairs. In 1960, there were about 160 pairs in Oberöstereich (Bauer and Glutz 1966). In 1968, 1971 and 1975, complete Austrian censuses were undertaken (Böck 1975) indicating about 250, 220 and 200 breeding pairs respectively.

In Hungary, 982 nests were counted in 1951 during a partial census. At that time, the total breeding population was estimated at 2000 pairs (Szijj, in Cramp and Simmons 1977). In 1988, the total breeding population of the Grey Heron in Poland was estimated at about 7000 pairs (M. Wielock, *in lit.*).

The first census of breeding Grey Herons in Italy was carried out in 1981, the total number of pairs being 680 (Fasola *et al.* 1981). The Grey Heron is not common in Spain. During a partial census in 1975, 218 nests were counted (Fernandez-Cruz 1975). In 1951, a pair of Grey Herons nested for the first time at Las Marismas (Valverde 1960). In 1973, the breeding population in this area was estimated at 50–100 pairs (Ree 1973). In Greece, the number of nesting pairs was estimated to be between 572 and 600 during 1985 and 1986 (Crivelli *et al.* 1988).

There are no national censuses available for Norway, Czechoslovakia, Romania, Yugoslavia and the USSR. The very scattered and transient breeding sites of Grey Herons in Norway have prevented any national census, although the species has bred in there since ancient times. As early as 1555, Grey Herons nested in numbers near Oslo (Haftorn 1971). Today, the number of breeding pairs may be estimated at some hundreds. In Czechoslovakia, the population decreased during the 1960s. In the lowlands of Slovakia, there were 700–800 pairs in 1956–1958 (Cramp and Simmons 1977). In Romania, persecution by fishermen has led to a fall in the number of nesting Grey Herons (Vasiliu 1968). In Yugoslavia, in the Kopacevski Reserve, the numbers of breeding pairs were put at (by census) 99 in 1955, 9 in 1957, none from 1958 to 1968 and 35 in 1970 (Cramp and Simmons 1977).

In the USSR, the Grey Heron is common along the lowland rivers flowing into the Black and Caspian seas. The Astrakhan Reserve had about 18,500 pairs in 1923 and 23,400 pairs in 1935 (Dementiev and Gladkov 1951). In the lower Volga Delta, 623 pairs were counted in 1951, 1805 in 1955 and 403 in 1958 (Lugovoy, in Cramp and Simmons 1977).

THE NUMBER AND SIZE OF HERONRIES IN EUROPE

The size of a heronry appears to be proportional to the richness of the foraging areas located within a radius of about 25 km. In Europe, the largest heronries are situated in coastal areas, presumably because of their proximity to extensive marshes, lagoons, estuaries and sea coasts, which provide, in a small area, a great variety of rich foraging grounds. Further inland, heronries are widely scattered along waterways, their size depending on the importance of the associated wetland areas. Large rivers, especially at junctions with tributaries, may support some hundreds of nests, a medium-sized river, some 50–100 nests. Along small streams where lakes and marshes are small in size, the heronries comprise only a few nests.

Most of the French heronries are established along the Atlantic coast from Bretagne to Aquitaine (about 4000 nests in 30 heronries in 1981) and in the northeastern third of France (about 3600 nests in 110 heronries in 1981; Duhautois and Marion, 1982) (see Table 16).

In the Netherlands in 1956, there were about 127 heronries, but no single, very large colony (see Table 17). In 1975, the number of heronries had increased to about 205 (some isolated nests were also found). Most of the heronries were to be found in the polder areas. In 1975, Friesland held about 2365 nests, Zuid-Holland 2080 nests and Noord-Holland 2660 nests (see Table 18).

In Britain, heronries are numerous but are generally small, 92% having less than 40 nests. Although there are numerous rivers and estuaries, they are not very large, and foraging territories are scattered in a great number of favourable but rather small sites. As early as 1872, L.H. Harting had estimated the number of heronries in the British Isles to be more than 200 (Lowe 1954; see Tables 19 and 20).

In Belgium, the mean colony size is 38.5 nests. The mean nest-density is 43 nests per 1000 km^2 (see Table 21). In Switzerland, the colonies are small or of medium size. In 1982, half the population bred in colonies of less than 20 nests and the other half in colonies ranging from 20 to 56 nests in size. Here, herons fish mostly along rivers that are not very large. There are no very large colonies because great concentrations of birds need extensive foraging areas, which this habitat cannot provide (see Table 22). In Poland, the total number of heronries was estimated at about 185 in 1988 (M. Wielock, *in litt.*).

In West and East Germany, six heronries had more than 100 nests in 1962 (the biggest, at Hoyerswort, had 340 nests, followed by Logabirum with 276 nests). Five of these big heronries are established in coastal areas and one on a lake crossed by an important tributary of the River Elbe. Twenty-five heronries contained between 50 and 100 nests. Those heronries with more than 50 nests were all situated in the northern half of West and East Germany, where low plains are crossed by numerous rivers. However, the great majority of the heronries had less than 50 nests and were scattered over the whole of both West and East Germany, near waters of lesser size (Krämer 1967). Austria had only 13 heronries in 1975, the largest containing 35 nests (Böck 1975).

In Italy, Grey Herons nest only in the northwestern part of the country. In 1981, there were 11 heronries with from 5 to 150 nests (mean number per heronry 56). All but one of them were situated in the dense rice-field area where the River Po and some of its tributaries from the Alps allow large-scale irrigation. The birds nested mostly in trees over 15 m high where they were often associated with other species of tree-nesting herons. However, some nests were found in reedbeds (Fasola *et al.* 1981a).

In Denmark in 1978, there were four heronries with more than 100 nests. The largest at that time held 242 nests. Eleven heronries had between 50 and 100 nests and 98 less than 50 nests (Møller and Olesen 1980).

In Norway, the colonies are small. In Rogaland, southwest Norway, 34% of the breeding sites have only 1–4 nests, 36% have 5–14 nests and only 30% more than 15 nests. The biggest colony had 40 nests. The mean size of the colonies is 9.3 nests for those established in trees and 12.0 for those on cliffs (Roalkvam 1984). The small colonies do not persist for many years, the birds changing nest-site almost every year. Only colonies of some size remain in the same breeding area long. This unusual breeding distribution makes census work difficult and explains why a general census has not been carried out.

The heronries in Sweden are rather small but quite numerous, and they are all situated south of 60°N. The biggest one held 75 nests, and most of the others 2–20 nests (see Table 23).

THE SURVIVAL RATE OF ADULT GREY HERONS IN ENGLAND AND WALES AND THE CAUSES OF DEATH

The national census of breeding Grey Herons in England and Wales undertaken since 1928 reveals that a significant decline of the breeding population occurs after exceptionally cold winters, followed by a more or less rapid return to normal conditions. The population normally recovers after 2–3 years, but took 7 years to recover after the particularly cold winter of 1962–1963. Mead *et al.* (1979) have shown from an analysis of ringing recoveries that during this period there was a long-term increase in adult mortality rates, possibly due to pesticides, though this is not proven (see Table 24).

However, a Dutch study in 1976 (van der Molen *et al.* 1982) seems to confirm the pesticide hypothesis. The bodies of 41 Grey Herons found dead during 14 days of cold weather during the winter of 1975–1976 were examined. A total of 20% of the birds had lethal and sub-lethal mercury residues in their kidneys and livers. Presumably, the birds with lethal mercury levels did not die before the cold spell due to the antagonistic effect of the high selenium residues also found in the birds' liver and kidneys. With one exception, all of the birds were found in a small area in the north. The local use of agricultural fungicides containing mercury may be considered as the primary source of this pollution. The combination of high mercury residues and the stress induced by cold weather and undernourishment seems to be the cause of the high mortality during the winter of 1975–1976. The result was a 19% decrease in the breeding population the following season.

The protection of the Grey Heron has allowed an increase in the survival rate of first-year birds and these young birds nested in greater numbers than previously during the difficult period following the winter of 1963. This increased input to the breeding population may have ameliorated the negative impact of the increased use of pesticides.

However, about 4600 Grey Herons are still shot each year in England at fish farms according to a study by Meyer (1981). This incredible number compares with the mean total breeding population for England and Wales of about 4000 pairs. If this estimate of mortality due to shooting is accurate, the persecution of Grey Herons is still, despite legal protection, the foremost mortality factor, and not to be forgotten when the species' population dynamics are studied.

After a succession of mild winters, Grey Herons may become numerous if the population has had time to recover from the last very cold winter. Since very short, severe spells do not necessarily lead to a noticeable decline, the duration of the frosty period seems a more important factor than that the actual minimum temperature itself.

BEHAVIOUR AND BIOLOGY

DAILY ROUTINE

Roosting Grey Herons have been studied in particular by Birkhead (1973). Each day, from September to March, they congregated either on the same field, or sometimes on one nearby. These fields were ploughed and sown during the winter months and throughout this period the soil remained bare. No herons were seen at these roosts before the beginning of September and after the first week of April. During periods of snow and mist, they tended to arrive later than usual and were less numerous. Each morning, the

> herons began to arrive, usually singly, about an hour after dawn and mostly between 09.00 and 10.00 hours. They continued to arrive at a slower rate throughout the day until 16.00–17.00 hours. Some started to leave the roost between 15.00 and 16.00, but the greatest number left approximately one hour before dark in the evening, and all had left by the time it was dark (Birkhead 1973a).

Upon arrival, each heron alighted with a low "muttering sound" given in greeting. The dorsal plumes were often slightly raised, though the crest and neck feathers remained sleeked. After landing at the roost, the birds remained there until their evening departure. Very little activity was observed: "The herons spent 76.8% of their time standing and awake, 5.9% asleep, 0.6% hunting and 16% preening" (Birkhead 1973a).

Herons generally leave their roosting site singly or in small groups of 2–3, uttering a loud, harsh "frank" call. At all times of the year, single birds may be found roosting by day or night at or near their foraging area. Some individuals may also roost in the deserted trees of the colony. Grey Herons feed to a large extent at dawn, at dusk and most probably during the night when there is little information available about their activities. Single birds have been observed foraging by night. Since they sleep little at their daytime roosts, it is likely that they spend a large part of the night asleep. Sleeping at or near their fishing stations is certainly less dangerous by night than by day, since persecution by man is their greatest danger. To what extent Grey Herons forage by night and whether or not they commonly sleep at night at or near their foraging areas should be the subjects of further study.

Of what use is a communal roost? Its defensive function is clear, it being more difficult for a predator to approach a group of herons unnoticed than a single individual. There is also much discussion as to whether communal roosts also act as information centres. In my opinion, this is very likely, since herons return to the roost each day. When a bird leaves in the evening, uttering its typical call, it is easy for another bird in search of a good foraging site to follow. If there is enough room for two, as is usually the case, the second heron will have found a new foraging area.

The daily routine at the heronry has been very little studied, though Marion (1976) has recorded all arrivals and departures from a heronry. Grey Herons are active throughout the day; the birds arrive at and leave the colony at any time from dawn to dusk with peaks of activity at dawn and dusk. They are less active during the middle of the day from about 11.00 or 12.00 h to 16.00 h (French time, which is Universal Time + 1 hour). The birds arrive and leave singly in 79.50 and 81.57% of cases respectively. In 13% of all observations, they form groups of two birds. When leaving the heronry, Grey Herons call on 13% of occasions. When arriving they are usually silent except for the Greeting Call, but may call in answer to the call of a departing bird (Marion 1976). Near a heronry there is usually a "standing ground", which is frequented both by non-breeding and breeding birds. Birkhead (1973) observed that, in late March and early April, incubating herons which had been relieved from the nest left immediately for the standing ground. Early in the morning, the standing grounds are usually empty. Most herons arrive there about 3 hours after dawn, when activity in the heronry is high. During the remaining part of the day, much movement to and from the standing ground occurs, but 2–3 hours before dark it is empty again. Birds at the standing ground were observed standing for 68.8% of the time, sleeping for 3.5%, lying for 2.8%, hunting for 1.3%, twig fiddling for 0.8% and preening for 22.8%. No sunbathing was observed. Sunbathing herons were seen at another spot near the heronry, suggesting "that there is a favoured place for this activity". The most common display observed at the standing ground was the Arched-neck Display. It was performed by an incoming bird in 73% of the arrivals observed by Birkhead (1973b). In one-third of these cases, the nearest bird or birds on the standing ground responded with the Arched-neck Display. This behaviour was also sometimes, though rarely, performed between individuals already at the standing ground. The Stretch Display was seen three times by Birkhead, performed by herons at the standing ground when another heron flew overhead. A landing heron may be chased by another, but the incoming heron may itself chase one of the birds already standing at the standing ground. These agonistic displays have been misinterpreted by authors in the past, who have wrongly taken them for a "dance"; that is to say, for sexual behaviour leading to pair-formation.

Maintenance behaviour

When resting, Grey Herons stand almost vertical, their necks completely retracted, the heads held just above the shoulders.

At the roost or in the heronry, they spend much of their time preening, treating all the feathers which can be reached. During preening, the bird rubs its head, neck and beak against its powder-puffs, which provide powder to dry any slime deposited from prey such as eels. Having preened, the bird then uses one of its two foot combs to remove the dried-up slime and powder. Grey Herons are also reputed to bathe (Creutz 1981) and to sunbathe on hot days (Boyd 1950). When sunbathing, they stand upright, with the neck fully extended and the bill nearly horizontal. The neck feathers are often slightly erected. The wings are usually unfolded sideways and downward in a typical Delta-wing Sunning Posture (Simmons 1986). They usually sunbathe facing the sun, but after a while may also turn their back to it. While sunbathing, they often preen a little.

Displays and calls

The displays of the Grey Heron are not so well known as may be expected. The best descriptions were written in 1930 by J. Verwey. In recent years, only the Snap Display has been studied in detail (Baerends and Van de Cingel 1962). Milstein *et al.* (1970), in an important study on the breeding cycle of the Grey Heron, comment on and discuss most displays but describe only some of them. All the displays are performed by males as well as by females. The characteristic Advertisement Call is only used by males during pair-formation. The other calls seem to be identical in both sexes but require further study.

Agonistic displays

The Aggressive Upright Display (Meyerriecks, 1960). This display has been called *Abwehr* by Bauer and Glutz (1966) and the "Arched-neck Greeting Display" by Milstein *et al.* (1970). The display is characterized by the following features:

○ the bird stands erect, facing its opponent;
○ the body is more or less raised;
○ the outstretched neck tends towards the vertical, except the upper part of the neck which is strongly arched;
○ the head and bill are inclined downwards;
○ the wings are held closed or slightly opened;
○ the crest, neck and scapular feathers are raised to varying degrees; and a soft call is sometimes given.

The Aggressive Upright Display does not seem to be purely aggressive. In my opinion, the aggressive component is tempered by the fact that the beak is pointed downwards and not at the opponent. The bird appears to be in a conflict situation. It shows its aggressiveness by raising its feathers, but at the same time does not seem willing to attack, if this can be avoided, and indicates this by pointing the beak downwards.

Milstein *et al.* (1970) consider this display to be a greeting display. I do not think this is the case, though it is often performed by a bird at the nest when its mate returns. In this case, the posture seems merely to be the result of a conflict between the desire to be released from guarding the nest and the urge to defend its territory.

The Snap Display (Meyerriecks 1960, Baerends and Van der Cingel 1962). *Schnappbewegung* by Verwey (1930). Verwey describes the Snap Display as follows (translated by Baerends and Van der Cingel, 1962):

> the neck is stretched and the head is lowered to the level of the feet or even lower, when the bird bends its legs. When the head is at its lowest, the bird opens its bill and then shuts it with a loud clash. The feathers of the crest and neck are erected during this ceremony.

Baerends and Van der Cingel (1962) add themselves "that the head is not always lowered to the same angle with the vertical or with the body axis" (Fig. 11). Figure 11 shows the distribution of the angles the neck made with the vertical in the 1977 Snap Displays observed.

A

B

C

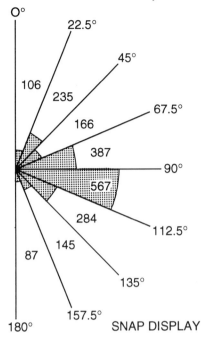

Figure 11   The angle that the neck makes with the vertical in 1977 Snap Displays (Baerends *et al.* 1962).

Although this distribution shows a marked peak in the sector between 90 and 112½ degrees, snapping also occurs rather frequently in other directions: a secondary peak lies between 22½ and 45 degrees. During snapping the neck and head need not always be in line with the body axis; the movement may also be directed sidewards. Sometimes one gets the impression that the head is purposively directed towards the partner, other times that it is turned away from the other bird. In a few cases the erection of the crest and of other feathers may be less intensive or may even, although very rarely be left out. The Bill Snap is sometimes barely audible and also the bending in the 'heel joints' may be incomplete. Sometimes a twig was seized at the end of the movement and released again, either almost immediately or after some head-shaking.

The clear presence of agonistic components in the Snap Display, its positive correlation with agonistic activities, the occasional appearance of transition forms between Forward and Snap Display and its occurrence in agonistic situations are a complex of arguments that in our opinion supports the interpretation of this display (or at least of a component of it) as an ambivalent movement controlled by the tendencies to attack and to flee (Baerends and Van der Cingel 1962).

A, Snap Display (after Baerends *et al.* 1962); B, Aggressive Upright Display (after Milstein *et al.* 1970); C. Delta-wing Sunning Posture.

The Snap Display is often performed by males at their nest sites during pair-formation, but is also given by both males and females throughout the breeding period. Both Meyerriecks (1960) and Baerends and Van der Cingel (1962) have classified this behaviour as a hostile one. These authors, however, admit a slight sexual component in it. The fact that the Snap Display is the result of a conflict situation is probably the cause of the difficulty in understanding it correctly. In my study of the Night Heron in 1970, I believed it was an entirely hostile display. However, in the Grey Heron, this display is more ritualized. In 1960 Meyerriecks wrote: "The movements of *Ardea cinerea* are few and smoothly performed indicating more advanced ritualization." Thus the hostile component is less obvious. That is probably the reason why this display has been mistaken for a sexual one by other authors such as Verwey and Milstein *et al.*

The Dancing Ground Display (Meyerriecks 1960). Lowe (1954) described this display briefly:

> It is on the gathering ground that the herons' somewhat primitive dance may be seen. It has always been started by a new arrival. The herons' dance may be shared by all the birds on the ground, but is a desultory affair of short duration. The incoming bird usually alights with open wings and runs or skips from the rear down the line already assembled, and they, activated by this stimulus, half unfold their wings and execute a few steps forwards. I have never seen the dance develop into anything more, nor has there been any resultant mating.

Meyerriecks also described a dance in the Great Blue Heron. The heron "raised its head and neck to about a 45° angle, erected its back plumes and strutted toward one of the other birds".

For Baerends and Van der Cingel (1962), the display observed on the gathering ground is only a variant of the Snap Display, but "In contrast with the Snap Display on the nest this display is always carried out on the ground with the crest and neck feathers down, and the bird does not bend at the heel joints." On the gathering ground "a heron approaches an opponent with stretched neck and after nearing it pecks downwards in the manner of the Snap Display. The bill may or may not reach the ground, but in the latter case the heron may seize a tuft of grass and pull at it. . . . Sometimes a twig is seized and then usually shaken".

According to Baerends and Van der Cingel (1962), when approached by a snapping heron, the attacked bird usually retreats. Sometimes one of the herons starts to chase another with a run or jump, often flapping its wings. In the past, probably by analogy with the cranes, this fighting has been taken for a "dance".

Birkhead's (1973b) observations do not agree with Baerends and Van der Cingel (1962). Birkhead wrote:

> The displays observed when a bird alighted on the standing-ground were all similar, they will be referred to as arch-neck displays. They always included the following. The neck was raised and arched, the crest, dorsal and ventral body plumes were erected. Arch-neck displays given by both incoming birds and birds

already on the standing-ground in response to individuals alighting near them were recorded. This included airborne displays immediately prior to landing. Previous observations at other heronries had shown that arch-neck displays also occurred apparently spontaneously among birds on the standing-ground. Generally one bird assumed the arch-neck posture then approached another.

Since all the sexual activities of herons take place at their nest-site, I think that to see a "dance", which is a sexual behaviour, in these displays is an error. But more observations are necessary to be certain that there is only one, rather than several, agonistic displays involved.

The Forward Display (Meyerriecks 1960). This display has been called *Stossbewegung* by Verwey (1930) and *Drohhaltung* by Bauer and Glutz (1966). This is the common threat display of herons and the bird assumes the following position when facing an opponent:

○ body in a nearly horizontal position;
○ legs slightly bent;
○ wings partly spread;
○ neck curved backwards in an "S" shape, bill pointing forwards ready to strike. The more the neck is curved backwards, the higher is the tendency to attack.

All the feathers are erected, particularly those on the neck and crest. From this position, the bird thrusts its head vigorously forwards with the bill open, giving loud Threat Calls. Milstein *et al.* (1970) have observed that the bird sometimes Bill-snaps instead.

Attack. The heron advances quickly to lunge at the intruder, and delivers sharp blows with the bill if it does not fly away. On fleeing, the intruder is often followed in flight by the territorial bird, which gives Pursuit Calls. The male Grey Heron does not only attack intruders on its own territory, but also other males displaying nearby.

Fear behaviour

Alert Posture. The heron stands erect, the neck extended, the feathers sleeked. Grey Herons also have a Warning Call which they use, for example, when humans approach too close to the roost or nest-site. It has a short, hard "rack" or "wäck" sound (Buckhart, in Bauer and Glutz 1966).

Courtship behaviour

Advertising Call (Meyerriecks 1960). Verwey (1930) called this *Liebeslockruf*. A male heron perched quietly in a tree may suddenly raise its head and give a sharp, single, yelping call. The yelp is repeated, and after some time is alternated with the Stretch Display and even with the Snap Display. This cry is only performed by lone males during courtship to attract females. The cry is usually uttered by day but sometimes continues at night with a lower frequency (Milstein *et al.* 1970). The difference between the Advertising Call and a similar call heard all year round, named *Lockruf* by Verwey, is not absolutely evident and Spillner (1968) thought that a sonogram would be necessary to be sure that the two are really different.

Stretch Display (Meyerriecks 1960). This display has been called *Reckbewegung* by Verwey (1930) and the *Bitterning Display* by Milstein *et al.* (1970). First, the bird makes an upward movement, and simultaneously:

○ stands erect and raises its body to an angle of about 45° with the horizontal; and
○ stretches the head and neck vertically to their fullest extents, bill pointing skywards.

Then follows a downward movement in which it simultaneously:

○ lowers its neck over its back, the bill still pointing upwards;
○ brings its body nearly to the horizontal; and
○ slowly bends its legs.

Forward Display (after Creutz 1981).

The display is accompanied by a distinctive double call. When the male extends its neck, it calls "hoo", the sound becoming more gurgling as its head is brought downwards and backwards (Lowe 1954).

During the Stretch Display, the feathers of the head are not raised. However, the feathers of the neck, especially the ones on either side of the upper part of the neck and the elongated feathers at the base of the neck, are raised to a maximum. (A photograph by G. Creutz, 1981, shows that the upper part of the neck is also probably slightly swelled.) The scapular feathers are raised as the bird crouches down. During this display, the most conspicuous feathers seem to be the elongated neck feathers and not the scapular feathers as in the case of the genus *Egretta*.

Feather-nibbling (Baerends and Van der Cingel 1962). This has also been called "Allopreening" by Cullen (1963). The bird lightly grips one of the other bird's feathers while making slight shaking movements with its bill (Baerends and Van der Cingel 1962).

Billing. According to Meyerriecks (1960), "Both birds extend their head and neck and gently grasp the mate's bill momentarily." Bill-sparring (Milstein *et al.* 1970) is a more aggressive variant of Billing. Feather-nibbling and Billing occur "during periods of excitement, particularly during the copulatory period, both before and after copulation and during nest relief, particularly at hatching" (Milstein *et al.* 1970).

Bill-clappering. According to Hudson (1965):

Frequently, but not invariably, the neck of the clappering bird is arched and the bill pointed towards the ground. After nibbling the feathers on various parts of the female, usually the neck and mantle, the male Common Heron may rapidly open and close the mandibles, a movement similar to that performed in feather nibbling except that in bill-clappering the bill is not held in contact with the plumage of the mate. Sometimes the clappering of the mandibles is clearly audible as a rattling noise, but often it cannot be heard at all. On a number of occasions movements of the mandibles down a scapular of the mate culminated in bill-clappering. Thus the movements of the head and bill respectively were continued after the end of the feather had been reached, so that allopreening and bill-clappering were one continuous movement.

The bird may shake its head from side to side during clappering but this is not an invariable feature. On other occasions, head-shaking occurred without movement of the mandible (Hudson 1965).

Only Hudson reports this display as being common. According to him, it is performed by both males and females during pair-formation and by males during the copulatory period. Verwey (1930) only recorded it on one evening, from two different individuals, and Lowe (1954) has heard it on rare occasions during copulation. Milstein *et al.* (1970) have hardly ever seen it. In Hudson's opinion, this behaviour is often confused with allopreening and thus goes unnoticed.

Since the same herons come to the same heronry year after year, and since

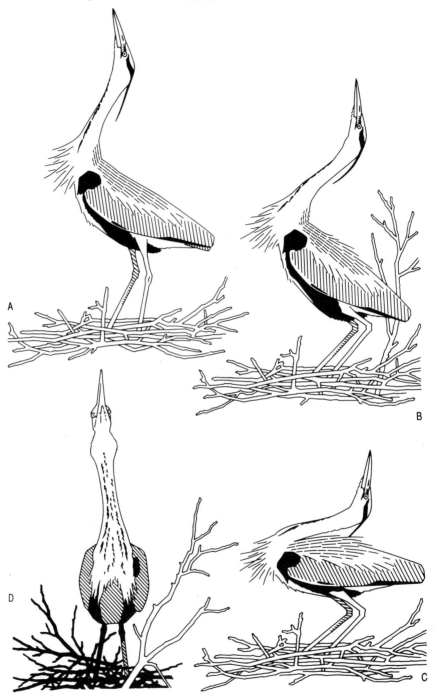

the young hatched there often also breed there, it is possible that certain behavioural peculiarities may appear in some colonies. Thus one type of behaviour, usually uncommon, may perhaps be common in certain specific populations. Hudson studied the heronry in the High Halstow Reserve. Bill-clapping is a common behaviour in some other heron species, e.g. the Little Egret.

Courtship Flights Observed by Verwey (1930) and Milstein *et al.* (1970), Courtship Flights are short circling flights, the bird returning to or near to the point of departure, though not always directly. The heron flies out with 3–4 loud heavy wing-beats, the neck remaining outstretched or somewhat bent during the flight.

Alighting Display (Milstein *et al.* 1970). In flight, and while still some 50 m away from the nest, the returning heron arches its neck, raises its crest feathers and fluffs out its body feathers. The incoming heron flies towards the nest in this posture with "almost laboured movements". At the same time, it utters a Greeting Call not heard in other situations "except occasionally as a toned-down reply from a welcoming heron". It is a series of "grunting squawks, diminishing in volume and often culminating in clucking as the heron alights on the nest" (Milstein *et al.* 1970).

REPRODUCTIVE BEHAVIOUR

Pair-formation

As long as the weather is bad, with cold, rain and wind, the first Grey Herons to arrive at the colony at the beginning of the nesting season use it only as a roosting place. However, on the first fair day, those males already present choose their nest-sites, which early in the season are often old nests from the previous year. The male starts to call from the nest-site, using the Advertising Call, and also to display, giving a Stretch Display now and then. Suddenly, another heron approaches and settles at some distance. The displaying male becomes very excited and Advertising Calls and Stretch Displays follow one another repeatedly. When a heron, usually a female attracted by the display, comes nearer to the nest or nest-site, it is driven away by the male. He usually adopts the Aggressive Upright Display as soon as the female approaches the nest, then threatens rapidly with a Forward Display, and even with Threat Calls. If the female does not retreat, she will be attacked. Usually she flies away but returns several times, each time the attacks of the male decreasing in intensity:

The Forward display becomes less frequent but now the Snap display appears

---

Stretch Display. A, B and C, three successive postures; D, front view of a Grey Heron in posture A. The erect feathers and the swelling of the upper part of the neck are clearly shown (A and C after Bauer and Glutz 1966; D after Creutz 1981).

with increasing frequency. At a further approach of the female the Forward display may occur again, usually, however, without a decrease in the number of Snap displays. From now on, the male only weakly resists the attempts of the female to get on the nest; both birds often grip each other's feathers while making slight shaking movements with their bills (Feather Nibbling); occasionally they may seize twigs on the nest with similar movements. Also, inhibited mutual bill fighting (Billing or Bill-sparring) frequently occurs (Baerends and Van der Cingel 1962).

Nest-building activities start as soon as the pair is formed. The male carries twigs gathered from trees, the ground or other nests to his own nest, usually given them to the female. The birds leave the colony to feed but the nest is not usually left unattended. When relieving each other on the nest, the birds perform greeting displays. Copulation occurs regularly from the time the female is admitted to the nest.

Greeting behaviour

When the Grey Heron returns to its nest, it performs the Alighting Display while still in flight. This display signals its friendly intentions and enables the bird at the nest to recognize its mate by its calls. The Alighting Display inhibits the aggressive tendencies of the bird on the nest, who instead of responding with the Forward Display and an attack, gives a less aggressive display. In fact, the responses of the resident bird are very variable. It may greet its mate with the Arched-neck Display or the Stretch Display. It may also ignore its arriving mate, sometimes not even rising. This great variation in response is particularly obvious during stick-bringing when the Arched-neck and Stretch Displays alternate with no display at all. Milstein *et al.* (1970) have observed that the Arched-neck Display tends to be replaced by the Stretch Display during the course of the breeding cycle but overlap considerably. The Arched-neck Display is the only display used commonly during the copulatory and egg-laying periods. From the beginning of the incubation period to the guardian period, the Stretch Display rapidly becomes more common than the Arched-neck Display.

There are two peaks of greeting activity during the reproductive period of the Grey Heron. The first occurs during the copulatory period (when the Arched-neck Display is the only display commonly used) and the second during the early guardian period (when the Stretch Display is the common one). The Arched-neck Display and the Stretch Display are only performed by the birds – male or female – at the nest, and never by the incoming bird. After these displays, both birds often become very excited, and both Allopreening and Billing commonly occur.

Sometimes, the bird at the nest does not rise but continues to sit, especially near to hatching, or when brooding the chicks. After a while, the newly arrived mate gently pushes the sitting bird from the nest. Milstein *et al.* (1970) once observed that "the male forced his head under the reluctant female, shouldering her until she rose", and Holstein (1927) observed "a relieving heron prod its incubating mate with its bill to get it off the nest". Sometimes, however, the bird at the nest is eager to be relieved, and leaves as soon as its mate arrives, without performing any display.

This description follows Milstein *et al.*'s (1970) observations, which seem accurate, but we must remember that the Arched-neck Display is considered by most authors to be an aggressive display of low intensity, also called the Aggressive Upright Display. While this interpretation does not change the sequence of displays observed, it is interesting to note that Grey Herons at the nest do not seem to have a specific greeting display, but use a low-intensity aggressive display (a distance-increasing display) progressively replaced by the display used by the male to attract the female during pair-formation (a distance-decreasing display). In most species studied so far, that is to say in the genera *Egretta*, *Nycticorax* and *Ardeola*, the Stretch Display is only performed by the male to attract females during pair-formation. In the Grey Heron, males also use it to attract females, but both sexes use it later in the breeding cycle as a greeting display at the nest. Besides the Grey Heron, this has only been observed in the Green-backed Heron (*Butorides striatus virescens*) by Meyerriecks (1960).

Copulation

This description follows Verwey (1930) and Milstein *et al.* (1970). Copulation always occurs on the nest or nest-site as soon as the pair is properly formed, that is to say once the female has been able to remain on the nest or nest-site for some hours, and ceases once the eggs are laid. Billing and Feather-nibbling often precede copulation and the male may engage in Neck-gripping, but it may occur without any preliminaries. The female usually stands up during copulation, though often loses her balance and rests on her tarsi. The male usually moves behind her and mounts by first placing one foot on her back. Sometimes, mounting is so quick that the male seems to jump onto the female. With the male on her back, the female extends her wings more or less to keep her balance, the male fully extending his for the same reason. The wings are not usually extended horizontally, as is the case for most herons, but raised above the bird's body, both humeri being almost vertical. Grasping the female's shoulders with his feet, the male lowers himself on his tarsi. At the same time, head turned sideways, he grasps the female firmly by the neck anywhere from just below the head to approximately halfway down. It sometimes happens that males copulate without grasping the neck or neck feathers of the female. In this position, the male lowers his tail to one side while the female raises hers and coition takes place. Although the male remains silent, the female often calls. Holstein (1927) describes it as a soft, plaintive call and Milstein *et al.* (1970) as a growling or wailing. After copulation, the male rises and steps to one side. The female usually fluffs her feathers out; the male may also do likewise. The maximum number of copulations recorded for a pair during one day is three. The copulations last between 8 and 16 seconds.

"Rape". Forced copulation may not be particularly common in Grey Herons, but Verwey (1930), whose study of their breeding behaviour is most thorough, has reported 10 cases. Two of the males involved were displaying, unmated males; the others had mates and nests, most already with eggs. Verwey (1930) also describes the furious attack on one of these males by the mate of the raped female.

Nest-building

After pair-formation, the two birds begin to build a nest on the site chosen by the male. However, further observations are necessary to be quite sure that Grey Herons only begin nest-building after pair-formation, since Verwey (1930) once observed an unpaired, courting heron bringing a stick to the nest-site.

The male usually displays on an old nest if one is available and in this case the newly formed pair starts to repair the old nest and then continues to build on it. However, males may begin to display on a new site even when an old nest is available. If an old nest is not available, the male chooses a favourable site to display and the newly formed pair begins a new nest. The foundation of the nest is the most difficult part of the building. Many sticks slide away and fall to the ground before some, by chance or by their particularly large size, get firmly stuck in the tree fork. Even so, new nests are often small, since the beginning of their construction takes several days. Verwey (1930) observed the foundation of a new nest which took 14 days to complete, although there was an interruption in building due to cold weather. Completion of the nest requires a further 3–5 days (Cramp and Simmons 1977), during which the birds are often in a great hurry as the female has to lay her eggs. Strijbos (1935) has observed nest-building at night and the gathering of nest material by moonlight. When the time comes for the female to lay her eggs, the newly built nest is often only about 50 cm wide and so thin that it is possible to see the eggs through the bottom of it (Creutz 1981).

Old Grey Herons nests are of very variable size but are always smaller than Stork nests. Typical of herons, it is built of sticks and twigs which protrude untidily. Some very old nests may weigh up to 75 kg, and be a cause of accidents, as spring storms may blow them down along with their eggs or young.

The bottom of the nest is built of large sticks stuck in the branches of a tree fork and bound together with smaller sticks or sometimes with rushes as well. Man-made materials have also been recorded, such as electric wires of various lengths (Creutz 1981). Smaller twigs are used for the upper part of the nest. A great variety of materials is used to line the nest cup, which is usually about 40–45 cm wide and very shallow. Small twigs, leaves and grass are most often used, but straw and roots are also found and sometimes earth and clay. Near the sea, wrack may be carried to line the nest. In reedbeds, the nests are built with reeds, rushes and other marsh vegetation. Feathers and even hairs have also been found in the nest structure.

Unlike other heron species, only Grey Herons sometimes line their nest with soft materials. This is certainly important to keep the eggs warm, as this species begins to lay its eggs in March or even February, and is the only heron adapted to live in the temperate zone of central Europe throughout the year.

The male brings most of the nest material (87.3% of the sticks; Milstein *et al.* 1970) and usually gives it to the female, who builds the nest, though the male may also place sticks in the nest himself. Milstein *et al.*'s (1970) observations confirm that females also bring sticks to the nest (12.7% of the sticks were brought by them). This behaviour is not observed in other European heron species (except in the very special case of the Bittern) where only males gather nest material.

Stick bringing, which begins during nest construction and before egg laying, continues during the whole incubating, hatching and guardian periods, but at a much slower rate. However, a peak of activity is observed again during the hatching period (Milstein *et al.* 1970). When the nest material is brought to the nest, a Greeting Ceremony is performed by the pair as previously described.

The sticks are gathered mostly from the ground in the woods of the heronry and also from the surrounding area, sometimes quite a distance away. Earnest attempts to break off green twigs occur now and then, but rarely with success. Sticks are also taken from old, unoccupied nests and, of course, unguarded nests are immediately robbed. However, Grey Herons may even try to rob an occupied nest:

> Normal robbing consists of a period of reconnaissance, then alighting alertly on the nest. If all is clear, the heron then stick-fidgets, possibly rejects up to four sticks, then flies off with the chosen one. The robber returns usually several times in quick succession until thwarted by the rightful occupant (Milstein *et al.* 1970).

Egg-laying and clutch size

The eggs of the Grey Heron are pale blue, often becoming stained during incubation. A sample of 300 eggs measured by Schönwetter (1967) gave the following measurements (mean and range): length 61 mm (52.8–68.0 mm), width 43 mm (38.5–49.5 mm). A sample of 100 eggs measured by Bauer (in Bauer and Glutz 1966) gave the following measurements (mean and range): length 60.6 mm (55.4–68.4 mm), width 43.0 mm (39.4–46.4 mm).

According to Bauer and Glutz (1966), the mean weight of full eggs is 60.8 g (range 48.2–68.5 g) (sample size not given). The mean weight of eggshell from a sample of 50 eggs was 4.63 g (range 3.76–5.78 g).

In England, egg-laying may commence as early as the beginning of February, but normally only begins in early March, with a peak at the end of March and early April. The last eggs are laid at the end of April, but those herons which have lost their clutch or brood may lay new clutches as late as June (Owen 1960). The egg-laying period seems to be the same in western Europe as in England. In northern countries, for example Sweden, it starts somewhat later. There the herons may lay as early as the end of March, but they do not normally start laying until the beginning of April, the peak period being the first 2 weeks of April (Curry-Lindahl 1959). Creutz (1981) found exactly the same egg-laying period in eastern Europe (at Oberlausitz, East Germany), adding that after a peak in April, eggs are normally laid in decreasing numbers until the end of the first 10 days of June. At the same heronry, the beginning of the egg-laying period varies from year to year according to the weather. Egg-laying commences early after mild winters and late after cold ones. The eggs are generally laid at 2-day intervals, but 3- and even 4-day intervals are possible.

According to Table 26, clutches of 4 eggs are most common, with a mean clutch size of 3.8–4.7 eggs. In addition to these data, the studies in France by Guichard (1949) and in Denmark by Holstein (1927), also found clutches of 4 eggs to be the most common. In a colony studied by Creutz in 1975, 4- and 5-egg clutches were equally common. The only heronry in which clutches of 5 eggs were most common, was that studied by Heckenroth in 1970 at Oberlausitz in East Germany.

Incubation and hatching

The incubation period ranges from 25 to 28 days, though it is usually 25–26 days; therefore, 31–32 days are necessary to bring a whole clutch to hatching. At the earliest, old females may lay their first egg 2 days after pair-formation (Bauer and Glutz 1966). Strijbos (1935) estimated that the first egg was usually laid about 6 days after pair-formation. Both sexes incubate. Milstein *et al.* (1970) noted an irregular start to incubation:

> The herons were restless on the first day and would stand on the nest often for long periods, alternated with periods of incubating. On the second and succeeding days, normal incubation behaviour was observed. This consisted of long periods of incubation by both sexes alternately, during which only short periods of non-incubation were interspersed.

Grey Herons incubate for long periods without being relieved from the nest by their mate. Holstein (1927) has observed one incubation spell of 12½ hours and Milstein *et al.* (1970) estimated that two birds which had incubated throughout the night had probably stayed at the nest for 14 hours 7 minutes and 14 hours 27 minutes respectively.

> Behaviour of herons during incubation follows a general pattern. They rise at irregular intervals for a short period, usually about three minutes. During this time they often stretch, preen and scratch their heads and necks. Herons often stick-fidget or turn their eggs at this time, and usually defaecate through the outer twigs or off the nest. They may also rise to shake off raindrops, yawn or re-arrange displeasing outer twigs, often after commencing this fidgeting from a prone position. Herons usually change direction randomly before settling to incubate again, although some indivduals seem to prefer one favorite direction. (Milstein *et al.* 1970).

Egg losses are very variable from one heronry to another and from year to year in the same heronry. For the years 1955–1959, Creutz (1981) estimated egg loss and hatching failure at between 13 and 28%, the mean loss being 21.5%. During this period, 52.1% of all clutches hatched without any egg loss, 25% of clutches lost one egg and 8.4% of clutches were lost altogether. Bernt (in Creutz 1981) found 15% egg loss, Lowe (1954) 10% and Knabe (in Creutz 1981) only 3%.

DEVELOPMENT AND CARE OF THE YOUNG

Three phases may be distinguished after hatching: the guardian period (the first 10 days of this period is often called the brooding period), when one of the parents is constantly at the nest; the post-guardian period, when the young are at the nest and their parents only visit the nest to feed them; and the fledgling period, when the young are able to fly and begin to hunt for themselves but are still fed by their parents.

The guardian period

For about the first 10 days of their lives, the chicks are continuously brooded by one of their parents. After that time, one of the adults remains constantly at the nest to watch the chicks, although it often only stands at the nest or near by. According to Milstein *et al.* (1970), the total guardian period lasts for about 26–31 days. Owen (1955) considers that it lasts for only 3 weeks, followed by a period of slow change in behaviour, in which neither parent stands for very long at the nest. In my opinion, Owen's observation is nearer the truth, though further observations on this point are needed.

When brooding, the adult is more attentive and more restless than during incubation. Spells at the nest are also shorter, averaging 4 hours 17 minutes (range 1 h 39 min to 8 h 24 min) (Milstein *et al.* 1970). During this period, if the weather deteriorates – cold, rain or snow – the young are protected by one of the parents. When small, they are brooded and when older, the adult stands over them. However, towards the end of the guardian period, Milstein has observed young that are incompletely feathered getting soaked in a rainstorm while the parent stood by. Lowe (1954) has made the same observation: during a thunderstorm with heavy rain, the chicks stood upright close together in the nest and suffered no ill-effect afterwards. When the sun is too hot, the attending adult stands for hours, its back turned towards the sun and its wings extended to shelter the chicks. Both adult and young gular-flutter, sometimes with a slightly open bill, to lower their body temperature by evaporation.

Heron chicks seem to spend most of their time just standing or dozing, waiting to be fed. However, their development is extremely rapid, especially during the guardian period. On the first day, the chicks lie on the nest bottom and are only able to raise their heads and open their beaks for short periods. Very soon after they are able to sit on their round bodies and small tarsi, and stretch their necks with open beaks giving the incessant hunger cry. During the first days, this soliciting call is a quiet chittering. Soon, however, a harsher call, "yek, yek, yek, yek", is heard. The cry is entirely vocal, "yet of such quality as to suggest bill-clappering" (Lowe 1954).

During their first 10 days of life, the chicks sleep a great deal, becoming much more active after the brooding period. By 2 weeks of age, they begin to stand on their legs. At about 18 days, instead of laying flat on the nest floor when danger draws near, they try to stand up, beak pointing towards the intruder (Creutz 1981). At 20 days, they stand easily, usually stretching and preening on the nest rim, returning to the centre of the nest to sleep.

When only a few days old, the chicks begin to preen their down. Later, "the young birds trim their growing feathers carefully following each feather-tract, nibbling the quills and generally giving much attention to their plumage" (Lowe 1954).

> There are many dropped sticks on the ground and the reason is not far to seek. When the adults are carrying sticks for actual building, very few are lost and even after the nest appears to be virtually complete the sticks brought as ceremonial offerings are worked into the structure; but the young, within ten days of being hatched, begin to pick up and rearrange any loose nesting material. Presently, in their eagerness to indulge in this practice, they pull sticks out of the nest and place them in another position. It is during this activity that so many sticks are dropped and the number increases vastly after the young are a month old (Lowe 1954).

The adults do not foul their nest much, and generally defecate over the edge of it. During early brooding, they even clean the nest, picking up eggshells and small refuse, which they deposit over the side. Later, when the chicks are moving about, they defecate where they stand so that the droppings percolate through the nest. Heron nests rapidly become "white-washed", as does the foliage and the ground below.

Grey Herons feed their young by regurgitation, usually depositing the food into the nest before giving it to the chicks. However, Lowe (1954) noted that "all food during the 10 first days is placed directly into the chicks' gullets". This may not be the rule, at least for such a long period, as this has only rarely been reported. Further studies are needed to improve our knowledge of the adults' means of feeding their young during the first days of life. Very soon, the chicks begin to pick up the regurgitated food from the nest floor without waiting for the adult to feed them.

At about 15 days when the young are stronger they seize the adult's beak in theirs and are fed directly from beak to beak. By the age of 14–17 days,

> the two largest nestlings still clamouring, reached up for the adult's bill, which was shortly lowered to them, and eagerly grasped by one young heron at either side. The ensuing rhythmic movements stimulated the older bird to disgorge, and bill grasping became henceforward the invariable practice (Lowe 1954).

Food still sometimes falls onto the nest floor where it is rapidly picked up by the hungry young.

The food is regurgitated in very different stages of digestion according to the age of the young. For newly hatched chicks, the food must be in an advanced state of digestion and is reduced to a semi-liquid state. Later, when food is regurgitated into the nest before being given to the chicks, "it is friable and disintegrates on impact" (Lowe 1954). Food items which are too big, or not digested enough, are re-eaten by the adult. Later, when the chicks are 2–3 weeks old, the food is regurgitated in almost fresh condition; fish, often eels, frogs and other food items being easily recognizable.

The post-guardian period

This period begins about 3–4 weeks after the first egg is hatched when the chicks are old enough to defend themselves. At about 25–27 days of age, they begin to venture outside the nest, climbing on the branches supporting it. At 30–34 days, they commonly climb from branch to branch to spend long periods at some distance from the nest, often in the shade of some thick foliage. At this stage they may already

> bring sticks when returning to their nests and sometimes there is much deliberation as to the best place to deposit the fresh material. Two or three young will hold a twig and try it in various positions before it is finally disposed of or, during an argument, dropped into the bracken.
> Particularly noticeable, now that the young are becoming more venturesome, is the prehensile use of their bills; as well as grasping with its mandibles, a young heron sometimes lays its bill across a branch either to help in climbing or to prevent a fall. Niethammer states that young herons from nests on the ground leave before they are fully fledged and it is a similarly precocious habit which causes them to scramble about the tree-tops before they can fly.
> Whenever a parent returns all the young greet it in the nest having scrambled back from their precarious 'flapping posts'. They grasp its bill and pump-handle it until there is no food left inside it; meantime their hunger-cries rise to squeals (Lowe 1954).

A heron feeding chicks is soon obvious by its dishevelled appearance. Its beautiful lanceolated breast plumes become stained and wavy and its long crest feathers are sometimes lost. The food is very unequally distributed during these struggles. Owen (1960) noted that:

> The first meal was taken almost entirely by the largest nestling, the second meal was shared among the three largest, the largest receiving the most, and the third meal was again shared among the three largest, but this time the third bird received the most. During this period (three-and-a-half hours) the smallest bird did not receive any food and was three times pushed out onto some branches by the other members of the brood.

The oldest chick of a brood observed by Lowe (1954) began to fly on its 41st day. Four days later, two more young of this brood were able to fly from branch to branch:

> Wing-exercises extend over the entire period the young are in the nest and after they have left it. Practice begins a few days after hatching; at a week old they stretch and raise their wings; in a fortnight they have begun their flapping

exercises; in three weeks they spend much time on the nest-rim and from then onwards they exercise regularly. From the earlier stretchings there gradually evolves a wing-beat so vigorous that the perch sways in rhythm, and so rapid as to exceed by far that of flying herons. Sometimes a bird will leap up and down, or run round the nest-rim, energetically beating the air with its wings. Another very precarious-looking antic is performed when a youngster, having climbed to some distant branch, clings to it firmly while flapping with such abandon that it seems in imminent danger of losing its balance (Lowe 1954).

The fledgling period

Eight weeks after hatching, Grey Herons are fully fledged and spend long periods away from the nest, though they still return to it to be fed and to roost. They acquire a new call, "a low and very short growl 'arr' uttered one or more times with a considerable interval between" (Lowe 1954). For a further 2 weeks or so, they stay in the vicinity of the heronry and begin to fish for themselves in the nearest water, often at the feet of the trees of the heronry and, after a few days, in pools, ditches and marshes nearby. At this age, young birds perching near the nests take an interest in adults flying over them on their way to distant fishing grounds. Some young try to follow the departing adults, but after some 100 m or so return to perch again on the trees of the heronry (Marion 1976). It is most probable that, after some false starts, their flying ability having improved, they follow the adults and leave the colony for good.

Chick aggression towards conspecifics

Parents never interfere when the chicks in their brood are quarrelling, no matter how dangerous for one of the chicks the fight may be. Fights usually occur during and after feeding, when some chicks are still hungry.

The chicks begin to quarrel when about 7 days old. Milstein *et al.* (1970) call these fights "pendulum fighting". Two chicks with stretched necks "would face each other at close range and exchange pecks, though the exchange was often one-sided. The pecking chick's head moved forward and returned to the vertical, while the pecked chick's head jerked backward and also returned to the vertical". When quarrelling, chicks seem to try to grasp each others' bills. This may be dangerous for the smallest sibling if, for example, it is weakened by a lack of food. Small chicks that have disappeared without any evidence of predation have usually been eaten by a sibling. Knabe (1938) found a chick choked to death while trying to swallow its sibling and the remains of a heron chick in the stomach of a larger one.

Lowe (1954) observed once, how a hungry heron chick succeeded "in grasping the bill of its sleeping nest-mate and wrestled it until the rhythmic motion induced it to throw up the fish". Quarrels become quite vicious when the chicks grow older, and genuine stabs may be given with the bill. Milstein *et al.* (1970) observed one 7-week-old chick which "had a red gash along the short white feathers overlying the mandible base". The youngest siblings are bullied and have the greatest difficulty in getting enough food. They are sometimes pushed out of the nest. Exhausted chicks may be pecked, often to death. When the chicks are about 3 weeks old, they begin to defend themselves against intruders. They have a typical threat squawk, and their crest feathers, which are always raised, certainly have a threatening effect. They also begin to perform the Forward Display and the Snap Display, especially the downward Snap Display. These threat displays are "much easier to release in the young while they have the habit of staying on the spot [nest] and hardly move about. When they grow older and begin to walk, flight responses become gradually more common" (Baerends and Van der Cingel 1962).

When the chicks are large enough to be left alone in the nest, they initially respond to a strange heron approaching the nest by begging. But after a while, they begin to threaten the intruder, which always leaves and flies away after having looked at the chicks for some time. Fledglings coming to a strange nest are always attacked by those owning the nest. They lunge at the intruder and then fence with their bills.

Breeding Grey Herons defend their nest and young against other adults but seem to ignore strange chicks and even fledglings. Beetham (1910) observed a strange chick being fed by the adults and some of Knabe's (in Milstein *et al.* 1970) small chicks introduced into nests with larger chicks were successfully fledged. Milstein *et al.* (1970) have observed strange fledglings coming to a nest with small chicks without the interference of the adult guarding the nest. There are not many cases of small Grey Heron chicks being introduced to strange nests, but the acceptance of small chicks by an adult is quite usual among birds. In contrast, there are many observations concerning the reactions of adult herons of various species to strange fledglings. In all cases so far recorded, they are savagely attacked, e.g. the Night Heron, Little Egret and Cattle Egret. Thus the indifference of Grey Herons towards strange fledglings, while typical of birds in general, seems very different from that of the other heron species.

Feeding the young

Owen (1955) and Milstein *et al.* (1970) both observed that Grey Herons feed their young mostly in the early morning (peak feeding being at 06.00 h) and in the late afternoon (with a less pronounced peak at 16.00–17.00 h) (see Fig. 12). Owen (1955) deduced the importance of the nocturnal fishing activity of Grey Herons, and wrote: "the peak of arrivals just after dawn indicates that many birds had been catching food some hours earlier, indeed some birds were arriving with food while it was still dark". During observations on windless nights, when sound carries well, Milstein *et al.* (1970) counted each feeding they heard, judged by the hungry cries and struggles of the chicks, confirming that chicks were fed at night as suspected (Fig. 13). They were fed more often during moonlit nights than during dark nights. During the day, six nests were watched from dawn to dusk (17 hours) and each feeding visit counted. The parents came to feed at mean intervals of 3.29 hours during the early guardian period (brooding), 3.61 hours during the

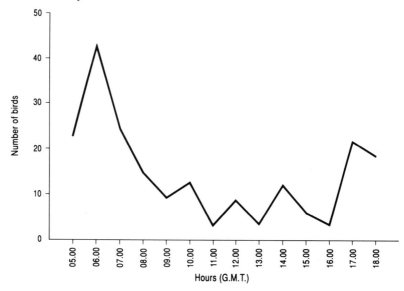

Figure 12   The number of Grey Herons arriving with food during each hour of daylight from 05.00 h onwards at Buscot on 3 days in April 1954 (after Owen 1955).

second part of the guardian period, 4.85 hours during the post-guardian period and 5.20 hours during the early fledgling period. During the brooding period, small chicks were fed up to four times by the same bird at the nest, which regurgitated small quantities of food each time. The mean interval between the first and the second regurgitation of the adult at the nest was 1.19 hours, between the second and the third regurgitation 1.34 hours and between the third and fourth 1.42 hours. Small chicks, which grow fast but have small stomachs, are thus fed most often. After the brooding period, the adult regurgitates at once all the food it has brought to the nest (Fig. 14).

The parents return to their nests to feed their young 5 times a day on

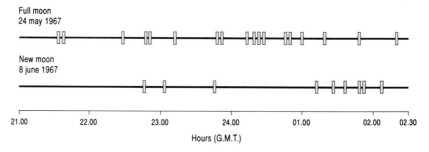

Figure 13   The incidence of feeding recorded by sound at night, when it is too dark to observe individual nests (after Milstein *et al.* 1970).

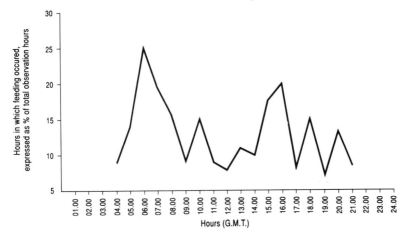

Figure 14   The ratio of hours spent feeding to hours of observation at different times of the day (after Milstein *et al.* 1970).

average during the early guardian period, 4–5 times during the late guardian period and 3–4 times during the post-guardian and fledgling periods. Milstein *et al.* (1970) thus noted that "it is a progressive decrease in feeding frequencies from brooding to fledgling". This occurs despite the fact that the time available for fishing by the adults is doubled after the guardian period. From Owen's observations on the time required to collect a complete meal (on average 7 h, but ranging from 3 h 50 min to 11 h) and the growth of the chicks, it is clear that they receive more food during the post-guardian period than at any time before. The young, being much larger, are able to eat greater quantities of food at each meal. Since it takes longer to digest big meals than small ones, the parents do not have to feed them as often. As long as the young have not reached their maximum weight (about 1500 g), which occurs at 3–4 weeks, their need for food is very great and the parents are obliged to fish as much as possible. Afterwards, the quantity needed by the young decreases and the adults are able to feed their offspring more easily. It is exceptional for the young to die of starvation when older than 4 weeks. Verwey (1930) and Strijbos (1935) noted a progressive decrease in the feeding rate during the fledgling period. Verwey considered this important as an excess of fat could hinder flight and is certainly detrimental in learning to fish.

Growth and mortality of nestlings

In order to study the growth of nestlings, it is necessary to weigh them regularly. In the wild, heron chicks become progressively more difficult to catch as they learn to escape, climbing away through the branches, instead of facing an intruder. Owen, who has weighed many broods, was able to catch young up to 3 and sometimes 4 weeks of age. Since herons hatch asynchronously, the chicks in a brood are of very different sizes. Owen (1960) found that the chicks which died in a brood were always the smallest and showed evidence of starvation. This was the only frequent cause of mortality:

> There was no evidence of disease, harmful endoparasites were not common, and apart from a few *Carnus hemapterus* (Diptera), blood-sucking ectoparasites were absent. Predation affected only eggs and very small young, and whenever small young were killed by a predator, the whole brood was destroyed. Such losses were infrequent (Owen 1960).

Once the young had grown older, and left the nest, there were also a few accidental deaths.

Owen (1960) has produced typical growth curves for a Grey Heron brood (Fig. 15). Only the first chick shows normal growth. The growth of the second chick was somewhat retarded due to insufficient feeding day 12. The third chick was in even greater difficulty from this moment, and only survived because the fourth, very weak chick died of starvation on the 18th day, allowing the third chick to obtain more food and increase its weight thereafter. The fifth chick never had a chance.

Heinroth (1967) studied the growth of heron chicks in captivity. His

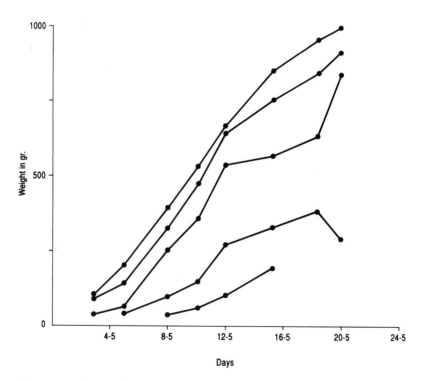

Figure 15   The weights of a brood of nestlings at Wytham Woods, Oxfordshire, 1955 (Owen 1960).

growth curve shows the very fast growth of a young Grey Heron between 9 and 25 days (Fig. 16). In the wild, during this period, only a few chicks will get enough food to approach this ideal: others will show slower growth and many will die. The quantity of food required increases rapidly each day as the chick grows larger. According to Heinroth's observations, by about 17 days a chick has reached its maximum food intake about 330 g per day. Thus, the demand for food is enormous from that day onwards. With the hungry young becoming more active each day, it is almost impossible for the adult on guard to remain in the vicinity of the nest. At this time, the young also begin to be able to defend themselves, and the adult, which is more or less obliged to escape from the begging chicks, leaves them more and more often and is thus free to fish. However, once they have reached about 1500 g and are 32–35 days old, the chicks are nearly full-grown and, in the wild, do not seem to put on much more weight. In contrast, Heinroth's captive chick continued to gain weight up to 3 months of age, when it weighed 1990 g.

Owen (1960) weighed five broods of between 1 and 5 chicks. He observed that:

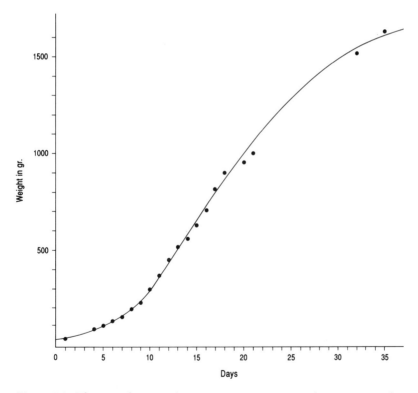

Figure 16   The growth curve of a young Grey Heron reared in captivity (after Heinroth 1967).

The broods of one to three grew normally, but in the brood of four the third and fourth birds did not grow as rapidly as the birds in the brood of three, and the fourth bird eventually died. In the brood of five, the third, fourth and fifth birds grew very slowly and all three eventually died, the smallest first.

He concluded that:

In this instance when five broods were followed simultaneously through the critical growing period, the broods of one to three were found to be completely successful, the brood of four lost one young, and the brood of five lost three young. Feeding conditions through the period must have been similar for each pair of adult herons and some food samples confirmed this, and the mortality in the larger broods was evidently due to a food shortage caused by the greater number of young in the nest.

The adaptive value of asynchronous hatching is that when food is scarce, the smallest young in the nest die of starvation, but when food is more plentiful all the young are raised. If all the young were hatched at the same time they would all be of the same size in the nest and each would run an equal risk of occasional deprivation, so that all might be so weakened as to die.

FEEDING BEHAVIOUR AND FOOD

Grey Herons fish mostly in shallow waters but also commonly hunt on dry land. They usually feed by day, especially in the morning and evening, but have also been observed fishing at night by moonlight or by the light of road lamps (Richner 1986).

Usual fishing methods

Grey Herons usually take fish up to a depth of 10 cm and exceptionally up to 17 cm (Bauer and Glutz 1966). They commonly use two methods of fishing (Meyerriecks 1960), the first being the Stand-and-wait method in which the bird stands motionless in shallow water, often for several minutes. The second is the Wade or Walk Slowly method, in which the legs and feet move very slowly so as to avoid disturbing the prey. During these two methods, the position of the body may vary from quite erect (body axis at an angle of 45° to the horizontal) to horizontal. The bird adopts a great variety of positions of the head and neck, so as to look into the water from different angles. However, the neck is always curved just before catching a prey to allow, by a sudden outstretch, the direct and swift strike of the beak. It seems that the more swift-moving the targeted prey, the more the heron curves its neck. Occasionally, prey may also be caught from the typical resting position – body erect and head between the shoulders.

The prey is usually seized between the mandibles. Rapid opening and closing of the beak manipulates it into a head-first position before the bird swallows it whole. Very occasionally, large prey may be stabbed with one or both mandibles. Cook (1978) has observed Grey Herons flying "to the river

Grey Herons foraging.

bank with their mandibles kept apart by the transfixed fish they had speared". The fish is then removed by pointing the beak downwards while shaking the head. It is then caught before it falls to the ground or into the water. Small prey are swallowed live, but large ones are killed before the bird tries to swallow them. "These prey are usually held crosswise in the bill, gripped just before the gills and shaken vigorously; possibly this breaks the vertebral column" (Cook 1978).

Very large fish, over 190–200 mm in length, and big eels which wriggle around the beak of the heron, are taken ashore and stabbed to death. Grey Herons sometimes take and kill fish too large for them to swallow and these are abandoned. Under normal conditions, herons do not eat fish by picking or tearing bits off them.

Unusual fishing methods

Grey Herons have occasionally been seen flying over deep water to fish. They fly low over the water, circling and even hovering. On landing, the bird drops its legs and lands feet and chest first. Then, floating on the water, it tries to catch any fish within reach of its beak (Stacey and Gervis 1967, Boyle 1967). This method is probably only used when fish are numerous or in a bad condition. A more efficient means is described by Pettitt (1950). When landing – in this case also feet first – the heron kept its wings outstreched at an angle of about 60° to the water surface and immediately upon touching the water jabbed its beak, and often also its head, under the water, to grab a prey. Another unusual fishing method was recorded by Pettitt (1950), who saw a heron successfully catching fish by jumping down from a perched position into the water below, where fish had been spotted. An interesting and unusual observation was related by Parsons (1947): a Grey Heron probed with its beak into the muddy bed of a small stream in winter, and after a short period of time took a frog.

Capture of mammals and birds

Grey Herons commonly catch mice, moles and rats. Large rats are repeatedly held under water to drown them (Banks 1982), mice and moles are swallowed alive. The method used to catch moles is described by Brooke (in Lowe 1966): "The heron was watching the movement of the earth as the mole tunnelled its way just below the surface and struck at the moment of exact range." Grey Herons are often reported to take birds, which are swallowed alive or drowned like rats. The birds taken are mostly chicks of various waterbirds such as the Little Grebe and Coot, or adults of small species, mostly passeriformes and charadriiformes. Very occasionally, Grey Herons may even take bigger birds, as one observation by Murphy (1976) shows:

on closer observation of the marshes, we could see Water Rails (*Rallus aquaticus*) seeking shelter from the incoming tide on rafts of floating vegetation. Small groups of herons landed nearby, seized rails in their bills and then flew to shallow water, where they drowned their prey. At one stage we saw four herons, each devouring a rail.

Kleptoparasitism and opportunistic hunting techniques

Kleptoparasitism by Grey Herons is very rare. However, it does happen that odd individuals discover this method of feeding and Cooper (1984) observed a Grey Heron taking food from Cape Cormorants:

> The heron was first observed roosting overnight on a rock that supported breeding Cape Cormorants. The next morning it was seen walking among the cormorants eliciting a great amount of threat behaviour from them. On three occasions it walked quickly with partially opened wings towards large feathered Cape Cormorant chicks being fed away from their nests. Each 'chase' resulted in cessation of feeding and the cormorants' rapid movement away from the heron. On the third occasion it succeeded in interrupting the chick being fed so that part of the meal being regurgitated by the adult was spilt onto the nest rock. The heron then picked up this material and swallowed it.

In Sweden, a heron – probably a juvenile – was seen to attack and pursue an Osprey, to rob it of the fish it had just caught. The attack was unsuccessful (Kullmann 1971).

Grey Herons, like most animals, try to catch prey with the minimum of effort, and are always on the lookout for good opportunities, as witnessed by Griffiths (1969):

> At Talybont Reservoir, Breconshire, we saw a Heron *Ardea cinerea* standing on the edge of a small concrete 'waterfall' about two feet high; it was leaning forward in such a manner that its open bill was just below the level of the overflow. The pool at the foot of the waterfall was full of small fish, approximately two inches in length, which were attempting to leap up to the stream above; a few were successful. The Heron remained motionless in the same position for five or ten seconds, with its bill in the vicinity of the leaping fish, and as soon as one of these jumped into the space between the bird's open mandibles they would snap shut and catch it. The Heron then raised itself so that it could adjust and swallow its prey. After a few seconds' rest, it returned to the original posture and repeated the procedure.
>
> The Heron had what appeared to be a very casual and leisurely approach to catching the fish: it was not seen to 'dart' its bill in any direction, apparently being quite content to wait for one to jump unintentionally into its mouth. There appeared to be a sufficient number of fish leaping the fall for the Heron to obtain two to four per minute in this manner.

Comparative foraging efficiency of adult and first-year birds

Catching agile prey is difficult. When young herons begin to hunt for themselves, there is plenty of food available and they have some months to learn to fish before the lean winter months. Cook's (1978) study shows that inexperienced first-year birds are much less efficient at catching prey than adult birds. First-year birds "made at least twice as many attempts to capture prey but attained only 62% of the adult catch rate in terms of grams per minute. Younger birds spent 1.8 times longer at foraging than adults." When foraging along the shore, they often chose less suitable tidal conditions, and also more often caught inanimate objects, which they then released.

Feeding territories

Some recent studies following individually marked or radio-tagged herons on their fishing grounds have tried to answer many questions concerning the behaviour of Grey Herons on their hunting grounds. Marion's (1984) observations of nine radio-tagged birds show that Grey Herons commonly defend feeding areas during the breeding season. Within its feeding area, a Grey Heron has a few, specific favourite watching posts. Birds which have a feeding territory fly back and forth by the same route between the colony and their territory each day. Marion studied birds from two colonies. The distance to the feeding area was 2.5–16 km for the colony at Guérande (Bretagne) and 15–33 km for that at Lac Grand-Lieu (except for 6.8% of the breeders which fed at the lake itself, where most of the favourable spots were used communally: probably too many birds were present to make it possible for one bird to keep all the others away).

A study of five radio-tagged Grey Herons (2 breeding adults, 1 nonbreeding adult and 2 non-breeding, first-year birds) by Van Vessem et al. (1984) also demonstrated the existence of feeding territories among breeding birds and the seasonal changes in exploitation of the environment by herons. All the radio-tagged birds remained within a radius of 3 km from the colony during the whole observation period, except for one of the breeding adults which flew 9–10 km to and from the feeding area each day in May. The two breeding adults were followed from March to June. During March and April, they explored different areas around the colony. In May, and at the beginning of June (probably from egg-hatching to the end of breeding), each bird was seen at its feeding territory, from which all other herons were chased. At the beginning of June, they again visited different areas and later seemed to have left as they could no longer be located. In April, the three non-breeding herons also explored various areas around the colony. After hatching, they very rarely visited the colony again and became more and more restricted to small areas at an increasing distance from the colony. These birds were never observed defending a territory. It therefore seems that, during incubation, adult breeders are on the lookout for the best feeding places, which they later occupy and defend only during the time they are feeding their young.

These two studies provide interesting results, but at the cost of disturbing the birds a good deal. Catching breeding adults always causes severe chick losses at a colony. Moreover, herons with radio-harnesses do not behave normally. Van Vessem et al. (1984), who used harnesses, do not discuss this point, though a few birds probably got used to them after a few days.

However, Marion's study was not successful when harnesses were used. Only when the transmitters were fixed directly onto the tail feathers, did the birds appear to behave normally.

Cook (1978) observed three herons in August and September, one colour-marked young and two adults individually recognizable by their plumage characteristics. His results are somewhat different from those of previous studies, as all of the herons observed defended territories – the adults, which at that time did not breed, as well as the first-year birds. Communal feeding occurred along one stretch of the estuary studied by Cook, where the birds could only feed occasionally. To defend the territories Cook (1978) observed three aggressive displays:

Beak Held Up

This display occurred commonly between neighbours when one bird was reaching the limits of its normal range and approaching its neighbour's. The latter would stiffen up, stand with wings drooping very slightly, neck upright and beak tilted back at an angle of about 45 degrees to the horizontal. Sometimes it would perform a very deliberate slow walk in this position towards or at right angles to the approach line of the other.

Spread-wings

The spread-wings display was often given by a pursued bird after it was once again well within its own area. It would then turn around and walk up . . . towards its pursuer with wings fully outstretched and the beak again up at an angle of about 45 degrees.

Crouched Run

This was seen on only four occasions, when the individuals concerned ran at another with body axis horizontal, neck held hunched on its shoulders and beak horizontal.

An interesting study was carried out by Richner (1986) in the winter. Nine herons were caught at their communal night roost using a catapult elastic-powered net. The birds were wing-tagged. It was clearly shown that some adults were territorial and some were not, while none of the juveniles defended a territory. Three groups could be distinguished: one which fished only in the estuary, one which fished only in streams, and a third, the "switchers". This last group fished in the estuary, as long as the state of the tide made fishing there more profitable than in the streams. They switched to stream fishing when the fishing conditions in the estuary worsened or became impossible at high tide. The "switchers" were in good condition, with a mean weight of 1993 ± 53 g. The stream-feeders had a difficult time and their mean weight was only 1378 ± 72 g. The estuary-only feeders, which were few in number, could not have survived had they not fished by night under a road lamp where small fish congregated, since the estuary was only fishable for a short period each day. They were not weighed.

Two juveniles, which that winter used to fish in the stream on the territories of several different adults, had a hard time. They were chased off as soon as the owner of the territory detected them and one was finally killed by an adult during a territorial interaction. This observation is particularly interesting. It shows that when Grey Herons are numerous and most available feeding sites are occupied, the mortality of first-year birds may be high, as it is unlikely that they will be able to fish undisturbed in a good area.

These four recent studies clearly establish that Grey Herons often defend individual fishing territories. It seems that most territories are held by breeders during the breeding season and by adults in the winter. First-year birds probably try to establish territories but do not seem to succeed in keeping them.

Food

Grey Herons take a great variety of prey. They capture mostly fish but also commonly take amphibians and small mammals. Reptiles and insects are also taken and occasionally crustaceans, molluscs, worms and birds. The diet varies considerably with the habitat and season, and has been evaluated by analyses of stomach contents, by the study of food regurgitated by chicks at the nest and, to a lesser extent by analyses of pellets.

Vasvàri (1948–51) studied the stomach contents of 200 birds in Hungary. They showed that Grey Herons ate (by weight) mostly fish (chiefly carp *Cyprinus*, bleak *Alburnus*, Crucian carp *Carassius*, sunfish *Eupomotis*, pike *Esox* and rudd *Scardinius*). In addition to fish, they also ate a sizeable quantity of amphibians (*Rana* and *Pelobates*) and some mammals (watershrew *Neomys*, mole *Talpa*, water-vole *Arvicola* and field-voles *Microtus*). They also took numerous insects (chiefly *Dysticus*, *Cybister*, *Hydrous* and *Hydrophilus*), though these did not contribute significantly to the diet.

Eighty-nine stomachs collected in Italy by Moltoni (1936) during the summer contained by frequency: 68.3% insects and their larvae (*Hydrophilidae, Dysticidae* and *Odonata*), 26% fish (chiefly sunfish *Eupomotis*), 24% frogs (*Rana*), 24% snakes (grass-snake *Natrix natrix*) and 12.5% small mammals (mole *Talpa* and water-vole *Arvicola*).

Eighteen stomachs collected in France from 1921 to 1926 had greater proportions of fish (perch *Perca*, tench *Tinca*, bleak *Alburnus* and eel *Anguilla*), mammals (water-vole *Arvicola*) and amphibians (*Rana*), but a smaller proportion of insects (Madon 1935).

Forty-three stomachs from the Danube Delta in Romania contained by volume 87% fish (chiefly pike *Esox*, Crucian carp *Carassius*, perch *Perca*, carp *Cyprinus*, sturgeon *Acipenser*, tench *Tinca* and loach *Cobitus*) weighing 1–125 g, with a preference for fish of about 70 g (Andone *et al.*, in Cramp and Simmons 1977).

A study in the Astrakhan Reserve, Volga Delta, USSR, from 1952 to 1954, of stomach contents, pellets and regurgitates showed that Grey Herons took mostly fish (chiefly roach *Rutilus*, carp *Cyprinus*, pike *Esox* and rudd

Scardinus) and a crustacean (*Apus cancriformis*). Only a very few reptiles, amphibians and mammals were taken (Skokova 1960).

Dementiev and Gladkov (1951) noted that in late autumn along the east coast of the Caspian Sea, Grey Herons were taking crabs (*Potambus leptodactylus* and *Potambus pachypus*).

A study of the prey regurgitated by chicks at the nest was undertaken by Owen (1955) between 1952 and 1954. The chicks were mostly fed on fish, though some mammals and insects were also present in the regurgitates.

PREDATION

Young Grey Herons at the nest are easy prey for the Eagle Owl during the post-guardian period. In southern Sweden, Olson (1979) observed a pair of Eagle Owls that brought several young herons to their nest from a nearby heronry.

Great Black-backed Gulls often try to steal food from Grey Herons. They are sometimes successful, as Forsberg (1979) observed, when a Grey Heron, frightened by the sudden sight of the observer, flew up with its prey. Attacked by a Great Black-backed Gull, the heron soon released its prey, which was taken by the gull before it reached the water. In contrast, Marshall (1956) observed a Grey Heron defending its catch with success. He wrote:

> I saw a Heron flying across the reservoir at Abberton, Essex, with a large fish in its bill. A Great Black-backed Gull (*Larus marinus*) then appeared in pursuit and the Heron dropped the fish into the water. The gull promptly retrieved it and flew off, while the Heron went on to the bank about forty yards away. After the gull had gone a hundred yards or more, the Heron uttered several long-drawn and grating

A Grey Heron swallowing an eel.

squawks (which gave the impression of extreme rage) and flew off after the gull which, to my surprise, it easily overhauled. A confused aerial skirmish then took place and the fish fell once more into the water, whereupon the Heron dropped to the surface and snatched it up again, while the gull flew off. The Heron made its way quickly to the bank and took cover under some willows. Although seven or eight Great Black-backed Gulls hovered over it during the five minutes or more that it took to swallow the fish, it now remained calm and unconcerned. I was particularly impressed by the Heron's apparent fury and its subsequent pertinacity in recovering its prey.

An attack on a Grey Heron by a Great Skua was observed at sea 4 miles northeast of Walls, Shetland (Campbell and Denzey). On 6 August 1953:

a few Herons were on the wing. A Great Skua suddenly swooped on a Heron from above, apparently striking with its feet at its victim's back, but also holding with its beak, for both fell together to the water. There the Skua, on the Heron's back, continued its attack by pecking repeatedly at the head of its prey, at the same time using a paddling action with its feet, as if to force the heron under water. The Heron finally succumbed.

Ravens and Carrion Crows are sometimes reported to nest in heronries with apparently little harm to the herons (Cox 1925, Thonen 1982). Carrion Crows have been observed mobbing Grey Herons apparently without damage, at least to healthy individuals (Cramb 1972, Birkhead 1972).

FISH FARMS, ANGLING AND THE PROTECTION OF THE GREY HERON

As Grey Herons in Europe are today generally protected, either during the breeding season or throughout the year, they have become quite numerous in some areas, thereby creating difficulties for fish farmers. Since herons fish for the easiest prey, many of the fish they catch are in a poor condition. On the other hand, if the fish are large, herons often try to capture them by stabbing, causing injuries to those fish that are missed and leaving wounds that may become infected.

When Grey Herons are not protected or a licence to shoot them is easy to get, the most commonly used method to eliminate them at fish ponds is to shoot them. This drastic method nearly caused the disappearance of the species in Europe. In England in the late 1970s, the number of Grey Herons shot at fish farms was estimated at 4600 ± 1000 (about 2400 of which were juveniles). The number of nestlings which died at the nest of starvation caused by the loss of one or both parents was estimated at 2150 a year (Meyer 1981). Thus, shooting at fish farms was the main cause of mortality among Grey Herons in England during this period.

There are, however, other ways to keep herons away from fish farms! Two approaches are possible. The first is to make sure that there are favourable fishing areas in the vicinity where herons can fish undisturbed, and the second is to make fish ponds unattractive to herons. When fish farms are established in areas favourable for Grey Herons, such as estuaries and extensive lowland marshes, they are often situated in places where the birds fished in the past. Keeping the remaining wetland areas as favourable as possible for herons by avoiding drainage is then of the utmost importance. If the pisciculture is established in drier areas where only streams are to be found, the river banks should be maintained in a suitable manner, gentle slopes with short vegetation being best. If some wetlands exist along the river they should be protected. If not, some suitable ponds ought to be created. When irrigation ditches and water reservoirs are constructed, the well-being of the herons should be taken into account. Only then will the various methods undertaken to protect the fish farmer's ponds have some chance of success.

Various methods have been tried to keep herons away from fish ponds (Van Vessem 1982), but only the ones that make fishing difficult or impossible are successful. Most methods which are meant to scare the birds away rapidly become ineffective, since herons do not react for long to warning stimuli that are not followed by real danger. Thus the use of scarecrows, as well as hanging up dead herons, has little effect. After a while, Grey Herons also get used to the firing of blank ammunition. The recorded cries of raptors are ineffective, as are most calls of the Grey Heron itself. Only the cries of frightened young at the nest and of frightened adults flying away seem effective, but only if broadcast at irregular intervals from various places, not more than 100 m from the bird to be chased away.

In the case of narrow, shallow containers, where numerous fish stay close together, as is often the case on trout farms, a very effective method is to cover the whole area with a net or wire mesh. In the case of large fish ponds, the most effective method is to make the ponds themselves unfavourable for heron fishing. Thus they should be made too deep for a heron to wade in them. The banks around the pond should be high and steep to prevent them from catching fish from the land. When old fish ponds are used which do not have steep borders, twines and floats are helpful to prevent fishing (see Fig. 17).

In areas where large fish farms are established, a good method would certainly be to employ one or two retired men with trained dogs who could walk around the ponds mainly in the early morning and evening to disturb the

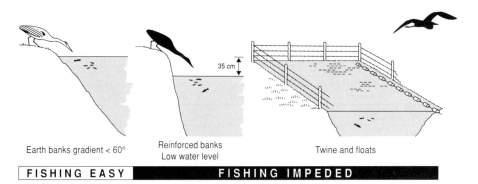

Earth banks gradient < 60°

Reinforced banks
Low water level

Twine and floats

FISHING EASY   **FISHING IMPEDED**

Figure 17   Methods of reducing the fishing success of Grey Herons at fish farms (after Meyer 1981).

fishing herons. To be really effective, these rounds should be made at various times of the day and also during moonlit nights.

Like fish farmers, anglers also dislike fishing Grey Herons. They are convinced that the herons will take most of the fish they intend to catch themselves. According to studies along streams (Geiger 1984, Krämer 1984), it seems that the density of fish in different parts of a stream does not depend at all on the presence or absence of herons. Fish density is linked with other factors such as disease, the physical characteristics of the stream (shape, depth and nature of the ground) and quality of the water (pH, oxygen content, etc.). These kinds of studies should be undertaken on a larger scale in order to convince anglers that the presence of scattered herons along a stream neither lessens the size nor the number of their catch.

Table 15.　The number of breeding pairs of Grey Herons in East Germany

Location	No. of breeding pairs	
	1960	1978
Rostock	399	520
Schwerin	178–183	440–450
Neubrandenbourg	229	719–755
Postdam	573–602	785–795
Frankfurt/Oder	222–254	468
Göttbus	276	384–404
Magdeburg	104	224
Suhl	24	30–32
Hälle	59–64	389

Table 16.　The size distribution of French heronries in 1974 and 1981[a]

No. of pairs	No. of heronries	
	1974	1981
2–20	32	59
21–90	31	70
91–250	6	23
251–1100	1	3

[a] After Brosselin (1974) and Duhautois (1981).

Table 17.　The size distribution of Dutch heronries in 1956[a]

No. of pairs	No. of heronries
1–15	24
16–30	62
31–100	29
101–200	8
>200	4

[a] After Van der Ven (1962).

Table 18.   *The size distribution of Dutch heronries in 1975*[a]

No. of pairs	No. of heronries
2–10	70
11–25	37
26–50	28
51–100	30
101–200	29
>200	10

[a] After Blok and Roos (1977).

Table 19.   *The size distribution of heronries in England and Wales in 1954 and 1976*[a]

No. of pairs	No. of heronries	
	1954	1976
1	54	43
2–10	117	189
11–20	66	74
21–30	18	38
31–40	21	23
41–50	9	7
51–60	2	5
61–70	6	2
71–80	1	2
81–90	2	1
91–100	2	0
>100	3	5
Total	301	389
Mean heronry size	15.7	13.9

[a] After Reynolds (1979).

Table 20.   *English heronries containing over 100 nests in 1954 and 1972–1977*[a]

Location	No. of heronries						
	1954	1972	1973	1974	1975	1976	1977
Brownsea Is. (Dorset)	64	124	114	127	114	101	107
High Halstow (Kent)	129	167	174	178	182	185	195
Walthamstow (Essex)	69	83	105	113	101	111	115
Islington (Norfolk)	127	63	58	48	42	51	38
Tabley (Cheshire)	111	91	95	88	102	103	103
Claughton (Lancashire)	c. 39	106	113	109	124	107	127

[a] After Reynolds (1979).

Table 21.   *The size distribution of Belgian heronries in 1981[a]*

No. of pairs	No. of heronries
1	5
2–10	11
11–50	7
51–100	6
>100	3

[a] After Van Vessem (1982).

Table 22.   *The size distribution of Swiss heronries in 1981 and 1982[a]*

No. of pairs	No. of heronries	
	1981	1982
1	22	10
2–5	36	31
6–10	21	18
11–20	18	13
21–30	7	8
31–60	6	5
Total	110	85

[a] After Geiger (1984).

Table 23.   *The size distribution of Swedish heronries in 1972[a]*

No. of pairs	No. of heronries
>30	16
10–30	46
<10 (including 13 isolates)	93

[a] After Swenson (1976).

Table 24.   *The mortality rates of British-ringed Grey Herons by age and dates of ringing[a]*

Date of ringing	Mortality rates (%)[b]		
	First-year	Second-year	Annually thereafter
1909–1941	69.7 ± 2.8 (267)	30.9 ± 5.1 (81)	24.7 ± 2.9 (56)
1942–1954	73.4 ± 3.1 (199)	32.1 ± 6.4 (53)	32.7 ± 4.5 (36)
1955–1975	55.9 ± 1.8 (775)	46.9 ± 2.9 (321)	30.3 ± 2.7 (153)

[a] After Mead *et al.* (1979).
[b] The percentage mortality is followed by the standard error. The sample sizes are given in parentheses.

Table 25.   The recovery circumstances of Grey Herons found in Britain and Ireland since 1909[a]

Reported cause of death	British-ringed		Foreign-ringed		Comments
	First-year	Older	First-year	Older	
Shot	118	45	42	8	Includes 2 allegedly mistaken for geese, and 1 shot attacking ducklings
Shot to protect fish	20	4	1	2	Mainly at trout hatcheries, but also 5 cases involving goldfish ponds
"Tangled"	10	6	1	1	Includes 6 in fishing lines and 8 in fish protection nets
Wires	75	26	7	3	Includes 8 caught on barbed-wire fencing
Traffic	7	7	2	—	8 each road and rail victims
Predated	8	1	—	—	6 by foxes, 3 juveniles mobbed by cows
Other causes (inc. unspecified)	630	253	167	60	Includes 2 which choked on prey (1 vole, 1 goldfish)
Total	868	342	220	74	

[a] After Mead *et al.* (1979).
Note: those birds which died of hunger, disease or pesticide use are usually classified as "unspecified", because the people that find the birds are unable to determine the cause of death.

Table 26.   *The clutch size of Grey Herons in Europe*[a]

Location	No. of clutches studied	No. of clutches of various size								Mean no. of eggs per clutch
		1	2	3	4	5	6	7	8	
Switzerland	85	2	1	17	55	9	1	—	—	3.83
England	220	—	4	41	136	39	—	—	—	3.96
East Germany										
Niedersachsen	27	—	—	2	5	19	1	—	—	4.70
Oberlausitz	484	—	22	61	168	213	18	2	—	4.30
Masury	461	1	16	73	231	124	13	2	1	4.10

[a] After Creutz (1981).

CHAPTER 16

The Purple Heron *Ardea purpurea*

GENERAL APPEARANCE AND FIELD CHARACTERS

The Purple Heron is 78–90 cm high with a wing-span of 120–150 cm.

Plumage. The sexes are alike, and the general colour of the plumage is rufous-brown and grey, with some black and white.

Adult: the crown and nape are black, the former with rather long, loose feathers. In breeding plumage, the bird has two long black, lanceolated plumes up to 15 cm long on the forenape. The crown and nape are followed by a broad black line running down half the length of the hindneck. The rest of the hindneck is slatey grey. The cheeks, chin and upper throat are white. The sides of the head and neck are rufous-brown marked with black, some-what broken, lines. One black line runs along each side of the head, from the base of the bill to the nape. The other follows each side of the head and neck, from the base of the bill to the chest. A narrow black line, which becomes gradually broader, follows the centre of the neck from the foreneck to the chest. These black lines are formed by black and rufous feathers. On the chest, the black lines disappear and the bird is streaked black. These feathers, which are coloured buff, rufous, black and white, are elongated, especially

241

during breeding. The upperparts from the lower half of the neck to the tail are slatey-grey; the mantle and upper scapulars often with a slight purple or olive-green gloss. The feathers of the lower mantle and upper scapulars are each split into several, long, lanceolated tips which are grey, buff to-cinnamon-chestnut and whitish. These feathers are longer during breeding. The shoulder-patches at the sites of the breast are deep vinous-chestnut. The flanks are grey. On the underparts, the feathers of the breast and belly are vinous-chestnut with a variable amount of black. The undertail-coverts are black. The thighs are buff to rufous-brown. On the upperwing, the primaries, primary coverts, secondaries and alula are black. The rest of the upperwing is grey, except the marginal upperwing-coverts which are tawny to cream-white. On the underwing, the primaries, secondaries, greater underprimary-coverts and axillaries are grey. The rest of the underwing is chestnut-brown.

Juvenile: the juvenile is mostly brown and tawny-buff with some black on the crown and wings. It has no black streaks on the head and neck. The forehead and part of the crown are black. The rest of the crown, the nape and the hindneck are chestnut brown. The chin, cheeks and upper throat are white, as in the adult. The side of the head, lower throat and neck are tawny-buff. The mantle, scapulars, back and upperwing-coverts are dark brown with wide tawny feather edges. The rest of the upperwing is as in the adults. The underwing is as in the adult but paler brown. The chest, breast, belly and undertail-coverts are pale buff streaked with brown.

In sub-adult (second calendar year) birds, brown streaks appear on the neck. The back and wing-coverts are brown tinged with grey. Purple Herons may breed when still in this plumage.

Downy young: the rufous-brown down on the upper parts is white-tipped, particularly on the crown and nape where it stands erect. The down is paler on the flanks and white on the underparts. In the Camargue, young Purple Herons are easy to distinguish from young Grey Herons as they are not tinged grey on the down or on the bare parts. In some populations of Purple Herons, the downy young seem to be much darker, as for example, the young of the subspecies *madagascariensis*. Further studies are needed to ascertain the variability in colour of the downy young, not only among the different subspecies but also among various populations of the same subspecies. In Botswana, Frazer (1971) noted that the nestlings of the subspecies *purpurea* had grey tinged down on the back. Tomlinson (1975) described the growth of the plumage:

> From hatching to 5 days old, the chicks are covered in soft down (neossoptiles). Between six and nine days spiky pin feathers push the neossoptiles out and at 10–11 days the teleoptiles break through the pin sheath and start to develop into proper feathers. These appear on the throat (white colour), in two rows down the pectorals to the abdomen, in two rows down each side of the back and also down the leading edge of the wings.
>
> From 12–20 days teleoptiles continue to grow out of their sheaths and cover bare patches of skin. Remnant neossoptiles are still present at the tips of some teleoptiles but they gradually begin to disappear towards the end of this stage. On about the 20th day, dark grey feathers appear on the neck, chest and back.

Primaries start to grow from this date onwards and flight is achieved at between 30–35 days of age, full juvenile plumage is attained at the age of 40–50 days, when they are capable of strong flight.

Bare parts

Adult: the iris is yellow. The bill is yellow with a green-brown tinge, darker at the tip and along the culmen. The bare skin of the head is yellow, tinged with green around the eyes. The legs and feet are dull brown, but the tibia, the back of the tarsus and the soles are mostly yellow. All the bare parts redden during pair-formation, except the brown ones.

Juvenile: resembles the adult but has more brown and less yellow on the bill and legs.

Downy young: the iris is green or yellow. The skin is green with a tinge of yellow along the dorsal spine, especially at the base of the neck. The upper mandible is olive-green with some yellow. The lower mandible is yellow with a tinge of olive-green.

Field characters. Purple Herons are generally seen during the early morning hours or in the evening when they fly, usually singly, between the breeding areas (which are almost always established in reed beds), and the foraging grounds. They are not easy to see when they forage, as they mostly stand motionless, often in water up to their tibias and even up to their bellies, among dense aquatic vegetation.

Juvenile Purple Herons may perhaps be confused with juvenile and adult Bitterns, *Botaurus stellaris*, by inexperienced observers. The Bittern is, however, a stocky bird with short legs and, for a heron, a short neck and bill. The plumage of the Bittern, both juvenile and adult, is much darker mottled than the juvenile Purple Heron. When flying, Purple Herons are often difficult to distinguish at a distance from Grey Herons (see chapter on the Grey Heron for differences between the two species). In Africa, the Purple Heron may also be confused with the much bigger Goliath Heron, *Ardea goliath*. However, this species has a proportionally longer and more massive bill, a rufous crown and no black lines on the sides of the head.

Measurements. The measurements (mm) of west Palearctic birds older than juveniles taken from skins are given below (see Cramp and Simmons 1977). The number of skins and the sex are indicated. Standard deviations are given in parentheses. The sex differences are significant.

wing	13 ♂♂ 357–383 (6.80)	9 ♀♀ 337–372 (11.20)
tail	13 ♂♂ 118–136 (4.44)	8 ♀♀ 112–127 (4.98)
bill	13 ♂♂ 120–131 (3.06)	8 ♀♀ 109–123 (3.87)
tarsus	13 ♂♂ 113–131 (4.58)	8 ♀♀ 112–125 (4.07)
toe	13 ♂♂ 121–139 (5.23)	7 ♀♀ 118–131 (4.46)

Juveniles have shorter wings: 8 ♂♂ 354–373 (6.03), 3 ♀♀ 339–342 (1.73). Birds from Russia tend to have longer wings than their western European counterparts: 10 ♂♂ 370–395, 9 ♀♀ 340–370 (Spangenberg, in Dementiev and Gladkov 1951).

The weight of Purple Herons is subject to great variations, according to the availability of food. The weights of adults in the Netherlands were recorded by Cramp and Simmons (1977): ♂♂ 617–1218 g, ♀♀ 525–1135 g. In the Camargue, Purple Herons weighed between 600 and 1345 g (Bauer and Glutz 1966). In Zimbabwe, two breeding males weighed 1265 g (full crop) and 1123 g (empty crop). One adult female weighed 905 g (Tomlinson 1975).

The mean wing-beat rate of the Purple Heron has been calculated as 135 wing-beats per minute by Voisin (unpublished).

DISTRIBUTION, MOVEMENTS AND HABITAT

GEOGRAPHICAL VARIATIONS

Four subspecies are recognized. *A. p. purpurea* Linnaeus has previously been described. *A. p. manilensis* Meyen is paler and more grey on the upperparts and blacker on the underparts than the nominate subspecies. The black streak on the foreneck is less developed and the elongated chest feathers are whiter. *A. p. bournei* de Naurois is very discoloured, as are many birds of arid areas. The upperparts are pale grey with whitish buff, elongated ornamental feathers. The elongated chest feathers are mostly cream-white and the underparts – except the shoulder-patches, which remain chestnut – are rufous with a few cream-white feathers. The black streaks on the head and neck are narrow and broken and are not as conspicuous as in the nominate subspecies. *A. p. madagascariensis* van Oort is darker than the nominate subspecies. On the upperparts only the ornamental feathers are tipped chestnut. The mantle, back and scapulars are slatey-grey. The belly and the undertail-coverts are black with only some rufous on the belly. The black streaks on the head and neck are very conspicuous.

BREEDING AND WINTERING AREAS

Purple Herons of the nominate subspecies breed in western Europe up to 52°N in the Netherlands and Poland. They breed in the Ukraine in the USSR up to about 50°N, and around the Caspian and Aral Seas up to about 48°N. The eastward limit seems to be the River Ili in Kazakhstan. Southwards, *A. p. purpurea* breeds in Turkey, Israel, Iraq and Iran. In Africa, it breeds in Morocco, Algeria, West Africa (nesting proven only in Sénégal), East Africa and South Africa. *A. p. manilensis* breeds in Pakistan, India, South East Asia to Celebes and the Philippines, in China up to about 50°N and in Taiwan. *A. p. bournei* breeds and winters on the Cape Verde Islands and *A. p. madagascariensis* breeds and winters in Madagascar, and is also found on the Seychelle Islands.

MOVEMENTS

The nominate, *A. p. purpurea* population is migratory. After leaving the heronry, the juveniles disperse in all directions before the autumn migration. A few individuals winter in the southern part of the breeding range and a small population winters in Arabia in Bahrain (Cramp and Simmons 1977). Most of the birds, however, winter in Africa south of the Sahara. The migration proceeds on a broad front as witnessed by records from numerous oases (Ahaggar, Bahariya, Colomb Bechar, Djanet, Ennedi, Fezzan, Chat, El Goléa and Kufra). The flight over the desert takes 30–60 hours (Moreau 1967, 1972). The autumn migration begins as soon as July, but most birds leave during the second half of August, in September and October. In the southern breeding range, stragglers leave in November and the first half of December. Most birds ringed in the Netherlands migrate through France and Spain but others migrate through Italy and Greece (den Held 1981). Recoveries have been made of birds ringed in Europe in Tunisia, Algeria, Morocco, Mauritania, Sénégal, Gambia, Mali, Niger, Sudan, Sierra Leone, Nigeria and Cameroon (Curry-Lindahl 1981). The autumn migration follows a south-southwest and southwest direction. Birds ringed in France have been recovered in the Gambia, Sierra Leone and Mali. Birds ringed in the USSR (Azov Sea) have been recovered in Nigeria and West Sudan. Some Purple Herons migrate through Egypt (Meinertzhagen 1930) and others follow the coast of Eritrea (Smith 1957), though there are no recoveries from East Africa. In the spring, the first migrants reach their breeding grounds in March but most do not arrive before April and even May. Overshooting is common during this period, as is northward post-breeding dispersal in July and August. Purple Herons have thus been observed outside their breeding range in Britain, Belgium, northern West Germany, Denmark and exceptionally Fennoscandia and central Siberia. Among the Asian population of *A. p. malinensis*, only birds breeding north of the Yangtze River leave the country in the autumn. They have been recorded on migration in Korea and as winter visitors in Japan (Vaurie 1965).

Purple Herons of the subspecies *bournei* do not seem to migrate and those of the subspecies *madagascariensis* stay in Madagascar during the non-breeding season. Further studies are needed however, to be sure that the whole population of *A. p. madagascariensis* is sedentary; some individuals may reach East Africa during the off-season.

HABITAT

Purple Herons usually both breed and winter in flooded lowland areas with a strong preference for those with extensive reedbeds. They forage in shallow water with a sandy or muddy bottom, among floating aquatic vegetation such as water crowfoot and water lilies, and on the fringes or in the cover of emerging aquatic vegetation such as reeds, rushes and even papyrus in Africa and Asia. They are found in natural or man-made habitats such as freshwater marshes, pools, rivers, canals and ditches. In rice culture areas, they forage in the ricefields when the rice is almost full-grown (from June in the Camargue). If numerous, they may also forage in nearby brackish water, in lagoons, deltas and estuaries where some aquatic vegetation has been able to maintain itself. On migration, Purple Herons may stop to forage in areas with no vegetation at all, along river banks or on sandflats at sea (Smith 1957).

Purple Herons prefer to breed in areas of extensive freshwater marshes covered by a luxurious vegetation of floating and emerging aquatic plants and where large reedbeds are available, such as are to be found in the Djoudj (Sénégal) and to a lesser extent in the Camargue. However, in Charente-Maritime (France), Purple Herons breed in an area of small, muddy rivers surrounded by gallery forest, small woods and frequently flooded prairies, drained by numerous ditches where cattle graze. The Purple Herons there nest in small reedbeds only a few acres wide and in trees, alone or with Night Herons, at a height of 3–10 m above the ground. Breeding in trees is exceptional for this species. In Botswana, a Purple Heron colony was found in fig trees (*Ficus verrucolosa*) 1.5–4 m above the water level on a flooded island in the Khwane River (Fraser 1971). Birds of the subspecies *bournei* seem to have adapted to a very uncommon habitat for Purple Herons, nesting in rubber and mango trees and foraging on the dry hillsides of the Cape Verde Islands (de Naurois 1969).

POPULATION SIZE AND TRENDS

In France, two national censuses of the breeding population of Purple Herons have been undertaken, one in 1974 by Brosselin and one in 1983 by Duhautois (see Tables 27 and 28).

The Atlantic coastal area had already been studied in depth in 1974. A significant increase in the population in that area was probably due to the total protection of the species in France in 1975. However, despite this protection, the population of Purple Herons has fallen in central and eastern France.

Little was known of the breeding areas in southern France in 1974. Only the Purple Herons breeding in the central part of the Camargue[*] – "La Grande Camargue" – were counted each year (Table 29). In 1974, 805 nests were counted in the area. The number of nests in the coastal areas of Languedoc and Rousillon, west of both La Grande Camargue and "La Petite Camargue", was estimated at about 50. Since 1980, Purple Heron nests in the French Mediterranean area have been counted each year using aerial photography. The low numbers of Purple Herons breeding in La Grande Camargue during years when surrounding areas were experiencing successful breeding, is probably due to the increasing salinity there. This began in the early 1980s, and has caused birds to move to less saline areas (Table 30).

---

[*]The Camargue can be divided into "la Grande Camargue" (between the two arms of the River Rhône) and "la Petite Camargue" west of la Grande Camargue (between the River Rhône and the canal "du Rhône à Sète). The "Plan du Bourg", east of the main arm of the River Rhône, is usually considered part of the Camargue.

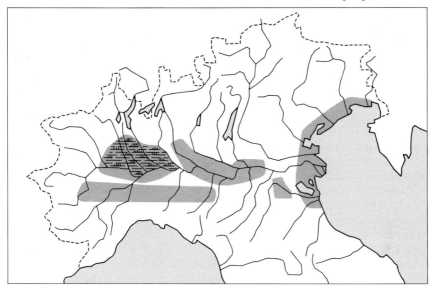

The breeding areas of both tree- and reed-nesting herons in Italy (Fasola *et al.* 1981).

In Italy, the first national census of Purple Herons was undertaken by Fasola *et al.* (1981). A total of 480 breeding pairs were counted in 27 heronries, all of them in northern Italy. The heronries comprised between 2 and 80 nests (mean size, 18 nests). As heronries numbering only a few nests are easily overlooked, and as all known heronries were not visited (27 out of 34 were visited), the total number of breeding pairs in 1981 was estimated at 800–1000.

Neither in Spain or Portugal has a census been undertaken of the breeding population of Purple Herons. A mixed heronry at La Albufera (Valencia) contained 33 Purple Heron nests in 1972 (Fernandez-Cruz 1975). Purple Herons breed in scattered places along rivers, especially the Ebro, the Tajo and the Guadalquivir. In the Las Marismas' area, a census undertaken from the air would be useful.

In the Netherlands during 1961–1979, about 750 pairs of Purple Herons bred each year (range 400–1000 pairs). Of the 14 heronries known, only 2 are large ones: Nieuwkoop and Maarsen, where the birds have been counted since 1961. Nieuwkoop usually contains more than 250 pairs (a maximum of 385 in 1968 and a minimum of 160 in 1973) and Maarsen (which started with a few nests in 1961) usually has more than 100 pairs (a maximum of 170 in 1968) (den Held 1981). In West Germany, Purple Herons breed in the Rhine Valley where 18–20 pairs were counted in 1970 (Cramp and Simmons 1977). Only a small, fluctuating population breeds in Switzerland: three pairs were found in 1941, though this increased to 54 pairs in 1955 (Bauer and Glutz 1966). In 1972, only 8–10 pairs were counted (Cramp and Simmons 1977). In Austria, Purple Herons breed at Neusiedlersee. During 1950–1955, the number of breeding pairs fluctuated between 240 and 350 (Bauer and Glutz 1966).

In Czechoslovakia, only a few pairs breed each year in Bohemia at Lomnice (Bauer and Glutz 1966). In Yugoslavia during 1954–1970, the number of breeding pairs fluctuated between 91 and 287 in the Kopačevski area and during 1959–1968, between 100 and 250 at Lake Ludaško (Cramp and Simmons 1977). In Hungary in 1951, about 315 pairs of Purple Herons nested in four large heronries at Velencer See, Kisbalaton, Karapancsa and Tiszaluc and in 10 other small ones (Szijj 1954). From 1968 to 1972, the number of breeding pairs at Kisbalaton declined from 107 to 37 pairs (Cramp and Simmons 1977). In Romania, Purple Herons are still common but their numbers are falling (Cramp and Simmons 1977). In Greece, about 300 pairs nested at Lake Mikra Prespa in 1969 (Terrasse *et al.* 1969). The total number of nesting pairs in the whole of Greece in 1985–1986 was estimated to be between 105 and 140 (Crivelli *et al.* 1988). In the Cape Verde Islands, Purple Herons breed only at São Tiago, where the total breeding population in 1969 was estimated at less than 200 pairs (de Naurois 1969).

A study undertaken by den Held in 1981 shows that the size of Purple Heron colonies in the Netherlands seem to depend greatly upon the amount of rain in the Sahel. The population needs to find this area well flooded to rest and feed before and after flying across the desert. A positive correlation was found between the size of the breeding population in the Netherlands each spring and the discharges of the rivers Sénégal and Niger during 1961–1979. The recoveries in West Africa of Purple Herons ringed in the Netherlands during the period 1934–1977 suggest that the wintering population from the Netherlands wintered further south during the drought period and that they experienced higher levels of mortality.

MORTALITY

A study of 64 recoveries of Purple Herons ringed at Neuenburger See (Switzerland), shows that more than half of the juveniles died during their first migration and that the major cause of mortality among birds of all ages was being shot. Of these, 40 (62%) were of birds in their first year, 7 (11%) of birds in their second year, 7 (11%) of birds in their third year and 5 (8%) of birds in their fourth year. Five (8%) were of birds older than 4 years. Most of these birds had been shot in France and Spain but, a few had been killed by electric wires (Bauer and Glutz 1966). The complete protection of Purple Herons since 1975 in France and since 1981 in Spain has been instrumental in helping to halt the decline of Purple Herons in western Europe.

The oldest ringed Purple Heron was found dead at the age of 23 years and 2 months (*CRMMO Bull.* 1964, Paris ringing centre).

BEHAVIOUR AND BIOLOGY

DAILY ROUTINE

Purple Herons forage by day, mostly in the morning and evening. There are no observations of them feeding by night, but further studies on this point are needed. During breeding, Purple Herons are a common sight flying over the reeds of the colony, to and from their foraging grounds. However, they remain in Europe only during their short breeding season, arriving late and leaving early.

MAINTENANCE BEHAVIOURS

These have been observed by Tomlinson (1974, 1975) who describes them briefly as follows:

Wing and Leg Stretch. "The wing and leg on one side of the body are stretched out and backwards and the appropriate half of the tail is spread sideways. The other side may then be similarly stretched."
Body-shake. "The neck is extended, all contour feathers ruffled, then the head is shaken from side to side while moving the wings in and out vigorously."
Head-scratch. "The neck is partially extended, one foot is brought directly up and the head is scratched with the largest toe."
Gular-flutter. "The gular region is rapidly fluttered . . . and the bill is held slightly open. This activity was observed only during hot weather."

DISPLAYS AND CALLS

The displays of Purple Herons have been studied only by Tomlinson (1974, 1975), who observed wild birds nesting among reeds and bullrushes along Lake McLlwaine in Zimbabwe, and hand-reared chicks kept in an aviary. He succeeded in observing most displays but not those of courtship, which still remain unknown. However, as we will see, the Stretch Display is used by Purple Herons as a greeting display. In all heron species studied until now, this display, when performed, is always a courtship display given by unmated males to attract a female. In addition, in some species, such as the Grey Heron, the Stretch Display is again used later in the season as a greeting display by both male and female at the nest to greet the returning mate. It is therefore likely that in Purple Herons the Stretch Display is also performed in courtship by unmated males earlier in the season.

Tomlinson observed that the degree to which the crown and nape feathers are raised, provide an accurate indicator of the levels of aggression and alarm in Purple Herons, as did Blaker in the case of the Cattle Egret.

Agonistic displays

Aggressive Upright Display. "The bird faces the intruder and, while keeping the whole length of the tarsus on the nest, stretches the neck and head vertically. It puffs out the gular region, half spreads the wings, raises the crest and looks under the beak at the intruder" (Tomlinson 1974). This form of the behaviour is typical of Purple Herons and has not been thus described in any other species until now. Herons such as the Great White Egret or the Grey Heron, when performing the Aggressive Upright Display, stay on the branch or nest and have their heads and bills either held horizontally or turned slightly downwards.

Forward Display. "The bird moved from the Aggressive Upright into Forward display where the neck is drawn back with the head held horizontal and crest flattened. The head then shoots forward at the intruder. This is often done sitting but occasionally the bird stands up to strike. The strike is usually accompanied by a high pitched squawk" (Tomlinson 1974).

Full Forward Display. "This display was observed . . . in hand-reared birds and it was triggered by intrusion of a dog in the cage area. It may be a method of territorial defence in the field. The bird erects all neck, pectoral and scapular feathers including the crest, hunches the shoulders and half spreads the wings. It advances slowly towards the intruder, stiff legged, with beak slightly open and pointing downwards. If the intruder persists the bird turns its eyes forwards and supplants its opponent by flying directly towards it. Twice the bird actually made contact with the dog" (Tomlinson 1974).

Aerial Combat. "Several *A. purpurea* were observed circling over a heronry when suddenly two birds attacked each other. They turned over on their sides, ventral surfaces opposed, then thrust out their legs at each other, before veering away." (Tomlinson 1974).

Alarm Displays

Alert Posture. "This was often observed in incubating birds when disturbed by a nearby movement or noise. The bird raises the neck with head horizontal and looks in the direction of the disturbance" (Tomlinson 1974).

Bittern Stance. "The bird faces the intruder, raises the bill, head and neck to an almost vertical position . . . the crest is flattened and gular region is not extended. The eyes look under the beak and are fixed on the intruder. The bird will remain in this position until almost touched and may then fly off" (Tomlinson 1974).

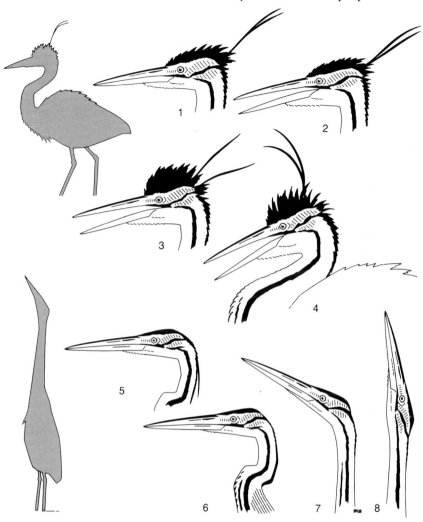

1–4 show increasing threat. The crown and nape feathers become more and more erect and the bill more and more open. 5–8 show increasing alarm: 5, a few nape feathers are still held erect; 6, all of the feathers are sleeked; 7, the bill begins to point upwards, which is a posture adopted prior to flight or the Bittern Stance; 8, Bittern Stance.

Breeding displays

Stretch Display. According to Tomlinson (1974):

The brooding bird rises slowly until its legs are fully extended, with head and neck stretched vertically and gular region puffed out. The eyes look skyward and the neck feathers are raised. As the brooding bird goes into this position it utters a noise which in the case of a female is a low 'craak' while the brooding male produces a musical 'whoop'. The brooding bird holds the upright position for about a second, then it suddenly retracts neck, flexes the legs and crouches down into the nest, all in one quick movement. The bill still points upwards but at a slightly lower angle. In the case of the male bird brooding it claps the bill loudly three times as it lowers itself into a crouching position. A female brooding utters a soft 'crak-crak-crak' as she crouches. The gular region is flattened and scapular and chest plumes start to erect during the crouch. The brooding bird then brings the head further down into a position slightly above horizontal, erects the scapular and chest plumes to their fullest extent, and slightly raises the feathers at the rear of the crest.

Sway-and-bob Display. This display has never been observed in any other heron and Tomlinson (1974) has only seen it performed once following a Stretch Display:

The brooding bird bent forward with head down and tail up as the mate approached from the rear. With feet stationary it swayed from side to side about six times, then rapidly lowered the tail and raised the head while keeping the beak at right angles to the body, in a bobbing movement. It then returned to the swaying position and repeated the whole performance three times.

A posture of slight alarm.

Allopreening. Immediately after a Stretch Display, the male "reached forward and nibbled the approaching partner's chest and wings with his beak, often grasping the mate's neck. Bill clappering accompanied this display and the scapular and chest feathers were partly raised" (Tomlinson 1974).

Greeting Stance. The male on the nest "first bows to the female, then stands up. . . . The female them moves in close to the male and lowers her head, placing it under the male's chest" (Tomlinson 1974). The Bow is not described by Tomlinson, but one Bowing bird has been drawn. When Bowing, the bird bends forwards with head and tail up as in the beginning of the Sway-and-bob Display. This behaviour is different from the Bow described by Wiese (1976) and Mock (1978), which Tomlinson (1976) called the Twig-shake.

Calls

In addition to the various calls mentioned above, the Purple Heron utters a typical call when leaving the colony. It is very like that of the Grey Heron, but is more highly pitched and not so loud. A low, guttural call – the greeting Call – is given when landing near the nest.

REPRODUCTIVE BEHAVIOUR

Greeting Behaviour. The bird returning to the heronry utters a low characteristic call, just before and landing on the vegetation at some distance from its nest. As the bird slowly approaches the nest, the brooding bird "turns itself to face either away from or side on to the arrival". This differs from other heron species, where the brooding bird usually faces the incoming bird. At this stage, the brooding bird begins a Stretch Display. The incoming bird stops near the nest and "stands with head and neck vertically extended, eyes fixed on its mate and neck feathers erect". This posture is held until the brooding bird has finished its Stretch Display.

Sometimes, when moving towards the nest, the incoming bird partially extends its wings horizontally and raises its crest feathers. At the same time, it pushes its wings backwards and forwards with short, jerky movements.

Allopreening and a Greeting Stance are often observed at this stage. Sometimes, the brooding bird does not readily leave the nest, and the incoming bird may make some pecks at it.

Twig-passing. According to Tomlinson (1974):

The arriving bird carried a freshly broken twig in its beak and after performing the Stretch Display, the twig was passed to the mate on the nest, who then placed it in the nest with a slight trembling of the beak. Both birds then repeated the Stretch Display and the newly arrived bird flew away. Fresh leaves and twigs were often found in nests containing eggs, indicating that twig passing was a common practice at this stage, although it was only observed once.

Nest-building

Purple Heron nests are usually built in reed beds, but sometimes also in bullrushes among *Typha* sp. and even *Scirpus* sp., and always in areas flooded to about 0.4–1.5 m. Nests may also be built on willows among the surrounding reeds. In a few places, where such vegetation is not available, nests may be built in trees. In Europe, when the first Purple Herons arrive in the breeding areas, only the old reeds from the previous year are tall enough to offer shelter and support for the nests. Colonies are therefore established in old vegetation from the previous year. Where reeds are cut and used by local people, it is of the greatest importance to retain protected areas with uncut reeds for Purple Herons to nest in. In Europe, new reeds are tall enough to offer shelter and nest material only in June. During years when Purple Herons are numerous, the last pairs to nest may use new reeds, as observed in Switzerland (Manuel 1957).

When nesting in reeds or among bullrushes, Purple Herons begin building by bending the stems over towards each other so as to form a platform. Sticks are then fetched and the nest is built, fixed firmly upon the bent stems and also to adjoining, unbent stems (Voisin, unpublished). According to Steinfatt (1939), nest construction takes 7–12 days, although the nest is added to throughout incubation. In the Camargue, nests are built only in reedbeds and constructed entirely out of reeds (including the stems, flowering heads and a few leaves). At Lake McLlwaine (Zimbabwe), birds nesting in reedbeds use only reeds as nest material, but those nesting in bullrushes also use *Polygonum* weed stems and Msasa (*Brachystegia* sp.) twigs in various proportions, in addition to Typha leaves.

Purple Heron nests are found in loose colonies, 5–20 m apart. New nests are built each year. They have a diameter of 0.5–0.8 m, very occasionally up to 1.35 m. They are only 5–10 cm deep and 20–25 cm high, but may be thicker, up to 40 cm (Hanzàk 1949–1950, Manuel 1957). They are thus very flat and usually smaller than those of the Grey Heron. They stand 0.8–2.3 m above the ground, depending in the main on the water level in the colony at the time of building, and are generally about 0.8–1.0 m above the water level. If the water level changes more than a few centimetres, the nests are in danger. In the Camargue, as soon as the water dries up under the nests, they are abandoned and plundered by raptors, rats, foxes and even perhaps snakes. Tomlinson (1974) stated:

> Most of the nests were abandoned as the water level receded causing them to be left over dry land. For a few days after this, eggs were still observed in the nests and no signs of nest disturbance were evident. However, the Marsh Harrier

The Stretch Display used as a greeting display (after Tomlinson 1974).

Circus ranivorus was observed to consume all of these eventually. Only those nests with well developed chicks was not abandoned after they had become situated over dry land.

Reproductive success will also be very poor if the water level under the colony and in the near vicinity drops too quickly, even if no dry land appears. In the Camargue in 1979 (Voisin, unpublished), when the water level did drop quickly, nest-building and incubation ceased and nests were abandoned, even those with newly hatched young. In contrast, when the water level rises too high and reaches the nests, as was the case in Chevroux in 1953 (Manuel 1957), both eggs and chicks were drowned, since the nests are firmly fixed and do not float like those of Grebes, for example. They are also loosely built, making it easy for rainwater to pour through, but also for water rising from underneath to reach the eggs and chicks. As we have seen, Purple Herons may also nest in trees, as in western France where no extensive reedbeds are available. Very occasionally, they may nest in trees even where reedbeds are found in the vicinity, probably where there is too much human disturbance during breeding. Purple Herons nesting high up in poplars, 15–20 m above the ground, have been observed in Switzerland (Manuel 1957, Hofstetter *et al.* 1949). The diameter of these nests was 40–60 cm. In western France, Purple Herons usually nest in small trees (oak, ash, elm and hawthorn) in frequently flooded areas, together with other tree-nesting herons. Their nests in this habitat are not much larger than those of Night Herons and are almost flat with few loose sticks. The blue-green eggs are often visible through the bottom of the nest. These poorly constructed nests suggest that the birds are not breeding in the habitat to which they are really adapted (Voisin, unpublished).

Egg-laying, clutch size and hatching success

The eggs of the Purple Heron are elongated ovals, light blue-green in colour. They are often stained during incubation. A sample of 300 eggs measured by Schönwetter (1967) gave the following measurements (mean and range): length 57 mm (50–61 mm), width 41 mm (37–44 mm).

According to Tomlinson (1974), the mean weight of full eggs is 47.4 g (range 39.0–59.0 g) and the mean shell thickness 0.28 mm (range 0.23–0.34 mm). Makatsch (in Bauer and Glutz 1966) found the mean weight of eggshell to be 3.15 g (range 2.24–3.97 g).

In temperate areas, egg-laying occurs in the spring. In the Camargue, the first eggs appear in the middle of April, but most are laid towards the end of April and the beginning of May. Egg-laying proceeds through May and the beginning of June with decreasing frequency. Further east in Europe, egg-laying begins later (about 3 weeks later in central Europe). In Africa, Purple Herons breed at the end of the main rainy season. The breeding season from the laying of the first eggs to the fledging of the last chicks is from September to January in the Djoudj, Sénégal (Dupuy 1975), from July to January in Zimbabwe (Tomlinson 1974), from March to July in Katanga (Ruwet 1965) and from June to January in the Transvaal (McLachlan and Liversidge 1957).

The incubation period, egg-laying and hatching intervals were studied by Tomlinson (1975) and Manuel (1957). Tomlinson found that of 31 eggs, 5 were laid about 1 day after the previous egg, 15 after about 2 days and 11 after about 3 days. The incubation period was 25 days for 10 eggs, 26 days for 19 eggs and 27 days for 2 eggs. Without exception, incubation began with the first egg laid. Manuel found an incubation period of 25–30 days, averaging 26 days. The eggs usually hatched with an interval of 1 day, sometimes 2.

The mean clutch size of 92 nests in Bourgogne and Dombes, France was 4.4 eggs (range 3–6 eggs) (Ferry and Blondel 1960). At Lake Neuchâtel in Switzerland, the mean clutch size of 154 nests was 4.1 eggs (range 2–6) (Manuel 1957). In 1957 in the Camargue, the mean clutch size of 28 nests was 3.3 eggs (range 2–5) (Williams 1959) and in 1977, the mean clutch size of 13 nests was 3.6 eggs (range 2–5) (Voisin, unpublished). However, I found one nest with 8 eggs (not included in the data above). These eggs were laid regularly between 18 May and 4 June. The egg-laying period was thus 17 days, suggesting that two females may have laid their eggs in the same nest. Groups of three birds – two females and a male – have been known to raise a brood together. Further studies of Purple Herons are required to discover the maximum number of eggs which a female can lay, and if polygamy occurs. A study of the clutch size of Purple Herons in central France published in 1932, mentioned clutches of 7 and 8 eggs. These were, of course, very rare, but they appeared often enough to give a mean clutch size of 5.1 eggs (Mayaud, in Ferry and Blondel 1960). At Lake McIlwaine in Zimbabwe, the mean clutch size of 34 nests was 3.25 eggs (range 2–5) (Tomlinson 1974).

Tomlinson (1975) visited the nests he was studying twice a day, often enough to disturb the birds and increase the rate of egg loss. In one colony, up to 56% of the eggs were lost. During good climatic conditions (when there is not too much rain, and the water level does not change too much) and when disturbances by humans remain low, hatching appears to be very successful. I followed 13 nests in the Camargue in 1977, visiting them only once every 3 days. In 12 nests, all the eggs hatched successfully. One nest with 3 eggs was plundered, the adult perhaps not returning quickly enough after my visit. Of 49 eggs laid, 46 hatched, giving a hatching success of 93.9%. Newly hatched chicks weighed 25–35 g (Voisin, unpublished).

DEVELOPMENT AND CARE OF THE YOUNG

Chick behaviour

The chicks were brooded by both parents and fed when the parents change-over duties at the nest. Change-over occurs two to three times daily.

In begging for food from the first day of hatching, the chicks assume a half-extended wing position and utter the characteristic begging noise (Chik, chik, chik, chik) at the same time shaking the wings slightly. After about 10 days the chicks sometimes mildly threaten parents when they approach the nest. Older chicks exhibit intense grasping behaviour at feeding times and with crest raised often take hold of the parent's beak and pull it down violently. This appears to stimulate regurgitation by the adult. The begging noise in young chicks up to 10 days is a continuous 'chik, chik', thereafter it becomes a raucous 'chak, chak'. After about nine days of age, the chicks often wiped their beaks against sticks after feeding. At this age, chicks often engaged in exploratory pecking, at a stick in the nest, for several minutes. Up until about 10 days the chicks feed by picking up the adult's regurgitated food off the base of the nest. Thereafter they begin to grasp the parents' beaks.

Sibling rivalry is intense up to the age of about 20 days, however no deaths due to fighting were actually observed. The largest chick in the nest asserts its dominance over the younger one by raising the neck into a stiff vertical position, then it drops forward to peck its sibling. Fighting can sometimes continue for two minutes until one chick admits defeat by going into a crouch position, often hanging its head over the edge of the nest. Fighting is generally very noisy but should the parent leave the nest all noise ceases although fighting may continue in silence (Tomlinson 1975).

As in all young herons, Purple Herons at first lie on their stomachs for a few days before standing, first on their tarsus and then fully upright. They have particularly large feet, which are very useful when they first move about in the dense flooded reeds, grasping several reed stems at a time between their long toes. They also use their bill to help in climbing through the reeds above water. By about 15 days, they begin to explore the area around the nest and from about the age of 20 days, are able to make a quick escape when danger threatens the nest. From about 30 days, the young leave the nest during the day, returning only to be fed, and at 45 days they are able to fly.

Growth of nestlings

Tomlinson (1975) and Voisin (unpublished) have studied the growth of young Purple Herons in the wild until they were 3 weeks old. They were captured, weighed and marked, at first with nail varnish and then, as soon as possible, with a ring. From the age of 20–25 days, chicks that escape into the reeds cannot be caught. In the Camargue, during the spring of 1977, only 2–3 chicks in each brood usually survived to 3 weeks of age. In 1974, at Lake McLlwaine in Zimbabwe, 3–4 chicks in each brood usually survived to the age of 3 weeks. Tomlinson (1975) also studied the growth of hand-reared chicks until they reached the adult weight at an age of 50–55 days (see Fig. 18).

Growth curves of chicks from both the Camargue and from Zimbabwe show that the first-hatched chick has an advantage over its siblings and grows fastest. The second-hatched chick, however, soon catches up with the oldest one. The third-hatched chick tends to develop more slowly but often survives. In broods with four chicks, the fourth one grows slower still. The fifth chick hardly ever seems to survive. Apart from a few newborn chicks which are never fed, the death of the smallest chick in a brood results in the quicker growth of the surviving chicks and often saves the smallest of those remaining. The youngest chicks in a brood hence form a reserve and are properly fed only when conditions are very favourable. They take the place of older chicks if they are killed by accidents, predators or illness. In one brood studied in the Camargue, the fourth chick suddenly began to grow rapidly after a very slow beginning. Its three older siblings, which had been ringed and were old enough to run into the reeds, were no longer seen. One of them at least had probably died, with the result that the youngest was fed enough to survive. The growth curves of two other broods are shown in Figs 19 and 20.

During the growth study in the Camargue, a healthy chick that had been ringed several days before, was captured quite by surprise while wandering about in the reeds. At 26 days of age, it weighed 870 g. The oldest in a brood of five, it had a weight equal to that of hand-reared chicks, showing that in the wild the oldest, and probably also the second chick (as they are of nearly the same weight), grow at an optimal rate.

The mean growth curve of chicks in the wild established by Tomlinson (1975) shows slower growth due to a lack of food. This slowed the growth of

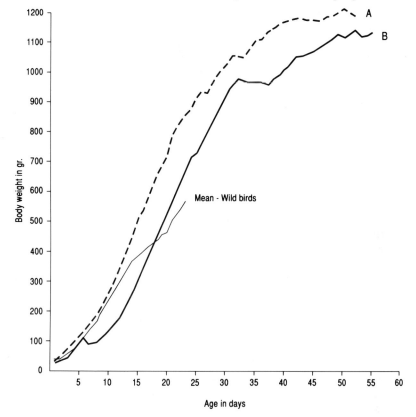

Figure 18   The daily body weight of two hand-reared Purple Heron chicks (A and B) compared with the mean of wild birds (Tomlinson 1975).

the youngest chicks, which often died. In addition, this growth curve shows a particularly low growth rate when chicks are aged 14–18 days. During this period, the parent birds do not seem to be able to bring enough food to their chicks and even the largest ones seem to starve temporarily. This clearly shows the importance of the crisis which occurs at the end of the guardian period. Both parents probably leave their brood in order to forage when the oldest chick is a little less than 3 weeks old. Thereafter the chicks are fed much more and the growth rate resumes its former value.

FEEDING BEHAVIOUR AND FOOD

Foraging methods

Purple Herons feed singly, standing and waiting for prey or walking slowly in shallow water among dense vegetation. They may also forage standing or

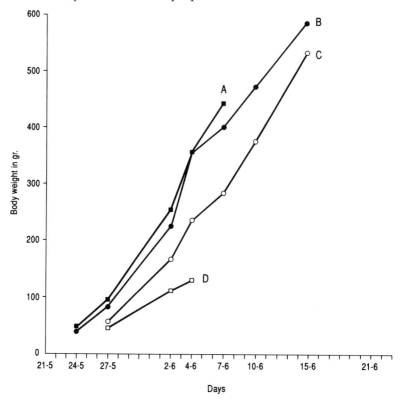

Figure 19   Nest I. The daily body weight of 4 Purple Heron chicks in the Camargue in 1977. On 21 May, 4 eggs were found in the nest; on 24 May, 2 young and 2 eggs; on 27 May, 4 young. On 7 June, chick D was found dead; on 10 June, chick A escaped and could not be caught again (Voisin, unpublished).

walking on floating aquatic vegetation where this occurs. They have also sometimes been seen hunting in meadows and fields, especially when rodents are abundant. They forage mostly in the morning and evening, but may be seen throughout the whole day. According to Bauer and Glutz (1966), they are also active by night. When hunting, Purple Herons either stand or walk, with body and neck erect at various angles above the surface of the water, or with body and neck horizontal just above it. They alternate between the Walk Slowly and the Stand-and-wait methods. They walk slowly, often with water up to their tibias, suddenly becoming completely immobile for several minutes. When walking, they sometimes move each leg so slowly that movement is hardly visible and even this slow movement is interrupted by frequent stops.

Observation of a Purple Heron hunting frogs. The bird walked slowly, body erect and neck stretched upwards. It suddenly stopped and took up a position with its body and neck horizontal just above the surface of the water. Its legs and body remained quite motionless, but the bill, head and neck

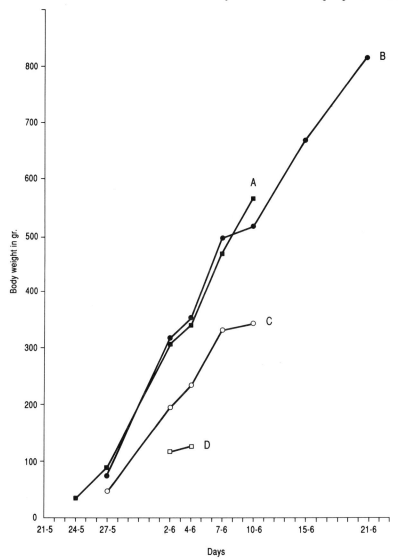

Figure 20   Nest II. The daily body weight of 4 Purple Heron chicks in the Camargue in 1977. On 21 May, 4 eggs were found in the nest; on 24 May, 3 eggs and 1 young; on 27 May, 3 young and 1 egg; on 2 June, 4 young. On 7 June, chick D was found dead in the nest; on 15 June, chick A escaped and could not be caught again (Voisin, unpublished).

moved rapidly and then froze, completely immobile. Suddenly, the bird grasped a frog between its mandibles, raised itself and swallowed it head first. In 27 minutes, the bird had caught four frogs, having missed or lost none.

A Purple Heron foraging.

Observation of a Purple Heron hunting eels. The bird rapidly seized a tuft of aquatic vegetation. It then walked to the shore and put it down. With its bill it searched for an eel hidden among the aquatic plants. Finding it, the bird swallowed it alive, with great difficulty, as it wriggled so much. If it had been a large eel, the bird would probably have had to kill it before swallowing it, as Grey Herons do (Voisin 1978).

An unusual method of feeding. Like many other herons, Purple Herons are able to land on deep water. At Lake Neuchâtel in Switzerland, they have been seen flying low over the water, feet hanging, towards the observer's small boat. The birds landed feet first on their belly and, folding their wings, grabbed the fish refuse thrown from the boat (Arm 1960).

Food

Purple Herons feed mostly on fish. They also take amphibians, snakes, lizards, birds, small mammals and insects. They occasionally capture crustaceans, molluscs and spiders.

The food of young Purple Herons was thoroughly studied in two heronries in Holland by collecting regurgitated food from 50 nests (Owen and Phillips 1956). The young ate mostly fish (usually 110–200 mm long). The prey were of about the same size as those taken by the Grey Heron. The authors could not find evidence of adults bringing smaller prey to small young and bigger ones to the larger young. The fish taken were pike *Esox lucius*, ten-spined stickleback *Pygosteus pungitius*, carp *Cyprinus carpio*, gudgeon *Gobio gobio*, tench *Tinca tinca*, rudd *Scardinius erythrophtalmus*, bream *Abramis brama*, eel *Anguilla anguilla*, perch *Perca fluviatilis*, ruffe *Acerina cernua* and burbot *Lota vulgaris*. The mammals taken were water-voles *Arvicola amphibius*, moles *Talpa europea* and shrews *Sorex* sp. A few frogs (*Rana* sp.) and a Skylark were also found in the regurgitates. Water beetle larvae *Dysticus* sp. were present in many samples in one of the heronries. The chief difference between this study and those that follow based on stomach contents was that the latter contained many more insects. This may have been due to the slow rate of digestion of insect remains, which means that any analysis of stomach contents tends to over-emphasize the insect part of the diet.

In France, Madon (1935) concluded after a study of 28 stomachs that the prey taken by Purple Herons were mostly fish (tench *Tinca tinca* and carp *Cyprinus carpio*) and insects. Twelve samples from Italy (Moltoni 1936) all contained fish, mostly sunfish *Eupomotis gibbosus* and many insects (chiefly aquatic larvae of Hydrophilidae). In 113 stomachs from Hungary studied by Vasvàri (1939), fish were found in 59, mammals in 28, amphibians in 25 and insects in most of them. The insects were mostly aquatic larvae.

Samples from Spain (1211 prey identified) collected in the Guadelquivir area contained mostly fish. Of the total prey items, 56.2% were fish (*Mugil* sp., *Anguilla anguilla* and *Cyprinus carpio*). The larvae of water beetles (*Cubister* sp.) constituted 29.6%. The remaining 14.2% comprised in order of decreasing numbers: dragonflies (Odonata larvae and adults), nestlings of water-birds (*Fulica atra* and some anatidae, rallidae and charadriidae), snakes (*Natrix maura*) and amphibians (*Pleurodeles walti, Pelobates cultripes*). By weight, the carp represented 67.8% of the total and nestlings 12.6% (Amat and Herrera 1975). In 70 stomachs from India, Purple Herons were also found to capture mostly fish. By number, 57% were fish (mostly *Mystus gulio, Anguilla bengalensis*), 20.57% reptiles (mostly *Natrix stolata* up to 190 mm), 14.34% crustaceans (mostly *Varuna litterata* and various Graspidae) and 7.65% insects (Dermaptera, Hemiptera, Odonata and Coleoptera) (Mukherjee 1977).

A chick still on its nest regurgitated a half-grown Little Grebe *Tachybaptus ruficollis* which had been swallowed whole (Belman 1974). In the Nairobi National Park in Kenya, Purple Herons hunting in small reservoirs where no fish were present, captured mostly the adults and tadpoles of the aquatic Clawed Toad *Xenopus* sp. (Reynolds 1974).

Table 27.   The size of the French Purple Heron population in 1974 and 1983[a]

Location	No. of breeding pairs	
	1974	1983
Mediterranean area	855	1693
Atlantic coast area	200	422
Central and eastern France	955	626

[a] After Brosselin (1974) and Duhautois (1983).

Table 28.   *The size distribution of French heronries in 1974 and 1983* [a]

No. of pairs	No. of heronries	
	1974	*1983*
1	9	19
2–10	35	80
11–70	36	30
> 100 (all in the Mediterranean area)	5	7

[a] After Brosselin (1974) and Duhautois (1983).

Table 29.   *The number of Purple Heron nests in the Grande Camargue, 1968–1974 and 1979* [a]

Year	No. of nests
1968	655
1969	660[b]
1970	476[b]
1971	825
1972	380[b]
1973	456
1974	805
1979	285

[a] After Walmsley *et al.* (1980).
[b] Not exhaustive counts.

Table 30.   *The numbers of Purple Herons in and around the Camargue, 1980–1985* [a]

Year	Camargue	Plan du Bourg and Petite Camargue	Languedoc and Roussillon	Total
1980	375	681	220	1276
1981	252	650	165	1067
1982	410	957	507	1874
1983	203	1038	400	1641
1984	235	781	229	1245
1985	363	599	27	989

[a] After Anonymous 1987b.

CHAPTER 17

The Little Egret *Egretta garzetta*

GENERAL APPEARANCE AND FIELD CHARACTERS

The Little Egret is a medium-sized heron, 55–65 cm high with a wing-span of 88–95 cm.

Plumage. The sexes are alike, both males and females having an entirely white plumage.

Adult: during breeding, Little Egrets have two, sometimes three, lanceolated feathers up to 16 cm in length on the hindcrown. During that period, they also have elongated chest, mantle and scapular feathers. The chest feathers have lanceolated tips. The scapular feathers have a long shaft (up to 24 cm in length) curved slightly upwards at the end and reaching down to the tip of the tail. The particular appearance of these beautiful scapular aigrettes is caused by an anatomical peculiarity. In these feathers (except at the base of their proximal part), the long barbs are set widely apart and the short barbules, visible only with a magnifying glass, do not hook the barbs together.

Juveniles and immatures: these have a wholly white plumage like the adults. Juveniles do not have any elongated feathers, though first-winter birds acquire slightly elongated chest feathers. It seems that after the first spring moult, 1-year-old birds take on the adult breeding plumage, the nuptial feathers being shorter than in older birds (Witherby *et al.* 1939).

Downy young: these are entirely white, the down being longer on the crown where it stands erect.

Bare parts

Adult non-breeding: the bill is usually black though sometimes the lower mandible may be yellowish horn in colour at the base. This light colour may extend more or less towards the tip, which is always black. The eyes are small compared with other herons of similar size. The iris around the pupil is thin and very pale-coloured, either yellow or blue.

The lores are grey near the eyes and blue towards the bill. The legs are black, and the feet yellow or sometimes yellowish green. The change in coloration between legs and feet is not always at the base of the tarsus. The yellow colour may extend up its lower part, especially behind.

Adult breeding: the bill is entirely black. The lores are purple-red and the feet bright red. The red colour of the bare parts is strongest during pairing and becomes paler as soon as the pair is formed, vanishing altogether during nest-building.

Nestlings and juveniles: the bill is light yellowish horn in colour, becoming deeper yellow and then darker: green-brown, dark-brown and at last black. The upper mandible darkens first, the lower mandible remaining yellowish for a much longer period, darkening only very slowly from the tip. There are great individual differences among nestlings, some having green-brown bills with a variable amount of yellow until the fledging stage. This may lead to confusion, as young Little Egrets at the nest often have quite a light-coloured bill, whereas young nestling Cattle Egrets have entirely black bills almost until the fledging stage (C. Voisin, unpublished data). Even fledgling Little Egrets do not always have a black bill but often only a dark brown one (Yésou 1984). At this stage, the basal part of the lower mandible of nearly all Little Egrets has a varying amount of yellow. Only the tip of the mandible is always dark. Even in July, juveniles often have some yellow colour at the base of their lower mandible. A good deal of yellow, especially on the upper mandible, as observed by Yésou (1984), is quite exceptional at this stage. The legs of nestlings darken very slowly from bright green to dark green (often with some amount of yellow), dark brown and black. At the fledging stage, many young still have dark green or dark brown legs. The feet are often green, but are more usually yellowish green. Fledgings are smaller than adult birds and have shorter bills.

Downy young: the bill is light horn-coloured. The skin is bright green.

Field characters. Little Egrets, with their entirely white plumage, black bill and yellow feet, are easy to observe as they forage in open areas with low vegetation or no vegetation at all. When foraging, they contrast sharply with the background of earth, dark water and vegetation. In contrast, in flight their white plumage offers very little contrast to the pale blue of the sky and even less to the white and grey of the clouds. In flight, Little Egrets are much less conspicuous than the coloured herons. Even the slightly rufous colour of

Cattle Egrets, *Bubulcus ibis*, which is not discernible at a distance, makes them easier to detect in flight. Although Little Egrets are commonly encountered singly in flight, when foraging they are mostly seen in small parties. When fishing in the same habitat as Cattle Egrets, they never perch on the backs of cattle or horses. Little Egrets may be confused with Cattle Egrets at a distance or when they do not have their breeding plumage, and with the Squacco Heron, *Ardeola ralloides*, but the shorter, yellow or red bill of the Cattle Egret and the dark body and heavier flight of the Squacco Heron are sure signs of each species.

The Great White Egret, *Egretta alba*, which is a vagrant to western Europe from eastern Europe and Africa, is very like the Little Egret and the difference in size between them is often difficult to appreciate in the field. The Great White Egret always has dark feet and, out of the breeding season, a yellow bill, making the distinction between the two species easy. During breeding, the bill of the Great White Egret becomes as black as that of the Little Egret, though the feet remain dark.

Although there is little difficulty in distinguishing a Little Egret from a Great White Egret, it is very difficult to tell a Little Egret from the white morphs of the Western Reef Heron, *Egretta gularis*, of which two subspecies, *gularis* and *schistacea*, may occur in Europe as rare vagrants from Africa. *E. g. gularis* is, however, a more stocky bird with a thicker, slightly downcurved bill which is dark brown, though this is often difficult to observe in the field. The legs are dark olive-green, the feet yellow or green and the soles always yellow. In breeding plumage, they cannot be told apart in the field, since the bill and legs are black. *E. g. schistacea* (= *asha*) has a yellow to light horn-coloured bill. The legs and feet are light olive-green. The bill and legs are not black, even in breeding plumage. The legs briefly flush reddish orange during courtship (Hancock and Elliott 1978, Hancock 1984).

The American Snowy Egret, *Egretta thula*, which may occur as an accidental in Europe, is indistinguishable at some distance from the Little Egret when not in breeding plumage. At close range, the bright yellow lores of the Snowy Egret may be visible and thus distinguish the two species (Hancock 1984). To tell them apart in breeding plumage is less difficult, as all the crest feathers of the Snowy Egret are elongated instead of only 2–3 in the case of the Little Egret. The distal part of the scapular feathers of the Snowy Egret curve upwards more strongly.

Measurements. The measurements (mm) of adult and juvenile birds taken from skins are given below (see Cramp and Simmons 1977). The number of skins and the sex are indicated. Standard deviations are given in parentheses. The sex differences are only significant for the bill measurements.

wing	17 ♂♂	245–303	(13.20)	17 ♀♀	251–297	(15.00)
tail	16 ♂♂	84–113	(8.03)	14 ♀♀	81–101	(5.91)
bill	17 ♂♂	67–93	(5.84)	17 ♀♀	68–89	(6.67)
tarsus	17 ♂♂	78–112	(8.24)	17 ♀♀	88–110	(6.36)
toe	15 ♂♂	65–79	(3.58)	14 ♀♀	64–96	(8.33)

Sterbetz (1961) measured 30 Hungarian birds, distinguishing between adults and young: wing, adults 276–330 mm, juveniles 235–330 mm; bill, adults 88–98 mm, juveniles 83–93 mm. These few measurements show that most juveniles are smaller than adult birds. It would appear, therefore, that Little Egrets are able to fly before becoming fully grown. Further studies are required on this point, which would probably allow the establishment of significant size differences between adult males and females and an interesting growth curve for juveniles who only probably reach their full size in August. The Hungarian specimens measured by Sterbetz are surprisingly large compared to those measured elsewhere in the world by Cramp and Simmons.

The weight of Little Egrets, which is subject to great variations, has not been studied in depth. In Hungary, Vasvàri (1948–51) weighed adult birds: ♂♂ 496–614 g, ♀♀ 490–530 g. In Italy, adult males weighed 450 to 460 g (Moltoni 1936). A total of 33 Little Egrets captured and then released in July and August in the Camargue, France, weighed between 280 and 555 g (Hoffmann, in Bauer and Glutz 1966).

On average, the wing-beat rate of the Little Egret is 156 wing-beats per minute.

TAXONOMIC PROBLEMS IN THE GENUS *EGRETTA*

The Western Reef Heron, *Egretta gularis*, has three subspecies: *E. g. gularis* (Bosc) from West Africa, *E. g. schistacea* (Ehrenberg) from East Africa and *E. g. dimorpha* (Hartert) from Madagascar and the surrounding islands. Western Reef Herons are found in Africa and Asia to India. Eastern Reef Herons, *Egretta sacra*, are found in East Asia, Australia and various islands in the Pacific Ocean.

The Little Egret, Western Reef Heron and Eastern Reef Heron are often considered to form a superspecies (Hancock and Elliott 1978), because they are morphologically very close to each other. However, Hancock and Kushlan (1984) recently lumped together *E. garzetta* and *E. gularis* on the basis of interbreeding – yet to be confirmed – between the two species at Lake Turkana in Kenya. In my opinion, these two species should be kept separate, as there are anatomical differences (i.e. strength of bill and length of legs) and important ecological differences between them. Little Egrets, *E. garzetta*, commonly breed in temperate areas in Europe and Asia as well as in tropical and subtropical areas in Africa and Asia, whereas the Western Reef Heron, *E. gularis*, belongs only to the tropical and subtropical areas of Afric and Asia. The Little Egret is not a coastal bird. Although it is often found near the coast, it usually lives somewhat inland. It also occurs very far inland; as far as central Europe, central Asia and central Africa. Such is not the case for the Reef Heron, which is never found far from the coast (except *E. g. dimorpha*, which is found inland in Madagascar). Furthermore, Reef Herons, with their strong bills, commonly forage along the shore. In contrast, Little Egrets, with their thin and slender bills, normally avoid the coast and forage inland in deltas, marshes and lagoons.

The other problem is knowing whether the very rare dark morph of the Little Egret really exists, as has commonly been alleged. The birds in question are grey to very dark slate-grey. The feather pattern of these melanistic specimens is not uniform, their feathers being various shades of grey. This apparent dark morph is not well known. Specifically, do they sometimes or do they always have a white chin and throat? These birds have a black bill and black legs. The feet are probably darker than in the white morph. Might these specimens actually belong to the Western Reef Heron?

The three subspecies of the Western Reef Heron also have dark morphs, though these are very common (in the subspecies *E. g. gularis*, the dark morph is by far the most common). The grey colour of their plumage varies from "dark sooty to blue (predominating in *schistacea*) or to lavender grey (a sign of immaturity) and they have an equally variable amount of white on the wing, usually restricted to primary coverts, sometimes absent all together . . . The most notable feature is the wholly white chin and throat" (Hancock and Elliott 1978). In non-breeding plumage, the bare parts of the subspecies *E. g. gularis* and *E. g. schistacea* differ slightly from those of *E. garzetta*. Compared to the Little Egret, the dark morphs of the Western Reef Heron have, as do the white morphs, a thicker and slightly downcurved bill, which is dark brown in the subspecies *gularis* and yellow, tinged with greenish grey in the subspecies *schistacea* (but black in the subspecies *dimorpha*). The three subspecies have black legs with dark yellow feet. All three have black bills in breeding plumage.

Comparative measurements (mm) by Cramp and Simmons (1977) and Vaurie (1965) give:

	Egretta garzetta garzetta	*Egretta gularis gularis*	*Egretta gularis schistacea*
bill	67–93	79–89	94–103
tarsus	78–112	82–94	92–116

When the bird is in hand, it is possible to calculate the tarsus-to-bill ratio, which varies from 1.06 to 1.41 in *E. garzetta* and from 0.97 to 1.16 in *E. gularis* (Hiraldo Cano 1971, Bernis 1969, Cramp and Simmons 1977). Since the ratios overlap in the region from 1.06 to 1.16, these measurements will only help to distinguish *E. garzetta* from *E. gularis* in extreme cases. Dark morph specimens of *E. garzetta* are very rare in collections and, according to Yésou (1986), only three are known. The first was captured in Bulgaria in the nineteenth century and is now in the Museum of Natural History in Cobourg, Germany. The specimen has a slender bill and looks like a Little Egret. The bill is 93 mm long and the tarsus 102 mm. The tarsus-to-bill ratio is thus 1.09, which is possible for both *E. garzetta* and *E. gularis*. The measurements of the bill and tarsus are those of *E. garzetta*, too large for *E. g. gularis* and possible, but somewhat small, for *E. g. schistacea* (Voisin, unpublished). The second specimen, taken on 26 May 1956 in the south of Spain, is considered by Bernis (1969) to be a hybrid between *E. gularis* and *E. garzetta*. The last specimen, captured in Hungary on 5 August 1964, looks like *E. gularis* in the photograph published by Fabian and Sterbetz (1965). The bill measures 95 mm and the tarsus 92 mm. The tarsus-to-bill ratio is thus 0.97, typical for

E. gularis. In conclusion, the very existence of the dark morph of the Little Egret may appear doubtful and further specimens are needed to be quite sure that it does, in fact, occur.

DISTRIBUTION, MOVEMENTS AND HABITAT

Geographical variation

Two subspecies of *E. garzetta* are commonly recognized: *E. g. garzetta* (Linnaeus) and *E. g. nigripes* (Temminck). The only difference between these two subspecies is that *E. g. nigripes* has entirely black feet instead of yellow ones. However, individuals with black feet but yellow soles have been observed in South East Asia.

Breeding range and wintering areas

Little Egrets, *E. g. garzetta*, breed in southern Europe from Spain to Russia, their northern breeding range extending to about 46°N. In central Asia, they are found breeding in the area around the Caspian and Aral seas. Their breeding range extends eastwards from Turkey, Israel, probably Iraq, south of the Himalayas and the mountains of China, to eastern and southern China. In Hopeh (China), Korea and Japan, Little Egrets breed up to 37°N (Hancock and Elliott 1978). In Africa, they have been recorded breeding in Morocco, probably Algeria, Tunisia and Egypt, and in scattered sites south of the Sahara to South Africa. The other subspecies, *E. g. nigripes*, breeds on the islands of South East Asia (Java, the Philippines and Taiwan) and the southwest Pacific (but not in New Zealand), as well as in northern, eastern and southern Australia.

Little Egrets winter in southern Europe, Africa, the Near and Middle East, southern and South East Asia, Australia and the southwestern Pacific.

Movements

This species is mainly migratory but when the climate permits, a more or less sizeable part of the population winters in the breeding range. The autumn migration commences as early as July, although most of the birds do not leave until August or September. The migration continues, with the final few birds departing in October, November and even during the first half of December. In many areas, the wintering population has a harsh time in particularly cold winters. In the south of France, and especially in the Camargue, cold periods regularly kill a considerable number of wintering Little Egrets. A study by Voisin (1985) of all recoveries of Little Egrets ringed in the Camargue during the years 1932–1977 shows very clearly the two migration routes taken by these birds, which are probably the ones used by all Little Egrets from western Europe (see Figs 21 and 22). No discernible pre-migratory vagrancy

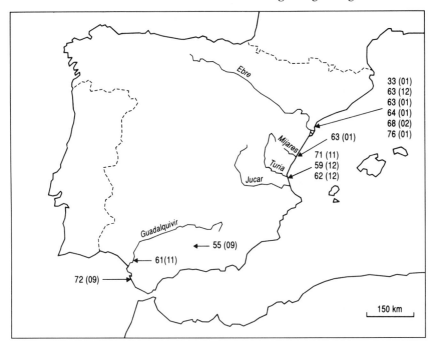

Figure 21   Recoveries in Spain of Little Egrets ringed in the Camargue. The arrows show the exact locations of the recoveries. Each bird is identified by its year of recovery and (in parentheses) the month of its recovery. The same notation is used for the maps of Italy, Africa and the Mediterranean area (Voisin 1985).

movements towards the north were found, the young dispersing immediately along the migration routes. One route lies westwards, along the lagoons of the Mediterranean Sea to Spain, where many birds remain along the eastern coast during the winter. Some birds fly farther south and recoveries have been made in Morocco and the Gambia. The second route lies eastwards towards Italy, the birds then flying south, mainly along the coasts to reach Sicily and Tunisia, where many birds winter. Some, however, follow the coast on to Libya, probably joining the Egyptian population, while others cross the desert to the flooded areas of Mali and even to tropical Africa (see Fig. 23). It seems that Little Egrets avoid crossing the Mediterranean Sea at least during the autumn migration, since there are no recoveries of Little Egrets ringed in France along the Algerian coast or along the Mediterranean coast of Morocco. A study of recoveries of Little Egrets ringed in Tunisia mostly between 1970 and 1977 (Voisin 1985), reveals that, in these more southern latitudes, the birds that do not remain disperse in all directions and are found throughout the Mediterranean area; only a few of them undertaking true migration across the Sahara to the Sahel and tropical Africa (see Fig. 24).

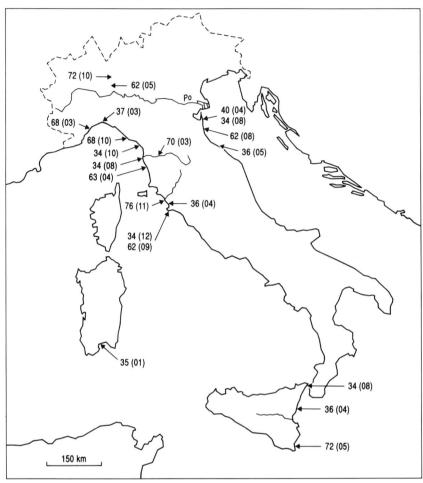

Figure 22   Recoveries in Italy of Little Egrets ringed in the Camargue (Voisin 1985).

Many eastern European and probably also Middle Eastern, birds seem to winter in Africa, as witnessed by the pronounced autumn passage along the coast of Eritrea (Moreau 1972). How many birds take the east African migration route and how many the trans-Saharan is not known. The trans-Saharan route has been proven by recoveries in Mali (Voisin 1985) and in Nigeria (Moreau 1972) of Little Egrets ringed in the USSR. Birds from China and Japan migrate south to Malaysia, the Philippines and Indonesia, where they meet the subspecies *E. g. nigripes*. Little Egrets from southern Australia have been found in New Guinea and New Zealand (Hancock and Elliott 1978).

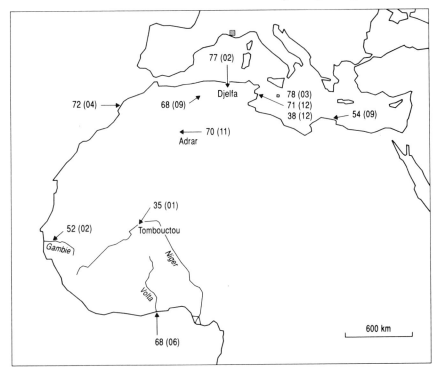

Figure 23   Recoveries in Africa of Little Egrets ringed in the Camargue (Voisin 1985).

In Europe, the return migration occurs in March, April and May. The heronries are occupied from early April in eastern Europe, and often as early as the second half of March in western Europe. As a rare exception, a heronry purely of Little Egrets established itself as late as May in the saltpans area of Aigues-Mortes (Camargue).

During the spring migration, Little Egrets have a strong tendency to overshoot (i.e. to migrate too far to the north where they cannot breed). Spring visitors have consequently been observed in all European countries except in Iceland. They are quite commonly reported in southern Germany, Switzerland, Austria, Britain and Ireland, where they may stay for several weeks or even months.

Three records of Little Egrets from the New World prove that they are able to cross the Atlantic ocean. The first observation came from Newfoundland in May 1954 (Cramp and Simmons 1977), and two birds ringed as nestlings in Spain in 1956 and 1962, were recovered in Trinidad in January 1957 and in Martinique in October 1962 respectively (Bernis 1962).

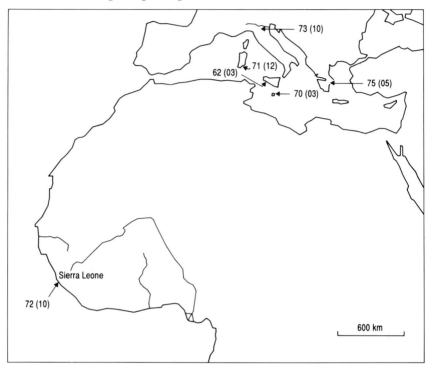

Figure 24   Recoveries outside Tunisia and eastern Algeria of Little Egrets
ringed in Tunisia (Voisin 1985).

HABITAT

Little Egrets are found at middle and low latitudes, usually in flooded
lowland areas. Judging from recoveries (Voisin 1985), they are to be found
mainly inland in coastal areas (in marshes, lagoons and deltas), but not
normally along the seashore itself. This is not the case, however, when the
birds migrate along the coast skirting a desert, such as in Mauritania and
Namibia. J. F. Voisin (unpublished) thus observed several Little Egrets
foraging at sea at Lüderitz. They also follow rivers upstream and are hence
found far inland, where a suitable habitat is provided, such as in the rice
district along the Po and Ticino rivers in Italy. On rare occasions they have
been seen at altitudes of up to 2000 m, e.g. in Armenia (Cramp and Simmons
1977). Little Egrets forage in lagoons, saltpans, estuaries, freshwater marshes,
rice fields and along streams and rivers. They fish in areas with low vegetation
or no vegetation at all, such as sandy river banks and salt- and brackish-water
areas. Amphibians and insects cannot tolerate much salinity, but some fish
(*Atherina boyeri* and *Anguilla anguilla*) commonly hunted by Little Egrets,
occur in water having salt concentrations up to about 50 g per litre.

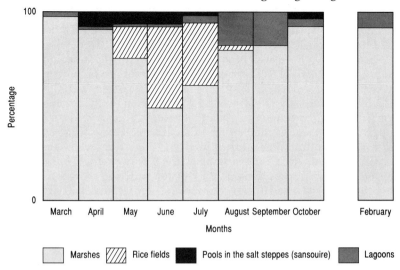

Figure 25   The percentage of the population of Little Egrets foraging in various biotopes in the Camargue during the months of March, April, May, June, July, August, September, October and February. The percentage is calculated over a 67-km route through the Camargue that was covered 85 times from 1971 to 1977 (Voisin 1978).

In freshwater marshes, Little Egrets are always found away from dense cover, where the vegetation is sparse and low. Unlike Grey Herons, they do not need large, bare areas to thrive, and are often seen hunting on small sandbanks not far from dense marsh and river vegetation. During my study in the Camargue, I noticed that Little Egrets actively seek pools, lagoons and marshes that are drying up, and where prey concentrate as the water recedes (see Fig. 25). Several Little Egrets usually forage in these favourable places, walking slowly or even running to catch their prey. They also hunt, to a lesser extent, in inundated grassland, mosty taking frogs. They may thus forage among cattle, in company with Cattle Egrets. It seems that they just happen to favour the same places. They do not get near to the feet of the cattle or take advantage of them as Cattle Egrets do; nor have I seen Little Egrets perching on the backs of cattle. Rice fields are used as foraging areas as soon as insects and frogs appear, and for as long as the young rice is still short – in the Camargue, from May to the beginning of August. Hence Little Egrets, like Grey Herons, fish in fresh-, brackish- and salt-water areas. They are very conspicuous birds, as they forage in open areas, often actively in small parties and often taking flight, especially during the breeding season when they fly several times each day between the heronry and their foraging grounds, often a distance of up to 20 km (Voisin 1978).

Little Egrets nest in mixed colonies in all kinds of trees – both deciduous and coniferous. The trees that they choose are usually tall, such as shoots growing from old alders, but may also be very large, old trees in well-protected reserves, such as the big cork-oaks of the Coto Doñana. Very small trees and bushes such as tamarisks and willows are used if no taller ones are available, as for instance in the reedbeds of the Ebro River Delta in Spain. Little Egrets' nests have even been found on reeds in African colonies (Hancock and Elliott 1978). In Europe, mixed heronries are often found among very dense vegetation in temporarily flooded areas along the margins of rivers, lakes and marshes. The ground vegetation in the surroundings of the heronry is usually extremely dense and it is often necessary to cut one's way through it; however, in the heronry, this ground storey becomes partially destroyed by the droppings of the birds and is never dense. Some heronries stand on dry land, often along a small channel or deep ditch, but many also occur on inundated spots. Despite the difficult access to most heronries, the birds are often persecuted during the breeding period. Small heronries may be found scattered in unprotected areas, but the important ones in Europe are established in protected places such as reserves or private estates. In France, and particularly in the Camargue, they are often quite close to human habitation (such as small farmhouses or wardens' houses) to gain the necessary protection against hunters and nest robbers.

In western Europe, Little Egrets nest mostly with Night Herons and to a lesser extent with Grey Herons. Because they breed later than these two species, they settle in previously established heronries, often in small numbers. In southern and eastern Europe, where they are more numerous, they often nest in greater numbers in company with Squacco Herons, Cattle Egrets and even spoonbills, as well as Night Herons and Grey Herons. In Africa and Asia, such colonies are often very large and number many thousands of breeding waterbirds, including spoonbills, ibises, cormorants and darters.

POPULATION SIZE, TRENDS AND DYNAMICS

Little Egrets are among the species which suffered greatly from the plumage trade at the end of the nineteenth and the beginning of the twentieth centuries, during which time they almost became extinct as breeding birds in Europe. The ending of the plumage trade, during the First World War, allowed the population to increase slowly. This increase has recently been hastened by the total protection of the species in most European countries.

In France, studies from the first half of the nineteenth century mention the Little Egret as a nesting bird in the Camargue (Voisin 1975). However, they had disappeared from the area by the end of the century and the British ornithologist, W. Eagle Clarke (1895), did not observe a single one during his spring and summer visit in 1894. In 1914, a few Little Egrets were nesting there again (l'Hermitte, in Voisin 1975). They increased in number very slowly until the Second World War, when hunting was allowed throughout the year in coastal areas.

The first census of the Camargue breeding population was carried out by J.A. Valverde (1955–1956), who counted 1150 breeding pairs; 3 years later, R. Lévêque found 1500 pairs (Hoffmann *et al.* 1959). Since 1968, breeding censuses have been undertaken each year and the wintering population has been counted since 1973 (Voison 1975, 1979, Hafner 1987).

National breeding censuses of Little Egrets in France were carried out in 1974 by Brosselin (1974) and in 1981 by Duhautois and Marion (1982), who recorded 1875 and 2253 breeding pairs respectively (see Tables 31–33).

The major events during 1975–1981 were the colonization of Mediterranean areas other than the Camargue, with two heronries appearing along the River Durance and one in the western coastal lagoon area, and the significant increase in the number of Little Egrets breeding in the Atlantic coastal areas from Nantes to Bordeaux. The reasons for the recent extension of the breeding range in France are two-fold: the complete protection of the species since 1962 and the lack of cold winters during the 1970s.

In 1981, Little Egrets nested in 29 colonies in France (Duhautois and Marion 1982). Some heronries were small, with only a few Little Egrets breeding among the Night Herons. These small heronries occurred mostly in inland areas. Heronries in coastal areas usually contained 50–300 nests. In the Camargue, one or two heronries usually held more than 500 nests (the maximum being 900 in one heronry in 1975) (Voisin 1979).

In Italy, the first national breeding population census was performed by Fasola *et al.* in 1981. Little Egret nests were found in 41 heronries, all situated in the Po River valley, mostly in tributaries in the rice-growing district, in the Po River Delta and along the coastal lagoons, which are scattered along the Adriatic Sea from Ravenna to the border with Yugoslavia. In the last two areas, the heronries were less numerous but larger. In Italy, the heronries ranged in size from just a few nests to 750 with one exception; this heronry, a little north of Ravenna, near a large lagoon, held 940 Little Egret nests. Two small heronries in more southerly coastal areas (one certain and one probable), as well as one probable colony in Sardinia, were not visited.

In Spain, the breeding census was undertaken by Fernandez-Cruz (1975) at the beginning of the 1970s. The breeding population was estimated at that time at about 3000 pairs, the great majority in the Marismas area (delta of the Guadalquivir River), where a large heronry was established at Donaña (Huelva) in the 1950s and 1960s, and at La Rocina (Huelva) in the 1970s. In 1970 and 1971, about 2000 pairs of Little Egrets bred at La Rocina (Ree 1973). The Donaña colony was still in existence in the 1970s, but was by then much smaller in size (see Table 34). The lagoon of La Albufera (Valencia) is the other location where Little Egrets breed in numbers in Spain. In 1973, 375 pairs nested in this area (Fernandez-Cruz 1975). Little Egret nests are few in number elsewhere in Spain, even in the Ebro Delta where two colonies housed 20 pairs in 1977 and 30 in 1978 (Martinez and Martinez 1983).

In Greece in 1972, 1500 pairs of Little Egrets bred in nine large heronries and several small ones (Cramp and Simmons 1977). During 1985 and 1986, the number of breeding pairs was estimated at 1055–1232 (Crivelli *et al.* 1988). In Turkey in the 1970s, 900 pairs bred in four large heronries (Cramp and Simons 1977). In Hungary, 150–203 pairs bred each year between 1959 and 1968. In Yugoslavia, during the same period, 600–800 pairs were breeding (Sterbetz and Slivka 1972). There are two major heronries in the coastal areas of Tunisia with about 100 pairs of breeding Little Egrets each

(Cramp and Simmons 1977). In Morocco, 150 nests were counted in a colony at Allal-Tazi in 1967 (Haas 1969).

The Camargue is the only place where sufficient nestlings have been ringed for a number of years to allow a study of the rate of survival of a population. The annual survival rates have been calculated using Seber's (1971) and Lebreton's (1977) methods for two periods: the first, from 1932 to 1939, when first-year birds had a survival rate of $20.9 \pm 7\%$ and birds more than 1 year of age a survival rate of $63.8 \pm 17\%$; the second, from 1958 to 1977, when first-year birds had a survival rate of $46.4 \pm 8\%$ and birds more than 1 year of age a survival rate of $81.6 \pm 6\%$ (Voisin 1985).

The population growth rate of Egrets for these two periods, estimated using Leslie's (1945) matrical model, showed that the population could hardly have maintained itself during the first period (1932–1939) without the immigration and breeding of adult birds born elsewhere, but that during the second period (1958–1977) the population increased of its own accord. (Little Egrets born in one colony may breed in others quite far away. Two birds ringed as nestlings in Spain were found dead in May in the Camargue, one of them in a heronry: Voisin 1985). The major difference between these two time periods was the existence of hunting laws during the latter, banning the hunting which was previously allowed throughout the year in coastal areas in the Camargue. At present, the population of the Camargue is rather stable, though according to our calculations it should now increase. The limited area of wetland available for the birds is probably responsible for the stable population. This conclusion is confirmed by the fact that the recent increase in the French population between 1974 and 1981 did not affect the Camargue, but rather new areas where Little Egrets had not bred before (Voisin 1985).

Ringing data clearly show that the principal cause of mortality is being hunted and shot and also, to a much smaller extent, being caught in nets in Africa. Accidental causes of death include one bird found dead in a well, one killed by an overhead electric cable and one by a raptor.

Another major cause of death in Europe, in addition to hunting, is cold weather. There was no really cold winter during the 1970s or early 1980s. However, every 10 or 15 years, one or several cold winters follow each other along the Atlantic coast as well as along the Mediterranean coast. Numerous Little Egrets wintering in southern and western France during the winter of 1985 were killed by the severe cold period in January, which lasted 3 weeks. In the Loire-Atlantique, 978 wintering Little Egrets were counted at two roosts at the end of December 1984. The minimum temperature during the January cold snap was $-13°C$, and at the end of it 67 Little Egrets were found dead at the roosts. In one, only one Little Egret was seen alive, in the other about 50 were counted. A month later, at the end of February, there were a few birds at the first roost and about 250 at the other (Recorbert 1985). They had probably not migrated very far, and had most likely foraged at sea on tidal flats, since at that time all the inland waters were frozen. In the Camargue, the water froze in marshes and even in the Vaccarès. The minimum temperature was $-10°C$ with the mistral blowing at 27 m per second. A total of 230 Little Egrets were found dead. The others must have left the

Camargue, as there were only 10 Little Egrets seen alive at the roosts in January and none in February (Hafner 1987). How many of them reached warmer climes in Spain or Italy one wonders? The breeding population in the Camargue in 1985 was the lowest since censuses began in 1954. Cold winters are thus an irregular but important cause of mortality among Little Egrets wintering in France and probably also in northern Italy.

BEHAVIOUR AND BIOLOGY

DAILY ROUTINE

Little Egrets often gather in small parties, both when flying and when fishing. In their winter quarters, they spend the whole day at the foraging grounds. When fully fed, they rest and preen on the banks bordering the marshes and lagoons where they fish, or perching on nearby trees and bushes, often tamarisks in the Camargue. At dusk, they fly singly or in small parties to the roosts. Little Egrets may congregate in great numbers at one roost, and use the same one each evening throughout the winter, and often year after year. There is no activity at the roost. The birds land directly in the trees and perch quickly on a suitable branch where they will sleep for the night. At dawn, they all leave the roost singly or in small parties to return to the foraging grounds. Little Egrets usually roost in large trees, but bushes may be used if trees are unavailable. Where they winter and breed in the same area, a few trees in one or two heronries are often used as roosts. In 1975, Little Egrets roosted in two locations in the Camargue, both situated in heronries, with 287 and 451 birds being present during February (Voisin 1976).

While breeding, Little Egrets sleep in the heronry at night. They generally leave at dawn, a few of them a little earlier still (on 22 June 1973, in the Allier, France, the first bird left at 03.20 Universal Time, with most departing at 03.30 U.T.). At the beginning of the breeding season, however, many birds do not leave the colony so early; males displaying within a territory and females looking for a mate often remain a few hours longer. Later, a parent incubating or guarding the nest will not depart from the heronry until its mate returns. At dusk, those birds not already in the heronry return, the last just as the bats emerge.

The weather also has an influence on the time birds return to the colony – and probably on their departure times as well. During fine weather, birds return to the colony on moonlit nights with no wind, probably having left distant foraging grounds too late in the day. I have never seen Little Egrets forage by night as Grey Herons sometimes do. During rainy and windy weather, Little Egrets return to the heronry earlier than usual. In Africa, when sandstorms darken the sky, nesting herons also return earlier than normal. However, at any time of the day when the sky suddenly darkens, for example before a thunderstorm, a few birds always return rapidly to their nests (Voisin 1976). During a solar eclipse in India, foraging Little Egrets took wing immediately, flying back to the roost as darkness suddenly fell at 15.46 h (Ashok Kumar 1981).

Like all herons, Little Egrets fly with retracted necks and legs stretched backwards along the body. The vigorous, regular wing-beats are never interrupted, even by short glides, except when landing. Observations at saltpans and lagoons bordering the sea in the Camargue have shown that when the wind is strong, Little Egrets adapt their flight accordingly. When flying against the wind, they fly just above the water surface, at a height of about 0.5–1.0 m. When flying with the wind, however, they fly at a height of at least 15–20 m. The wind probably blows stronger higher up, since dykes and dunes lessen its strength near the water surface. In addition, when flying with the wind, the precision of flight is certainly less than when flying against it. Thus flying low over the water with strong winds from the rear could be dangerous. In one heronry established among the pine trees in a lagoon area near the sea where the wind was often strong, Little Egrets landed into the wind. Those flying with the wind came in very fast over the trees. When landing, they often glided for 3–7 seconds to lessen their speed, sometimes making a wing-beat to adjust direction and perhaps to increase speed a little. They flew past the place in the branches where they were about to land, turning up against the wind at just the right distance to land very slowly on their perch, having lost much of their speed when turning and spending the rest of it reaching their perch. Their behaviour recalled that of a sailing boat when landing at a buoy (Voisin 1976).

However, Little Egrets usually nest further inland. When flying to and from their foraging grounds, over dry land or marshes, they usually fly 15–20 m above flat land and at greater heights over hills and valleys. Flying at higher altitudes provides more security and removes the need to follow the topography, thereby shortening flying distances. Little Egrets leaving their foraging grounds along the Allier River, for example, which is surrounded by hills, flew up high and maintained this altitude until reaching the heronry. They often began their downward flight only when directly above the heronry, using a particular form of flight to lose height rapidly. They came down to the heronry in a rapid "side slipping swerving flight" (a term used by Blaker in 1968 for the Cattle Egret, which also uses this specific flight), which recalls falling leaves in autumn (Voisin 1976). Meyerriecks (1960) has observed it in the Green- backed Heron and has described it as a "whirling and twisting" flight. It would be useful to film and analyse it, using slow-motion photography, as it is too rapid and too complex to be completely understood and described when observed only in the field.

In the heronry, Little Egrets spend much time alternately preening and resting, especially during good weather. They always preen thoroughly when returning from the foraging grounds. This complete cleansing of the plumage takes about 1 hour each time and usually begins as soon as the bird returns to the heronry. During nesting, the mate at the nest is relieved first and the young fed. When leaving the nest, Little Egrets usually perch on a nearby branch and preen briefly for about 10 minutes before flying off to forage. To preen, they both nibble and stroke their feathers. When nibbling, they seize one feather – or several small ones – between their mandibles, which are closed and opened alternately in quick movements of small amplitude. They either work along

Little Egrets preening and stretching (A and B after photographs by D. Robert; E after a photograph by J. Delpech).

the whole feather from the base to the tip, or concentrate their attention at the base of the calamus and the adjacent skin. To stroke a feather, they pass it slowly through the slightly closed mandibles. During preening, Little Egrets also rub their head and upper neck against the powder patches on the breast, rump and flanks, those on the breast being used the most. Preening usually begins with the breast and lower neck feathers and moves on to the belly feathers. The back is usually attended to only briefly and not every time. The upperwing feathers are thoroughly cleaned by nibbling and stroking. To clean the underwing-coverts, Little Egrets stretch the unfolded wing upwards and forwards and nibble the feathers with the bill held vertically against the wing. They are unable to use the bill to preen the head and upper neck, and therefore use the pectinated claws to scratch away the powder that has been rubbed on them once it has absorbed the moisture and dirt. Little Egrets seem to use their oil gland sparingly, since there is no record of its use.

They commonly body-shake to get their plumage in order, particularly females after copulation. They lean forwards, the wings slightly apart, body feathers erect, and shake vigorously. Little Egrets also body-stretch by leaning forwards and stretching the head, neck and body as much as possible. They also stretch their legs by extending one leg backwards as much as possible. Sometimes, they also stretch the wing back at the same time and on the same side as the leg. I have never seen a Little Egret bathe or sunbathe. When resting, they adopt the typical heron position (Voisin 1976).

DISPLAYS AND CALLS

Only two studies have been undertaken of the displays of the Little Egret: a preliminary work by Blaker (1969) and my own (1976–1977). All of the agonistic and fear displays are performed by both sexes. The Alarm Call seems to be the same for both males and females. In contrast, the typical sexual display, and Stretch Display is only performed by males, who use two different calls during its performance. Unmated males also have a very characteristic Advertisement Call.

Agonistic displays

The forward displays are a succession of increasingly intense threat displays, used at the heronry to maintain individual distances and to defend the nest territory.

Full Forward Display. This is the common threat display of herons, and takes the following form in the Little Egret:

○ body in a near horizontal position;
○ legs slightly bent;
○ wings partly spread;

○ neck curved backwards in an "S" shape, bill pointed forwards ready to strike (the more the neck is curved backwards, the higher is the tendency to attack);

○ all the feathers are held erect, particularly on the neck and crest. The long crest feathers are erected beyond the vertical and fall forwards. The nearly horizontal breast feathers point straight forwards.

From this position the bird thrusts its head vigorously forwards with open bill, giving loud Threat Calls. If the intruder is some metres away, the bird walks slowly towards him maintaining the threatening posture (but with legs less bent and neck less arched). At a distance of 1–2 m, it stops to resume the

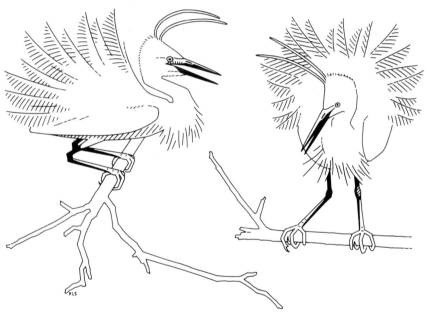

Full Forward Display.

Full Forward Display, aiming vigorous stabs at its opponent (which is still too far away to be reached), and making harsh Threat Calls. If the intruder does not retire, the bird moves a few steps closer and displays again. Finally, it comes within striking distance and the stabs of the dagger-shaped bill become real, at which stage the intruder always flees. When feeling very aggressive, a Little Egret may threaten a bird at some 10–12 m, away, in which case the bird threatening often flies off to land a few metres from its opponent, where it displays and then starts its slow threatening walk towards the intruder. The gradual approach gives intruders time to flee and avoids a fight. If a stranger lands within 1 m of the nest, the occupant displays on its nest. During the Full Forward Display, the neck is curved backwards in an "S" shape for several seconds before stabbing, which gives the intruder time to leave before getting hurt.

Other forward displays. Little Egrets often threaten with much less intensity. At the lowest threat level, only the crest feathers are raised a little and the bird may even remain in the resting posture. The crest and neck feathers are progressively raised as the degree of aggressiveness increases and the neck is more or less stretched depending on the activity of the bird. For example, a bird may try to look at an intruder through branches and thick foliage. Becoming more aggressive, it moves towards the intruder, neck held straight, head and neck feathers held very erect, the breast feathers and scapulars only slightly raised. When verging on the Full Forward Display, the legs are not as bent, the neck is not curved as much and not all of the feathers are raised to a maximum. The degree of aggressiveness of a bird is recognized by others in the colony by its posture and how far its feathers are raised. In a group, dominance and level of aggression are related.

A particular form of forward display is the Stab-and-counter-stab, often performed by Little Egrets on nearby nests in the same way as by Cattle Egrets. When threatening each other, the two birds involved remain on their nests, each in turn lungeing rather slowly at the other. They do not hurt each other, though their nests are often so close that they are able to reach each others' head and neck. Stab-and-counter-stab is a common display in dense colonies.

The Direct Attack. This usually occurs when a strange male tries to copulate with a paired female at her nest. The female gives loud calls which can be heard at a distance. If her mate is in the vicinity (if he has not left the heronry, he is usually collecting sticks), he flies back to the nest at once and attacks the strange male without any preliminary display, delivering strong blows with his sharp bill as he lands on the nest. The attack continues until the stranger flees. Often, however, the interloper sees the male returning and flies off at the last moment. The swiftness of the attack leaves no time for further flight, and to avoid being attacked from the rear, the stranger usually faces the attacking bird head on. Both birds become engaged in an aerial struggle some metres above the trees of the heronry. They strike at each other with their bills while flapping their wings to try to keep their balance and remain aloft. Their legs dangle, their feathers raised to a maximum. After a short struggle, both birds crash down into the foliage where the struggle ends, since they must try to land without breaking their necks. This behaviour is quite common during the copulation period and has often been mistaken for a sexual display.

The Supplanting Run. On the foraging grounds, Little Egrets never use forward displays to threaten each other. They attack directly but without the violence of the Direct Attack used at the heronry. The Supplanting Run is not commonly used on the foraging grounds and occurs only when food is scarce. With the body held horizontal, the neck withdrawn between the shoulders and the bill pointing straight forward, the attacking bird moves quickly or runs towards its opponent. The feathers are neither raised nor sleeked, but held in the normal position. In order to avoid being pecked, the bird being attacked backs off a little and begins to fish again at some distance away.

Fear, curiosity and conflict displays

Alarm Posture. The Little Egret takes up this posture when in fear of humans, predators or strange machines in the heronry. The bird stands with legs, body, neck and head held nearly vertical. The bill is pointed upwards. If the danger comes from under the trees, they may look down as if peering over a high fence, bill pointed slightly downwards. All the feathers are sleeked against the body. Birds threatened by others in the heronry do not adopt the Alarm Posture, but try to flee with their plumage sleeked, either rapidly slipping through the branches or flying away. Little Egrets do not perform the Bittern Stance.

Alarm Call. Little Egrets have a loud, typical heron call, which is used when flying away when alarmed or sometimes by birds remaining in the trees when danger approaches.

Curiosity Posture. When Little Egrets are interested in, but not afraid of, some interaction between others in the heronry, for example a fight or a strange noise, they stretch their neck, hold their scapular feathers slightly erect, and look in the direction of the noise. Though this is the best posture for looking around, it is also used at other times. For example, the same posture is adopted by females when perching near a displaying male whom they could easily observe with their necks retracted. The retracted neck, however, denotes indifference, while the stretched neck is a posture showing interest.

Wing-touch. This is a typical conflict display given by both unmated males and females when in the presence of a bird of the opposite sex. The movement is exactly the same as in Cattle Egrets.

Courtship displays

Advertising Call. During pair-formation, and before having found a mate, the male alternates courtship display with a special, long gargling call that carries over a long distance. This Advertising Call is only given within the heronry, is loud enough to be heard easily by an observer outside the heronry.

Supplanting Run.

A, a male performing its typical Advertising Call; B, Alarm Posture characteristic of both males and females; C, a male leaving for a Direct Attack.

It is not only easy to recognize but, once heard, is impossible to confuse with any other call of either the Little Egret or any other European heron. It lasts about 0.4 of a second and is interrupted 4–6 times, these very short interruptions being specific to the Advertising Call. During many observations of advertising males, I have found that they all gular flutter, as though it is too hot. It seems that the sound, produced in the syrinx, is modified by this fluttering, which probably causes the interruptions in the call and gives it its gargling sound. Having heard the call at a distance, an observer will know that Little Egrets are displaying and will nest nearby, without having to cause any disturbance by approaching the birds during a particularly sensitive period. The number of nests is easily counted during another visit later in the season. The Advertising Call of males is thus very useful to field observers.

Stretch Display. In Little Egrets, the Stretch Display is only performed by unmated males to attract females, and proceeds as follows:

(a)   In a nearly horizontal posture, the bird bends its legs and points its bill vertically towards the sky. The long scapulars are erected to a maximum but the feathers of the head and neck are not erected (the two or three elongated crest feathers are thus not used during this display).

(b)   The bird then slowly stretches its neck vertically and gives a succession of very soft calls – "ko, ko, ko". After stretching the neck upwards as much as possible, it begins to retract it slowly, while the bill, head and neck remain held vertical. The bird is silent during this phase.

(c)   At the end of the display, the head and bill become horizontal again and the bird returns to the ordinary resting position.

(d)   At the end of the movement described in (b), the bird may begin the display again, usually performing it 1–5 times in succession.

(e)   The same movement as that described in (b) may also be performed in a very rapid fashion. The neck, head and bill shoot rapidly upwards as the bird utters a loud, short "kock". The following downward movement, when the neck is retracted, is as rapid as the upward movement.

Usually, the male stretches slowly several times and ends with the rapid stretch, but these two versions of the display are given in every possible combination. The bird may only use the slow one or the rapid one or begin with the rapid one and end with the slow one.

Circle Flights and Pursuit Flights. When Circle Flying, both male and female Little Egrets fly in a circle, landing at or near their former perch in the heronry. During this flight, males often give the Advertising Call. In Pursuit Flights, one of the birds (usually the male) flies off and lands in another part of the heronry. Usually, the other bird follows. However, the other bird may not follow, in which case the first bird usually flies back after a short period. Pursuit Flights are more complicated when several females are perched close to a displaying male, since when the male flies off, several females follow. During Pursuit Flights, males often give the Advertising Call as they do during Circle Flights. During both Circle Flights and Pursuit Flights, the birds fly with legs stretched backwards along the body, but with extended necks. The fact that they fly with an extended neck is not, in my opinion, part of a ritualization, but only a matter of convenience. During nest-building, Little Egrets fly with an extended neck to fetch sticks from nearby. During long Pursuit Flights, Little Egrets often fly with retracted necks, though some birds fly with extended necks even during long Pursuit Flights (over 100 m).

I have never observed any Flap Flight Display, in which birds make a sound with their wings as they fly, though Blaker (1968) has noted such a display in which Little Egrets produce a weaker sound than do Cattle Egrets.

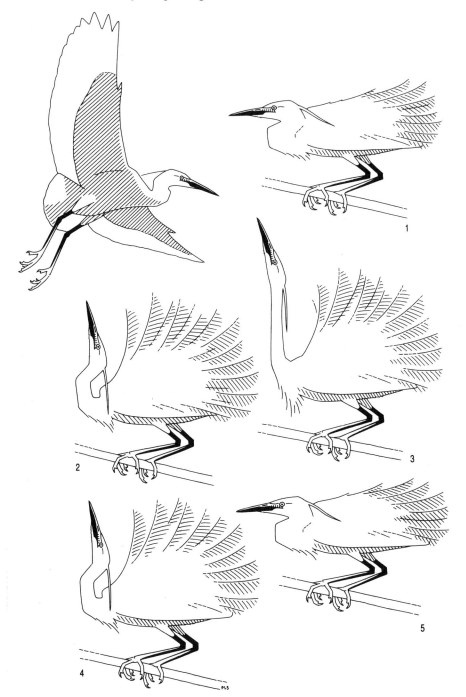

Twig-shake. This is a common behaviour in Little Egrets during pair-formation. To attract females, males seize a twig in their bills on the branch where they perch, and draw hard on it while shaking the head horizontally. At this stage, the twigs are not actually picked. Both males and females also seize twigs in their bills and, not drawing at them, shake their heads horizontally, looking like birds arranging twigs in their nest.

Breeding displays

Bill-clappering. The bird rapidly opens and closes its bill, the mandibles being only slightly parted. The amplitude of the movement is too small to produce a sound audible at any distance and, this behaviour is very inconspicuous and easily goes unnoticed. Bill-clappering appears as soon as the pair is formed and is much used during the first hours after pair-formation when the birds have to learn to recognize each other. Still very frequent during the beginning of the incubation period, it becomes less so at the end of it and is not heard after hatching.

Bill-clappering is directed either towards the mate or towards the nest. After greeting, the incoming bird usually begins to Bill-clapper, soon followed by its mate. Both birds perform facing each other or behind each other's back in the same position as other species adopt during Back-biting. They may also Bill-clapper towards the nest, with the bill directed downwards. During incubation, the incoming bird, after some mutual Bill-clappering, often begins to push its mate gently away from the eggs while still Bill-clappering.

Back-biting. I have not observed this behaviour in Little Egrets, though it is common in most heron species, particularly Night Herons, Cattle Egrets, Squacco Herons and Grey Herons. In Little Egrets, the pair bonds are thus strengthened without any tactile stimuli.

REPRODUCTIVE BEHAVIOUR

Pair-formation

The unmated male, perched on a prominent branch in the heronry, gives the Stretch Display, and the soft "ko, ko, ko" and the short, hard "kock" calls, the latter sometimes sounding slightly gargled. When not performing the Stretch Display, the male very often gives Advertising Calls, and also sometimes Twig-shakes. Between these displays, he takes long pauses during which he remains very alert, looking around and taking a great interest in every movement in the heronry. At this time, he adopts a characteristic posture such that an experienced observer can easily identify him as an unmated male. He looks around with his body less vertical than a resting bird and with the neck stretched. The long scapulars are slightly erected; the head and neck feathers are sleeked.

A female in flight and successive postures of a male performing the Stretch Display.

After a while, one or several females surround him at distances of 1–5 m. Though attracted by him, they remain at a distance, seeming for long periods to take no notice of him and often preening thoroughly. However, they may threaten each other when a newcomer lands too near a preening bird.

Suddenly, one female shows some interest in the displaying male, often after having threatened a newcomer. She adopts the Curiosity Posture, but, when moving towards the male, keeps all her feathers sleeked. At this stage, the Wing-touch is a common behaviour. Now and then, she takes a number of steps towards the male, with the result that, after a while, she gets quite close to him. During the first attempts to approach, the male is not ready to accept a female on his territory. He threatens, using the Full Forward Display and, with harsh calls, moves towards her. During these first attempts, the female always flees before being attacked. Sometimes, the male takes off, Circle Flies and lands right on top of the fleeing female, before perching on the spot she had earlier occupied. After such an attack, the male usually returns to the place from which he previously displayed but may also begin to display from this new spot.

Often, especially when attempts to approach the male have been numerous, instead of moving progressively towards him, the female makes a jump with extended wings and lands near him. She often makes this jump when a new female lands in the vicinity. She may also land after a Pursuit Flight, often quite abruptly, near the male who usually threatens her. At this stage, the female, having already attempted many approaches, stays even though the male is threatening. Sometimes, the male stops threatening and the female is accepted, but often he attacks, pecking her with his bill. However, if she does not flee, he soon halts his attack. From that moment, the female is finally accepted and the pair is formed. Sometimes the female is attacked again later and must flee, but this is rare. The male, alone again, starts to display almost immediately, and the female has once more to resume the difficult process of approach.

Frequent Circle Flights and Pursuit Flights complicate greatly this generalized description of pair-formation. The male does not establish one single territory on which to display, as do many other heron species. The male Little Egret is on the move all the time and displays form various places in the heronry, establishing several display territories which he defends against intruders. Heronries with only a few Little Egrets are easier to study, since groups are formed by a male and only one or two females. In heronries where Little Egrets are numerous, 5–6 and even more females surround each male. In addition, the displaying males are more numerous. When one flies off, females follow singly, not all together. Some follow immediately, others after a while. Sometimes, a female Circle Flies or leaves to land at another location in the heronry. The male often follows after a short period of time, especially if he is alone. Females also fly off to join other males, calling and displaying. Little Egrets – individually or in groups – are thus constantly on the move during pair-formation.

When a male followed by 2–3 females lands in the branches in one of his territories, the females almost inevitably trespass on the borders of adjacent territories of other Little Egrets, Night Herons, Squacco Herons or Cattle

Egrets. The owner of the territory gives the Full Forward Display, harsh threat calls and sometimes even attacks. After much threatening, calling and at times fighting, the group of Little Egrets flies off and with luck lands in a less crowded area. During pair-formation, Little Egrets are particularly boisterous and noisy birds, and Night Herons who have established themselves first and who are now quietly incubating have a hard time with them.

When the pair is newly formed, there is not usually any copulation, though it can happen. The paired male gives no further Advertising Calls nor Stretch Displays and the birds settle down to get to know each other. They stand together, Bill-clappering for long periods. They also move about in the heronry looking for a suitable nest location. The nest is usually established in, or near to, one of the spots at which the male displayed. At this stage, when the following bird lands near its mate, it uses the Greeting Call (see Nest-building). It is at the end of this period, when the paired birds have been together for about 6–12 hours, that they usually copulate (Voisin 1976).

Copulation

Copulation occurs at the nest – or on a branch if the birds do not yet have a nest – and without any previous display. The female either stands, legs slightly bent, or crouches. The male stands on her, bending his legs until the two cloaca are in contact. To maintain his balance, the male unfolds his wings, the female often keeping her wings folded, though she may also unfold them. In this case, the male lightly touches the wings of the female with his own to keep better balance still. The male does not usually grasp the female's neck or neck feathers with his bill. During copulation, the feathers of both birds are slightly erected. A soft call is often heard, reminiscent of the soft "ko, ko, ko" of the male during a Stretch Display. Further study is needed to know if both birds call and if the calls are identical. Copulation is most frequent when the paired birds are seeking a suitable nest-site and during the beginning of the nest-building period. It continues but becomes rapidly less and less frequent towards the end of nest construction and the beginning of incubation.

Extramarital copulations are frequent among Little Egrets. During nest construction and incubation, males often leave their own nest and eggs and try to copulate with a female on a nearby nest. These copulations often succeed, as some females more or less cooperate. Others do not and rise from their nests, calling loudly. In my opinion, these copulations play an important role in suppressing the negative impact of sterile males (Voisin 1976).

Greeting Behaviour

When a Little Egret returns to the heronry, it lands in the branches at some distance from its mate and nest, uttering soft Greeting Calls: "kak, kak, kak". With stretched neck and continuous calling, the bird walks slowly through the branches towards the nest and its mate. When the two birds are newly paired, the incoming bird carries its crown and neck feathers very erect, but not to their maximum, as the long crest feathers do not usually fall forwards. The scapulars are slightly erected. Later in the season, when the members of the pair know each other well, the incoming bird erects its feathers only slightly.

When the bird at the nest hears the calls of the incoming bird, it immediately stretches its neck and listens closely for some seconds. Having recognized its mate, it answers with soft calls very like those of the incoming bird. Further studies are needed to know if the calls of both birds are identical. Early in the season, the bird at the nest rises if it is lying down, erects all its feathers, the crown feathers to a maximum, the long crown feathers falling forwards, and answers the incoming bird in this posture. Later in the season, the bird at the nest erects its feathers only slightly and may even remain lying in the nest, only stretching its neck to answer the incoming bird.

When both birds face each other, their crown and neck feathers fall slowly back. The scapulars, however, remain slightly erected for a long time. The two birds often Bill-clapper. The Greeting displays occur whenever the newly paired birds meet each other, even before nest construction and continues until the end of the guardian period.

The incoming bird's slow walk towards the nest and the vocal exchange, give the birds time to recognize each other and avoid the errors that would inevitably lead to fights if the bird landed directly at the nest. I once saw a Little Egret approach the wrong nest near its own newly built one. The bird at the nest answered the incoming bird's greeting calls with the Full Forward Display and harsh warning calls. The incoming Little Egret stopped, bewildered. It looked around and, understanding its error, and perhaps hearing its own mate calling, changed direction, walking towards its own nest and mate, calling softly again (Voisin 1976).

Nest-building

Only the males gather sticks, a conclusion based on observations of pairs where the male could be identified during copulation, and another where the male was ringed. The males collect only one stick at a time, which is given to the female after the Greeting displays. The female generally places the twig in the nest and is the one who does most building. However, if the female is not at the nest, the male places the stick himself. I have observed three behaviour patterns during nest-building. The most important is Tremble-shove (Lorenz 1955), in which the bird grasps a stick and pushes it slowly downwards while shaking its head with short lateral movements. Another movement is Push-pull (Blaker 1968) and is used to remove an unwanted twig. The bird grasps it in its bill and "violently jerks it back and forth". In the third movement, the bird changes its grasp on the twig, for example, to hold it more in the middle. The bird opens and shuts the bill with rapid movements of small amplitude letting the stick glide to one side or the other.

The birds often have great difficulty fixing the first twigs in the chosen tree fork and, at the beginning, the twigs usually fall to the ground. The male will not fly down to fetch them from under the tree, but flies off to gather new ones. Usually, after several failures, the pair – mostly by chance – succeeds in firmly fastening some twigs which have a size and shape that allows them to be stuck in the tree fork. The ability of the pair also seems to vary, older birds being more experienced than younger ones, especially first-year breeders. Once the first twigs are secured, nest-building continues at a more or less rapid pace, depending on how soon the female is going to lay her eggs. The fastest nest-building I have observed was by a pair whose male collected nine sticks in 21 minutes, all of which were placed in the nest by the female. When the birds build with such speed, they hardly perform any Greetings. A nest takes about 4–5 days to build. There are sometimes so few sticks in a nest, that when the first egg is laid it is possible to view it through the bottom of the nest, but nest-building activity continues during the whole incubation period, though with decreasing frequency.

The nest and territory are always guarded. The female remains at the nest when she is in the heronry and, when she is away hunting, the male is to be found either at the nest or nearby collecting sticks. Unguarded territories may be taken by another pair and unguarded nests are always plundered by other stick-gathering herons, as this is the easiest way to collect them. Abandoned nests disappear within a few hours. Little Egrets collect sticks mostly from the ground, and sometimes those floating on the water, in the vicinity of the heronry and beneath it. They prefer dry sticks, often from old nests which were blown down during the previous winter, but also sometimes try to pick growing twigs from branches. This is a difficult way to gather them, since the male has to pull very hard with all his weight, often giving up after a prolonged attempt. If he does succeed in picking the twig, he often falls backwards, but does not lose his grip on the branch, and with a few wing-beats comes up again. After some seconds' rest, he flies back to his nest with a stick bearing green leaves. Most stick-collecting activity takes place during the morning and afternoon change-over at the nest.

When there is little room left in the colony, the last pairs settle down near other nests. The first time a newcomer lands near an occupied nest, it is threatened and attacked, at which point it flees. If the intruder returns several times again shortly after, the nest owner may become too tired to chase it away. It may also perhaps get used to the newcomer's presence. The bird at the nest continues to threaten but no longer leaves its nest, and the newcomer and its mate begin building just out of reach of its bill. The newcomers, while building, occasionally mildly threaten the birds in the old nest, their crest and neck feathers raised. When the new nest is established, both pairs are equally at home in their own nests. When there is some movement in one nest, as for example a change of incubating bird, the Little Egret in the other nest becomes aggressive and threatens, and vice versa. The birds of each pair use the Stab-and-counter-stab to mark possession of their small territory, consisting of their own nest and half the space between the two nests, without a real fight or significant disturbance (Voisin 1976).

One nest measured by I. Sterbetz (1961) was a platform 30–35 cm in diameter and 10–15 cm high. The sticks that made up the nest were mostly 10–15 cm in length.

Egg-laying and clutch size

The eggs of the Little Egret are elongated ovals, matt green-blue in colour, often becoming discoloured with time. A sample of 200 eggs measured by Schönwetter (1967) gave the following measurements (mean and range): length 46 mm (42–54 mm), width 34 mm (31–38 mm).

According to Géroudet (1967), the weight of full eggs is 22–27 g. Bauer and Glutz (1966) found the mean weight of eggshell to be 1.90 g (range 1.44–2.36 g).

Little Egrets lay only one brood but, after early egg loss, replacement clutches are laid. The eggs are laid at 24-hour intervals, occasionally 48 hours, and incubation begins as soon as the first egg is laid. In temperate areas, egg-laying occurs in spring. In the tropics, it occurs at the end of the main rainy season. In the Camargue in France, the first eggs are laid at the end of the first week of April. Most are laid in April and May with egg-laying continuing with decreasing frequency until the end of June. Further east, Little Egrets begin to lay later in the spring (the middle of May in the Balkans). In Hungary, egg-laying continues until the end of July and in some years even until the beginning of August (Sterbetz 1961). In Italy, Fasola and Barbieri (1975) followed the development of eggs and young in six nests in 1973 and in four nests in 1974. Clutches of 3 eggs were found in two nests, 4 eggs in three nests, 5 eggs in two nests and 6 eggs in three nests. In the Camargue, the mean clutch size in 22 nests was 4.3 eggs in 1972. Three-egg clutches were found in 23% of the nests, 4-egg clutches in 36%, 5-egg clutches in 32% and 6- to 7-egg clutches in 9%.

Incubation and hatching

The incubation period ranges from 21 to 22 days, but may take up to 25 days. Both adults incubate. Change-over occurs mostly during the morning and late afternoon, and the eggs are never left unguarded. One of the two adults incubates at the nest while the other is away fishing. The birds need to eat well after pair-formation and nest-building, when hunting is somewhat neglected. The incubating Little Egret never leaves the nest for more than a few seconds, usually to threaten another heron, as egg thieves are numerous (other herons, Magpies and Carrion Crows). If great care is taken not to disturb the incubating birds, egg losses seem to be of little importance. In the Camargue, 91.6% of the eggs from 22 nests hatched with success, 6.3% did not hatch and 2.1% were lost (Voisin 1976).

DEVELOPMENT AND CARE OF THE YOUNG

The guardian period

During the oldest chick's first 10–14 days of life, one of the parents is at the nest all the time. For the first 4–5 days, the young are brooded constantly, later the parent on guard often stands on the nest rim or even on a nearby.

branch. The chicks grow very rapidly, and within a few hours after hatching, they can just lift their heads a little, giving some low peeping cries. After a few days, they sit on their tarsi and, when, about 1 week old, they stand in the nest. At this stage, they are not able to flee, and instead turn to face intruders, trying to defend themselves. At this time, they are easy to catch for ringing and other studies. Side-by-side in the nest, they sleep for long periods. When they are hungry they beg and quarrel. They also preen, peck at the nest bottom and try to catch insects, mostly flies (Voisin 1976).

The post-guardian period

The young are alone at the nest during the day. Both parents go to fish and return to the nest only to feed the chicks. At this age, the young are very active. They leave the nest and begin to climb in the branches, at first venturing only onto those that support the nest. Their agility increases rapidly and soon they wander several metres away, getting to know the surrounding area. When danger threatens the nest, they flee rapidly by running along the branches, and become more and more difficult to catch each day. They wing-beat for long periods. By the end of the post-guardian period, they are not often to be found in the nest but walk, sleep and rest on the surrounding branches, coming back to the nest only to be fed, to keep warm during cold weather and to sleep by night. During the night, one of the parents always sleeps at the nest or on a nearby branch. Those adults that are not on guard at their nests, always seem to roost together on the same branches in the heronry. Once in the Camargue, at the end of this period, when most of the young are 18–25 days old, I counted 35 young from 13 nests, or a mean number of 2.7 young per nest (Voisin 1976). In Italy, Fasola and Barbieri (1975) counted 23 young from 10 nests.

The fledgling stage

When the young are 4 weeks old, they begin to fly from branch to branch and, about 1 week later, start to land on the ground or in shallow water at the foot of the heronry. They spend about 1 month improving their flying skills and learning to hunt for themselves, while still being fed by their parents. In the Camargue, the first young are seeen on the foraging grounds away from the heronries in early July, and are thus independent at about 2 months of age (Voisin 1976).

Feeding the young

Both parents feed the young. During the first days, the chicks just touch the bill of the adult when begging for food. The adult can feed them several times without having to forage after each feeding. The food has time to become well digested before being fed directly into the open bills of the chicks. After the brooding period, the incoming adult feeds the chicks all the food it has immediately upon arrival at the nest. The feeding adult often holds the feathers of its head and neck erect and even the scapulars are more or less erected. When not actually regurgitating, the neck is held in a threatening "S" shape, since the growing young become very aggressive in their eagerness to be fed. Just before regurgitation, the adult retracts its neck several times in order to throw up the food. Once it succeeds, the young are fed rapidly. Only a few seconds are needed to feed each chick. Night Herons take longer but Little Egrets probably regurgitate more easily as they usually catch smaller prey. The Little Egret usually brings food for two, sometimes three chicks. Struggling, the chicks try to grasp the adult's bill, and beg by flapping their wings alternately. Curiously, this is not a flying movement but recalls walking or running. The oldest chick usually succeeds first and the food regurgitated by the adult falls directly into its open bill. A second chick is usually fed soon afterwards and sometimes also a third. When the chicks are of almost equal size, the fourth one may be fed, and one of the older chicks receiving nothing. Usually, the smallest chick gets very little food, especially if it was hatched several days after the oldest. It rapidly disppears from the nest, having been eaten by one of its older, larger siblings. The larger chicks that die do not disappear immediately, but their remains stay in the nest until completely dried up.

During the post-guardian period, the chicks run along the branches towards the incoming adult, who lands some distance from the nest. The first chick to meet the adult graps its bill and is fed where it stands. Sometimes, the second chicks is also fed. Usually, the adult leaves the young in the branches after having fed one or two of them and flies to the nest to feed any less well-grown chicks remaining there. Sometimes, the adult lands very close to the nest and feeds the small chicks first. Seeing this, the larger ones run back to the nest from their perches in the branches. Young Little Egrets do not quarrel as violently as Night Herons. Nevertheless, when the young grow older, the incoming adult is often met with such violence that it flies off and lands some distance away in the branches. The young that are beginning to fly immediately follow it and land abruptly nearby. One or two get fed, while the presence of the group arouses wild protestations from surrounding nest-owners, both adults and large young giving the Forward Display and harsh calls. They soon calm down as the group leaves after 1–2 minutes. The adult usually flies back to feed one or two of the younger chicks who are not yet able to fly. Later, during the fledgling period, young birds even follow the adult as it leaves the heronry and land beside it on the foraging grounds, for example in a lagoon near the heronry. There the adult often begins to run away from the young, but usually stops after a short pursuit to feed one, two or three fledglings who come running through the water after it. If it has nothing more to give, it flies away again, heading for more distant foraging grounds. The young birds, running, raising their legs high above the water, jumping and even flapping their wings in their eagerness to be fed, quieten down as soon as the adult leaves. Walking slowly, they now peer into the water and begin to fish, at first with no success. After a short period of time, they fly back to the heronry and their nest territory. In time, they stay for longer periods at the lagoon, finally returning to their territory and nest only to be fed and to sleep during the night. At this stage, the young may not be at the nest when the adult returns to feed them. Perching in the vicinity of the nest, the adult starts calling several times, very loudly. Hearing this, the young fly back as fast as possible, clearly able to recognize their own parents' voices.

As they grow older, the chicks follow the adult over greater distances. I saw one adult followed by two young cross a 3500-m wide lagoon before the adult landed and rapidly fed the chicks. After a while, it flew away and was no longer pursued by its young. Later, they probably follow the adult further away from the heronry to better fishing grounds and remain there until the time for migration. The young are no longer fed by the adults once they have definitively left the heronry.

In early July 1973, I counted the number of young in several clutches in which all the young flew well and followed an adult in order to be fed. A total of 69 such clutches were observed and the mean number of young per clutch was 2.4. There was one young in 8.7% of the clutches, two in 49.3%, three in 34.8% and four in 7.2%.

Little Egrets feed their young from dawn until dusk. I have observed numerous Little Egret nests with young during moonlit nights (using special field glasses), and have never seen nor heard a single adult feeding them. Once certain that the young were not fed by night, I was able to estimate the feeding frequency of chicks at three stages of development.

Three nests were continuously observed from 03.40 h to 20.45 h on 21 June and 02.40 h to 4.30 h on 22 June 1973. The nests were chosen so as to sample young of different ages. The 4- to 5-day-old chicks in the first nest were still being brooded. The second nest held four young of about 10 days of age (guardian stage), all of which looked in good health. The third nest held five young about 3 weeks old (post-guardian stage): two large, one medium-sized and two smaller chicks, all in good health. In the first nest, the brooded young were fed six times in 15 hours. The shortest interval between two successive feeds was 1 hour 56 minutes; the longest interval during the middle of the day, 6 hours 40 minutes. The four young in the second nest were fed eight times. Here, the shortest interval between two successive feeds was 1 hour 36 minutes, the longest 2 hours 57 minutes. In these two nests, one of the adults stayed on guard at the nest while the other was fishing.

The five young in the third nest were fed 15 times. Here, the shortest interval between two successive feeds was only 2 minutes, when both adults were feeding the young successively. The longest interval was 2 hours 42 minutes in the early afternoon. Neither parent stood guard at this nest, both of whom were busy foraging throughout the day, with the result that the large young were nourished nearly twice as often as those in the two first nests. The young were not fed during the night, from a little past 20.00 h until 04.00–05.00 h in the morning. They therefore fast 8–9 hours in every 24 hours (Voisin 1976).

Growth of the young

The young were captured, marked and weighed (Voisin 1976). The best way to mark young chicks is to paint their bare tibia with nail varnish of various colours, renewing the marks each time the chicks are weighed until they are large enough to be ringed. The fact that the young are able to run on the branches from an early age, thus becoming impossible to catch, limits the duration of growth studies in the wild. Little Egrets can be caught up to about 12 days of age. Their weight is equivalent to their development and is a better indicator of growth than age. It is almost impossible to catch Little Egrets weighing more than 270 g. Blaker (1967) encountered the same difficulty with Cattle Egrets, which were impossible to catch when older than 11–13 days of age. As the larger species of herons do not develop as quickly as the smaller ones, Owen (1955) and Tomlinson (1975) were able to catch, respectively, Grey Herons and Purple Herons up to about 3 weeks of age. I noticed that among 10 Little Egrets whose mean growth during the first 11 days of life was more than 14 g per day, all of the young survived. Among five young whose mean growth was less than 14 g per day, two died.

This growth study (see Fig. 26) also shows the existence of a crisis at the end of the guardian period. When comparing the increase in weight per day of small, young chicks and of larger ones, it is obvious that the demand for food increases greatly as the chicks age. By the end of the first week, some pairs are already unable to gather enough food for their offspring. It was, for example, the case in clutch no. 2, where the smallest chick did not receive enough food after the fifth day, thus allowing the second chick's weight to catch that of the first chick. Usually, the adults are able to gather enough food for the brood until the oldest chick is 10–15 days old. After this time, the brood always faces a period of starvation. This situation seems to bring about the end of the guardian period, since both parents are forced to forage throughout the day to catch enough food to keep the young from starving. The increasing growth of the chicks after the guardian period can clearly be seen on the growth curves in Fig. 26 (Voisin 1976).

Interactions between adults and young

During my observations on Little Egret, chicks alone at the nest during the post-guardian period were never seriously threatened by other herons. At this stage, they are too large to be considered as prey by other herons, which take no interest in them. The greatest danger for these young is to trespass within the territorial limits of other herons, whether Little Egrets or other species, because the owner of the territory will immediately attack the trespassing young who must flee or risk being wounded. If the young happen to venture onto several territories, either because their owners are temporarily absent or because they have fallen from above, they face the danger of never being able to climb back to their nest because of the hostile behaviour of other territory owners. When the young are alone in their territory during the post-guardian period, they do not defend it against other herons who steal sticks from the nest or settle down to preen. The adult, coming back to feed the young, chases away these intruders after feeding; the young remain unconcerned (Voisin 1976).

Effects of weather

During the guardian stage, the adult at the nest protects the young against the sun by standing over them and shading them, and from rain and wind by lying

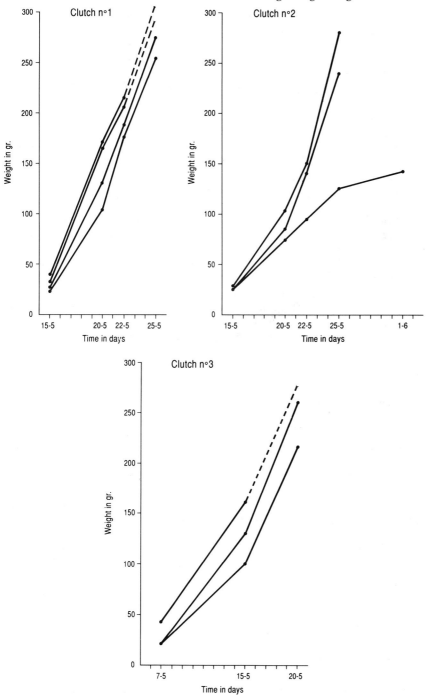

Figure 26   Growth curves of young Little Egrets (Voisin 1976).

on them in the nest. After the guardian period, the young are able to hold onto the branches firmly enough to withstand strong winds. However, during severe storms, some young are always unlucky enough to fall. After the storm, they may be found dead on the ground or strangled in a tree fork. Little Egrets fear the rain and when old enough to be left alone, always return to the nest when it starts raining. They stand close together, their backs turned outwards, waiting for the rain to stop. With their white colouring and small eyes, older chicks are able to endure with ease any sunshine which may occur in Europe. I have never seen them gular-flutter in the Camargue, not even those which nested at the heronry in the lagoons (Voisin 1976).

FEEDING BEHAVIOUR AND FOOD

Little Egrets usually fish by wading up to their tibias, and sometimes even to their bellies in shallow water. They may, on rare occasions, fish in deep water, or from dry land. They forage during the day, especially in the morning and evening.

Usual methods of foraging

Little Egrets commonly use two methods of fishing: the Wade-or-walk-slowly and Open-wing methods (Meyerriecks 1960), the former being by far

Little Egrets Foot-stirring.

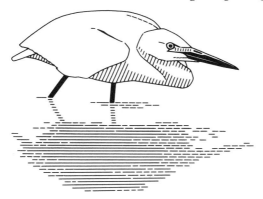

A Little Egret foraging for swift prey, body held very close to the water and neck very bent. The bird Walks Slowly while Head-tilting (after a photograph by D. Robert).

the most common. When wading-or-walking slowly, the body and neck may be held in various positions from the horizontal to nearly vertical. The neck is more or less stretched. The legs are moved slowly with frequent stops, the feet raised high. Now and then, in order to see into the water better, the bird Head-tilts (Meyerriecks 1960), its head and neck strongly inclined to one side as it peers into the water. If the bottom is muddy or sandy, and especially if there is some aquatic vegetation, the bird stops now and then, extends one leg forwards and rapidly vibrates it. This stirring motion of the foot, which rakes the bottom, moves sand, mud and aquatic vegetation around, disturbing the small animals which hide there. After having Foot-stirred (Meyerriecks 1960) for a moment, the Little Egret looks down into the water. If no prey is seen, the bird sometimes tries again with the same foot or with the other one, but usually resumes the Wade-and-walk-slowly tactic. If the disturbed prey is a slow-moving one, the Little Egret catches it immediately. If it is fast-moving, such as a fish, the bird – with head, neck and body held horizontal – aims carefully before catching its prey. Small prey are swallowed as soon as they are caught. To swallow a somewhat larger prey, the Little Egret must lift its head a little and stretch the distal part of its neck. If the prey is more than about 3 cm long (or if it has particularly long legs), the Little Egret stands up and swallows it with a stretched neck. In this case, fish and frogs are turned in the bill so as to be swallowed head-first.

Foot-stirring is not used when Little Egrets are hunting abundant prey which swarm in the water such as, for example, *Triops*. In this case, the birds merely pick them up as rapidly as possible.

Little Egrets use the Open-wing Feeding technique when hunting swift prey such as fish. They move rapidly, generally running in a zig-zag manner, raising their legs very high to enable more rapid running. After a while, they begin to wing-beat, still running so as to move faster. Eventually, some birds even jump, giving some wing-beats while in the air. Having landed again, they

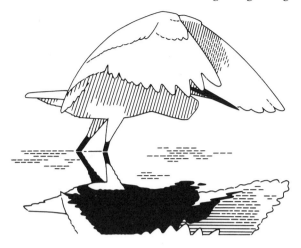

A Little Egret Double-wing Feeding (after Robert and Voisin, 1991).

resume their zig-zag running, while still wing-beating. While dashing about in this way, they now and then catch a prey. Most of the time, however, they stop as soon as a prey is seen, body and neck held horizontally above the water, aiming carefully to catch it. This running frightens the fish, which flee and are more easily seen and caught by a nearby Egret. Little Egrets do not use their wings to frighten fish by casting a sudden shadow as has been described in North American Egrets by Meyerriecks (1960). In Little Egrets, the wing-beats observed are those necessary to balance and speed the bird, even if they do also frighten the fish. Thus Little Egrets can be said to perform a primitive Open-wing Feeding technique (Voisin 1978).

Unusual methods of foraging

In August 1988, D. Robert (pers. comm.) observed several Little Egrets in the Kopacki Rit Reserve in Yugoslavia actively catching fish swept along by the current of a small stream. One of the Egrets, facing the sun, suddenly unfolded both wings and brought them over its head, efficiently sheltering its eyes from the dazzling light, in the same way that a person might place his or her hands over the eyes. This behaviour probably allows a better view of the prey in the water, rather than attracting the prey into the very restricted shadow of the bird. This foraging behaviour, called Double-wing Feeding (Kushlan 1978), is seldom observed, and has not until now been described for the Little Egret.

I once observed a Little Egret who stood near a shallow steam and picked up *Gammarus* sp. Although it was standing still, it was certainly extremely busy picking up the food items. This is the closest to a Little Egret using the

Little Egrets foraging, A, B and C, Walking Slowly; D, Open-wing Feeding; E, Walking Slowly while Head-tilting.

Stand-and-wait technique that I have seen. Little Egrets seem to be too active in their fishing behaviour to use it generally. Fishing mostly for small prey, they need to catch them in great numbers, which the slow Stand-and-wait technique cannot provide. Spitzer (1967) describes a Little Egret Jumping-Upwards, helping itself with one wing-beat to get higher in order to catch dragonflies. Walter (1967) describes a Little Egret flying over the water among Herring Gulls, snatching fish scraps floating near a fish factory. Little Egrets nesting near Luanda in Angola were commonly seen around fishing boats at sea (up to 1 mile offshore) snatching fish offal while flying low over the water (Sinclair 1974). Brooke (1971) has described how Little Egrets took fish scraps in Luanda harbour:

> Their technique was to fly slowly at about 10 m above the water and when they saw a manageable item to hover with dangling legs, arched neck and bill pointing straight down. They would slowly lose height until they were able to pick up the item when they would rise clumsily and swallow it.

Abduladi (1967) describes the same method used by a Little Egret to catch live fish in a lake near Bombay where the water level had fallen to a very low level.

Association between Little Egrets and other foraging birds

There are some very interesting observations of Little Egrets associating with other foraging waterbirds to take advantage of the other birds' activity to increase their own foraging success. J. Reynolds (1965) noted:

> A Little Egret *Egretta garzetta* was deliberately feeding in close proximity to an African Spoonbill *Platalea alba*. This species has very similar habits to the Eurasian Spoonbill *P. leucorodia*, striding vigorously through the water while sweeping its bill from side to side. The egret kept close to, and a little behind, the spoonbill, catching prey disturbed by the latter's movements. Eventually the spoonbill stopped feeding and went to sleep. While it was asleep the egret moved some distance away, but when the spoonbill started feeding again the egret at once flew back to resume the association.

F. T. Morris (1978) wrote:

> As the Ibises fed on the mud and among the draining channels, an Egret selected an Ibis and began to follow it, staying one or two metres behind it. When the Ibis began to probe the mud, the Egret moved closer, until alongside the larger bird. As the Ibis forced its bill deeply into the ooze, the Egret hurriedly fed in shallow water and surface mud surrounding the probed area.

F. Fraser (1974) recorded

> a feeding association between Little Egrets *Egretta garzetta* and Reed Cormorants *Phalacrocorax africanus*. The fish kept mainly to the deeper water of the river where they were inaccessible to the egrets. However, the cormorants frequently drove shoals to the banks where in the shallow water the fish were in

reach of the egrets. To exploit this food-source the egrets had to be at, or close to, the spot where a shoal was briefly forced against the bank. Each egret watched a fishing cormorant, following its progress and keeping abreast of it on the bank. Often a diving cormorant was lost to sight in the murky water but immediately it surfaced the egret ran or flew to the spot on the bank closest to it. Usually the egret was present when a shoal was driven into the shallow water and was able to catch a fish before they darted back into the deeper water. The cormorant usually caught one or two of the fish while in the shallows but the egret made no attempt to rob it.

When the cormorants left the water the egrets stopped patrolling the bank and stood and preened close to them. Immediately the cormorants took to the water again, the egrets resumed their activities.

Fishing rates

I have recorded the number of prey captured by Little Egrets actively fishing in various habitats in the Camargue. In marshes, the mean number of prey caught per minute was 3.8, in lagoons 2.9 and in rice-fields 3.6 (not counting Little Egrets capturing swarms of the crustacean *Triops*). The mean number of *Triops* taken per minute was 22.9. Even in marshes, Little Egrets sometimes caught swarming small prey, catching up to 23 per minute. The mean number of prey taken per minute in all habitats was 7.2 including the capture of swarming *Triops*, and 3.43 otherwise. With 3.43 prey taken per minute, the Little Egret takes more prey per minute than any other European heron, rates varying from 0.5 per minute for the Purple Heron to 1.48 per minute for the Cattle Egret. The Little Egret is the only European heron which specializes in very small prey, often swift ones such as small fish, but also small swarming ones such as *Triops* and *Gammarus*. Their great agility and active hunting techniques have allowed this species to occupy a very specialized ecological niche (Voisin 1978).

Food

Little Egrets usually take small prey 2–6 cm in length, the majority of which are fish, but also amphibians, crustaceans, insects (both terrestrial and aquatic) and worms. They have also been reported taking lizards, snakes, small mammals and snails.

Studies of their diet are numerous. Since this species is commonly protected nowadays, the most usual study technique is to examine food regurgitated by chicks at the nest. However, some studies of stomach contents have also been undertaken. The first study was published by Moltoni (1936), which was followed by those of Vasvàri (1948–1951), Valverde (1956), Skokova (1960), Kosugi (1960), Sterbetz (1961), Mukherjee (1971), Hafner (1977) and Voisin (1978).

Their prey in Europe are generally the same over their whole range, the most commonly taken items being: crustaceans (*Triops cancriformis, Gammarus* sp.), spiders (*Agyroneta* sp.), insects (Dytiscids, Tipulids, Syrphids,

Notonectids and Naucorids), fish (carp *Cyprinus carpio*, rudd *Scardinius erythrophtalmus*, eel *Anguilla anguilla*, stickleback *Gasterosteus aculeatus*, gambusia *Gambusia affinis*, atherine *Atherina boyeri*, sunfish *Lepomis gibbosus*, mullet *Liza* sp., syngnatiidae *Syngnatus abaster*) and amphibians (tadpoles of *Pelobates cultripes*, tadpoles and adults of *Rana esculenta*, adults of *Hyla arborea*).

Fish is the most important source of food for Little Egrets. Figure 27 shows the relative importance by weight of various prey taken in the spring and early summer in the Camargue. In winter, when there are no amphibians and no insects, the importance of fish in the diet is increased. Five of the nine species of fish commonly taken by them have no commercial value (rudd, stickleback, gambusia, sunfish and syngnathid).

The prey taken by Little Egrets varies from heronry to heronry in the same

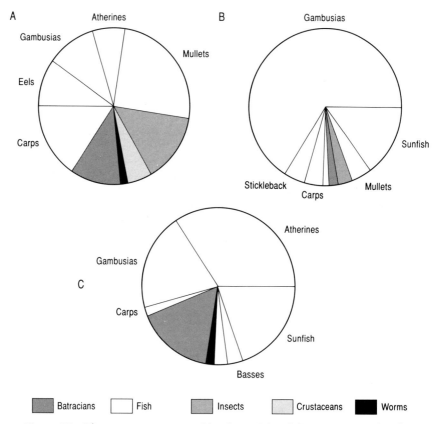

Figure 27   The percentage composition by weight of the prey items taken by Little Egrets in three different heronries in the Camargue. The complete circle represents 100%. A, A heronry established along the River Rhône with nearby rice-fields; B, a heronry in the centre of the Camargue; C, a heronry in the western Camargue established in lagoons.

area depending on the nature of the surrounding foraging grounds. I have studied regurgitated food samples in three heronries in the Camargue. In one, surrounded by large rice-fields, a large number of insects was taken. However, the presence of mullet and atherines (which can tolerate salinities of 50 g per litre) shows that the birds flew 11–17 km to forage in the nearest lagoons. This was probably necessary, since insects and small *Triops* must be captured at a very high rate to provide sufficient food.

Marshes of brackish-water covered huge areas near the second heronry. Fish which can tolerate modest concentrations of salt were taken in numbers. Gambusias, the most commonly taken fish, were introduced from America to the Camargue in 1927, to eat mosquito larvae (which they do). These are very small fish: the male, which is smaller than the female, weighs only about 0.18 g. They are not numerous in winter but become very abundant from May to October, though with marked variations from year to year. The third heronry was surrounded by lagoons and saltpans where Little Egrets fished and took atherines and bass coming in from the sea. The Little Egrets in this heronry also flew to brackish- and fresh-water areas 5–12 km distant to take other fish species and frogs.

In west Bengal in India, Mukherjee (1971) studied the food taken on estuarine tidal mudflats and rice-field areas. In both cases, they ate mostly fish but the proportion of insects captured was important in the rice-field areas. Kosugi (1960), who studied the diet of Little Egrets foraging in rice-fields in Japan, also found that fish was the main food (mostly *Misgurus anguillicaudatus*) but numerous amphibians were also taken (*Rana nigromaculata*). Little Egrets also commonly captured crayfish (*Procambarus clarki*, a species recently introduced to Japan from America), which they swallowed whole, tail first. A study from the Natal in South Africa (Whitfield and Blater 1979) also showed that Little Egrets take mostly small prey. The fish eaten (mostly *Glossogobius giuris* and *Sarotherodon mossambicus*) ranged in weight from less than 1 g to almost 14 g, but the great majority weighed less than 1 g. Aquatic invertebrates were caught in numbers. Other common prey of Little Egrets were the crown crab *Hymenosoma orbiculare*, the gasteropod *Assiminea bifasciata* and the bivalve *Musculus virgiliae*.

Predation

Little Egrets are easy prey for the Eagle Owl and their remains were found in pellets regurgitated in the south of France (Hérault). In 1972, I once observed a Long-eared Owl which was sleeping on a branch in one of the trees of the heronry. It probably could have captured young which had accidentally strayed from the nest, but not adult Little Egrets on guard at the nest or sleeping in the common roost.

In one heronry in the Camargue in 1975, I saw a Marsh Harrier capture a 4- to 5-week-old Little Egret. During the short struggle, which I could not actually see from my hide, I could hear the harsh alarm calls of all the Little Egrets in the tree. Many Jackdaws which happened to be in the vicinity were also calling fiercely. Since the Little Egret that was captured was heavy, the

Marsh Harrier could not fly away with it, but had to fly down to the ground and landed quite near my hide. As soon as the Marsh Harrier was out of sight of the Little Egrets in the tree, they ceased their alarm calls and rapidly settled down, totally unconcerned by what was happening on the ground where the Marsh Harrier began to tear bits off the dead bird. The Jackdaws, on the contrary, followed the bird of prey to the ground and landed around it, both on the ground and in the low branches, continuously giving high-pitched alarm calls. After a while, a party of about 10 Jackdaws tried to attack the harrier. They ran towards it trying to peck it, retreating rapidly after each peck to avoid the harrier's sharp bill. The Marsh Harrier stood above its prey in the threatening posture typical of raptors, wings unfolded and bill open, turning slowly to face the Jackdaws which soon stopped their attacks and even their alarm calls, perhaps because the dead prey neither moved nor shrieked any longer. Only two Magpies stayed as they tried to steal bits of the prey from the raptor.

Table 31.   *The number of breeding pairs of Little Egrets in the Camargue, 1968–1985* [a]

Year	No. of pairs	Year	No. of pairs
1968	1340	1977	1227
1969	1126	1978	1498
1970	1234	1979	1335
1971	1370	1980	1224
1972	2280	1981	1441
1973	1640	1982	2251
1974	1619	1983	2456
1975	1760	1984	1931
1976	1249	1985	1016

[a] After Voisin (1975, 1979) and Hafner (1987).

Table 32.   *The number of Little Egrets wintering in the Camargue* [a]

Winter	December	January	February
1973–74	162	201	375
1974–75	860	750	773
1975–76	856	572	599
1976–77	308	187	–
1977–78	325	291	110
1978–79	454	125	298
1979–80	839	497	851
1980–81	771	355	726
1981–82	755	535	801
1982–83	935	1159	966
1983–84	1064	1205	1220
1984–85	1037	10	0

[a] After Hafner (1987).

Table 33.   *National censuses of Little Egrets breeding in France in 1974 and 1981*[a]

Location	1974	1981
Camargue	1650	1441
Other Mediterranean areas	0	147
Atlantic coastal areas	65	570
Inland areas	160	95
Total	1875	2253

[a] After Brosselin (1974) and Duhautois and Marion (1981).

Table 34.   *The number of breeding pairs of Little Egrets at Donaña*[a]

Year	No. of pairs
1952	600–750
1953	2060
1954	1500
1955	3000
1956	3000
1963	1400
1964	1500

[a] After Fernandez-Cruz (1975).

CHAPTER 18

The Great White Egret *Egretta alba*

GENERAL APPEARANCE AND FIELD CHARACTERS

The Great White Egret is 85–102 cm high with a wing-span of 140–170 cm. Four subspecies are recognized: *Egretta alba alba* (Linnaeus), *E. a. egretta* (Gmelin), *E. a. melanorhynchos* (Wragler) and *E. a. modesta* (Gray), which differ from each other slightly in size (see Measurements) and coloration of the bare parts, principally during the breeding season (see Bare parts).

Plumage. The sexes are alike, both males and females at all ages having a wholly white plumage.

Adult: in the breeding season, the feathers of the crown, nape and chest are only slightly elongated, loose and soft, but not lanceolated. In contrast, the scapulars are particularly conspicuous, being by far the longest aigrettes known (30–50 cm in length) and reaching *c.* 10 cm beyond the tip of the tail feathers. These special plumes have the same anatomical particularities as those of the Little Egret, but they are stronger due to their much thicker shafts.

Juveniles and immatures: these resemble non-breeding adults. They have a wholly white plumage and no elongated feathers.

Downy young: these are also entirely white, slightly tinged with grey, at least in the subspecies *melanorhynchos*. The longer down on the crown forms a kind of crest.

Bare parts

Adult: non-breeding adults have yellow bills (often tipped black in the American subspecies), yellow irises and dull yellow to pale green lores. The legs and feet of the subspecies *egretta* and *melanorhynchos* are black. Those of the subspecies *alba* are dark grey-green, except the tibias which are yellow – in some individuals, the soles are also often yellow. The legs and feet of the subspecies *modesta* are brown, with the tarsus and feet dark brown and the tibias light brown. When breeding, these subspecies differ more from each other than when not breeding, and may be identified in the field by the colour of their legs and feet.

In the subspecies *egretta*, the "bill changes from dull streaked yellow to bright orange. The legs and feet remain black, the irises acquire an outer ring of red surrounding the yellow and the yellow-green lores brighten" (Mock 1978). However, according to Mock, numerous displaying Great White Egrets had lores which remained yellow. As these birds also had shorter aigrette plumes and as only a few of them eventually bred successfully, Mock suspects them to be first-year birds. In the subspecies *melanorhynchos*, the bill becomes wholly black. When the bird is displaying, the irises are red and the lores bright green-blue. As soon as the bird is paired, the irises revert to yellow once more and the lores turn first pale-green and then yellow. The colour of the bill changes more slowly, becoming yellow from its proximal part. I have observed an adult which had a half yellow and half black bill when its young hatched. However, usually only the tip of the bill remains black at that stage. The legs and feet remain black (Voisin 1983).

In the subspecies *alba*, the bill becomes black with a variable amount of yellow at the base. According to Hancock (1984), the bill may even become red with black streaks during courtship displays. As the black bare parts never redden, these birds probably keep a variable amount of yellow, which is able to redden even on the distal part of the bill. The tibias are pinkish, this colour often extending in narrow strips down the side of the tarsus which are black, as are the feet (the soles are sometimes pinkish). The lores are bright green (Hancock 1984).

In the subspecies *modesta*, as in the subspecies *melanorhynchos*, the bill becomes black turning yellow from the base after pair-formation. The lores become bright green, the legs pink to purple-red and the feet black (sometimes briefly red) (Hancock 1984).

Juvenile: the bare parts of juveniles are the same colour as those of non-breeding adults. However, juveniles often have a blackish bill tip, which adults do not have except in the subspecies *egretta*.

Nestlings: those of the subspecies *alba* and *modesta* have not been described. In the subspecies *egretta*, the iris is off-white. The upper mandible is grey with a black culmen and tip, and the lower mandible is yellow-grey, the whole mandible becoming yellow later. The orbital skin is at first pale blue-grey, also becoming yellow later. The skin is dark blue-grey dorsally and lighter ventrally. The throat is pink in colour. The legs are pale pink-flesh with a blue tinge, becoming grey-green later (McVaugh 1972). In the subspecies *melanorhynchos*, the skin of nestlings is green as are their legs and feet. At hatching, the bill is horn-coloured with a green tinge. During the following days, it becomes progressively yellow. The iris is green. When the chick is 15–20 days old, feathers cover its entire body. The bill is yellow with a black tip, the irises and lores are yellow and the legs and feet are black (Voisin 1983). Thus the young have the same colour pattern as adult birds at a very early stage.

Field characters. In the field, the Great White Egret is a conspicuous bird when it forages in shallow water among scattered aquatic vegetation. Like the Little Egret, this entirely white bird is more difficult to detect in flight, when it offers little contrast against the pale colour of the sky. It is a large heron with a particularly long, thin and sharply kinked neck, long legs and a proportionally short body (mean body length 40–45 cm). It is easy to distinguish from the Little Egret, since it has black feet and, when not breeding, a yellow bill. In western Europe, the Great White Egret is a rare vagrant. It is difficult to distinguish it from other rare, vagrant white herons except at close range, when the extension of the black line of the gape to about 1 cm behind the eye differentiates it from the Intermediate, Little and Snowy Egrets and from the white morphs of the Reef Heron (Hancock and Elliot 1978).

Measurements. The measurements (mm) of European Great White Egrets, *Egretta alba alba*, by Witherby (1943) are as follows:

wing	12 ♂♂ 410–465	12 ♀♀ 400–450
bill	12 ♂♂ 110–135	12 ♀♀ 110–132
tail	12 ♂♂ 140–185	

Vaurie (1965) gives the following measurements (range and mean) for males of the same subspecies:

wing	10 ♂♂ 410–485 (437.5)
bill	10 ♂♂ 117–130 (123.3)
tarsus	10 ♂♂ 170–215 (190.0)

Vaurie (1965) also gives the following measurements (range and mean) for males of the subspecies *modesta* from China:

wing	10 ♂♂ 340–380 (366.4)
bill	10 ♂♂ 98–125 (112.0)
tarsus	10 ♂♂ 135–167 (153.8)

A few measurements of the subspecies *melanorhynchos* (both males and females) in South Africa (Roberts 1942) show that the African subspecies is also probably smaller than the nominate subspecies *alba*:

wing   ♂♀ 345–395
tail   ♂♀ 133–163
tarsus   ♂♀ 130–170
bill   ♂♀ 104–115

The weight of three European birds, as measured by Bauer and Glutz (1966), was as follows: one juvenile 1680 g, and two lean winter birds, 1 ♂ and 1 ♀, 1030 and 960 g respectively.

According to Blake (1948), the average wing-beat rate of the Great White Egret is 2.3 ± 0.1 wing-beats per second.

DISTRIBUTION, MOVEMENTS AND HABITAT

BREEDING AND WINTERING AREAS

Despite the worldwide range of the Great White Egret, which spans all five continents, this bird is far from common. At the end of the nineteenth and beginning of the twentieth centuries, they were killed in great numbers during the breeding season for their beautiful nuptial plumes, which were used to adorn ladies' hats. This trade nearly caused the extinction of the species, and its recovery since then has been painfully slow. Thus the present distribution of Great White Egrets within their immense breeding range is in fact very patchy, the known breeding sites remaining separated by huge areas where none now occur.

The subspecies *E. a. alba* breeds in Europe from southern Czechoslovakia and eastern Austria south to Albania, southern Yugoslavia, Bulgaria and Romania, eastwards to the Ukraine (north to about 48°30′N) and the plains around the lower Volga and lower Ural rivers (north to about 50°N). In Asia this nominate subspecies breeds from Turkey (south to 37°50′N), Iran and the Russian Turkestan eastwards to Mongolia, northern Manchuria and Ussuriland (Vaurie 1965).

E. a. modesta breeds in Pakistan, India and Ceylon eastwards to Indochina, the Sunda Archipelago, the Philippines, New Guinea, Australia and New Zealand, and northwards through eastern China to southern Japan, Korea and southern Ussuriland.

E. a. melanorhynchos breeds from Senegal, Sudan and Ethiopia to the Cape Province in South Africa, Madagascar and the Comores.

E. a. egretta breeds in North America along the eastern seaboard as far north as Massachussetts and along the western seaboard as far north as Oregon. This subspecies also breeds in Central America, in the Caribbean and in South America as far south as the Strait of Magellan (Hancock and Elliot 1978).

The western population of the nominate *E. a. alba* winters mostly in the eastern part of the Mediterranean basin. More eastern populations winter in Turkey, Iraq and Iran, some reaching Pakistan and India as rare stragglers. The far eastern populations winter in Japan, Korea, Ussuriland and China where they encounter the subspecies *E. a. modesta*.

In North America, about 40% of the birds winter in Florida, around the Gulf of Mexico and in California, but others move farther south to Central and South America. A northward post-breeding migration in the southern parts of South America, where the Great White Egret breeds, is still unproven but very likely. *E. a. modesta* migrates only in its northeastern range when it becomes too cold in the winter.

MOVEMENTS OF THE WESTERN POPULATION OF THE NOMINATE SUBSPECIES

When leaving the heronry, the young disperse in all directions. This post-fledging dispersal begins in July and continues into August and September, during which time juveniles may be recovered up to 400 km from their natal heronry. The autumn migration, in eastern Europe and the USSR west of the Ural River, begins in late September and continues into early November, though during mild winters a few birds remain in the breeding area or nearby. Thus Great White Egrets are only absent from Lake Kisbalaton in Hungary when it is frozen over. Austrian Great White Egrets (at Neusied-lersee) and Hungarian birds winter mainly along the northeastern coast of Italy, in Yugoslavia, Albania and Greece (Kuhk 1955). However, a part of this population migrates farther south and is found in small numbers in Turkey, Israel, Egypt and Tunisia. The trans-Saharan migration route may even be used, at least by a few individuals, and one Great White Egret ringed in western Russia was recovered in the Central African Republic (Hancock and Elliott 1978). The birds return to the heronries from late February to early April, but mostly during March (Bauer and Glutz 1966). Immatures rarely seem to return to the colonies and may account for the late spring passage and early summer vagrant records (Cramp and Simmons 1977).

The Great White Egret has been found as an accidental in Britain, Belgium, the Netherlands, Norway, Denmark, Sweden, Finland, West Germany, Poland, Czechoslovakia, Switzerland, France, Spain, Malta, Algeria, Morocco, Libya, Mauritania and the Canary Islands (Cramp and Simmons 1977).

HABITAT

Great White Egrets occur in temperate and tropical lowland areas where extensive wetlands still exist. However, in Asia, they have on rare occasions been found nesting up to 1800 m (Dementiev and Gladkov 1951). They forage mostly in freshwater marshes, but also along rivers and channels, in lakes and estuaries and even along the coast when on migration or wintering. They may also forage in pools that are drying up, on meadows and in rice-fields. They nest and roost in reeds, shrubs and sometimes trees, such as acacia and mangrove and occasionally pines.

POPULATION SIZE, TRENDS AND DYNAMICS

Only small relict populations still breed in Europe. Great White Egrets have bred at Neusiedlersee since at least 1682. In 1946, 100 pairs nested. By 1951, the population had increased to 140 breeding pairs, in 1959 to 200 (Bauer and Glutz 1966) and in 1976 to 260 (Schmidt 1977). Between 1981 and 1987, the population remained stable, with 200–300 nesting pairs (Grüll 1988).

In Hungary, the main colony is at Lake Kisbalaton and numbered 100 pairs in 1886. The breeding population more or less deserted the area between 1915 and 1930. In 1966, 40 pairs were counted, but despite protection the colony declined again and between 1968 and 1972 only 4–11 pairs were found. In another colony at Lake Velence, 12 breeding pairs were counted in 1966 (Cramp and Simmons 1977), but by 1976 the number of nesting sites had increased from 2 to 14. In 1976, 80 breeding pairs were counted at Lake Kisbalaton and 32 breeding pairs at Lake Velence. About 50 pairs bred that year in the 12 other known nesting sites (Schmidt 1977).

Only a few pairs breed in Yugoslavia, Albania and Greece (12–15 breeding pairs were counted in 1971 at Lake Mikra Prespa) (Cramp and Simmons 1977). Great White Egrets were once numerous in Romania, especially in the Danube Delta, but only 80 pairs bred in the delta in 1939 and none in 1950. After protection, the birds began to nest again. Their number was estimated at 120 breeding pairs in 1960–1962, but during the following years the population decreased rapidly again and in 1968 only 30–40 pairs nested in the delta region (Vasiliu 1968). The breeding population in Turkey was estimated at about 50 pairs in 1971. In the USSR, the species was nearly extinct in the lower Volga Delta from the end of the nineteenth century to 1917. In 1935, after protection, the population was estimated at 1070 adults and juveniles (Dementiev and Gladkov 1951) and in 1951 at about 557 breeding pairs, but none were found breeding in 1958 (Lugovoy, in Cramp and Simmons 1977).

The mortality rate of Great White Egrets, determined from American ringing recoveries, was 76% at the end of the first year and 26% each following year. If the birds begin to breed at 2 years of age, each pair must raise 2.92 young to fledging each year to maintain the population (Kahl 1963). The oldest recovered bird was 22 years old (Kennard 1976).

BEHAVIOUR AND BIOLOGY

DAILY ROUTINE

When not breeding, Great White Egrets feed away from the roost or colony during the day, returning individually or in small groups about an hour before sunset:

On clear, calm days egrets flew high and directly over the 2.7 km of open water to Smith Island (Florida). In fog, heavy rains and high winds they follow the chain of oyster bars to the island, flying within 2 m of the water surface. Great White Egrets left the roost individually at sunrise, generally after the smaller species of ardeids had already gone. After nights below freezing temperatures Smith Island egrets commonly sunned on wind-protected oyster bars before flying to the mainland to feed (Wiese 1976).

Great White Egrets usually forage alone, but roost together in the vicinity of the feeding area during a few hours in the middle of the day (Wiese 1976).

When breeding, they divide their time between foraging and breeding activities, such as displaying, incubating and caring for the young. During this period, they leave the heronry at dawn when not guarding the nest. Birds fly to and from the heronry throughout the day, though arrivals and departures are few during the middle of the day and numerous in the morning and evening (in the Djoudj from about 07.00–10.30 h and from about 16.30–19.30 h), with a peak at dawn and dusk. When the sky darkens, as it does in the Djoudj when high dust clouds blow in from the desert, Great White Egrets return to the heronry about 30 minutes earlier than usual, as do other herons breeding there (Voisin 1983).

DISPLAYS AND CALLS

The displays of the Great White Egret have been studied by D.A. McCrimmon (1974), D.N.S. Tomlinson (1976), J.H. Wiese (1976), D.W. Mock (1978) and C. Voisin (1983). These observations on the American *E. a. egretta* and the African *E. a. melanorhynchos* show no substantial differences in behaviour between them. However, small differences in behaviour would only be discovered if the same observer had studied the different subspecies.

The male Great White Egret has a particular display, the Bow, in addition to the usual Stretch Display. The very conspicuous aigrettes seem to have produced a number of displays specifically to show them. An important difference between the male Little Egret and the male Great White Egret is that the latter does not use a loud, characteristic Advertising Call during pair-formation.

Agonistic displays

The forward displays comprise a succession of more and more intense threat displays, reaching their highest intensity with the Full Forward Display.

Full Forward Display. The bird adopts the following position while facing an intruder:

○ body in a nearly horizontal position;
○ legs slightly bent;
○ wings partly spread;

○ neck curved backwards in an "S" shape, bill pointing forwards ready to strike. The more the neck is curved backwards, the higher is the tendency to attack.
○ feathers of head and neck held fully erect, scapulars only slightly erect.

In this position, Threat Calls are given: "a harsh skok or less commonly, a high-pitched eeee-i-eeee" (Mock 1978). During the ensuing stab, the wings flick quickly out, which helps both to maintain balance and to act as a threat by increasing the apparent size of the bird.

Forward Display. Great White Egrets often threaten at a lower intensity. The posture changes from normal relaxed feathers, to partly erect feathers, (the "fat head" of Mock 1978), and Threat Calls may be given. The precise posture adopted by the bird varies and has not yet been studied in detail.

Forward Display.

Aggressive Upright Display. This display was first described by Meyer-riecks in 1960 for several species of North American herons. It is the same behaviour as the "Erect stance" of Wiese (1976) and the "Fluffed neck" of Mock (1978):

> In the Erect stance Great White Egrets extend the neck vertically while holding the head and bill horizontally. The head and neck plumage is fully erect and the scapular plumes slightly so. The bill is open, and the egret repeatedly gives 'raah' calls. The Erect stance was most commonly performed after landing on a nest site, or directed toward closely passing conspecifics. Nestlings threatened younger siblings and neighbouring young with the Erect stance. Egrets of both sexes regularly performed an Erect stance after landing on their territories, and the display became a major component of the greeting ceremony following pair formation (Wiese 1976).

According to Mock, this behaviour "functions as a mild threat/warning".

Stab-crouch. In the Stab-crouch posture, a Great White Egret

> erects its crest and scapular plumes and strikes with closed bill . . . At the fullest extension of the stab, the legs flex rapidly at the heels, producing a full crouch. . . . The wings are usually flicked out and back during the crouch. Afterwards the bird resumes a normal standing position. Most performances are silent but some are accompanied by a mechanical bill-clack during the stab (Mock 1978).

This behaviour has only been described by Mock.

Supplanting Flight. This is a commonly observed agonistic behaviour among herons:

> With a harsh squawk an egret flies suddenly and lands either atop its opponent or on the spot just vacated by the fleeing bird. Occasionally the attack results in physical contact with the receiver, involving grasping feet and thrusting bill. The fleeing opponent may be pursued briefly and pecked in flight, but usually the attacker simply lands on the empty perch, remains there for a minute or two, and returns to its original location. Supplanting is usually done by bachelor males (toward satellite females) and by satellite females (among themselves). Occasionally, when a bachelor male flies an unusually long distance (up to 20 m) to supplant a satellite female, the display appears to draw attention to him. A few such distantly supplanted females actually moved closer and grew more attentive after being attacked. Since females presumably are evaluating the male's aggressiveness (among other things) in their choice of mates, this act could sometimes be viewed as a form of male advertisement (Mock 1978).

Bill-duel. According to Mock (1978):

> If a newly mated (or very close satellite) female egret raises her head while a male is facing her, a ritualized attack may follow. The male strikes with his bill toward the female's face and she recoils, avoiding the contact. Repeated stabs by the male and recoils by the female produce a very rapid see-sawing motion. Occasionally

the female manages to catch the male's bill-tip in her mandibles, in which case she can render him immobile and end the duel. Otherwise it ends when the male ceases his stabbing usually within 5 s.

The Bill-duel described by Mock occurs in newly paired birds and is not the same behaviour as Stab-and-counter-stab, which occurs between birds of different pairs. In Stab-and-counter-stab, the bill of the opponent is not seized.

Stab-and-counter-stab. This has been observed in the Great White Egret and is exactly as performed by the Little Egret.

Fight. Real fights seldom occur between Great White Egrets. Sometimes, however, when one bird makes an attack, it meets with resistance. The attacked bird flies up into the air to meet its opponent and, as in the Little Egret, the birds fight in the air about 5 m over the heronry, calling loudly and snatching at each other as they fall down into the branches. In order to avoid crashing onto the ground, they put an end to their fight often even before reaching the trees.

Courtship displays

At the beginning of the breeding period, the males choose a conspicuous branch on which to stand. When not displaying, they adopt a characteristic position which Tomlinson (1976) has called the Hunched Neck position and

Inter-display Stance (after Mock 1978).

Mock (1978) the Inter-display Stance. This posture has also been described by myself (Voisin 1983), but not named. The male keeps his neck, crest and body feathers slightly erect and appears larger than a non-displaying bird. His throat is puffed out, and his scapulars either slightly or fully fanned. He either rests on his branch in a hunched position or with his neck more or less outstretched and looks around in an interested way at what is going on in the heronry. The displaying males are thus recognizable even when resting. Mock has observed that prior to display, a male in the Inter-display Stance often "shifts his weight slowly from leg to leg, producing a gentle swaying motion of the long aigrettes".

Stretch Display. The Stretch Display is performed as follows. First, an upward movement in which:

○ the male raises his body to an angle of about 45° to the horizontal;
○ the bill is pointed towards the sky and the neck is slowly stretched upwards and slightly backwards.

Stretch display.

Secondly, a downward movement: in which

○ the male slowly retracts his neck, bill still pointing upwards and then curves his neck, his head coming slowly back to a horizontal position.
○ At the beginning of this downward movement, the male bends his legs and, at the end of it, he stands up again.

In the Stretch Display, Great White Egrets do not erect the feathers of the head and neck but do erect the long white aigrettes of the back as far as possible. Tomlinson (1976) alone has heard a vocalization – "a brief nasal stammering noise" – only audible at very close quarters. Other authors, including myself, were probably too far away to hear this call. This courtship display is only performed by unpaired males (Wiese 1976, Tomlinson 1976, Mock 1978, Voisin 1983), as is also the case for the Little Egret. In contrast, the Grey Heron performs the Stretch Display on two occasions: first, when unpaired males display and later when both males and females greet each other when one of the pair returns to the nest.

During the Stretch Display, the male Great White Egret bends his neck backwards only very slightly, as little, or nearly as little, as the Little Egret and not as much as the Grey Heron, which lowers its neck over the back during the downward movement. However, there are differences in detail between Great White and Little Egrets. The Little Egret bends its legs more than the Great White Egret and also keeps its body closer to the horizontal, unlike the Great White Egret which holds its body at an angle of about 45° to the horizontal, as does the Grey Heron. The most conspicuous difference, however, is the position of the aigrettes, which being longer and stronger in the Great White Egret than in the Little Egret are much more fanned when fully erected.

Bow. This behaviour, observed by Wiese (1976), Tomlinson (1976) and Mock (1978), is a ritualized Twig-shaking. The Bow of Wiese and Mock is identical to the Twig-shake of Tomlinson. When Bowing:

the egret lowers its head and firmly grasps a branch or nest-stick in its bill. In this hunched position it briefly sways its head from side to side and then suddenly crouches with a shallow flex, causing the scapular plumes to bounce upwards. Finally it releases the stick and resumes standing. Bows are quite stereotyped in form, varying in degree of neck extension, depth of crouch, choice of stick to grasp and overall vigor of performance. Bows usually involve a stick about 10–20 cm from the egret's toes, but occasionally sticks are chosen that are directly beneath the toes and as far away as 60 cm, producing a range of neck extensions. Few Bows involve a stick higher than the bird's feet. The depth of the crouch of course, influences the bouncing motion of the plumes and therefore the visual effect of the display. Bows are an extremely frequent and conspicuous part of the male repertoire. I have seen Bows performed only twice by females, both by satellites attending a bachelor male. Like Stretch and Snap, the Bow seems to be a conspicuous mate-attracting signal in the repertoire of courting males (Mock 1978).

No other heron species so far studied has such a ritualized Twig-shaking behaviour, though it may have gone unnoticed in other species if performed in a more subtle form.

Twig-shake. Mock (1978) describes Twig-shaking as follows:

> The egret extends its neck out and down, grasp a stick in its bill, and gently shakes it. The bird does not appear to be trying to snap the branch off for nesting material and there is no leg flex component. The Twig Shake is a spontaneous male display, the frequency of which greatly increases in the presence of a satellite female. I have seen only five Twig Shake performances by females.

Snap Display. The Snap Display of the Great White Egret has been observed by every observer. It is usually performed by males, but females may do it too. It has been described in detail by Mock (1978):

> With scapular aigrettes fully fanned, a Great Egret smoothly extends its neck horizontally until the neck is nearly straight. Then, with a sudden deep flex of the legs (crouch), the neck drops well below horizontal and the mandibles are clacked together once. As the torso drops, the aigrettes bounce upwards. The only acoustic component is the mechanical bill-clack. The Great Egret's Snap is highly stereotyped, showing only minor variability in neck angle (at the time of the clack), degree of plume erection, depth of leg flex, and overall speed of performance.

After the first copulation, the Snap Display becomes infrequent. Mock and I have never observed paired birds performing the Snap Display after the first

Snap Display.

copulation, but Wiese has observed it throughout pair-formation and incubation. Mock, Wiese and I have classified the Snap Display as a mate-attracting display when performed by unpaired males and Wiese believes that it strengthens the pair-bond later on (see discussion in Chapter 5, p 23).

Circle Flight. Circle Flights have been observed by Wiese (1976), Tomlinson (1976), Mock (1978) and Voisin (1983):

> The egret leaps off its perch with deep, exaggerated wingbeats, neck extended, feet trailing. The bird resumes normal flight after 5–15 m, and usually flies once around the colony. The circle flight posture is resumed 15–25 m from the nest platform, and the male lands calling loudly (Wiese 1976).

> A few Circle Flights are performed by bachelor males during spontaneous courtship but most are flown by satellite females. After a Circle Flight a satellite female usually lands a few meters closer to the bachelor male's nest. Thus the display seems to be a tactic for approaching an aggressive male gradually (and perhaps submissively) (Mock 1978).

Extended-neck Flight. The Extended-neck Flight has been observed by Mock (1978) and Voisin (1983):

> An egret takes off with its bill pointing 45°–60° above horizontal and usually flies with the neck recurved and almost fully outstretched. It may fly this way for a short distance and land, or it may retract the head against the shoulders and continue flying some distance. A few flights are accompanied by a kraack call. In landing, the egret extends its neck and points the bill upwards as it brakes to perch. The distinction between this display and the Circle Flight may be artificial. In the Great Egret many display flights are short and straight, between two points in the colony. I have seen it performed by unpaired males moving to new display sites, visiting nearby nests for stick-theft, or flying home with a stick in the bill. Bachelor males often begin aerial attacks (Supplants) on satellite females with an Extended Neck takeoff posture and satellite females use it commonly when Supplanting each other near a bachelor male (Mock 1978).

Aerial-stretch Display. This display has only been observed in the eastern subspecies *E. a. modesta* by Hancock (1984), who gives the following description:

> The bird took up a position on a bush at some height above its nest and some 500 m from it. It stood erect, stretched its neck forward, dropped its wings and uttered a harsh croak. It then launched itself into the air, and descended to the nest in a direct line. Its flight was undulating, occasioned by the backwards and forwards movement of the neck and legs. The arching backwards and forwards of the neck during this spectacular flight was done quickly but gracefully, and the final outstretching of the legs brought it close to the edge of the nest.

This display is very similar to the Extended-neck Flight observed in both *E. a. egretta* and *E. a. melanorhynchos*. Its existence in only one of the subspecies, if confirmed, would show that in a few cases behaviours may differ between subspecies. Since the Aerial-stretch Display has not been observed in the genus *Ardea*, but is observed in the genus *Egretta*, Hancock does not agree with the new classification of Payne and Risley (1976) and the *Check-List of the Birds of the World* (Mayr and Cottrell 1979), where the Great White Egret is classified as an *Ardea*.

Feather-nibbling (Baerends and Van der Cingel 1962). This behaviour is performed by the Great White Egret in the same way as by the Grey Heron, and it is given by both sexes after a female has been accepted by the male. It is the only display that commonly precedes copulation. Little Egrets have not been observed performing it and so make no physical contact prior to copulation. However, this is not a characteristic of all *Egretta* spp., since Meyerriecks has observed Feather-nibbling in both the Snowy Egret and the Reddish Egret.

Conflict display

Wing-preen (Mock 1978). This is the same display as the Wing-touch (Blaker 1968):

> With scapular plumes usually half-erect or less, the Great White Egret leans over and runs its bill-tip along the entire leading edge of one wing. The bill is partially open and surrounds some primaries in most performances. Most Wing Preens include holding the wing out and slightly forward. The entire display takes 2 to 3 s. Often the bill does not even touch the wing, but travels parallel to its leading edge 3–5 cm away. When actively courting, males perform Wing Preens at a

Feather-nibbling while walking (after a photograph by D. Robert).

mean rate of 2 per min, making this display and the Bow the most frequent displays in the unpaired male egret's repertoire. Satellite females perform Wing Preens only occasionally while watching a bachelor male (Mock 1978).

Fear and appeasement displays

Alert Posture. The bird stands erect, the neck stretched upwards, the feathers sleeked, and looks towards the danger (Voisin 1983).

Upright Display (Meyerriecks 1960). This display is different from the Aggressive Upright Display (Meyerriecks 1960):

> In the Upright display the egret sleeks its plumage and extends neck, head and bill upwards in a straight line at 45°–50° angle. The bill remains closed while the bird utters a loud, single syllable 'kroogh'. The Upright display of Great Egrets occurs primarily during conspecific disputes over feeding and roosting sites. It was not seen in nest site defense (Wiese 1976).

This display is also described by Meyerriecks (1960) and Mock (1978) in several species of North American herons, but has not been described by Tomlinson (1976) for the Great White Egret nor by Milstein *et al.* (1970) for the Grey Heron. It has been classified as an antagonistic behaviour incorporating a high degree of fear because the bird has a sleeked plumage and an erect posture. I think that both these characteristics show that this behaviour is an appeasement behaviour and not an agonistic one. The bird, in the Upright Posture, foresees a possible attack and wants both to remain where it is and to avoid a fight, which does not mean that if attacked it will not fight back. In my opinion, the Upright Display is very close, if not identical, to the Alert Display, which I and other authors have described in several heron species.

REPRODUCTIVE BEHAVIOUR

Pair-formation

Pair-formation has been studied by Wiese (1976), Tomlinson (1976), Mock (1978, 1979) and Voisin (1983). The male Great White Egret chooses a nest-site from which he displays, performing Stretch, Bow and Snap Displays. The females, named satellite females by Mock, try to approach but are repeatedly repelled. They often perform the Wing-preen Display while watching the males. At this stage, Circle Flights and Pursuit Flights are common. Mock (1978):

> suspects that this stalling tactic gives a male time to appraise each female (and vice versa). Females often have an assortment of males from which to choose. A satellite female can reject one male simply by moving over to another. On the other hand, a male egret exercises his choice by selective rejection. Before accepting a mate on his nest, a male usually has chased off many other females. One might speculate that females are accepted or rejected on the persistence of

their approaches and that males are chosen according to some optimal standards of site-tenacity, aggressiveness, and display vigor. Exactly what cues are most important is unknown.

When newly paired, the bonds between male and female are still fragile and, in the heronry observed by Mock (1978), 10–20% of all pairs were not maintained to egg-laying. In contrast, in the colonies observed by Tomlinson and myself, once paired the birds nearly always stayed together throughout the breeding cycle. The pair-bonds are strengthened by Feather-nibbling, nest-building, nest-defence and copulation. A pair copulates on average 20 times per season. The displays observed at this stage are the Forward and Full Forward Displays, given against intruders, as well as Feather-nibbling, Bill-duel and Fluffed-neck.

When coming to the nest, a Great White Egret gives a characteristic Landing Call while still in flight. It lands on a branch some distance from the nest and, still calling, walks towards the nest. The mate recognizes the call and answers. During the Greeting Display, the crest feathers of both birds are completely erected; the neck and scapular feathers are only slightly erected. When the birds are newly paired, the Bill-duels, Feather-nibbling and Fluffed-neck Displays are given following the mate's arrival. Later, during incubation and brooding, as soon as the mate has reached the nest, the bird on guard usually leaves and, walking out onto the branches, brings its plumage back into order before flying away.

Mock (1979) discovered a behaviour not observed before. One or two days after pairing, the male, when alone at the nest while the female is away foraging, begins the courtship display exactly as if not already paired, performing the Stretch, Bow and Snap Displays. Satellite females watch him and try to approach the nest. Now and then the paired female returned briefly to chase them away (Mock was able to recognize several individuals). The newly paired female is off foraging most of the time, so is rarely at the nest and may often not return at all. In this case, the male keeps the new female he has acquired during her absence and no time is wasted in what is often a very short reproductive period.

However, these observations do not mirror either Tomlinson's or my own. In the African heronries, the newly paired birds stay together on the nest for most of the day, engaged in various activities which serve to strengthen the pair-bond. Mock's observations most probably occurred in an area where food was scarce, so the female must forage a good deal to get enough food to produce her eggs. The male is left alone and, bewildered by this – in my opinion – abnormal situation, begins to display again as if he had lost her. If this interpretation (see also Nest-building) is correct, Great White Egrets show considerable behavioural plasticity in the face of difficult ecological conditions.

Behaviour and taxonomy

In this book, the Great White Egret has been retained in the genus *Egretta* due to its behavioural similarities to the Little Egret, *Egretta garzetta*. The

Stretch Display is only used by unpaired males in order to attract females, both in the Great White Egret and in the Little Egret. In the Grey Heron, *Ardea cinerea*, as in the Great Blue Heron, *Ardea herodias*, the Stretch Display is not only used in this way, but also by both sexes when the birds are paired, as a greeting display during nest-building, incubation and brooding. Since the Stretch Display is one of the most important displays among herons, this provides a very strong argument for maintaining the Great White Egret in the genus *Egretta*. Further studies of species belonging to the genera *Ardea* and *Egretta* will be necessary to establish definitively these differences as being a characteristic of the two genera.

The observation by Hancock (1984) of an Aerial Stretch Display in one subspecies of the Great White Egret, is also an argument in favour of it remaining in the genus *Egretta*, since this display has been observed in at least two other *Egretta* species, *Egretta thula* and *Egretta rufescens*, but not in any *Ardea* species.

Nest-building

To build their nests, Great White Egrets use only sticks; larger ones for the initial platform and smaller ones to complete the nest-rim and cup. Their nests are much smaller than those of the Grey Herons. In the Djoudj, Sénégal, where the birds nest in trees, the nests are about the same size as those of the Night Heron and Little Egret. Tomlinson (1976) measured 20 nests at hatching time in Zimbabwe. Their mean outer diameter was 34.4 cm (range 29–41 cm) and their mean depth 11.5 cm (range 9–15 cm). Those of the eastern European Great White Egrets seem to be much larger, since at Lake Kisbalaton they had a mean outer diameter of 100 cm (range 80–120 cm) (Warga 1938).

According to Mock (1978), the males start repairing old nests and even building new ones before finding a mate. This behaviour has not been observed in other European herons but has been noticed in the Louisiana Heron and the Green Heron. Once paired, only the male collects sticks, as in all the other European herons. He places about half the sticks into the nest himself, much more than is usual among other heron species. When the male presents a stick to the female, the Greeting Display is often reduced to a weak Fluffed-neck Display performed by the female. Sometimes the male only lays the stick onto the nest for the female to take it. In contrast, Tomlinson and I noted that when a male lands, with his typical Landing Call, he nearly always gives the stick to the female after a Greeting Display. This difference in behaviour is, in my opinion, adaptive. Mock (1978) had noted that the females in the heronry he observed were very often away foraging. The male, being alone, had to do most of the nest-building himself. Since the female helped less than is usual, the birds were probably in a hurry and I have observed that in such cases the Greeting Display during twig passing is often reduced.

In the Djoudj, Great White Egrets were eager to steal sticks from other nests, even from occupied ones. Nest-building continues during incubation, and to some extent also during the first days after hatching.

Copulation

The male approaches his mate with crown feathers slightly raised (the "Fat Head") and often performs Feather-nibbling before mounting (Mock 1978). Wiese (1976) has described copulation in detail. He wrote:

> Females were mounted either from the side or the rear. The male placed one foot on the female's back, causing her to squat on the nest platform. The male climbed up and forward as the female extended her neck and wings for balance, and raised her tail sideways to expose the protruding cloaca. The male hooked his toes around the base of the females' humeri, and moved his tail laterally until he made cloacal contact. No sounds were emitted by either bird during the 15–20 sec copulations, nor was the female's neck ever grasped.

In contrast to these Louisiana birds, those observed by me in the Djoudj uttered a succession of calls during copulation.

Neither Tomlinson (1976), Mock (1978) nor myself (1983) have observed a single case of rape among Great White Egrets. In contrast, Wiese (1976) reports that "both hetero- and homosexual rapes were commonly observed at Avery Island (Louisiana)" and that "males copulated nonselectively with any female landing on their nest platforms". It is probable that these behaviours were induced by overcrowding, the colony of Avery Island being established on closely spaced man-made platforms.

Egg-laying, clutch size and breeding success

The eggs of the Great White Egret are oval in shape and pale blue in colour. A sample of 120 eggs measured by Schönwetter (1967) gave the following measurements (mean and range): length 61 mm (41–68 mm), width 43 mm (40–54 mm). A sample of 64 eggs measured by Tomlinson (1976) gave the following measurements (mean and range): length 55.6 mm (54.5–65.5 mm), width 39.9 mm (30.9–44.0 mm).

The mean weight of eggshell is 4.54 g (range 3.7–5.8 g) and the mean weight of full eggs is 61 g (Schönwetter, in Bauer and Glutz 1966).

Tomlinson found that the average interval between pair-formation and the laying of the first egg was 7.4 days (range 5–8 days). The Great White Egret lays only one brood, but after egg loss may lay new clutches. Incubation begins as soon as the first egg is laid. Egg-laying occurs in the spring in temperate areas and at the end of the main rains in tropical areas. In eastern Europe, laying begins in April and continues to the end of June. Most eggs are laid at the end of April and in May (Bauer and Glutz 1966). The average incubation time at Lake Kisbalaton (Hungary) is 25–26 days (Warga 1938) and at Lake Kyle, Zimbabwe 26.4 days ± 1 day (range 24–27 days) (Tomlinson 1976).

In Europe, clutches range in size from 2 to 6 eggs, 4-egg clutches being most common (Bauer and Glutz 1966). Clutches seem to be on average somewhat smaller in Sénégal and in Zimbabwe. The mean clutch size in the Djoudj in

1981 was 3.2 eggs (Voisin 1983) and at Lake Kyle in 1974, 3.7 eggs (Tomlinson 1976). The clutches range in size from 2 to 5 eggs in these areas.

Of a sample of 121 eggs observed at Lake Kyle, 16 in four nests were destroyed by strong winds, 4 failed to hatch and 7 disappeared, leaving a total of 94 that hatched successfully, giving a hatching success of ˙77.6%. Of a sample of 34 eggs observed in the Djoudj, 4 eggs in different nests did not hatch. The other 30 hatched successfully giving a hatching success of 88%. A sample of nine pairs breeding in the Djoudj gave a mean number of young per nest at hatching of 2.7, at 15 days 2.4 and at 20 days only 1.9 (Voisin 1983). During a 6-year study at Lake Kisbalaton, the young of 80 nests were followed until fledging. A total of 159 fledglings were recorded, the mean number of young reared per nest ranging from 1.13 in bad years to 3.06 in good ones (Warga 1938).

DEVELOPMENT AND CARE OF THE YOUNG

Both parents take care of the young, nest change-overs occurring in the morning and evening. In the Djoudj, Sénégal, the guardian period lasted only until the oldest chicks were 12–15 days old. At this stage, the young were able to gular-flutter and to give threat displays. At Lake Kyle, Zimbabwe, the feeding conditions were probably better, because Tomlinson observed that the guardian period lasted until the chicks were nearly 30 days old. During the post-guardian period, the chicks were left alone during the day while both parents were away foraging, but one of the adults always stayed at or near the nest during the night. When about 30 days old, the young began to leave the

A Great White Egret feeding young.

nest to explore their surroundings. The fledging stage began at about 40 days, when the young were able to fly short distances. At 50–60 days of age, the young began to leave the colony, which was established on an island in the lake, and flew with their parents to forage on the mainland about 300 m away.

When the chicks are still too young to leave the nest, the adults come to the nest rim to feed them. When old enough to walk on the branches, the chicks move towards the incoming adult, which lands some distance from the nest, and are fed in the branches. One of the chicks – usually one of the two largest – soon succeeds in grasping the bill of the adult, usually at the base. It draws the adult's bill downwards, which the adult resists. The two birds remain in this position for several seconds until the adult begins to regurgitate. Once this happens, the young, its mandible gliding along the bill of the adult, places its open gape at the bill tip in order to catch the regurgitated prey in its throat. It swallows the food, often with difficulty. The other large chick often succeeds in grasping the bill of the adult and gets fed also. The third chick does not have much chance of being fed, since once the first has swallowed its food it usually tries to grasp the adult's bill again. The third chick is therefore fed only if the larger ones are sated. The fourth chick did not have a chance of being fed in the Djoudj in 1981. When the difference in size between the largest chicks and the smallest ones is such that the largest are able to swallow the small ones, they often do so.

Growth of the young

A growth study of young Great White Egrets was undertaken by J.-F. Voisin and I in the Djoudj in 1981 (Voisin 1983). The young were captured, marked and weighed using the same techniques as for the Little Egrets in the Camargue (see chapter on the Little Egret). Being larger, Great White Egrets have a slower development than Little Egrets, which makes their capture possible for a somewhat longer period of time. They could be caught at the nest up to 2 and sometimes 3 weeks of age. When facing capture, the chicks try to flee long before the age at which they would normally leave the nest to explore their surroundings. The one or two oldest young should therefore be captured first, before they escape. If missed, they should not be pursued, since they may fall from the tree or stray too far into unknown surroundings. The long accacia thorns are an additional danger for escaping young.

During our study, we weighed the young of nine nests and drew growth curves. As in the case of the Little Egret, these curves demonstrate the existence of a crisis at the end of the guardian period. In the Djoudj in 1981, Great White Egrets left the young at about 12–15 days of age. Several growth curves show a reduction in growth rate between the age of 5 and 15 days. During the first days of life, the 2 or 3 first-hatched young seem to have enough food, but after about 5–15 days the quantity of food brought by the parents is not enough to maintain the high initial growth rate. The whole brood faces the danger of starvation. At this point, both parents leave to forage, forced away from the nest by the incessant begging of their offspring. Most of the growth curves that had shown a reduction in growth rate towards the end of the guardian period, show a sharp increase due to the greater quantity of food provided by both parents once the post-guardian period begins.

The weights of the young at 5, 10 and 15 days have been calculated from the growth curves. From the weights of the chicks at those ages, and the ones which died before the age of 3 weeks, I have been able to produce a diagram showing the normal weights of young in relation to their age and the critical age/weight which will rapidly cause their death. Between these are the weights at which the young are placed in danger, but which do not always prove fatal. Only a slight reduction in growth seems sufficient to doom them. From a total of 25 young, 7 died (most probably of hunger) before the age of 20 days and 1 between 20 and 25 days (probably of illness). The death rate was thus 30%. The very fast growth rate of herons, which is unable to withstand much perturbation, is probably a consequence of the often very short favourable conditions found in the temporarily flooded habitats in which they usually breed.

FEEDING BEHAVIOUR AND FOOD

Foraging methods

Great White Egrets usually forage among tall aquatic vegetation, wading in water up to their bellies. In the Djoudj, only their heads and parts of their neck could be seen as they walked in the deep aquatic grasses. Fortunately, they also foraged in openings in the swamps at the edge of the vegetation where they could easily be observed. Occasionally, they forage in open areas in fresh-, brackish- and salt-water.

Great White Egrets fish using either the Stand-and-wait or the Walk Slowly methods. They usually walk with the body held at an angle of about 45° above the horizontal, their long kinked neck more or less outstretched, often Head-tilting in order to see into the water better.

Freezing postures are combined with wading and the birds tend to take a step, then freeze for a few seconds, take another step and freeze again, and so on. Three times a bird was observed to pull at floating and submerged debris with its bill and then strike in an area adjacent to the debris. Each time the bird was successful in catching a fish and these were always swallowed head first (Tomlinson 1976).

They may exceptionally alight in deep water to catch a prey and have also been observed following Double-crested Cormorants in shallow water in order to feed near them (Palmer 1962). A few observations have shown that they will catch small birds when the opportunity arises. Sprunt (1936) saw a Great White Egret catch a Red-winged Blackbird and fly off with it. Genelly (1964) saw one prey on a Meadow-lark and Repenning (1977) observed one taking a Sandpiper (*Calidris* sp.). Finally, Great White Egrets have been observed on a few occasions foraging in fields around cattle in Florida and Cuba (Palmer 1962). I have never seen Great White Egrets run after prey, nor Foot-stirring as Little Egrets do. Great White Egrets therefore forage in much the same way as Purple Herons do probably due to the size of the birds; only small herons can move about much to capture prey. In general, fishing methods differ markedly between closely related species, being a consequence of size and preferred habitat, and thus of very little use in taxonomy. In the Djoudj, Great White Egrets caught a mean number of 0.42 prey per minute; the maximum number caught during 1 minute was three.

Food

Great White Egrets prey mainly on fish but also catch small mammals, birds, amphibians, crustaceans, molluscs, worms and insects.

Only the stomach contents of two west European Great White Egrets have been studied. They were taken in Italy during the winter of 1941 by Moltoni (1948). Both birds had fed on fish only. One stomach contained; 1 sunfish *Eupomotis gibbosus*, 4 small carps *Cyprinus carpio* and 4 tenches *Tinca vulgaris*. The other contained only a few remains of fish. In Hungary, 20 stomachs contained mainly fish (Crussian carp *Carassius*, rudd *Scardinius*, bleak *Alburnus*, carp *Cyprinus*, dace *Leuciscus* and bitterling *Rhodeus*) and a few insects (*Dysticus, Hydrophilus, Cybister, Gryllotalpa, Aeschna* and *Naucoris*) (Vasvàri 1948–1951). In Romania, 16 stomachs contained fish with 3 Great Reed Warblers *Acrocephalus arundinaceus*, 1 grass snake *Natrix natrix* and various insects (Dombrowski, in Cramp and Simmons 1977).

Some 70 stomachs from Sundarban, West Bengal, India, contained chiefly fish: 1166 specimens were found belonging to 26 species (3 freshwater species and 23 brackish-water species). The length of the fish varied from 5 to 175 mm. By weight, these stomachs contained 80% fish, belonging mostly to five species (*Mystus gulio, Periophthalmus, Mugil tade, Aplocheilus panchax* and *Anguilla bengalensis*), 6% molluscs (mostly *Lymnaea* and *Melanoides*), 5% crustaceans (mostly crabs among which *Scylla serrata* was the most common), 2% reptiles (which were water snakes belonging chiefly to the species *Natrix stolata*) and various insects (*Odonata* and *Coleoptera*) (Mukherjee 1971).

Small mammals have been found in stomach contents from the USSR together with fish and insect remains. A social vole *Microtus socialis*, 2 water shrews and several voles where found in three different stomachs (Dementiev and Gladkov 1951).

Studies on the prey of Great White Egrets in America are few. The fish taken are mostly sunfish *Lepomis* sp., gizzard shads *Dorosoma cepedianum*, large-mouthed bass *Micropterus salmoides*, needlefish *Belonidae* and mullet *Mugillidae*. They take also frogs *Leptodactylus albilabris* and various species of *Odonata* and *Coleoptera*.

A Great White Egret foraging

A Great White Egret foraging.

The unusual death of a Great White Egret

A dead Great White Egret was found in a mangrove swamp bordering the west edge of the Indian River at Vero Beach, Florida. "Examination of the macerated skeleton revealed a seven-cm forked twig protruding from the foramen magnum and right optic foramen of the skull. The twig had evidently pierced the brain when the bird thrust its bill into the dark swamp water while feeding" (Weigel 1962). This accident is very interesting as it shows how fragile avian pneumatized bones are. Such accidents among herons may not be as exceptional as might be thought as they forage in turbid, debris-strewn waters.

CHAPTER 19

Protection of herons in Europe

In all European countries, the progress of laws for the protection of animals and plants has followed the same trend. In particular, they have all increased the protection given to birds with the result that, within the last few years, all the herons in western Europe, except the Grey Heron, are protected everywhere throughout the year:

Under British law, all bird species are protected in the Wildlife and Countryside Act of 1981. This makes it illegal to take any bird species from the wild at any time, with certain species carrying special penalties if disturbed at or near the breeding site, or with dependent young of such a bird. The Grey Heron *Ardea cinerea* falls into the former category, but may be killed under licence to protect food crops, such as salmon or trout in fish farms. The Bittern *Botaurus stellaris*, however, falls into the later category, and as already stated, if disturbed on or near a nest containing eggs or depending young, then the person involved could be fined up to £2000.00 (S. Dudley, *in litt.*).

In Switzerland,

all herons have been fully protected by an earlier law and are again fully protected (during the whole year, everywhere) by our new Hunting Law of 1986. There is

335

one exception: if herons cause really serious damage the Cantons can give permissions to official hunters, to game wardens and to the police to persecute such birds. Such permissions are given only in rare cases and only for the persecution of Grey Herons" (H. Schmid, *in litt.*).

In France, all heron species as well as their nests and eggs are totally protected and trade and transport of living or dead herons has been forbidden since the Nature Protection Law was passed on 10 July 1976. Up to 1962 for the Little Egret and 1974–1975 for the other species, herons could be hunted inland during the hunting season for waterbirds. A list of birds which could never be hunted was established in 1962 and among these was the Little Egret. On 26 June 1974, the Squacco Heron and the Cattle Egret were put on the list and on 15 October 1975, all the other herons were finally added. Before 1950, hunting was allowed in coastal areas throughout the year. Thus herons could be hunted along the coast, in lagoons, on coastal marshes and estuaries at any time. Since 1950, coastal areas have been submitted to the same regulation as the nearest inland area. In Belgium, all herons have been totally protected since 20 July 1972 (by *arrêté Royal*).

In the Netherlands, the Bird Protection Act of 1912 as well as that of 1936 provides the following definition of "protected birds":

> all birds belonging to species living in the wild in Europe, with the exception of the birds mentioned in the Game Act. None of the European heron species was in the Game Act since 1912, so in principle all herons are protected. However, there was a possibility in the Bird Act to declare certain birds unprotected during a continuous period of two years at the maximum. The Grey Heron was in the list of species which could thus be declared unprotected till 1985 and it was in effect unprotected till 1963 during a certain period of the year (mostly from 15 August to 15 March). The Grey Heron is fully protected now. However, every year a small number of licences (less than 10) is given to shoot Grey Herons in fish ponds and in view of air safety (A.J. Binsbergen, *in litt.*).

Nature protection laws in Austria are established by each province (*Land*). Neusiedlersee in Burgenland is the only really favourable area for herons in Austria and all herons are totally protected there. It is the only place in western Europe where Great White Egrets still breed. They have been protected since very ancient times and this has allowed the population to survive. The Grey Heron is protected in most provinces but not in all, and may be shot everywhere under licence.

All herons, except the Grey Heron, are protected at the federal level in West Germany since the Bonn Convention was ratified on 1 October 1984, but in West Germany, as in Austria, protection laws are established by the provinces (*Länder*). Thus herons were protected before 1984 but in various ways according to each province. The precise protection given to the Grey Heron still depends on the *Länder* concerned. Hence it is protected in some regions and not in others, where it can be shot during the hunting season. The specific protection afforded to heronries also depends on each *Land*.

In East Germany, all herons except Grey Herons are totally protected. Hunting Grey Herons is allowed between 1 July and 31 January. The two species of Bitterns breeding in East Germany are afforded special protection status.

In Italy, a few heron species were protected before 1977 but since that time all herons are protected. In Spain, all heron species have been protected since 6 March 1981 by Law 3181/1980 of 30 December 1980. In Greece, herons were protected for the first time in 1979 by Ministerial decree and all heron species occurring in Greece are now totally protected throughout the year.

In Denmark, all herons with the exception of the Grey Heron, are protected throughout the year by the Game Laws of 1931, 1959 and 1967. The Grey Heron was protected from 1 January to 30 June only until the Game Law of 25 December 1982, since when it has been protected throughout the year. In Sweden the two species breeding there, the Grey Heron and the Bittern, are protected throughout the year, but in a few cases Grey Herons are hunted at fish farms by permission of the Environment Protection Board. In Norway, all heron species are totally protected.

In Poland, all heron species except the Grey Heron have been totally protected since April 1949. Grey Herons are only protected from 1 April to 15 August outside fish farms. In Hungary, Great White Egrets, Little Egrets and Squacco Herons have been totally protected since 1912. Purple Herons, Cattle Egrets, Night Herons, Little Bitterns and Great Bitterns were added to the protected species list in 1954. At that time, Grey Herons were also protected except at fish ponds. On 1 October 1988, Grey Herons became protected at fish ponds also, except between 1 July and 31 January. In 1982, the protection of Great White Egrets, Little Egrets and Squacco Herons was reinforced when they were classified as strictly protected species.

An international convention – the Convention on the Conservation of Migratory Species of Wild Animals usually referred to as the Bonn Convention – was concluded on 23 June 1979. The Convention entered into force on 1 November 1983 after 15 countries had ratified it (Cameroon, Chile, Denmark, Egypt, the European Economic Community, Hungary, India, Ireland, Israel, Italy, Luxembourg, the Netherlands, Niger, Portugal and Sweden). Several other countries have signed but not ratified the convention, among them France and the United Kingdom. The fundamental objective of the Bonn Convention is to protect migratory species and strict protection for species listed in Appendix 1 (which includes all of the European herons except the Grey Heron and the Cattle Egret) is required. These species are the migratory ones in danger of extinction throughout all, or a significant portion of, their range and the Convention seeks to protect them by imposing strict conservation obligations on Parties in whose territory the species occur (Lyster 1985).

Therefore herons are protected today in all the European countries, but this protection is for most of them quite recent. The situation regarding the Grey Heron remains worrying. The disastrous state of the population during the 1960s led to its total protection in most European countries. However, because the population recovered rapidly, the Grey Heron is not listed in Appendix 1 (strictly protected species) of the Bonn Convention. Countries when ratifying it may thus take advantage of this situation to suppress the year-round protection of the Grey Heron. This would be very unfortunate as these beautiful birds, despite their increasing numbers, are as yet far from numerous.

The situation of herons in many countries outside Europe is still quite disastrous. The protection laws taken in Europe can only be effective if excessive hunting pressure on the migration routes and wintering areas stops. Particularly distressing is the situation in Malta where the local ornithological society struggles to stop the wholesale slaughter of migratory species. In Malta, herons are protected only from 22 May to 31 August, which means that they are hunted both on the autumn and spring migrations. The following average annual totals of herons killed in Malta has been established by members of the Ornithological Society of Malta:

Ardea cinerea	500–1000	*Ardeola ralloides*	500
Ardea purpurea	400–800	*Nycticorax nycticorax*	1000–2500
Egretta garzetta	1000	*Ixobrychus minutus*	500

Comparing the numbers of herons killed on migration each year on only one island such as Malta with the number of birds breeding each year in Europe, shows the incredible slaughter which occurs during migration. The only hope of survival for rare species is that countries such as Malta ratify and police international protection laws as soon as possible. The existence of international conventions such as the Bonn Convention is of the utmost importance since local associations for nature protection have only to ask for the ratification of already existing regulations, something which has much more chance of rapid success than the establishment of quite new laws.

Another major problem is the disappearance of wildlife habitats. It is no use protecting species if their habitats are destroyed. The Convention on the Conservation of European Wildlife and Natural Habitats or the Berne Convention, tries to limit their destruction in Europe. It came into force on 1 June 1982:

> The aims of the Berne Convention are to 'conserve wild flora and fauna and their natural habitat', to promote cooperation between countries in their conservation efforts and to give 'particular emphasis to endangered and vulnerable species including endangered and vulnerable migratory species'. The Berne Convention is an extremely important conservation treaty. It imposes a clear and unequivocal legal obligation on Parties to protect all important breeding and resting sites of the hundreds of species of animals in Appendix II. It imposes an equally clear obligation on Parties to prohibit the picking, collecting, cutting or uprooting of the 119 species of plants in Appendix I, and it requires Parties to take such measures as are necessary to maintain populations of all species of animals and plants at levels corresponding to ecological, scientific and cultural requirements even if this means over-riding economic interests (Lyster 1985).

Austria, Denmark, Greece, Ireland, Italy, Luxembourg, Lichtenstein, the Netherlands, Portugal, Sweden, Switzerland, Turkey and the United Kingdom are full parties to the Convention. Belgium, Cyprus, Finland, France, West Germany, Norway and Spain have signed but not ratified it.

Bibliography

Abdulali, H. 1967. Unusual method of fishing by Little Egret *Egretta garzetta*. *Journal of the Bombay Natural History Society*, 64: 557–558.

Abramson, I.J. 1960. Cattle Egrets on dry tortugas. *Auk*, 77: 475.

Ali, S. and Ripley, S.D. 1968. *Handbook of the Birds of India and Pakistan together with those of Nepal, Sikkim, Bhutan and Ceylon*. Oxford University Press, Bombay.

Allen, R.P. 1937. Black-crowned Night Heron colonies on Long Island. *Proceedings of the Linnaean Society of New York*, 49: 43–51.

Allen, R.P. and Mangels, F.P. 1940. Studies of the nesting behaviour of the Black-crowned Night Heron. *Proceedings of the Linnaean Society of New York*, 50–51: 1–28.

Amat, J.A. and Herrera, C.M. 1977. Alimentacion de la Garza Imperial en las Marismas del Guadalquivir durante el periodo de nidificacion. *Ardeola*, 24: 95–104.

American Ornithologists' Union 1983. The AOU Check-list of North American Birds, 6th edn. AOU,

Andrews, S. 1981. Black-crowned Night Heron predation on Black-necked Stilt. *Elepaio*, 41: 86.

Andrle, R.F. and Axtell, H.H. 1961. Cattle Egrets in Mexico. *Wilson Bulletin*, 73: 320.

Anonymous 1986. How many herons? *The British Trust for Ornithology News.* March–April 1986. Number 143, p 12.

Anonymous 1987a. 1986 Heronries Census. *The British Trust for Ornithology News.* September–October 1987. Number 152, p 16.

Anonymous 1987b. Réserve Nationale de Camargue. Compte rendu ornithologique camarguais pour les années 1984–1985. *Revue d'Ecologie (La Terre et la Vie)*, 42: 167–191.

Arm, R. 1960. Nouveau procédé de pêche des Hérons pourprés. *Nos Oiseaux*, 25: 227.

Ashok Kumar, S. 1981. Solar eclipse – Notes on behaviour of Egrets. *Journal of the Bombay Natural History Society*, 78: 594–597.

Axell, H.E. 1967. Pursuit flights of Bitterns. *British Birds*, 60: 415.

Baerends, G.P. and Van der Cingel, N.A. 1962. On the phylogenetic origin of the Snap display in the Common Heron (*Ardea cinerea*). *Symposium of the Zoological Society of London*, 8: 7–24.

Baillie, J.L. 1963. Three bird immigrants from the old world. *Transactions of the Royal Canadian Institute*, 34: 95–100.

Banks, S. 1982. Grey Heron dunking and swallowing large rat. *British Birds*, 75: 181.

Bannerman, D.A. 1957. *The Birds of the British Isles*, Vol. 6. Oliver and Boyd, Edinburgh.

Bannerman, D. and Bannerman, W.M. 1968. *Birds of the Atlantic Islands, Vol. 4: History of the Birds of Cape Verde Islands*. Oliver and Boyd, Edinburgh.

Batten, L.A. and Marchant, G.A. 1976. Bird population changes for the years 1973–1974. *Bird Study*, 23: 11–22.

Bauer, K.M. and Glutz von Blotzheim, U.N. 1966. *Handbuch der Vögel Mitteleuropas*, Band I. Akademische Verlagsgesellschaft, Frankfurt am Main.

Bauer, K.M., Freundl, H. and Lugitsch, R. 1955. Weitere Beiträge zur Kenntnis der Vogelwelt des Neusiedlersee-Gebietes. *Wissenschaftliche Arbeiten aus dem Burgenland*, 7: 1–123.

Beckett, T.A. 1964. Black-crowned Night Heron feeding behaviour. *Chat*, 28: 93–94.

Beetham, B. 1910. *The Home-life of the Spoonbill, the Stork and Some Herons*. H.F. and G. Witherby, London.

Belman, P.J. 1974. Purple Heron chick regurgitating young Little Grebe. *British Birds*, 67: 439.

Belton, W. 1974. Cattle Egrets in Rio Grande del Sul, Brazil. *Bird-Banding*, 45: 59.

Benson, C.W. and Penny, M.J. 1971. Land birds of Aldabra. *Philosophical Transactions of the Royal Society of London*, B260: 417–527.

Bent, A.C. 1926. Life histories of North American marsh birds. *United States National Museum Bulletin*, 135: 490.

Bernhardt, P. 1929. Von der Rohrdommel. *Beiträge zur Fortflanzungsbiologie der Vögel mit berüchsichtigung der Oologie*, 5: 121–124.

Bernis, F. 1961. Cuatro notas sobre Garzaz. *Ardeola*, 7: 204–217.

Bernis, F. 1966. *Aves Migradoras Ibericas I*. Sociedad Espanola de Ornitologia, Madrid.

Bernis, F. 1969. Reconsideración del ejemplar melnico de *Egretta* spp., obtenido en Doñana en 1956. *Ardeola*, 15: 107–110.

Bibby, C.J. 1981. Wintering Bitterns in Britain. *British Birds*, 74: 1–10.

Bigot, L. and Jouventin, P. 1974. Quelques experiences de comestibilité de lépidoptères gabonais faites avec un Mandrille le Cercocèbe à joues grises et le Garde-Boeufs. *Terre et Vie*, 28: 521–543.

Birkhead, T.R. 1972. Carrion crows mobbing Grey Herons. *British Birds*, 65: 356.

Birkhead, T.R. 1973a. A winter roost of Grey Herons. *British Birds*, 66: 147–156.

Birkhead, T.R. 1973b. Observations at a standing-ground adjoining a heronry. *The Naturalist*, 924: 13–19.

Blake, C.H. 1948. More data on the wing flapping rates of birds. *Condor*, 50: 148–151.

Blake, E.R. 1939. African Cattle Heron taken in British Guiana. *Auk*, 56: 470–471.

Blaker, D. 1969a. The behaviour of the Cattle Egret *Ardeola ibis*. *Ostrich*, 40: 75–129.

Blaker, D. 1969b. The behaviour of *Egretta garzetta* and *Egretta intermedia*. *Ostrich*, 40: 150–155.

Blaszkiewitz, B. 1981. Bemerkenswertes Alter beim Nachtreiher. *Gefiederte Welt*, 105: 8–9.

Blok, A.A. and Roos, M. 1977. Grey heron censuses for 1970–1976. *Het Vogeljaar*, 25: 205–223.

Blondel, J. 1965. Le héron cendré *Ardea cinerea* nicheur en Camargue. *L'Oiseau et la Revue Française d'Ornithologie*, 35: 59–60.

Boada, M. 1975. Sobre una nueva coloña de Ardeidas en Gerona. *Ardeola*, 21: 59–63.

Boas, J.E.V. 1929. Biologische-anatomische Studien über den Hals der Vögel. *Det Kongelige Danske Videnskabernes Selskabs Skrifter*, ser. 9, 1: 105–122.

Böck, F. von 1975. Der bestand des Graureihers (*Ardea cinerea*) in Österreich. *Egretta*, 18: 54–64.

Bock, W.J. 1956. A generic review of the Family Ardeidae (Aves). *American Museum Notivates*, 1779.

Bond, J. 1956. *Second Supplement to the Check-list of Birds of the West Indies*, 4th edn. Academy of Natural Sciences of Philadelphia, Philadelphia, Penn.

Bond, R.M. 1957. The Cattle Egret in Jamaica, British West Indies. *Condor*, 59: 269.

Boswall, J. 1977. Tool-using by birds and related behaviour. *Avicultural Magazine*, 83: 88–97, 146–159, 220–228.

Bowen, T.V. and Nicholls, G.D. 1968. An Egret observed on St-Paul's Rocks, equatorial Atlantic Ocean. *Auk*, 85: 130–131.

Bowen, W. 1962. Communal nesting of *Phalacrocorax africanus*, *Bubulcus ibis*, and *Anhinga rufa* in southern Ghana. *Ibis*, 104: 246–247.

Boyd, A.W. 1950. Herons sun-bathing. *British Birds*, 43: 125.

Boyle, G. 1967. Heron fishing in deep water. *British Birds*, 60: 215.

Braaksma, S. 1958. Aanvullende gegevens over de stand van de Roerdomp, *Botaurus stellaris* L., als broedvogel in Netherland. *Ardea*, 46: 158–166.

Braaksma, S. 1968. Der verspreiding van het Woodaapje (*Ixobrychus minutus*) als broedvogel. *Limosa*, 41: 41–61.

Braschler, K., Lengweiler, O., Feldman, G. and Egli, V. 1961. Zur Fortpflanzungsbiologie des Zwergrohrdommel, *Ixobrychus minutus*. *Der Ornithologische Beobachter*, 58: 59–75.

Bredin, D. 1985. Première preuve de nidification du Héron Garde-Boeufs (*Bubulcus ibis*) en Charente-Maritime. *Alauda*, 53: 144–145.

Breese, P. 1959. Information on Cattle Egret. A bird new to Hawaii. *Elepaio*, 20: 33–34.

Broberg, L. 1971. Rördrommen, *Botaurus stellaris*, i Sverige 1969. *Vår Fågelvärld*, 30: 91–98.

Brodkorb, P. 1963. Catalogue of fossil birds. Part I (Archaeopterygiformes through Ardeiformes). *Bulletin of the Florida State Museum*, 7: 179–293.

Brodkorb, P. 1971. Origin and evolution of birds. In *Avian Biology* (Farner, D.S. and King, J.R., eds). Vol. I, pp 20–51. Academic Press, London.

Brooke, R.K. 1971. Avian scavenger in Luanda harbour. *Bulletin of the British Ornithologists' Club*, 91: 46.

Brosselin, M. 1974. *Hérons arboricoles de France*. Société Nationale de Protection de la Nature, Paris.

Browder, J.A. 1973. Long-distance movements of Cattle Egrets. *Bird-Banding*, 44: 158–170.

Brown, A.G. 1949. Unidentified Egret. *Emu*, 49: 25.

Brown, B. 1980. Possible early record of Cattle Egrets in New Zealand. *Notornis*, 27: 400.

Buerkle, U. and Mansell, W.D. 1963. First nesting record of Cattle Egret (*Bubulcus ibis*) in Canada. *Auk*, 80: 378–379.

Burger, J. and Gochfeld, M. 1982. Host selection as an adaptation to host-dependent foraging success in the Cattle Egret (*Bubulcus ibis*). *Behaviour*, 79: 212–229.

Burton, J.F. 1956. Report on the National Census of Heronries, 1954. *Bird Study*, 3: 42–73 (additions and corrections in *Bird Study*, 4: 50–52).

Byrd, G.V., Zeillemaker, C.F. and Telfer, T.C. 1980. Population increases of Cattle Egrets on Kauai. *Elepaio*, 41: 25–28.

Campbell, W.D. and Denzey, F.J. 1954. Great Skua killing Heron. *British Birds*, 47: 403.

Carlson, L. 1978. Häger, *Ardea cinerea*, häckande på kala skär i Blekinge. *Vår Fågelvärld*, 37: 364–365.

Chapin, J.P. 1922. The function of the oesophagus in the Bittern's booming. *Auk*, 39: 196–202.

Chapin, J.P. 1932. The birds of Belgian Congo, Part I. *Bulletin of the American Museum of Natural History*, 65: 443–444.

Chapman, B.R., Grantland, T.L. and Ricklefs, R.E. 1981. Growth and development of temperature regulation in nesting Black-crowned Night Herons. *Colonial Waterbirds*, 4: 114–119.

Christman, G.M. 1957. Some interspecific relations in the feeding of estuarine birds. *Condor*, 59: 343.

Collins, G.T. 1970. Black-crowned Night Heron as predator of tern chicks. *Auk*, 87: 584–585.

Cook, D.C. 1978a. Grey Herons *Ardea cinerea* holding feeding territories on the Ythan Estuary. *Bird Study*, 25: 11–16.

Cook, D.C. 1978b. Foraging behaviour and food of the Grey Herons *Ardea cinerea* on the Ythan Estuary. *Bird Study*, 25: 17–22.

Cooper, J. 1971. Wing-beat rate in the genus Ardea. *Honeyguide*, 67: 23–25.

Cooper, J. 1984. Grey Heron *Ardea cinerea* kleptoparasitizes Cape cormorants *Phalocrocorax capensis*. *Cormorant*, 12: 94.

Courser, W.D. and Dinsmore, J.J. 1971. Red-tailed Hawk preys on Cattle Egret. *Auk*, 88: 669–670.

Cox, A.H.M. 1925. Raven nesting in heronry. *British Birds*, 19: 149–150.

Cramb, A.P.D. 1972. Grey Heron squatting and being attacked by Carrion Crow. *British Birds*, 65: 167.

Cramp, S. and Simmons, K.E.L. 1977. *The Birds of Western Palearctic. Handbook of the Birds of Europe, the Middle East and North Africa*, Vol. I. Oxford University Press, Oxford.

Craufurd, R.K. 1966. Notes on the ecology of the Cattle Egret, *Ardeola ibis*, at Rokupr, Sierra Leone. *Ibis*, 108: 411–418.

Creutz, G. 1981. *Der Graureiher. Die Neue Brehm-Bücherei*. A. Ziemens Verlag, Wittenberg.

Creutz, G. and Schlegel, R. 1961. Das Brutvorkommen des Graureihers der DDR. *Falke*, 8: 377–386.

Crivelli, A.J., Jerrentrup, H. and Hallmann, B. 1988. Preliminary results of a complete census of breeding colonial wading birds in Greece, spring 1985–1986. *Newsletter of the Hellenic Ornithological Society*, 4: 31–32.

Crosby, G.T. 1972. Spread of the Cattle Egret in the western hemisphere. *Bird-Banding*, 43: 205–212.

Cullen, J.M. 1963. Allo-, Auto-, and Hetero-preening. *Ibis*, 105: 121.

Cunningham, R.L. 1965. Predation on birds by the Cattle Egret. *Auk*, 82: 502–503.

Curry-Lindahl, K. 1959. Våra fåglar i norden. Bokförlaget Natur och Kultur, Stockholm.

Curry-Lindahl, K. 1981. *Bird Migration in Africa*. Academic Press, London.

Custer, W.T., Hensler, G.L. and Kaiser, T.L. 1983. Clutch size, reproductive success and organochlorine contaminants in Atlantic coast Black-crowned Night Herons. *Auk*, 100: 699–710.

Dahlbeck, N. 1946. Hägerstammens storlek i Sverige under åren 1941 och 1943. *Vår Fågelvärld*, 5: 114–118.

Day, J.C.U. 1981. Status of Bitterns in Europe since 1976. *British Birds*, 74: 10–16.

Day, J.C.U. and Wilson, J. 1978. Breeding Bitterns in Britain. *British Birds*, 71: 285–300.

Dean, A.R. 1973. Night Herons fishing in deep water. *British Birds*, 68: 385.

Deignan, H.G. 1964. Birds of the Arnhem Land. In *Records of the American-Australian Expedition to Arnhem Land* (Specht, R.L., ed.), Vol. 4, pp. 345–425. Melbourne University Press, Melbourne.

Dementiev, G.P. and Gladkov, N.A. 1951. *Birds of the Soviet Union*, Vol. 2 (English translation 1968). Israeli Programme for Scientific Translations, Jerusalem.

Den Held, J.J. 1981. Population changes in the Purple Heron in relation to drought in wintering area. *Ardea*, 69: 185–191.

Devitt, O.E. 1962. Further additions to the birds of Simcoe County, Ontario. *Canadian Field-Naturalist*, 76: 153–158.

Dickerman, R.W. 1964. Cattle Egrets nesting in Mexico. *Wilson Bulletin*, 76: 290.

Dinsmore, J.J. 1973. Foraging success of Cattle Egrets, *Bubulcus ibis*. *The American Midland Naturalist*, 89: 242–246.

D'Oliveira, P. 1896. *Aves da Peninsula Iberica e especialamte de Portugal*. Impressa da Universidade, Coimbra.

Dorward, D.F. 1957. The Night Heron colony in the Edinburgh Zoo. *Scottish Naturalist*, 69: 32–36.

Drinkwater, H. 1958. Black-crowned Night Heron using bill motion to lure prey. *Wilson Bulletin*, 70: 201–202.

Duhautois, L. 1983. *Hérons paludicoles*. Société Nationale de Protection de la Nature, Paris.

Duhautois, L. 1984. Hérons pourprés et Butors. Le déclin. *Le Courrier de la Nature*, 92: 21–29.

Duhautois, L. and Marion, L. 1981. *Inventaire des colonies de hérons arboricoles en France: statut 1981*. Société Nationale de Protection de la Nature, Paris.

Duhautois, L. and Marion, L. 1982. Protection des hérons: des résultats? *Le Courrier de la Nature*, 78: 23–32.

Dupuy, A.R. 1975. Nidification de Hérons pourprés (*Ardea purpurea*) au Parc National des Oiseaux du Djoudj, Sénégal. *L'Oiseau et la Revue Française d'Ornithologie*, 45: 289–290.

Dusi, J.L. 1966. The identification and characteristics of nests, eggs and nestlings of some herons, ibises and anhingas. *Alabama Birdlife*, 14: 4–6.

Dusi, J.L. and Dusi, R.I. 1970. Nesting success and mortality of nestlings in a Cattle Egret colony. *Wilson Bulletin*, 82: 458–460.

Dybbro, T. 1970. Fiskehejrens (*Ardea cinerea*) udbredelse i Danmark 1968. *Dansk Ornithologisk Forenings Tidsskrift*, 64: 45–69.

Eagle Clarke, W. 1895. On the ornithology of the Delta of the Rhône. *Ibis*, 31: 173–211.

Edwards, M.H. 1965. Cattle Egret in Guerrero, Mexico. *Condor*, 67: 191.

Eisenmann, E. 1955. Cattle Egret, Marbled Godwit, Surfbird and Brown-chested Martin in Panama. *Auk*, 72: 426–428.

Elgood, J.H., Fry, C.H. and Dowsett, R.J. 1973. African migrants in Nigeria. *Ibis*, 115: 1–45.

Elliot, H.F.I. 1957. A contribution to the ornithology of the Tristan da Cunha group. *Ibis*, 99: 545–586.

Emlen, T. and Ambrose, H.W. 1970. Feeding interactions of Snowy Egrets and Red-breasted Mergansers. *Auk*, 87: 164–165.

Etchécopar, R.D. and Hüe, F. 1964. *Les Oiseaux du Nord de l'Afrique*. Boubée, Paris.

Fabian, G. and Sterbetz, I. 1965. Black Little Egrets (L.) in Europe. *Aquila*, 71–72: 99–112.

Falla, R.A., Sibson, R.B. and Turbott, E.G., 1970. *A Field Guide to the Birds of New Zealand*, 2nd edn. Collins, London.

Fasola, M. 1984. Activity rhythm and feeding success of nesting Night Herons *Nycticorax nycticorax*. *Ardea*, 72: 217–222.

Fasola, M. and Barbieri, F. 1975. *Aspetti della biologia riproduttiva degli Ardeidi gregari. Ricerche di Biologia della Selvaggina 62*. Laboratorio di Zoologia Applicata alla Caccia, Bologna.

Fasola, M., Barbieri, F., Prigioni, C. and Bogliani, G. 1981a. Le Garzaie in Italia 1981. *Avocetta*, 5: 107–131.

Fasola, M., Galeotti, P., Bogliani, G. and Nardi, P. 1981b. Food of Night Heron *Nycticorax nycticorax* and Little Egret *Egretta garzetta* feeding in rice fields. *Rivista Italiana di Ornitologia*, 51: 97–112.

Fernandez-Cruz, M. 1975. Revision de las actuales colonias de Ardeidas de España. *Ardeola*, 21: 65–126.

Ferry, C. and Blondel, J. 1960. Sur le nombre d'oeufs du Héron pourpré. *Alauda*, 28: 62–64.

Fogarty, M.J. and Hetrick, W.M. 1973. Summer foods of Cattle Egrets in north central Florida. *Auk*, 90: 268–280.

Forsberg, B. 1979. Havstrut som näringsparasit på Häger. *Vår Fagelvärld*, 38: 107.

Fox, N.C. 1975. Falcon killing Cattle Egret. *Notornis*, 22: 183.

Fraser, W. 1971. Breeding Herons and Storks in Botswana. *Ostrich*, 42: 123–127.

Fraser, W. 1974. Feeding association between Little Egret and Reed Cormorant. *Ostrich*, 45: 262.

Frazier, F.P., Jr 1964. New records of Cattle Egrets in Peru. *Auk*, 81: 553–554.

French, R.P. 1966. The utilisation of mangroves by birds in Trinidad. *Ibis*, 108: 423–424.

Frith, H.J. and Davies, S.J.J.F. 1961. Breeding seasons of birds in subcoastal Northern Territory. *Emu*, 61: 97–111.

Fujioka, M. and Yamagishi, S. 1981. Extramarital and pair copulations in the Cattle Egret. *Auk*, 98: 134–144.

Gauckler, A. and Kraus, M. 1965. Zur Brutbiologie der Grossen Rohrdommel (*Botaurus stellaris*). *Die Vogelwelt*, 86: 129–146.

Geiger, C. 1984a. Bestand und verbreitung des Graureihers *Ardea cinerea* in der Schweiz. *Der Ornithologische Beobachter*, 81: 85–97.

Geiger, C. 1984b. Graureiher *Ardea cinerea* und Fischbestand in Fliessgewassern. *Der Ornithologische Beobachter*, 81: 111–131.

Genelly, R.E. 1964. Common Egret preys on Meadowlark. *Condor*, 66: 274.

Gentz, K. 1959. Zur Lebenweise der Zwergrohrdommel. *Falke*, 6; 39–47, 81–87.

Gentz, K. 1965. *Die Grosse Rohrdommel. Die Neue Brehm-Bücherei*. A. Ziemsen Verlag, Wittenberg.

Géroudet, P. 1955. L'évolution de l'avifaune Suisse dans la première moitié du XX ième siècle. *Acta XI Congressus Internationalis Ornithologici*. Birkhäuser, Basel.

Géroudet, P. 1967. *Les Echassiers*. Delachaux et Niestlé, Neuchâtel.

Goddard, M.T.M. 1955. Notes on the breeding of the Cattle Egret in North-eastern New South Wales. *Emu*, 55: 275–277.

Goering, D.K. 1971. Nestling mortality in a Texas heronry. *Wilson Bulletin*, 83: 303–304.

Gollop, B. 1981. The nesting season June–July 81. Prairie provinces region. *American Birds*, 35: 950–952.

Goodwin, D. 1948. Washing food by Buff-backed heron. *British Birds*, 41: 121.

Green, R. 1981. Osprey carrying Black-crowned Night Heron. *Nebraska Bird Review*, 49: 11.

Griffiths, J. and Griffiths, G. 1969. Fish jumping into Heron's mouth. *British Birds*, 62: 382–383.

Gross, A.O. 1923. The Black-crowned Night Heron of Sandy Neck. *Auk*, 40: 191–214.

Grüll, A. 1988. *Zur Bedeutung des Südlichen Neusiedlerseebekens für den Vogelschutz*. Biologische Station, Neusiedlersee.

Guichard, G. 1949. La héronnière de Pierre Rouge. *L'Oiseau et la Revue Française d'Ornithologie*, 19: 85–91.

Guth, R.W. 1971. New bird records from Guadeloupe and its dependencies. *Auk*, 88: 180–182.

Haas, W. 1969. Observations ornithologiques dans le nord-ouest de l'Afrique. *Alauda*, 37: 28–36.

Hafner, H. 1970. A propos d'une population de hérons Garde-Boeufs en Camargue. *Alauda*, 38: 249–254.

Hafner, H. 1977. Contribution à l'étude de quatre espèces de hérons pendant leur nidification en Camargue. Thèse, Université Paul Sabatier, Toulouse.

Hafner, H. 1987. Compte rendu ornithologique camarguais pour les années 1984–1985. *Revue d'Ecologie (La Terre et la Vie)*, 42: 166–191.

Hafner, H., Johnson, A. and Walmsley, J. 1982a. Compte rendu ornithologique camarguais pour les années 1980 et 1981. *Revue d'Ecologie (La Terre et la Vie)*, 36: 573–601.

Hafner, H., Boy, V. and Gory, G. 1982b. Feeding methods, flock size and feeding success in the Little Egret *Egretta garzetta* and the Squacco Heron *Ardeola ralloides* in the Camargue, southern France. *Ardea*, 70: 45–58.

Haftorn, S. 1971. *Norges Fugler*. Universitetsforlaget, Oslo.

Halley, M.R. and Wayne, D. 1978. A Cattle Egret–Deer mutualism. *Wilson Bulletin*, 90: 291.'

Hancock, J. 1984a. Field identification of West Palearctic white herons and egrets. *British Birds*, 77: 451–457.

Hancock, J. 1984b. Aerial stretch display of the eastern race of the Great White Egret *Egretta alba*. *Ibis*, 126: 92–95.

Hancock, J. and Elliot, H. 1978. *The Herons of the World*. London Editions Limited, London.

Hancock, J. and Kushlan, J. 1984. *The Herons Handbook*. Croom Helm, London.

Harrington, B.A. and Dinsmore, J.J. 1975. Mortality of transient Cattle Egrets at dry tortugas, Florida. *Bird-Banding*, 46: 7–14.

Haverschmidt, F. 1950. Occurrence of Cattle Egret *Bubulcus ibis* in Surinam, Dutch Guiana. *Auk*, 67: 380–381.

Haverschmidt, F. 1953. The Cattle Egret in South America. *Audubon Magazine*, 55: 202–204, 256.

Heather, B.D. 1982. The Cattle Egret in New Zealand, 1978–1980. *Notornis*, 29: 241–268.

Heatwole, H. 1965. Some aspects of the association of Cattle Egrets with cattle. *Animal Behaviour*, 13: 79–83.

Heim de Balzac, H. and Mayaud, N. 1962. *Les Oiseaux du Nord de l'Afrique.* Paul Lechevalier, Paris.

Heinroth, O. 1967. *Die Vögel Mittel-Europas.* Verlag für Kunst und Wissenschaft, Leipzig.

Henny, C.J. 1972. An analysis of the population dynamics of selected avian species with special reference to changes during the modern pesticide era. *Wildlife Research Report I.* US Fish and Wildlife Service, US Department of the Interior, Washington DC.

Hewitt, J.M. 1960. The Cattle Egret in Australia. *Emu*, 60: 99–102.

Hiraldo Cano, F. 1971. Primera captura segura de *Egretta gularis* en España. *Ardeola*, 15: 103–107.

Hoffmann, L., L'Évêque, R., Aguesse, P. and Bigot, L. 1959. Esquisse écologique de la Camargue à l'intention des Ornithologistes. Actes de la Réserve de Camargue. *La Terre et la Vie*, 30: 26–60.

Hofstetter, J., Chmetz, I., Baumann, R. and Crousaz, G. 1949. Une colonie romande de Hérons pourprés sur des arbres. *Nos Oiseaux*, 20: 81–85.

Holstein, V. 1927. *Fiskehejren.* Gad's Forlag, København.

Hölzinger, J. 1970. Ornithologischer Sammelbericht für Baden-Würtenberg. *Anzeiger der Ornithologischen Gesellschaft in Bayern*, 9: 155–169.

Hölzinger, J. 1973. Ornithologischer Sammelbericht für Baden-Würtenberg. *Anzeiger der Ornithologischen Gesellschaft in Bayern*, 12: 130–139.

Hubbard, J.P. 1966. The Cattle Egret on the Pacific Coast of Chiapas, Mexico. *Wilson Bulletin*, 78: 121.

Hubbs, C.L. 1968. Dispersal of Cattle Egret and Little Blue Heron into northeastern Baja California, Mexico. *Condor*, 70: 92–93.

Hudson, M.J. 1965. Bill-clappering display in the Common heron *Ardea cinerea. Ibis*, 107: 460–465.

Hunter, R.G. and Morris, R.D. 1976. Nocturnal predation by Black-crowned Night Heron at a Common Tern colony. *Auk*, 93: 629–633.

Huxley, J.S. 1924. Some points in the breeding behaviour of the Common Heron. *British Birds*, 18: 155–163.

Irby, L.H.L. 1895. *The Ornithology of the Straits of Gibraltar.* R.H. Porter, London.

Jefferies, D.J. and Pendlebury, J.B. 1967. Pursuit flights of Bitterns. *British Birds*, 60: 414.

Jenkins, C.F.H. 1960. The Cattle Egret and its Symbiont in South-western Australia. *Emu*, 60: 245–249.

Jenkins, J. 1981. Trans-Tasman Cattle Egrets. *Notornis*, 28: 102.

Jenni, D.A. 1969. A study of ecology of four species of herons during the breeding season at Lake Alice, Alachua county, Florida. *Ecological Monographs*, 39: 245–270.

Jenni, D.A. 1973. Regional variation in the food of nestling Cattle Egrets. *Auk*, 90: 821–826.

Johnson, A.W. 1965. *The Birds of Chile and Adjacent Region of Argentina, Bolivia and Peru.* Establecimientos Gráficos S.A., Buenos Aires.

Jósefik, M. 1969–1970. Studies on the Squacco Heron, *Ardeola ralloides. Acta Ornitologica Warzawa*, 11: 103–262; 12: 57–102, 394–504.

Jouanin, C. and Roux, F. 1963. Une race nouvelle de Héron Cendré *Ardea cinerea monicae. L'Oiseau et la Revue Française d'Ornithologie*, 33: 103–106.

Junor, F.R.J. 1972. Estimation of the daily food intake of piscivorous birds. *Ostrich*, 43: 193–205.

Kadry, I. 1942. The economic importance of Buff-backed Egret (*Ardea ibis*) to Egyptian agriculture. *Bulletin of the Zoological Society of Egypt*, 4: 20–26.

Kahl, M.P. 1963. Mortality of Common Egrets and other herons. *Auk*, 80: 295–300.

Kahl, M.P. 1971. Observation on the breeding of the Abdim's Stork at Lake Shala, Ethiopia. *Ostrich*, 42: 233–241.

Kale, H.W. 1965. Nesting predation by herons in a Georgia heronry. *Oriole*, 30: 69–70.

Keenan, W.J. 1981. Green Heron fishing with may-flies. *Chat*, 45: 41.

Kennard, J.H. 1975. Longevity records of North American birds. *Bird-Banding*, 46: 55–73.

Kérautret, L. 1969. Notes sur le comportement diurne du Butor étoilé (*Botaurus s. stellaris*), *L'Oiseau et la Revue Française d'Ornithologie*, 39: 176–178.

King, B. 1975. Vagrant Squacco Heron feeding in dry habitats. *British Birds*, 68: 76.

King, B. 1981. Presumed advertising flight of Little Bittern. *British Birds*, 74: 396.

Klag, S. and Boswall, J. 1970. Observations from a water bird colony, Lake Tana, Ethiopia. *Bulletin of the British Ornithologists' Club*, 90: 97–105.

Kosugi, A. 1960. On the food habits of some herons. *Miscellaneous Reports of the Yamashina Institute for Ornithology*, 15: 89–98.

Krämer, A. 1984. Zum Einfluss des Graureihers *Ardea cinerea* und Fischbestand von Forellenbacken. *Der Ornithologische Beobachter*, 81: 149–158.

Krämer, H. 1962. Das Vorkommen des Fischreihers (*Ardea cinerea*) in der Bundesrepublik Deutschland. *Journal für Ornithologie*, 103: 401–417.

Krüger, C. 1946. Kolonier af Fiskehejre *Ardea c. cinerea* i Danmark. *Dansk Ornithologisk Forenings Tidsskrift*, 40: 216–245.

Kuhk, R. 1955. Beringungs-Ergebnisse beim Silberreiher. *Ornithologische Beobachter*, 52: 2–5.

Kullmann, L. 1971. Försök till näringsparasitism hos häger *Ardea cinerea?* *Vår Fågelvärld*, 30: 126.

Kummerloeve, H. 1960. Zur Verbreitung des Rallenreihers *Ardea ralloides* in Vorderasien. *Acta Ornithologica Warszawa*, 5: 301–306.

Kushlan, J.A. 1973. Black-crowned Night Heron diving for prey. *Florida Field Naturalist*, 1: 27–28.

Kushlan, J.A. 1978. *Feeding Ecology of Wading Birds*. Wading Birds Research Report 7. National Audubon Society.

Kuyt, E. 1972. First record of Cattle Egrets in the Northwest Territories. *Canadian Field Naturalist*, 86: 83–84.

Lamm, D.W. 1975. Symbiotic relationships within a mixed waterfowl assembly. *Condor*, 77: 207.

Lancaster, D.A. 1970. Breeding behaviour of Cattle Egret in Colombia. *The Living Bird*, 9: 167–194.

Land, H.C. 1963. A collection of birds from the Caribbean lowlands of Guatemala. *Condor*, 65: 49–65.

Langley, C.H. 1983. Biology of the Little Bittern in the Southwestern Cape. *Ostrich*, 54: 83–94.

Lebreton, J.D. 1977. Maximum likelihood estimations of survival rates from bird band returns: Some complements to age-dependent methods. *Biometrie-Praximetrie*, 17: 145–161.

Lehmann, F.C. 1959. Observations on Cattle Egrets in Colombia. *Condor*, 61: 265–269.

Leslie, P.H. 1945. On the use of matrices in population mathematics. *Biometrica*, 33: 183–212.

Lévêque, R., Bowman, R.I. and Billet, S.L. 1966. Migration in the Galapagos area. *Condor*, 68: 81–101.

L'Hermitte, J. 1915–1916. Contribution à l'étude ornithologique de la Provence. *Revue Française d'Ornithologie*, 4; 161–166, 331–337.

Lippens, L. and Wille, H. 1969. Le Héron Bihoreau, *Nycticorax nycticorax* en Belgique et en Europe occidentale. *Le Gerfaut*, 59: 123–156.

Lippens, L. and Wille, H. 1972. *Atlas des Oiseaux de Belgique et d'Europe occidentale*. Tielt, Lannoo.

Litvinenko, N. 1982. Nesting of Grey Heron (*Ardea cinerea L.*) on Sea Islands of South Primorye. *Miscellaneous Reports of the Yamashina Institute for Ornithology*, 14: 220–231.

Londot, F. 1971. Contribution à l'étude de la héronnière de S. Jacinto (Aveiro) en 1970. *Cyanopica*, 1: 5–35.

Lorenz, K. 1955. Morphology and behaviour patterns in closely allied species. In *Group Processes, Transactions of the First Conference on Group Processes 1954*, pp. 168–220. Bertham Schaffner, Ithaca, N.Y.

Lovell, H.B. 1958. Baiting of fish by a Green Heron (*Butorides virescens*). *Wilson Bulletin*, 70: 280–281.

Lowe, F.A. 1954. *The Heron*. Collins, London.

Lowe, F.A. 1966. Heron swallowing Mole. *British Birds*, 59: 37–38.

Lowe-McConnell, R.H. 1967. Biology of the immigrant Cattle Egret *Ardeola ibis* in Guyana, South America. *Ibis*, 109: 168–179.

Lundevall, C.F. 1953. Anteckningar om en rördrom (*Botaurus stellaris*) i fångenskap. *Vår Fågelvärld*, 12: 1–8.

Lyster, S. 1985. *International Wildlife Law*. Grotius Publications, Cambridge.

Madon, P. 1935. Contribution à l'étude du régime des oiseaux aquatiques. *Alauda*, 7: 177–197, 183–197.

Majić, J. and Mikuska, J. 1972. Zum Brüten der Reiher im Reservat von Kopacevo und in seiner näheren Umgebung in den Jahren 1954 bis 1970. *Larus*, 24: 65–77.

Manuel, F. 1957. Nouvelle vue d'ensemble sur le Héron pourpré *Ardea purpurea* en Suisse. *Nos Oiseaux*, 24: 35–59.

Marion, L. 1976. Contribution à l'écologie des populations de Hérons cendrés, *Ardea cinerea* en Bretagne. D.E.A., Université de Rennes, Rennes.

Marion, L. 1979. Stratégies d'utilisation du milieu des colonies de Hérons cendrés *Ardea cinerea* L. en Bretagne. Thèse de troisième cycle, Université de Rennes, Rennes.

Marion, L. 1984. Mise en évidence par biotélémétrie de territoires individuels chez un oiseau colonial, le Héron cendré. Mécanisme de répartition et de régulation des effectifs des colonies de hérons. *L'Oiseau et la Revue Française d'Ornithologie*, 54: 1–78.

Marion, L. and Marion, P. 1982. Le Héron Garde-boeufs (*Bubulcus ibis*) niche dans l'ouest de la France. *Alauda*, 50: 161–175.

Marshall, R.V.A. 1961. Attack and counter attack between Great Black-backed Gull and Heron. *British Birds*, 54: 116.

Martinez, A. and Martinez, I. 1983. Nuevas colonias de Garzas en el Delta del Ebro. *Ardeola*, 30: 105–108.

Maxwell, G.R. and Putnam, L.S. 1968. The maintenance behaviour of the Black-crowned Night Heron. *Wilson Bulletin*, 80: 467–478.

Mayr, E. 1941. *List of New Guinea Birds*. American Museum of Natural History, New York.

Mayr, E. and Cottrell, W. 1979. *Check-list of the Birds of the World. Revision of the Work of J. Peters*. Museum of Comparative Zoology, Cambridge, Mass.

McCaskies, R.G. 1965. The Cattle Egret reaches the west coast of the United States. *Condor*, 67: 89.

McCrimmon, D.A. 1974. Stretch and Snap display in the Great White Egret. *Wilson Bulletin*, 86: 165–167.

McFarlane, R.W. 1975. Heron expansion in the Atacama Desert. *Auk*, 92: 378–379.

McLachlan, G.R. and Liversidge, R. 1957. *Roberts' Birds of South Africa*. The Trustees of the J. Voelcker Bird Book Fund, 5. Central New Agency, Cape Town.

McVaugh, M. 1972. The development of four North American herons. *Living Bird*, 11: 155–173.

Mead, C.J., North, P.M. and Watmough, B.R. 1979. The mortality of British Grey Herons. *Bird Study*, 26: 13–22.

Meyer, J. 1981a. Easy pickings. *Birds Magazine*, 8: 51–52.

Meyer, J. 1981b. Room for bird and fish. RSPB's survey of heron damage. *Fish Farmer*, July.

Meyerriecks, A.J. 1960a. *Comparative Breeding Behaviour of Four Species of North American Herons*. Publications of the Nuttall Ornithological Club 2, Cambridge, Mass.

Meyerriecks, A.J. 1960b. Success story of a pioneering bird. *Natural History*, 39: 45–56.

Milon, P., Petter, J.J. and Randrianasolo, G. 1973. *Faune de Madagascar 35. Oiseaux*. Centre National de Recherches Scientifiques (CNRS), Paris.

Milstein, P. le S., Prestt, I. and Bell, A.A. 1970. The breeding cycle of the Grey Heron. *Ardea*, 58: 171–257.

Mock, D.W. 1978. Pair-formation displays of the Great Egret. *Condor*, 80: 159–172.

Mock, D.W. 1979. Displays repertoire shifts and "extramarital" courtship in herons. *Behaviour*, 69: 57–71.

Møller, N.W. and Olesen, N.S. 1980. Bestanden af ynglende Fiskehejre *Ardea cinerea* i Danmark 1978. *Dansk Ornithologisk Forenings Tidsskrift*, 74: 105–112.

Moltoni, E. 1936. Le Garzaie in Italia. *Rivista Italiana di Ornithologia*, 6: 109–148, 210–269.

Moltoni, E. 1948. L'alimentazione degli Ardeidae (Aironi) in Italia. *Rivista Italiana di Ornitologia*, 18: 87–93.

Moreau, R.E. 1967. Water-Birds over Sahara. *Ibis*, 109: 232–259.

Moreau, R.E. 1972. *The Palaearctic-African Bird Migration Systems*. Academic Press, London.

Morris, F.T. 1978. Feeding association between Little Egret and Sacred Ibis. *Emu*, 78: 164.

Mukherjee, A.K. 1971. Food-habits of water-birds of the Sundarban, 24-Parganas District, West Bengal, India. Part II and III. *Journal of the Bombay Natural History Society*, 68: 37–64, 691–716.

Murphy, C.M. 1976. Grey Herons eating Water Rails. *British Birds*, 69: 369.

Murton, R.K. and Isaacson, A.J. 1962. The functional basis of some behaviour in the Woodpigeon *Columba palumbus*. *Ibis*, 104: 503–521.

Narosky, S. 1973. Primeros nidos de la Garcita Bueyera en la Argentina (*Bubulcus ibis*). *El Hornero*, XI: 225–226.

Narosky, S. 1978. *Aves Argentinas*. Associación Ornitólogica del Plata, Buenos Aires.

Naurois, de R. 1966. Le Héron Pourpré de l'archipel du Cap-Vert *Ardea purpurea bournei* ssp. nov. *L'Oiseau et la Revue Française d'Ornithologie*, 36: 89–94.

Naurois, de R. 1969. Notes brèves sur l'avifaune de l'archipel du Cap-Vert. Faunistique, endémisme et écologie. *Bulletin de l'Institut Fondamental d'Afrique Noire*, 31: 143–218.

Newton, I.P., Adams, N.S., Brown, C.R., Enticott, S.W. and Fugler, S.R. 1983. Non marine vagrant birds at the Prince Edward Islands, June 1981, May 1983. *The Cormorant*, 11: 35–38.

Nicholson, E.M. 1929. Report on the British Birds Census of Heronries,1928. *British Birds*, 22: 269–323, 333–372.

Niethammer, G. 1938. *Handbuch der deutschen Vogelkunde.* Akademische Verlagsgesellschaft, Leipzig.

Niethammer, G. 1955. Der Kuhreiher (*Bubulcus ibis*) in Bolivien. *Journal für Ornithologie*, 96: 222–223.

Noll, H. 1924. *Sumpfvogelleben. Eine Studie über die Vogelwelt des Linthriedes, Schweiz.* Deutscher Verlag für Jugend und Volk, Wien.

Norris, D. 1975. Green Heron (*Butorides virescens*) uses feather lure for fishing. *American Birds*, 29: 652–654.

North, P.M. 1979. Relating Grey Heron survival rates to winter weather conditions. *Bird Study*, 26: 23–28.

Olson, S.L. 1985. The fossil record of birds. In *Avian Biology* (Farner, D.S. and King, J.R., eds). Vol 8, pp 79–238. Academic Press, London.

Olsson, V. 1979. Studies on a population of Eagle Owls *Bubo bubo* in southeast Sweden. *Viltrevy*, 11: 1–99.

Owen, D.F. 1955. The food of the heron *Ardea cinerea* in the breeding season. *Ibis*, 97: 276–295.

Owen, D.F. 1960. The nesting success of the heron *Ardea cinerea* in relation to the availability of food. *Proceedings of the Zoological Society of London*, 133: 597–617.

Owen, D.F. and Phillips, G.C. 1956. The food of nestling Purple Herons in Holland. *British Birds*, 49: 494–499.

Owre, O.T. 1959. Cattle Egrets in Haiti. *Auk*, 76: 359.

Palm, B. 1962. Beobachtungen an zwei Grossen Rohrdommeln. *Der Falke*, 9: 68–69.

Palmer, R.S. 1962. *Handbook of North American Birds*, Vol. I. Yale University Press, New Haven, Conn.

Parks, J.M. and Bressler, S.L. 1963. Observations of joint feeding activities of certain fish eating birds. *Auk*, 80: 198–199.

Parsons, A.G. 1947. Heron feeding by probing under water. *British Birds*, 40: 313–314.

Payne, R.B. and Risley, C.J. 1976. *Systematics and Evolutionary Relationships Among the Herons (Ardeidae).* Miscellaneous Publications 150. Museum of Zoology, University of Michigan, Michigan, Ill.

Penny, M. 1974. *The Birds of Seychelles and Outlying Islands.* Collins, London.

Percy, W. 1932. The use of powder-down patches in the Bittern. *Bulletin of the British Ornithologists' Club*, 52: 136–138.

Percy, Lord W. 1951. *Three Studies in Bird Character.* Country Life, London.

Peters, J.L. 1931. *Check-list of the Birds of the World*, Vol. I. Harvard University Press, Cambridge, Mass.

Pettitt, R.G. 1950. Feeding behaviour of Common Heron. *British Birds*, 43: 376.

Phelps, W.H. 1944. *Bubulcus ibis* in Venezuela. *Auk*, 61: 656.

Piette, V. 1986. Contribution à l'étude des parades du Héron Bihoreau (*Nycticorax nycticorax*) en période de reproduction. Observation d'une colonie captive à la station d'acclimatation du Zwin. *Cahiers d'éthologie appliquée*, 6: 313–358.

Portielje, A.F.J. 1926. Zur Ethologie bezw. Psychologie von *Botaurus stellaris* (L.). *Ardea*, 15: 1–15.

Post, P.W. 1970. First report in Chile and range extensions in Peru. *Auk*, 87: 361.

Power, D.M. and Rising, J.D. The Cattle Egret in central Baja California, Mexico. *Condor*, 77: 353.

Pratt, E. 1979. The growth of a Cattle Egret colony. *Notornis*, 26: 353–356.

Prytherch, R. 1980. Squacco Heron possibly using insects as bait. *British Birds*, 73: 183–184.

Recher, H.F. and Recher, J.A. 1969. Comparative foraging efficiency of adult and immature Little Blue Herons (*Florida caerulea*). *Animal Behaviour*, 17: 320–322.

Recher, H.F. and Recher, J.A. 1980. Why are there different kinds of herons? *Transactions of the Linnaean Society of New York*, 9: 135–158.

Recorbert, B. 1985. Ornithologie, hiver 1984–1985. *Groupe Ornithologique de Loire Atlantique*, 5: 7–14.

Ree, V. 1973. Dagens avifaunistiske situasjon i Las Marismas i sør- Spania. *Sterna*, 12: 225–268.

Repenning, R. 1977. Great Egret preys on Sandpiper. *Auk*, 94: 171.

Rey, E. 1872. Zur Ornis von Portugal. *Journal für Ornithologie*, 20: 140.

Reynolds, C.M. 1974. The census of heronries, 1969–1973. *Bird Study*, 21: 129–134.

Reynolds, C.M. 1979. The heronries census: 1972–1977 population changes and review. *Bird Study*, 26: 7–12.

Reynolds, J.F. 1965a. Association between Little Egret (*Egretta garzetta*) and African Spoonbill (*Platalea alba*). *British Birds*, 58: 468.

Reynolds, J.F. 1965b. Feeding habits of Cattle Egrets (*Ardeola ibis*). *British Birds*, 58: 509.

Reynolds, J.F. 1974. Palearctic birds in East Africa. *British Birds*, 67: 70–76.

Rice, D.W. 1956. Dynamics of range expansion of Cattle Egrets in Florida. *Auk*, 73: 259–266.

Richner, H. 1986. Winter feeding strategies of individually marked herons. *Animal Behaviour*, 34: 881–886.

Riddell, W.H. 1944. The Buff-backed Heron *Ardeola ibis* (L). *Ibis*, 86: 503–511.

Ried, E.T. 1955. Insect diet of the Buff-backed Heron or Tick-bird (*Bubulcus ibis*), in the southern Soudan. *The Entomologist's Monthly Magazine*, 91: 169–173.

Roalkvam, R. 1984. Reirhabitat hos gråhegre *Ardea cinerea* i Rogaland. *Vår Fugelfauna*, 7: 145–148.

Roberson, D. 1982. *Rare Birds of the West Coast of North America*. Woodcock Publications, Pacific Grove, Calif.

Robert, D. and Voisin, C. 1991. Un comportement de pêche inhabitud l'Aigrette garzette. *L'Oiseau et la Revue Français d'Ornithologie*, 61: 51–52.

Roberts, A. 1942. *The Birds of South Africa*. H.F. & G. Witherby Ltd., London.

Rodgers, T.H. 1978. The nesting season June 1 – July 31. Northern Rocky Mountains–Intermountains region. *American Birds*, 32: 1186–1190.

Ruiz, X., Jover, L. and Montori, A. 1981. Primeros datos sobre la reproduccion de Garcilla Bueyera – *Bubulcus ibis* (L) – en delta Ebro, Taragona (España). *Publicaciones Departamento Zoologia Universidad Barcelona*, 7: 77–86.

Rumboll, M.A.E. and Canevari, P.J. 1975. Invasion de *Bubulcus ibis* en la Argentina. *Neotropica*, 66: 162–165.

Rutschke, E. 1982. Der Brutbestand des Graureihers in D.D.R. *Falke*, 92: 51–58.

Ruwet, J.C. 1965. *Les oiseaux des plaines et du lac-barrage de la Lufira Superieure (Katanga Méridional)*. FULREAC, Liège.

Rydzewski, W. 1956. The nomadic movements and migrations of the European Common Heron *Ardea cinerea* (L.). *Ardea*, 44: 71–188.

Schlatter, R.P. 1980. Nuevos registros ornitologicos en la Antartica chilena, 1979–1980. Serie científica. *Instituto antartico chileno*, 25–26: 45–48.

Schmidt, von, E. 1977. Auffallende Zunahme des Silberreihers (*Casmerodius albus*) in Ungarn im Jahre 1976. *Egretta*, 20: 68–70.

Schönwetter, M. 1967. *Handbuch der Oologie*, vol. I. Akademie Verlag, Berlin.

Schuster, L. 1928. Einige brutbiologische Beobachtungen aus dem Jahre 1928. *Beiträge zur Fortflanzungsbiologie der Vögel mit berücksichtigung der Oologie*, 4: 209–214.

Schüz, E. and Kuhk, R. 1972. Stand 1970 der Ausbreitung des Kuhreihers (*Ardeola ibis*). *Beiträge zur Vogelkunde*, 18: 70–80.

Seaman, G.A. 1955. Cattle Egrets in Virgin Islands. *Wilson Bulletin*, 67: 304–305.

Seaman, G.A. 1958. Nesting of Cattle Egrets in Virgin Islands. *Wilson Bulletin*, 70: 93–94.

Seber, G.A.F. 1971. Estimating age-specific survival rates from bird-band return when the reporting rate is constant. *Biometrik*, 58: 491–497.

Sermont, E. 1980. Observation sur la pêche du Grand Butor, *Botaurus stellaris*. *Nos Oiseaux*, 35: 242–243.

Serventy, D.L. and Whittell, H.M. 1962. *Birds of Western Australia*. Paterson Brokensha, Perth.

Sharma, B.D. 1981. Cobra and Little Bittern *Ixobrychus minutus*. *Journal of the Bombay Natural History Society*, 77: 350.

Siegfried, W.R. 1965. The status of the Cattle Egret in the Cape Province. *Ostrich*, 36: 109–116.

Siegfried, W.R. 1966a. The number of Cattle Egrets in the Cape Province. *Ostrich*, 37: 57.

Siegfried, W.R. 1966b. The status of the Cattle Egret in South Africa with notes on neighbouring territories. *Ostrich*, 37: 157–169.

Siegfried, W.R. 1966c. Age at which Cattle Egrets first breed. *Ostrich*, 37: 198–199.

Siegfried, W.R. 1966d. On the food of nestling Cattle Egrets. *Ostrich*, 37: 219–220.

Siegfried, W.R. 1966e. Time departure from the roost in the Night Heron. *Ostrich*, 37: 235–236.

Siegfried, W.R. 1969. Energy metabolism of the Cattle Egret. *Zoologica Africana*, 4: 265–273.

Siegfried, W.R. 1971a. The food of the Cattle Egret. *Journal of Applied Ecology*, 8: 447–468.

Siegfried, W.R. 1971b. Feeding activity of the Cattle Egret. *Ardea*, 59: 38–46.

Siegfried, W.R. 1971c. Plumage and moult of Cattle Egret. *Ostrich*, 9: 153–164 (suppl.).

Siegfried, W.R. 1971d. The nest of the Cattle Egret. *Ostrich*, 42: 193–197.

Siegfried, W.R. 1972a. Aspects of feeding ecology of Cattle Egret in South Africa. *Journal of Animal Ecology*, 41: 71–78.

Siegfried, W.R. 1972b. Food requirements and growth of Cattle Egrets in South Africa. *Living Bird*, 11: 193–206.

Siegfried, W.R. 1972c. Breeding success and reproductive output of Cattle Egret. *Ostrich*, 45: 43–55.

Siegfried, W.R. 1978. *Habitat and Modern Range Expansion of the Cattle Egret.* Wading Birds, Research Report 7, National Audubon Society.

Simmons, K.E.L. 1986. *The Sunning Behaviour of Birds.* The Bristol Ornithological Club, Bristol.

Sinclair, J.C. 1974. Fish offal scavengers off Luanda. *Bulletin of the British Ornithologists' Club*, 94: 58.

Sisson, R.F. 1974. Aha! It really works. *National Geographic Magazine*, 145: 142–147.

Skead, C.J. 1952. The status of the Cattle Egret in the eastern Cape Province. *Ostrich*, 23: 186–218.

Skead, C.J. 1956. The Cattle Egret in South Africa. *Audubon Magazine*, 59: 206–209, 221, 224–226.

Skinner, J.D. and Skinner, C.P. 1975. Predation on Cattle Egret (*Bubulcus ibis*) and Masked Weaver (*Ploceus velatus*) by the Vervet Monkey (*Cercopithecus aethiops*). *South African Journal of Science*, 70: 157–158.

Skokova, N.N. 1960. Food of the breeding birds of the Volga Delta (Astrakhan Reserve). *First Ornithological Congress of U.S.S.R., Papers of the Thematic Conferences*, 9: 205–215 (in Russian).

Slott, K., Jr 1957. A first record of Cattle Egrets in Peru. *Condor*, 59: 143.

Slud, P. 1957. Cattle Egret in Costa Rica. *Condor*, 59: 400.

Smallwood, J.A., Woodrey, M., Smallwood, N.J. and Kettler, M.A. 1982. Foraging by Cattle Egrets and American Kestrels at a fire's edge. *Journal of Field Ornithology*, 53; 171–172.

Smith, K.D. 1957. An annotated check list of the birds of Eritrea. *Ibis*, 99: 1–26.

Smith, W.J. 1958. Cattle Egrets (*Bubulcus ibis*) nesting on Cuba. *Auk*, 75: 89.

Snow, B.K. 1974. The Plumbeous Heron of the Galapagos. *Living Bird*, 13: 51–72.

Spillner, W. von 1968. Zur Paarungs- und Brutbiologie des Graureihers (*Ardea cinerea*). *Beiträge zur Vogelkunde*, 14: 29–74.

Spizer, G. 1967. Ein Seidenreiher jagt Fluginsecten. *Egretta*, 10: 28–29.

Sprunt, A. Jr 1939. Predatory instincts in the American Egret. *Auk*, 56: 469.

Sprunt, A. Jr 1954. The spread of the Cattle Egret. *Annual Report of the Smithsonian Institution*, pp. 259–276.

Sprunt, A. Jr 1956. The Cattle Egret in North America. *Audubon Magazine*, 58: 174–177.

Stacey, J.V. and Gervis, G.R. 1967. Heron apparently fishing in deep water. *British Birds*, 60: 49–50.

Stafford, J. 1969. The census of heronries 1962–1963. *Bird Study*, 16: 83–88.

Stafford, J. 1971. The Heron population of England and Wales 1928–1970. *Bird Study*, 18: 218–221.

Sterbetz, I. 1961. *Der Seidenreiher. Die Neue Brehm-Bücherei*. A. Ziemsen Verlag, Wittenberg.

Sterbetz, I. 1962. The Squacco Heron in the Sasér Bird Sanctuary. *Aquila*, 69–70: 246.

Sterbetz, I. and Slivka, L. 1972. Der Seidenreiher, *Egretta g. garzetta* L., im Karpathenbecken in dem Jahren 1959–1968. *Larus*, 24: 141–148.

Stettenheim, P. 1972. The integument of birds. In *Avian Biology* (Farner, D.S. and King, J.R., eds). Vol. II, pp 2–54. Academic Press, London.

Strange, I.J. 1979. Distribution of Cattle Egrets (*Bubulcus ibis*) to the Falkland Islands. *Le Gerfaut*, 69: 397–401.

Strijbos, J.P. 1935. *De blauwe Reiger*. L.J. Veen, Amsterdam.

Stronach, B.W.H. 1968. The Chagana heronry in western Tanzania. *Ibis*, 110: 345–348.

Suchantke, A. 1960. Herbstlicher Reiherzug an der Camargue-Küste. *Die Vogelwelt*, 81: 33–46.

Sullivan Caldwell, G. and Wolff Rubinoff, R. 1983. Avoidance of venomous Sea Snakes by naive Herons and Egrets. *Auk*, 100: 195–198.

Svenson, S. 1976. Hägerns *Ardea cinerea* utbredning och antal i Sverige 1972. *Vår Fågelvärld*, 35: 26–35.

Szlivka, A. 1958. The Little Bittern breeding in a colony. *Aquila*, 65: 339.

Taylor, D.W. 1979. Cattle Egret eating Yellow Wagtail. *British Birds*, 72: 475.

Teal, J.M. 1965. Nestling success of Egrets and Herons in Georgia. *Wilson Bulletin*, 77: 257–263.

Terrasse, J.-F., Terrasse, M. and Brosselin, M. 1969. Avifaune d'un lac des Balkans: Mikra Prespa (Grèce). *L'Oiseau et la Revue Française d'Ornithologie*, 39: 185–201.

Thonen, W. 1982. Kolkrabe *Corvus corax* brutet in Reiherkolonie. *Der Ornithologische Beobachter*, 79: 131–132.

Tomlinson, D.N.S. 1974. Studies of the Purple Heron. Part 1: Heronry structure, nesting habits and reproductive success; Part 2: Behaviour patterns. *Ostrich*, 45: 149–160, 209–223.

Tomlinson, D.N.S. 1975. Studies of the Purple Heron. Part 3: Eggs and chicks development. *Ostrich*, 46: 157–165.

Tomlinson, D.N.S. 1976. Breeding behaviour of the Great White Egret. *Ostrich*, 47: 161–178.

Tosi, G. and Toso, S. 1979. Night Herons (*Nycticorax nycticorax*) wintering in the Po River valley. *Ibis*, 126: 336.

Tully, H, 1950. Herons sun-bathing and sitting on the ground. *British Birds*, 43: 374–375.

Turbott, E.G., Brathwaite, D.H. and Wilkin, F.W. 1963. Cattle Egret: A new bird for New Zealand. *Notornis*, 10: 316.

Turner, E.A. 1911. The return of the Bittern to Norfolk. *British Birds*, 5: 90–97.

Tyler, S.J. 1979. Underwing-feeding by Night Heron. *British Birds*, 72: 475.

Utschick, H. 1983. Die Brutbestandsentwicklung des Graureihers (*Ardea cinerea*) in Bayern. *Journal für Ornithologie*, 124: 233–250.

Valentine, J.M. 1958. The Cattle Egret at Chincoteague, Virginia. *Raven*, 29: 68–96.

Valverde, J.A. 1955–1956. Essai sur l'Aigrette Garzette en France (*Egretta garzetta*). *Alauda*, 23: 145–171; 24: 1–36.

Valverde, J.A. 1958. Description du poussin d'*Ardeola ralloides*. *Alauda*, 21: 250–252.

Valverde, J.A. 1960. *Vertebrados de las Marismas del Guadalquivir*. Archivos del Instituto de Aclimatacion, Almeria.

Van der Molen, E.J., Blok, A.A. and De Graaf, G.J. 1982. Winter starvation and mercury intoxication in Grey Herons (*Ardea cinerea*) in the Netherlands. *Ardea*, 70: 173–184.

Van der Ven, J. 1962. Het aantal broedparen van de Blauwe Reiger (*Ardea cinerea*) in Nederland in 1956 en 1961. *Limosa*, 35: 266–269.

Van der Ven, J. 1964. De Blauwe Reiger in 1963 en 1964 in Nederland. *Limosa*, 37: 308–309.

Van Ee, C.A. 1973. Cattle Egrets prey on breeding Queleas. *Ostrich*, 44: 136.

Van Vessem, J. 1982. Aspects écologiques de la protection des cultures contre les Hérons Cendrés. *L'Homme et l'Oiseau*, 20: 270–280.

Van Vessem, J., Draulans, D. and De Bont, A.F. 1982. De status van de Blauwe Reiger (*Ardea cinerea*) als broedvogel in België van 1966 tot 1981. *De Giervalk*, 72: 327–335.

Van Vessem, J., Draulans, D. and De Bont, A.F. 1984. Movements of radio-tagged Grey Herons *Ardea cinerea* during the breeding season in a large pond area. *Ibis*, 126: 576–587.

Vasiliu, G.D. 1968. *Systema Avium Romaniae*. Alauda, Paris.

Vasvàri, M. 1929. Beiträge zur Ernärungsökologie von *Botaurus stellaris* L. und *Ardetta minuta* L. *Aquila*, 34–35: 342–374.

Vasvàri, M. 1938. Die wichtigsten Ergebnisse meiner Untersuchungen über die Ernährungsoekologie der Reihervögel (Ardeidae). *IX Congrès Orntologique International*. J. Delacour, Rouen.

Vasvàri, M. 1948–1951. Food-ecology of the Common Heron, the Great White Egret and the Little Egret. *Aquila*, 55–58: 23–38.

Vaurie, C. 1963. Systematic notes on the Cattle Egret (*Bubulcus ibis*). *Bulletin of the British Ornithologists' Club*, 83: 164–166.

Vaurie, C. 1965. *The Birds of the Palearctic Fauna: Non-Passeriformes*. H.F. and G. Witherby, London.

Verheyen, R.F. 1966. Het voorkomen van de Blauwe Reiger, *Ardea cinerea* in Belgie. *De Giervalk*, 56: 374–403.

Verwey, J. 1930. Die Paarungsbiologie des Fischreihers. *Zoologische Jahrbücher*, 48: 1–120.

Vincent, J. 1947. Habits of the Cattle Egret in Natal. *Ibis*, 89: 489–491.

Vinokurov, A.A. 1960. On the food digestion rate in herons. *Moskovske Obshchestvo Ispryatelei Pirody Bjulletin. Otdel Biologii Moscow*, 65: 10 (in Russian).

Voisin, C. 1970. Observations sur le comportement du Héron Bihoreau *Nycticorax n. nycticorax* en période de reproduction. *L'Oiseau et la Revue Française d'Ornithologie*, 40: 307–339.

Voisin, C. 1975. Importance des populations de hérons arboricoles, *Egretta garzetta, Nycticorax nycticorax, Ardeola ralloides* et *Ardeola ibis* dans le delta du Rhône. Données historiques et situation actuelle. *L'Oiseau et la Revue Française d'Ornithologie*, 45: 7–25.

Voisin, C. 1976–1977. Etude du comportement de l'Aigrette garzette (*Egretta garzetta*) en période de reproduction. *L'Oiseau et la Revue Française d'Ornithologie*, 46: 387–425; 47: 65–103.

Voisin, C. 1978a. Utilisation des zones humides du delta rhôdanien par les Ardéidés. *L'Oiseau et la Revue Française d'Ornithologie*, 48: 217–261, 329–380.

Voisin, C. 1978b. Etho-écologie de quelques espèces d'Ardéidae nichant en France. Thèse de Doctorat d'Etat, Université Pierre et Marie Curie, Paris.

Voisin, C. 1979. Les populations d'Ardéidés arboricoles dans le delta du Rhône de 1968 à 1977: Évolution des effectifs et période de reproduction. *Alauda*, 47: 151–156.

Voisin, C. 1980. Etude du comportement du Héron crabier (*Ardeola ralloides*) en période de reproduction. *L'Oiseau et la Revue Française d'Ornithologie*, 50: 149–160.

Voisin, C. 1983. Les Ardéidés du delta du fleuve Sénégal. *L'Oiseau et la Revue Française d'Ornithologie*, 53: 335–369.

Voisin, C. 1985. Migration et stabilité des populations chez l'Aigrette garzette *Egretta garzetta*. *L'Oiseau et la Revue Française d'Ornithologie*, 55: 291–311.

Voisin, C. and Voisin, J.F. 1975. Observations sur l'abondance de quelques espèces d'oiseaux en basse Camargue au cours du printemps et de l'été 1973. *L'Oiseau et la Revue Française d'Ornithologie*, 45: 127–137.

Voisin, C. and Voisin, J.F. 1976. Observations sur l'abondance de quelques espèces d'oiseaux en basse Camargue. *L'Oiseau et la Revue Française d'Ornithologie*, 46: 157–165.

Voisin, J.F. 1979. Observations ornithologiques aux îles Tristan da Cunha et Gough. *Alauda*, 47: 73–82.

Wackernagel, H. 1950. Zur Fortflanzungsbiologie der Zwergrohrdommel, *Ixobrychus m. minutus* (L.). *Der Ornithologische Beobachter* 47: 41–56.

Walmsley, J., Hafner, H. and Johnson, A. 1980. Compte rendu ornithologique camarguais pour les années 1978 et 1979. *Revue d'Ecologie (La Terre et la Vie)*, 34: 621–647.

Walsh, J.F., Grunewald, J. and Grunewald, B. 1985. Green-backed Heron (*Butorides striatus*) possibly using a lure and using apparent bait. *Journal für Ornithologie*, 126: 439–442.

Walter, H. 1967. Seidenreiher (*Egretta garzetta*) fangt Beute im Flug. *Die Vogelwelt*, 88: 58–59.

Warga, K. 1938. Phänologische und nidobiologische Daten aus den Kolonien von *Egretta a. alba* (L.) am Kisbalaton. *Proceedings of the Eighth International Ornithological Congress*, Oxford, 1934, pp. 655–663. Oxford University Press, Oxford.

Watmough, B.R. 1978. Observations on nocturnal feeding by Night Herons, *Nycticorax nycticorax. Ibis*, 120: 356–358.

Weibüll, V. 1912. Hejren (*Ardea cinerea*) i Danmark nu og tidligere. *Dansk Ornithologisk Forenings Tidsskrift*, 6: 80–89.

Wetmore, A. 1920. Observations on the habits of birds at Lake Burford, New Mexico. *Auk*, 88: 435–437.

Wetmore, A. 1963. An early record of Cattle Egrets in Columbia. *Auk*, 80: 547.

Whitfield, A.K. and Blaber, S.J.M. 1979. Feeding ecology of piscivorous birds at Lake St-Lucia, Part 2: Wading birds. *Ostrich*, 50: 1–9.

Wiese, J.H. 1976. Courtship and pair formation in the Great Egret. *Auk*, 93: 709–724.

Williams, G. 1959. Some ecological observations on the Purple Heron in the Camargue. *La Terre et la Vie*, 30: 104–120.

Williams, L.E., Jr 1961. Three new birds for the Mississippi list. *Wilson Bulletin*, 73: 389.

Witherby, H.F., Jourdain, F.C.R., Ticehurst, N.F. and Tucker, B.W. 1939. *The Handbook of British Birds*, 3rd impression. Witherby, London.

Wolfe, L.R. 1961. Cattle Egrets in Mexico. *Auk*, 78: 640–641.

Wolford, J.W. 1966. An ecological study of the Black-crowned Night Herons in southern Alberta. Thesis, University of Alberta, Edmonton, Alberta.

Wolford, J.W. and Boag, D.A. 1971a. Distribution and biology of Black-crowned Night Herons in Alberta. *The Canadian Field Naturalist*, 85: 13–19.

Wolford, J.W. and Boag, D.A. 1971b. Food habits of Black-crowned Night Herons in southern Alberta. *Auk*, 88: 435–437.

Woods, R.W. 1975. *The Birds of Falkland Islands*. Anthony Nelson: Oswestry, Shropshire.

Woolfenden, G.E., White, S.C., Mumme, R.L. and Robertson, W.B., Jr 1976. Aggression among starving Cattle Egrets. *Bird-Banding*, 47: 48–53.

Yeates, G.K. 1940. Some notes on the Bittern. *British Birds*, 34: 98–99.

Yésou, P. 1984. Little Egrets with uncommon bare-parts coloration. *British Birds*, 77: 315–316.

Yésou, P. 1986. L'Aigrette des récifs *Egretta gularis* une espèce à part entière sur la liste des oiseaux de France. *L'Oiseau et la Revue Française d'Ornithologie*, 56: 321–329.

Zimmerman, D.A. 1973. Cattle Egrets in northern Mexico. *Condor*: 75: 480–481.

Zimmermann, R. 1925. Am Neste der Grossen Rohrdommel. *Pallasia*, 2: 185–194.

Zimmermann, R. 1929. Zur Oekologie und Biologie der Grossen Rohrdommel *Botaurus stellaris* L. in der Oberlausitzer Niederung. *Journal für Ornithologie*, 77: 249–266.

Zimmermann, R. 1931. Zur Fortpflanzungsbiologie der Grossen Rohrdommel, *Botaurus stellaris* L. *Journal für Ornithologie*, 79: 324–332.

Zimmermann, R. 1934. Zur Fortpflanzungsbiologie der Grossen Rohrdommel. *Mitteilungen der Vereinigung der Sächsischen Ornithologen*, 4: 129–133.

Zink, G. 1958. Vom Zug der Grossen Rohrdommel (*Botaurus stellaris*) nach den Ringfunden. *Die Vogelwarte*, 19: 243–247.

Zink, G. 1961. Ringfudergebnisse bei der Zwergrohrdommel (*Ixobrychus minutus*). *Die Vogelwarte*, 21: 113–117.

Index

Index   361

Grey Heron – *contd*
  fledging period 220
  food 232
  foraging
    areas 230
    efficiency 229
  Forward Displays 207
  Foot 14
  greeting 212
  growth 223
  guardian period 217
  habitat 192
  hatching 216
  heronries 194, 198
  incubation 216
  interactions with other species 233
  Kleptoparasitism 229
  maintenance behaviours 202
  measurements 189
  migration 190
  mortality
    of adults and juveniles 200
    of nestling 223
  nest 214
  pair formation 211
  plumage 186
  population size 195
  post-guardian period 219
  predation 233
  protection 234
  Snap Display 23, 203
  Stand and Wait 226
  Stretch Display 24, 208
  subspecies 189
  Walking slowly 226
  weight 189
  wing beat rate 189
  wing span 186
  young 217
Gular flutter 249

Habitat 31, 55, 79, 100, 131, 149, 192 245, 274, 314
Hanging Upside Down 37, 48
Hatching 69, 90, 118, 141, 159, 216, 256, 294
Head Flick 154
Head-neck swaying 37, 39, 49
Head tilting 37, 49, 301
Head swinging 37, 49
Heronries
  descriptions 194, 198
  society 20
Hopping 37, 48, 228, 301
Hovering 37, 48, 124

Incubation 28, 70, 89, 118, 141, 159, 216, 256, 294, 328

Information centres 44
Interactions with other birds 73, 92, 126
Ixobrichus minutus 75, 96
  minutus 78
  novaezelandiae 78
  payesii 78
  podiceps 78

Jumping 37, 48, 228
Jumping Upward 37, 48, 304

Kleptoparasitism 38, 49, 229

Larus delawarencis 41
Larus hermani 41
Larus mazinus 233
Larus pipixcan 126
Leapfrog feeding 37, 48, 162
Learning to forage 44
Little Bittern
  Advertising call 84
  additional broods 91
  agonistic displays 81
  Allopreening 89
  bare parts 76
  Bill-quivering 89
  Bittern Stance 82
  breeding 78, 84
  calls 84
  care of the young 90
  clutch size 88
  copulation 87
  daily routine 80
  dispersion 78
  distribution 78
  eggs 88
  fear displays 82
  Feather nibbling 89
  feeding behaviours
    foraging 91
    feeding the young 90
  field characters 77
  food 92
  Forward Displays 81
  habitat 79
  hatching 90
  incubation 89
  measurements 77
  migration 78
  Naja naja 93
  Neck-crossing 89
  nest 86
  pair formation 84
  plumage 75
  population size 79
  predators 92